T0323390

Employment Discrimination

Employment Discrimination

A Concise Review of the Legal Landscape

Stephen J. Vodanovich and Deborah E. Rupp

OXFORD
UNIVERSITY PRESS

OXFORD
UNIVERSITY PRESS

Oxford University Press is a department of the University of Oxford. It furthers
the University's objective of excellence in research, scholarship, and education
by publishing worldwide. Oxford is a registered trade mark of Oxford University
Press in the UK and certain other countries.

Published in the United States of America by Oxford University Press
198 Madison Avenue, New York, NY 10016, United States of America.

Library of Congress Cataloging-in-Publication Data
Names: Vodanovich, Stephen J., editor. | Rupp, Deborah E., 1975- editor.
Title: Employment discrimination : a concise review of the legal landscape /
Stephen J. Vodanovich and Deborah E. Rupp.
Description: New York, NY : Oxford University Press, [2022] |
Includes bibliographical references and index. |
Identifiers: LCCN 2021037330 (print) | LCCN 2021037331 (ebook) |
ISBN 9780190085421 (hardback) | ISBN 9780190085445 (epub) |
ISBN 9780190085452
Subjects: LCSH: Discrimination in employment—Law and legislation—United
States. | Pay equity—Law and legislation—United States. | Age
discrimination in employment—Law and legislation—United States.
Classification: LCC KF3464 .E439 2022 (print) | LCC KF3464 (ebook) |
DDC 344.7301/133—dc23
LC record available at https://lccn.loc.gov/2021037330
LC ebook record available at https://lccn.loc.gov/2021037331

DOI: 10.1093/oso/9780190085421.001.0001

1 3 5 7 9 8 6 4 2

Printed by Sheridan Books, Inc., United States of America

*Nothing presented herein should be interpreted as legal advice, and both individuals and organizations should
consult attorneys for guidance with matters relevant to potential discrimination*

SJV: To my wife, Donna, and to my parents, for their boundless love and for always being there for me.

DER: To my son, Tom, please don't forget to always be fair and just.

SJV and DER: To Art Gutman, for his generosity and extraordinary contributions to our understanding of EEO law. And to the late Jim Outtz for bringing many important aspects of adverse impact to the attention of industrial-organizational psychologists.

Contents

Acknowledgments

We are deeply indebted to Jessie Cannon, who provided unparalleled editorial assistance with all aspects of our book preparation and who also prepared the supplementary lecture slides. We also wish to thank Abby Gross and the staff at Oxford University Press for allowing us to fulfill our vision for this book and supporting us all along the way.

Stephen J. Vodanovich: I would like to additionally thank my previous students in the Legal Issues in I-O Psychology course at the University of West Florida. Their astonishing interest in learning discrimination law was contagious and inspired me to be a better teacher.

Deborah E. Rupp: I would like to additionally thank Nicole Strah; the students of my legal issues seminars at Purdue University and George Mason University; as well as Andrew Lee and the social sciences and law libraries at George Mason University. I also extend my utmost appreciation to Ron Laschever for providing the love and support required to complete this project and, finally, to Steve Vodanovich for decades of mentoring and friendship.

About the Companion Website

www.oup.com/us/employmentdiscrimination

Oxford University Press has created a website to accompany Employment Discrimination: A Concise Review of the Legal Landscape. This website is designed to feature supplementary material for instructors and readers, including powerpoint slides and a list of related hyperlinks. We encourage readers to consult this resource alongside the book.

Introduction

> Even when laws have been written down, they ought not always to
> remain unaltered.
>
> **—Aristotle**

This book seeks to provide readers with a straightforward and understandable presentation of the major laws and regulations concerning employment discrimination. For many, legal material can be difficult to comprehend. This is especially true given the terminology (e.g., Latin phrases) and writing style involved. Consistent with the opening quote from Aristotle, to further complicate matters, the legal landscape is constantly changing. Fortunately, the Internet provides convenient access to many useful legal resources that allow one to stay current with the ever-changing nature of the law (see the "Useful Legal Sites" box).

This text is meant to be useful for readers at all levels: from those new to equal employment opportunity (EEO) and employment discrimination law, to those who are moderately familiar, and for readers with advanced knowledge. Our intention is to allow individuals (including instructors) to choose which level of detail they desire. For those interested in a basic but reasonably thorough introduction to employment discrimination law, reading only the text itself may be sufficient. Readers can also learn about practical applications of laws in the boxes titled "EEO in the Wild," which may be especially helpful for those new to employment discrimination law. Additionally, the "Insights from Social Science" boxes provide empirical research findings that inform both academic and applied pursuits related to employment discrimination. For those interested in more in-depth coverage, access to more detailed information is provided via links to a variety of external sources. These links include court decisions, various laws and regulations, videos, legal commentaries and reviews, as well as oral arguments before the US Supreme Court.[1]

---

[1] Relatively few people will have the opportunity to physically attend oral arguments at the US Supreme Court. Listening to oral arguments is both intellectually stimulating and quite impressive to hear.

Employment Discrimination. Stephen J. Vodanovich and Deborah E. Rupp, Oxford University Press. © Oxford University Press 2022. DOI: 10.1093/oso/9780190085421.003.0001

Readers with a physical copy of the text may refer to the links written out in the footnotes, and readers with the online version may click on the hyperlinked footnotes in the body of the text. Some of this information will also be included in the "Supplemental Readings" sections in addition to links embedded within the text. When supplemental readings are grouped together in tables under specific topics, they will be denoted as applicable to those interested in beginner, intermediate, or advanced follow-up material. Generally speaking, outside readings intended for beginners consist of popular press writings on the topic, such as those from newspapers and magazines. Intermediate material includes summaries from articles for practitioner audiences and various websites/blogs that specialize in covering employment discrimination. Advanced information is comprised of, among other sources, peer-reviewed academic journal publications and papers published in law review journals. Each chapter includes a glossary at the end containing legal terms mentioned in the text. The glossary terms are also italicized in the text so readers can connect what they are reading to the glossary definitions. Finally, the content of the book will be regularly updated online. Updates will allow readers (including instructors) to stay current with recent court cases (and associated precedent), new and amended legislation, legal trends, and much more. Please note that nothing we present should be interpreted as legal advice, and both individuals and organizations should consult attorneys for guidance with matters relevant to potential discrimination. Enjoy your venture into employment discrimination law!

Useful Legal Sites

Equal Employment Opportunity Commission. https://www.eeoc.gov/
Supreme Court Home. https://www.supremecourt.gov/
Scotus (Supreme Court of the United States) Blog. https://www.scotusblog.com/
FindLaw. https://caselaw.findlaw.com/
Legal Information Institute at Cornell University. https://www.law.cornell.edu/supremecourt/text/home
Oyez Project (contains audio files of oral arguments and/or opinions of cases). https://www.oyez.org/
Open Jurist (Case Law, U.S. Code). https://openjurist.org/
UScourts.gov (federal courts, rules, policies).
DCI Consulting Blog (information regarding EEO/Affirmative Action topics). https://blog.dciconsult.com/

Justia.com (cases, codes). https://www.justia.com/

Department of Labor (laws & and regulations). https://www.dol.gov/

Department of Justice. https://www.justice.gov/

National Archives & and Records Administration (federal regulations, public laws). https://www.archives.gov/

Office of Federal Contract Compliance Programs. https://www.dol.gov/ofccp/

1

Overview of Employment Discrimination Law and the Civil Court System

United States Civil Court System
Employment Discrimination Law
Constitutional Amendments
- 1st Amendment
- 5th Amendment
- 11th Amendment
- 13th Amendment
- 14th Amendment

Major Employment Discrimination Laws
Group-Specific Discrimination Laws
Title VII
Some Title VII Exemptions
Bona Fide Seniority Systems
- *US Airways v. Barnett* (2002)

- *Lorance v. AT&T* (1989)
Bona Fide Occupational Qualifications
- *Diaz v. Pan Am World Airways* (1971)
Key Administrative Agencies
Equal Employment Opportunity
Commission
- Important Links Related to the Equal
Employment Opportunity Commission
EEOC Settlements
Office of Federal Contract Compliance
Programs
- Recommendation/Best Practices
Summary and Take-Aways

United States Civil Court System

The US civil court system consists of three levels: (1) District Courts ("Trial Courts"), (2) Circuit Courts of Appeal ("appellate courts"), and (3) the Supreme Court (see Figure 1.1). The United States has a total of 94 districts, representing distinct geographic regions (see Table 1.1). The number of districts varies by state. For instance, some states have only one district (e.g., Arizona, Colorado, Delaware), while others have multiple districts, such as California, Florida, and Michigan (e.g., Southern District of California, Central District of California).

These 94 districts are nested within larger geographic areas, or circuits, which constitute the Courts of Appeals (appellate courts; see Figure 1.1). There are a total of 13 appellate courts within the Courts of Appeals. Twelve of these represent regional circuits (comprising several states) and are designated by numbers (1–11) with the exception of the District of Columbia

Employment Discrimination. Stephen J. Vodanovich and Deborah E. Rupp, Oxford University Press. © Oxford University Press 2022. DOI: 10.1093/oso/9780190085421.003.0002

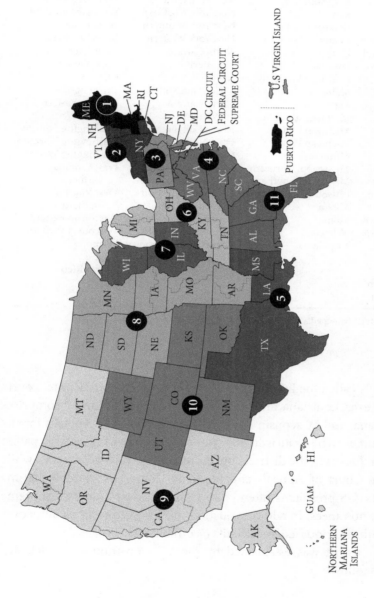

Figure 1.1 Geographic boundaries of US Courts of Appeals (see also Table 1.1) and US District Courts

Source: https://www.uscourts.gov/about-federal-courts/federal-courts-public/court-website-links

Table 1.1 US District Courts

Alabama Middle	Indiana Northern	New Hampshire	South Carolina
Alabama Northern	Indiana Southern	New Jersey	South Dakota
Alabama Southern	Iowa Northern	New Mexico	Tennessee Eastern
Alaska	Iowa Southern	New York Eastern	Tennessee Middle
Arizona	Kansas	New York Northern	Tennessee Western
Arkansas Eastern	Kentucky Eastern	New York Southern	Texas Eastern
Arkansas Western	Kentucky Western	New York Western	Texas Northern
California Central	Louisiana Eastern	North Carolina	Texas Southern
California Eastern	Louisiana Middle	Eastern	Texas Western
California Northern	Louisiana Western	North Carolina Middle	Utah
California Southern	Maine	North Carolina Western	Vermont
Colorado	Maryland		Virginia Eastern
Connecticut	Massachusetts	North Dakota	Virginia Western
Delaware	Michigan Eastern	Ohio Northern	Washington Eastern
Florida Middle	Michigan Western	Ohio Southern	Washington Northern
Florida Northern	Minnesota	Oklahoma Eastern	Washington Western
Florida Southern	Mississippi Northern	Oklahoma Northern	West Virginia Northern
Georgia Middle	Mississippi Southern	Oklahoma Western	West Virginia Southern
Georgia Northern	Missouri Eastern	Oregon	Wisconsin Eastern
Georgia Southern	Missouri Western	Pennsylvania Eastern	Wisconsin Western
Hawaii	Montana	Pennsylvania Middle	Wyoming
Idaho	Nebraska	Pennsylvania Western	D.C.
Illinois Central	Nevada	Rhode Island	Puerto Rico
Illinois Northern			
Illinois Southern			

Retrieved from https://ballotpedia.org/United_States_District_Court

Circuit (simply called the DC Circuit). As an example, the 5th Circuit covers the states of Texas, Louisiana, and Mississippi, while the 7th Circuit comprises Illinois, Indiana, and Wisconsin. There is also the Court of Appeals for the Federal Circuit, which has jurisdiction over certain types of cases (e.g., patent appeal cases). Judges in the district courts are limited to 10-year terms, while those on the Court of Appeals and Supreme Court are afforded lifetime appointments. US presidents often choose circuit court judges as Supreme Court justice nominees. In addition, justices are assigned responsibility over cases filed within various federal circuits (see Table 1.2).

The Supreme Court was established by the US Constitution (Article III, Section 1), as follows:

> [t]he judicial Power of the United States, shall be vested in one Supreme Court, and in such inferior Courts as the Congress may from time to time ordain and establish.

Table 1.2 Circuit Court assignments of Supreme Court Justices

Circuit	Assigned Justice	States within circuit
District of Columbia Circuit	Chief Justice John Roberts	Washington, DC
First Circuit	Stephen Breyer	Maine, Massachusetts, New Hampshire, Puerto Rico, and Rhode Island
Second Circuit	Sonia Sotomayor	Connecticut, New York, Vermont
Third Circuit	Samuel Alito	Pennsylvania, New Jersey, Delaware, and the Virgin Islands
Fourth Circuit	Chief Justice John Roberts	Maryland, North Carolina, South Carolina, Virginia, and West Virginia
Fifth Circuit	Samuel Alito	Louisiana, Mississippi, and Texas
Sixth Circuit	Brett Kavanaugh	Kentucky, Michigan, Ohio, and Tennessee
Seventh Circuit	Amy Coney Barrett	Illinois, Indiana, and Wisconsin
Eighth Circuit	Brett Kavanaugh	Arkansas, Iowa, Minnesota, Missouri, Nebraska, North Dakota, and South Dakota
Ninth Circuit	Elena Kagan	Alaska, Arizona, California, Hawaii, Idaho, Montana, Nevada, Oregon, Washington, Guam, and the Northern Mariana Islands
Tenth Circuit	Neil Gorsuch	Colorado, Kansas, New Mexico, Oklahoma, Utah, and Wyoming
Eleventh Circuit	Clarence Thomas	Alabama, Florida, and Georgia
Federal Circuit	Chief Justice John Roberts	

Retrieved from https://www.supremecourt.gov/about/circuitassignments.aspx

Originally the Court was composed of only six justices, and the judiciary was considered to be a comparatively weak branch of government. Today, the Supreme Court consists of nine justices and generally accepts fewer than 100 cases a year. Several groups (e.g., legal scholars, politicians) have made proposals to increase the number of justices on the Court and/or to limit their terms. This idea has received some support among the public[1] and from Justice Breyer.[2] It has also received the backing of some members of the House of Representatives: a bill was introduced in the House that, among other things, proposes to limit the terms of Supreme Court Justices to 18-years.[3]

The Supreme Court decides to take cases for a variety of reasons, such as to resolve conflicting decisions across circuits, interpret lower court decisions that are at odds with previous Court rulings, and consider cases with

[1] https://www.reuters.com/article/us-usa-court-poll-idUSKCN0PU09820150720
[2] https://www.washingtonpost.com/news/wonk/wp/2016/02/13/why-its-time-to-get-serious-about-supreme-court-term-limits/
[3] https://khanna.house.gov/sites/khanna.house.gov/files/KHANNA_070_xml.pdf

Table 1.3 Different standards of proof

Highest standard of proof	Beyond a reasonable doubt	Used in criminal cases. No reasonable, additional alternatives exist that the accused is guilty. Evidence is strong enough to negate the presumption of innocence.
	Clear and convincing	Used in some civil cases. A high likelihood exists that the evidence presented is true. Can be used when a court wants to use a more difficult burden of proof.
Lowest standard of proof	Preponderance of evidence	Used in a majority of civil cases. Evidence exists that it is more likely than not that the facts are true.

particular constitutional significance. Supreme Court sessions begin on the first Monday in October and continue until the latter part of June or early July.

The standard of proof in civil cases requires the establishment of a *preponderance of evidence*[4] that the alleged discrimination transpired. The preponderance standard essentially requires the demonstration that, more likely than not, discrimination has occurred. Sometimes civil cases can require *clear and convincing* evidence (e.g., a high probability exists that discrimination is present) if a court wants to use stricter evidentiary criteria. Finally, the *beyond a reasonable doubt* standard is used in criminal cases. It is a standard designed to be more difficult to meet given the severe penalties that can occur in criminal trials, such as deprivation of life or liberty. Essentially, it requires that the evidence presented creates a reasonable certainty, sometimes referred to as a "moral" certainty, that the accused is guilty and that no viable facts or explanations exist to conclude otherwise (see Table 1.3).

Supplemental Readings on the Supreme Court

How the Court Works. (n.d.). The Supreme Court Historical Society. http://supremecourthistory.org/htcw_home.html

Nix, E. (2019, October 7). 7 Things You May Not Know About the Supreme Court. History.com. https://www.history.com/news/7-things-you-might-not-know-about-the-u-s-supreme-court

Justices 1789 to Present. (n.d.). Supreme Court of the United States. https://www.supremecourt.gov/about/members.aspx

Supreme Court Blog. https://www.scotusblog.com/author/scotustalk/

---

[4] Italicized technical terms are defined in the glossary at the end of this chapter.

Public Opinion Trends About the Court (Gallup). https://news.gallup.com/poll/4732/
    supreme-court.aspx
Interviews with Supreme Court Justices (C-Span). https://www.c-span.org/series/
    ?theSupremeCourt

Employment Discrimination Law

Constitutional Amendments

One category of law relevant to equal employment opportunity (EEO) involves some of the Constitutional Amendments. [5] Although the amendments were not designed to apply to workplace discrimination, several of them have been used in employment-related cases. These largely include the 1st, 5th, 11th, 13th, and 14th Amendments. Amendments can be useful in employment discrimination cases since, compared to legislation specific to employment discrimination law (e.g., Title VII of the Civil Right Act of 1964),[6] they can result in wider coverage, have fewer constraints, and can allow greater damage awards. Therefore, it is not uncommon for discrimination suits to be filed under both Title VII and one or more constitutional amendments.

The 1st Amendment pertains to freedom of religion, free speech, freedom of the press, the right to assemble, and the right to petition the Government. Specifically, the amendment states that "Congress shall make no law respecting an establishment of religion, or prohibiting the free exercise thereof; or abridging the freedom of speech, or of the press; or the right of the people peaceably to assemble, and to petition the government for a redress of grievances."

Although religious discrimination claims are more commonly filed under Title VII, the 1st Amendment has sometimes been used to challenge religious discrimination using both the "establishment clause" (separation of church and state) and the "free exercise clause" of the amendment (the protection of religious beliefs and the expression of those beliefs). Discrimination based on religion is the focus of Chapter 4.

The 5th Amendment guarantees, among other things, that individuals cannot be "deprived of life, liberty, or property without due process of law." In other words, individuals cannot be denied such rights without notice and the opportunity to defend themselves. The 5th Amendment only applies to

---

[5] https://constitution.findlaw.com/amendments.html
[6] https://www.eeoc.gov/laws/statutes/titlevii.cfm

discrimination by the Federal government and covers discrimination based on race as well as other suspect classifications.

The 11th Amendment protects the sovereign immunity of states and their right to govern themselves by limiting the power of the Federal government in cases against states. From the 11th Amendment:

> The Judicial power of the United States shall not be construed to extend to any suit in law or equity, commenced or prosecuted against one of the United States by Citizens of another State, or by Citizens or Subjects of any Foreign State.

An example of how the 11th Amendment has been used in lawsuits to guarantee state immunity is a decision by the Supreme Court in *Kimel v. Florida Board of Regents*, 2000).[7] Here, a private Age Discrimination in Employment Act (ADEA) suit was filed by university employees against the state alleging the denial of promotions because of age and age-based retaliation. The state employer claimed that 11th Amendment precluded private suits against states under the ADEA. The Court ruled in favor of the state. Essentially, the data presented in the case was not judged to be sufficiently persuasive to deny state immunity in private ADEA suits filed against state employers. Further, the text of the ADEA was found to lack clarity regarding its ability to nullify state immunity granted by the 11th Amendment. However, the Court concluded that "Our decision today does not signal the end of the line for employees who find themselves subject to age discrimination at the hands of their state employers. We hold only that, in the ADEA, Congress did not validly abrogate the States' sovereign immunity to suits by private individuals." It is important to note that the EEOC can file ADEA suits for private individuals against state agencies. Also, the *Kimel* decision does not deny private suits to be filed against municipal entities (e.g., police and fire departments).

The 13th Amendment outlawed slavery.[8] Section 1 of the 13th Amendment states: "Neither slavery nor involuntary servitude, except as a punishment for crime whereof the party shall have been duly convicted, shall exist within the United States, or any place subject to their jurisdiction." In the context of employment law, the amendment has been applied in cases of workplace discrimination based on race, color, and national origin. There are some advantages to employing the 13th Amendment in such cases. For instance, Title VII limits back pay to two years and only organizations with 15 or more employees must

---

[7] https://www.law.cornell.edu/supct/pdf/98-791P.ZO

[8] The 13th and 14th Amendments were enforced by earlier Civil Rights Acts in 1866 and 1871, respectively, and the Acts have been amended and codified by various statutes in the U.S. Code (e.g., Title 42 Sections 1981, 1982, 1983).

comply (Title VII is discussed later in this chapter). Neither of these limitations exist under the 13th Amendment. However, the amendment is only applicable to private entities and does not pertain to sex discrimination.

Finally, the 14th Amendment guarantees due process *and* equal protection by states as well as local governmental entities. Section 1 of the Amendment includes the following: "All persons born or naturalized in the United States, and subject to the jurisdiction thereof, are citizens of the United States and of the state wherein they reside. No state shall make or enforce any law which shall abridge the privileges or immunities of citizens of the United States; nor shall any state deprive any person of life, liberty, or property, without due process of law; nor deny to any person within its jurisdiction the equal protection of the laws."

In pragmatic terms, the amendment has been employed in (but has not been limited to) discrimination suits against private, state, and municipal agencies (e.g., police and fire departments) for alleged race and sex discrimination. For instance, it is not uncommon for the 14th Amendment to be applied in affirmative action and so-called reverse discrimination cases under the premise that such programs may violate the equal protection clause of the amendment. "Reverse discrimination" cases typically involve allegations of discrimination against individuals in a majority group (e.g., White applicants) by favoring those within underrepresented groups (e.g., Black applicants), often as a result of affirmative action programs. The issue of affirmative action is covered in Chapter 9. Finally, under the 14th Amendment, Congress can waive state 11th Amendment rights if federal laws are being infringed upon.

Supplemental Readings on Constitutional Amendments

Beginner
Constitutional Amendments (n.d.). *The New York Times.* https://www.nytimes.com/topic/subject/constitutional-amendments

Schmidt, A. (2018, December). The US Constitution has 27 amendments that protect the rights of Americans. Do you know them all? Insider. https://www.insider.com/what-are-all-the-amendments-us-constitution-meaning-history-2018-11

Intermediate
Fifth Amendment (n.d.). Cornell Law School. https://www.law.cornell.edu/constitution-conan/amendment-5

Eleventh Amendment (n.d.). Cornell Law School. https://www.law.cornell.edu/constitution-conan/amendment-11/state-sovereign-immunity

Thirteenth Amendment (n.d.). Cornell Law School. https://www.law.cornell.edu/constitution-conan/amendment-13#amdt13_hd4

Fourteenth Amendment (n.d.). Cornell Law School. https://www.law.cornell.edu/wex/fourteenth_amendment_0

Advanced
Vázquez, C. M. (1999–2000). Eleventh Amendment schizophrenia. *Notre Dame Law Review, 75*, 859–918. https://scholarship.law.georgetown.edu/facpub/549/

Wolcher, L. E. (2016). Reconciling state sovereign immunity with the Fourteenth Amendment. *Harvard Law Review, 129*, 1068–1089. http://cdn.harvardlawreview.org/wp-content/uploads/2016/02/1068-1089-Online.pdf

Major Employment Discrimination Laws

Group-Specific Discrimination Laws

Separate laws prohibit discrimination based on age (the Age Discrimination in Employment Act of 1967 [ADEA];[9] 29 U.S.C. Sec. 621 *et seq.*) and individuals with disabilities (the Americans with Disabilities Act of 1990 [ADA];[10] 42 U.S.C. Sec. 12111 *et seq.*). Other laws also exist, such as the Equal Pay Act of 1963[11] (EPA; 29 U.S.C. Sec. 206(d)), the Family and Medical Leave Act of 1993[12] (FMLA; 29 U.S.C Sec. 2601 *et seq.*), and the Pregnancy Discrimination Act[13] (PDA), which was inserted into the Civil Rights Act in 1978. Table 1.4 offers a basic summary of these major employment discriminations laws, which are discussed in depth in future chapters. In this chapter, we introduce a broader piece of legislation, Title VII of the Civil Rights Act of 1964 (42 U.S.C. Sec. 2000e *et seq.*).

Title VII

The Civil Rights Act of 1964 was a comprehensive, landmark bill. It contains 11 sections (Titles) that provide protections regarding a range of issues such as voter registration, access to public accommodations, and school desegregation. For the purpose of this book, we focus on Title VII of the Civil Rights Act of 1964,[14] which bans discrimination in employment for private- and public-sector companies with 15 or more employees on the basis of race, color, religion, sex, or national origin.

---

[9] https://www.eeoc.gov/laws/statutes/adea.cfm
[10] https://www.ada.gov/pubs/adastatute08.pdf
[11] https://www.eeoc.gov/laws/statutes/epa.cfm
[12] https://www.ecfr.gov/cgi-bin/text-idx?c=ecfr&sid=d178a2522c85f1f401ed3f3740984fed&rgn=div5&view=text&node=29:3.1.1.3.54&idno=29
[13] https://www.eeoc.gov/laws/statutes/pregnancy.cfm
[14] https://www.eeoc.gov/laws/statutes/titlevii.cfm

Table 1.4 Summary of major employment discrimination laws

Group protection	Law	Who needs to comply	Basic protections or requirements	Key points
Discrimination based on race, color, religion, sex, and national origin	Title VII of the Civil Rights Act (1964, 1972, 1978, 1991)	Public and private companies with 15 or more employees	Illegal to discriminate in personnel decisions (e.g., hiring, promotion, pay) and in terms and conditions of employment	Some Title VII exemptions include bona fide seniority systems (BFSS) and bona fide occupational qualifications (BFOQs) Illegitimate to alter, adjust, or use different passing scores based on race, color, religion, sex, and national origin Suits filed with the EEOC must be done in a timely fashion; 300 days in deferral states and 180 days in non-deferral states Jury trials are allowed
Pay discrimination	Equal Pay Act (1963); Lily Ledbetter Fair Pay Restoration Act	Public and private entities of all sizes Public and private companies with 15 or more employees	Mandates the same rate of pay for men and women doing substantially equal work Altered the time frame for filing a Title VII pay discrimination claim	Jobs are deemed equal if they require equal skill, effort, responsibility, and working conditions Market forces is not an allowable defense of pay disparities between men and women If pay discrimination exists, each pay check is considered a new violation of law An unlawful pay decision occurs when it is put into effect, people become subject to it, or individuals are impacted by its use
Pregnancy discrimination	Pregnancy Discrimination Act (1978)	Public and private companies with 15 or more employees	Pregnant employees must be treated the same as others in their ability or inability to work	It is illegal to not hire female applicants because of pregnancy After taking leave, females must be allowed to return to their same (or equivalent) job Disparate treatment process can be used to decide pregnancy discrimination cases

(continued)

Table 1.4 Continued

Group protection	Law	Who needs to comply	Basic protections or requirements	Key points
Sexual harassment	(a) Title VII of the Civil Rights Act[1]	Public and private companies with 15 or more employees	Illegal to (a) Make personnel decisions dependent on receipt of a sexual favor (quid pro quo) or (b) perform an unwelcomed sexual behavior that creates a hostile work environment	Sexual harassment can be committed by supervisors, co-workers, and clients Organizations can be found vicariously liable (e.g., behavior of supervisors) but companies have an affirmative defense Men and women are protected Same-sex harassment is covered
Family and medical leave	Family and Medical Leave Act (FMLA; 1993)	Organizations with 50 or more employees	Requires granting 12 weeks of unpaid leave for those with serious medical conditions, including childbirth and caring for an immediate family member	Leave is available to both mothers and fathers Seniority does not have to accumulate during FMLA leave Organizations can ask for medical information from a health care provider regarding am employee's serious medical condition
Disability discrimination	Rehabilitation Act (RE '73); Americans with Disabilities Act ADA); Americans With Disabilities Amendments Act (ADAAA)	Public and private organizations affecting commerce with 15 or more employees	Outlaws employment discrimination for qualified individuals with a disability	To be considered as a disability an impairment must substantially limit a major life activity Both physical and mental impairments are covered Individuals must be qualified to perform the job (able to perform essential job duties with or without a reasonable accommodation) Disabilities are assessed without considering possible corrective measures (e.g., medicine) Accommodations are not required if they pose an undue hardship for organizations
Age discrimination	Age Discrimination in Employment Act (ADEA; 1967)	Public and private organizations with 20 or more employees	Bans discrimination against those 40 years old or older	Adverse impact cases are allowed but with different criteria than Title VII An ADEA violation can occur even if the more favorably treated employee/applicant is also in the protected age group Mixed-motive cases are *not* allowed under the ADEA Claims can be filed if a substantially younger person was treated more favorably or the favored individual was a "similarly situated" younger individual

Affirmative action	Executive Order 11246	Federal agencies; Federal contractors with minimum contracts of $10,000	Requires preferences for racial minorities and females regarding personnel decisions if under-represented in the workforce	The use of minority status as a "plus factor" is legitimate if it constitutes a relatively small part in the decision-making process and other factors were involved Strict scrutiny must be met for affirmative action programs to be legal Affirmative action approaches are generally legitimate if they address a compelling state interest (e.g., diversity in higher education), are narrowly tailored, and do not trammel on the rights of those in the majority States can ban the use of affirmative action programs
Retaliation	Title VII of the Civil Rights Act, Section 704(a)	Public and private companies with 15 or more employees	Illegal to retaliate against employees who challenge an employment practice (opposition clause) or file a claim against an organization (participation clause)	Evidence must exist that employees suffered a material adverse action (one that would deter a reasonable person from engaging in a protected activity) Organizations must have *prior knowledge* that employees engaged in protected activities Retaliation against third parties is protected Mixed-motive cases are *not* allowed for retaliation Plaintiffs must show that retaliation was the (*but for*) reason for the adverse employment action (not a motivating factor)

1 Sexual harassment is considered a form of sex discrimination.

Although sex discrimination suits are relatively common today, it was not the initial intention of lawmakers to include sex as a protected class within Title VII.[15] An amendment to include sex as a protected group was introduced at the last minute in the House of Representatives—two days before the House vote (e.g., Freeman, 1991[16]; Gold, 1980[17]). There has been a lively discussion as to why sex was introduced into Title VII. Was it done to defeat the bill, as a joke, or as a genuine effort to protect women from employment discrimination? Title VII was ultimately passed by the Senate (June 19, 1964) and the House (July 2, 1964) and quickly signed into law by President Johnson on the same day the House approved the bill (see Vaas, 1966).[18] By virtue of sex being added as a protected group at the last minute, there was little discussion or legislative history accompanying its inclusion. Consequently, Congress and various legislative agencies were not properly equipped for future sex discrimination cases.

Legal Commentary: What Motivated the Introduction of "Sex" into Title VII of the Civil Rights Act of 1964?

There has been a lot of discussion regarding the motivation for including "sex" within Title VII, especially given its late addition into the bill. One long-standing view is that it was introduced as a means to stop the bill's passage (see Berry, 2003; Guion, 1998). This position was reinforced by the Equal Employment Opportunity Commission (EEOC) when discussing the history of Title VII on its 40th anniversary.

Others have noted that sex was possibly incorporated as a joke (see Vaas, 1966). This view is reinforced by the humorous manner in which the Amendment that included sex was introduced, as well as several House of Representative members employing the phrase "Ladies Day" when the amendment was proposed. Also, in an interaction between the since-retired Representative Howard Smith (who introduced the amendment) and Representative Martha Griffiths (who led the support for Smith's amendment) lends some credence to the joke position. After Griffiths reminisced with Smith about the inclusion of sex into Title VII, Smith replied to her that he had proposed the amendment as a joke.

---

[15] More than 40 amendments were introduced into the House bill. The vast majority of these were not incorporated within to the Senate version.

[16] https://heinonline.org/HOL/P?h=hein.journals/duqu19&i=465

[17] https://heinonline.org/HOL/P?h=hein.journals/duqu19&i=465

[18] https://lawdigitalcommons.bc.edu/cgi/viewcontent.cgi?referer=https://scholar.google.com/scholar?hl=en&as_sdt=0,10&q=Vaas,+F.+J.+(1966).+Title+VII:+Legislative+history.+Boston+College+Industrial+%26+Commercial+Law+Review,+43&httpsredir=1&article=3038&context=bclr

Highhouse contends that placing sex into Title VII was not a joke (Highhouse & Gutman, 2011). His rationale includes the fact that Representative Smith repeatedly discussed supporting a "sex amendment" since the mid-1950s. Smith also had a friendly connection with the National Women's Party, which considered him an ally. Furthermore, Smith stated on the television program *Meet the Press*, in response to a question, that he might incorporate equal rights for women into Title VII. Finally, as Highhouse notes, Representative Smith, who harbored racist views, was worried that Title VII could be disadvantageous to White females. Given that the bill had widespread support, Highhouse contends that Smith, by introducing sex into Title VII, may have sought to guarantee legal protection for women.

This view was reinforced by Gutman, who adds that several female Congressional Representatives strongly supported having sex included in Title VII (Highhouse & Gutman, 2011). This was particularly true of efforts by Representative Martha Griffith to pass the amendment. Consistent with the view of Highhouse and that of Gold (1980), Gutman asserts that Representative Smith was keenly aware that Title VII had enough votes to pass and wanted to protect women from employment discrimination. Gutman further asserts that introducing sex into Title VII at the last minute without much debate hampered the enforcement of sex discrimination for many years (because the addition included little guidance for handling sex-based claims). However, there is no doubt that placing sex into Title VII was a "big deal," one that has led to numerous legal protections for women and the LGBTQ+ community.

As mentioned earlier, organizations with 15 or more employees must comply with Title VII. An "employee" in this case is defined as an individual who has been in an "employment relationship" with an organization full-time, part-time, or on a temporary basis for a minimum of 20 weeks during the current or previous year. Evidence of a so-called employment relationship can include things like organizational control over supervision and work duties or the presence of the individual on the organization's payroll. Those who are considered independent contractors do not count as employees.

The goal of Title VII was to offer widespread safeguards for protected group members from workplace discrimination (see Gutman & Dunleavy, 2013, for a summary of four ongoing "controversial" Title VII issues involving adverse impact theory, reverse discrimination, retaliation, and sexual harassment). This protection includes nondiscrimination in compensation, terms, conditions, or privileges of employment, as well as in hiring, promotion, and

Table 1.5 Summary of amendments to Title VII of the Civil Rights Act (CRA)

Amendment	Summary
CRA 1972	Added public sector coverage, gave EEOC power to sue, expanded organizations covered from those with 25 to those with 15 employees, increased time frame to file EEOC suits (from 90 to 180 days in non-deferral states [ones without EEO laws]; from 210 to 300 days in deferral states [ones with EEO laws])
CRA 1978	Reorganization Plan. EEOC given authority to enforce anti-discrimination laws and coordinate federal equal employment opportunity programs, passed the Pregnancy Discrimination Act[1] (PDA); administration of Equal Pay Act[2] and ADEA[3] moved to EEOC (from Department of Justice; DOJ)
CRA 1991[4]	Clarified burden of proof in adverse-impact and mixed-motive scenarios, banned test score adjustment based on minority status, allowed compensatory and punitive damages for intentional discrimination, jury trials, and coverage for expert witness fees. CRA '91 overturned several Supreme Court cases, most of which will be discussed later in the text. Appendix A contains a summary of cases that were affected by CRA '91.

[1] https://www.eeoc.gov/laws/statutes/pregnancy.cfm
[2] https://www.eeoc.gov/laws/statutes/epa.cfm
[3] https://www.eeoc.gov/laws/statutes/adea.cfm
[4] https://www.eeoc.gov/eeoc/history/35th/thelaw/cra_1991.html

termination decisions (see EEOC list of prohibited practices/policies).[19] As is shown in Table 1.5, Title VII has been amended on multiple occasions, most notably in 1972, 1978, and 1991. Some key features of the amended versions include granting the right of the EEOC to sue, adding coverage to the public sector, increasing time frames for filing suits with the EEOC, legal protection for pregnant employees, the banning of test score adjustment based on protected group status, allowing compensatory and punitive damages, and the permitting of jury trials. The Civil Rights Act of 1991 (Pub.L.No. 102-166, 105 Stat. 1071) also overturned several employment discrimination decisions by the Supreme Court (see Table 1.6).

Some Title VII Exemptions
Bona Fide Seniority Systems
Several exemptions exist within Title VII.[20] One involves the use of seniority systems as a basis for making employment decisions (e.g., when an individual with more years with a company is given preference for a promotion or is last to be terminated when layoffs are implemented). Such seniority systems can

[19] https://www.eeoc.gov/laws/practices/index.cfm
[20] Title VII exemptions also exist for religion and are discussed in Chapter 4.

Table 1.6 Supreme Court cases overturned by the Civil Rights Act of 1991 (CRA-91)

Case	Issue	Court decision	Codified in CRA-91
Price Waterhouse v. Hopkins (1989)[1]	Proof and liability in mixed-motive cases	In mixed-motive cases (where illegal and legal factors are used), organizations could escape liability if they presented evidence that they would have made the same decision absent the illegal factor used	It is unlawful if the plaintiff demonstrates that *race, color, religion, sex, or national origin was a* motivating *factor in their decision.* Liability is minimized if defense proves they would have made the same decision absent use of the illegal factor
Lorance v. AT&T (1989)[2]	Challenges to seniority systems	The challenge to the seniority system was filed too late. Filing period begins when the plan is adopted	Seniority systems can be challenged when *adopted*, when a person *becomes subject* to them, or when a person is injured by its *application*
Martin v. Wilks (1989)[3]	Challenges to existing consent decrees	Plaintiffs could challenge a consent decree, after the fact, because one party (White firefighters) chose not to participate in the process. The Court ruled that the White firefighters were denied an opportunity to have input into the contents of the decree	Consent decrees cannot be challenged at a later date if plaintiffs were available to present objections, had a reasonable opportunity to present, or had interests that were adequately represented by another person
Wards Cove v. Atonio (1989)[4]	Defense burden in adverse impact cases	The defense must articulate, not prove	Defense in adverse impact cases must demonstrate (burden of production and persuasion) that the challenged practice is job-related and consistent with business necessity
Patterson v. McClean Credit Union (1989)[5]	Racial harassment	Civil Rights Act of 1866 does not cover racial harassment on the job of current employees	The phrase "make and enforce contracts" in the Civil Rights Act of 1866 covers racial harassment of those in a contractual relationship (current employees)

[1] http://caselaw.findlaw.com/scripts/getcase.pl?navby=search&linkurl=%3C%LINKURL%%3E&graphurl=%3C%GRAPHURL%%3E&court=US&case=/data/us/490/228.html
[2] https://supreme.justia.com/cases/federal/us/490/900/case.html
[3] https://www.law.cornell.edu/supremecourt/text/490/755#writing-USSC_CR_0490_0755_ZO
[4] https://www.law.cornell.edu/supremecourt/text/490/642#writing-USSC_CR_0490_0642_ZO
[5] https://www.law.cornell.edu/supremecourt/text/491/164#writing-USSC_CR_0491_0164_ZO

disadvantage traditionally underrepresented subgroups (e.g., women, people of color) who have traditionally acquired fewer years on the job than have White men. Given this, traditionally underrepresented subgroups can be the first to be negatively affected by various personnel practices such as reduction in force efforts and promotion decisions.

Nonetheless, seniority systems have been utilized by numerous organizations to make personnel decisions and are a common element in *collective bargaining agreements* with unions. Overall, Title VII (e.g., Section 703(h)) and case law (e.g., *International Brotherhood of Teamsters v. United States*; 1977)[21,22] state that it is legitimate to use seniority systems (which in this context are termed *bona fide seniority systems* [BFSS]) as long as they are not designed with the intent to discriminate (see also Zimmer, 1980).[23] Seniority systems can be upheld (absent proof of intent) even if discrimination is found to exist.

One case that involved a seniority system was *US Airways v. Barnett* (2002).[24,25] Here, Robert Barnett hurt his back and could not perform his job of cargo handler (see also Anderson, 2002).[26] Barnett was transferred to a job that did not require much lifting (a mailroom position). After two years had passed, an official posting for a mailroom job appeared. Barnett applied but was not given the job since two other employees with greater seniority were also in the applicant pool. He sued the airline under Title VII as part of a broader disability lawsuit claiming that the company failed to reasonably accommodate his disability. Barnett noted that the seniority system was not part of a collective bargaining agreement—it was developed unilaterally. Fundamentally, the case was about whether the requirement to reasonably accommodate a disability is greater than rights of employees under a seniority system. The Court ruled in favor of US Airways, favoring the seniority system. As the Court stated,

> In our view, the seniority system will prevail in the run of cases. As we interpret the statute, to show that a requested accommodation conflicts with the rules of a seniority system is ordinarily to show that the accommodation is not "reasonable."

---

[21] https://caselaw.findlaw.com/us-supreme-court/431/324.html
[22] https://www.oyez.org/cases/1976/75-636
[23] https://scholarship.law.marquette.edu/cgi/viewcontent.cgi?article=2050&context=mulr
[24] https://www.law.cornell.edu/supct/html/00-1250.ZO.html
[25] https://www.oyez.org/cases/2001/00-1250
[26] https://lawreviewdrake.files.wordpress.com/2015/04/anderson.pdf

Another seniority-related case that centered around *when* a lawsuit needs to be filed is *Lorance v. AT&T*, 1989.[27,28] In this case, a collective bargaining agreement was reached in 1979 between AT&T and the labor union in which *job* seniority (not overall seniority within the company) would be used as criteria for employees in the "tester" position—a job mostly occupied by men. The economy worsened a few years later, and, given the new collective bargaining agreement, several women in the tester position were demoted. This was because they had less job tenure in the tester position than did men. A Title VII sex discrimination suit was filed in 1982, alleging that the collective bargaining agreement violated Title VII.

The Supreme Court ruled that the plaintiffs had waited too long to file their claim. In *Lorance*, the suit was filed past the deadline of 300 days after the seniority system was adopted. Strict time frames exist for filing a lawsuit with the EEOC. Lawsuits not meeting established deadlines can lead to claims being dismissed. The filing deadlines vary by state. In states with employment discrimination laws ("deferral" states), claims need to be filed with the EEOC within 300 days. In states without employment discrimination laws ("non-deferral" states), claims must be filed within 180 days.[29,30] So, in the end, the Court concluded that the suit in *Lorance* was time-barred but also took the opportunity to reiterate its longstanding position that, for seniority systems to be illegal, *intent* to discriminate needs to be proved even if adverse impact exists. Quoting from its decision in *Trans World Airlines, Inc. v. Hardison* (1977), the Court noted that "absent a discriminatory purpose, the operation of a seniority system cannot be an unlawful employment practice even if the system is discriminatory in its effect." In *Lorance*, the plaintiffs were unable to prove that the seniority system was intentionally designed to discriminate against women.

The *dissent* in *Lorance* contended that the decision encourages plaintiffs to sue in *anticipation of*, or before, an actual violation. In *Lorance*, women in the tester job were not affected by the collective bargaining agreement until after 300 days had passed. Consequently, prior to being harmed by the

---

[27] https://supreme.justia.com/cases/federal/us/490/900/case.html
[28] https://www.oyez.org/cases/1988/87-1428
[29] https://www.eeoc.gov/employees/timeliness.cfm
[30] https://www.eeoc.gov/employees/howtofile.cfm

agreement (demotions), the ability to provide evidence for a sex discrimination suit would have been legally problematic. The view of the dissent was supported when the Civil Rights Act of 1991[31] overruled the *Lorance* decision. The Act states that an illegal action occurs when

- the seniority system is adopted,
- when individuals become subject to a seniority system, or
- individuals are injured by the application of the seniority system.

Bona Fide Occupational Qualifications

Bona fide occupational qualifications[32] (BFOQs) are another exception to Title VII. Basically, the BFOQ defense permits organizations to discriminate against certain protected groups "where religion, sex, or national origin is a bona fide occupational qualification reasonably necessary to the normal operation of that particular business or enterprise." The BFOQ defense has applied to age-related job requirements as well.

BFOQs are meant to be interpreted rather narrowly. That is, they are literally exceptions to the rule. As such, BFOQs must be supported by facts and cannot be defended by using assumptions, stereotypes, convenience, or the preference of others.[33] For instance, organizations cannot limit their hiring practices to only women simply because of customer preference. An early case rejecting customer preference as a rationale for only hiring female flight attendants (an alleged BFOQ) was illustrated by *Diaz v. Pan Am World Airways* (1971). As the 5th Circuit stated,

> Pan Am argues that the customers' preferences are not based on "stereotyped thinking," but the ability of women stewardesses to better provide the non-mechanical aspects of the job. . . . [S]ince these aspects are tangential to the business, the fact that customers prefer them cannot justify sex discrimination.

When defending the use of a BFOQ, organizations need to show that (1) they have a reasonable cause (factual basis) that members of a given protected group as a whole (e.g., women, older individuals) cannot perform job tasks efficiently or safely, (2) that individual assessment of group members is impractical, and (3) no useful alternatives are available. The use of BFOQs for

[31] https://www.eeoc.gov/laws/statutes/cra-1991.cfm
[32] https://www.law.cornell.edu/wex/bona_fide_occupational_qualification_(bfoq)
[33] https://www.law.cornell.edu/cfr/text/29/1604.2

specific protected groups (e.g., sex, age) will be covered in relevant chapters later in the text.

Supplemental Readings on Seniority Systems and Bona Fide Occupational Qualifications

Beginner

Dick, J. (2019 May). Longshoremen claim sex discrimination, abuse of seniority system. Beaumont Enterprise. https://www.beaumontenterprise.com/news/article/Longshoremen-claim-sex-discrimination-abuse-of-13827263.php

Glasser, N. M., Forman, A. S., & Savage Aibel, M. (2019 November). INSIGHT: Online ads targeting job applicants under scrutiny from EEOC, Plaintiff's Bar. Bloomberg Law. https://news.bloomberglaw.com/daily-labor-report/insight-online-ads-targeting-job-applicants-under-scrutiny-from-eeoc-plaintiffs-bar

Intermediate

Cavico, F. J., & Mujaba, B. G. (2016). The bona fide occupational qualification (BFOQ) defense in employment discrimination: A narrow and limited justification exception. *Journal of Business Studies Quarterly, 7*, 15–29.

Gutman, A. (2002). The Supreme Court ruling in US Airways v. Barnett. *The Industrial-Organizational Psychologist, 40*, 90–94.

Advanced

Brandon, B. W. (1984). The seniority system exemption to Title VII of the Civil Rights Acts: The impact of a new barrier to Title VII litigants. *Cleveland State Law Review, 32*, 607–640. https://engagedscholarship.csuohio.edu/cgi/viewcontent.cgi?referer=https://scholar.google.com/scholar?hl=en&as_sdt=0%2C10&q=The+seniority+system+exemption+to+Title+VII+of+the+Civil+Rights+Acts%3A+The+impact+of+a+new+barrier+to+Title+VII+litigants.+Cleveland+State+Law+Review%2C+32%2C+607--640&btnG=&httpsredir=1&article=2047&context=clevstlrev

Manley, K. (2009). The BFOQ defense: Title VII's concession to gender discrimination. *Duke Journal of Gender Law & Policy, 16*, 169–210. https://scholarship.law.duke.edu/cgi/viewcontent.cgi?article=1160&context=djglp

---

Key Administrative Agencies

Equal Employment Opportunity Commission

The primary federal agency responsible for issues of employment discrimination is the Equal Employment Opportunity Commission[34] (EEOC; see

---

[34] https://www.eeoc.gov

also important links listed here). The headquarters of the agency is located in Washington, DC, but more than 50 locations exist throughout the United States.

Important Links Related to the Equal Employment Opportunity Commission

- Timeline of important EEOC events. https://www.eeoc.gov/youth/timeline-important-eeoc-events
- What You Should Know About COVID-19 and the ADA, the Rehabilitation Act, and Other EEO Laws. https://www.eeoc.gov/wysk/what-you-should-know-about-covid-19-and-ada-rehabilitation-act-and-other-eeo-laws
- Filing a Charge of Discrimination with the EEOC. https://www.eeoc.gov/filing-charge-discrimination
- EEOC multimedia gallery. https://www.eeoc.gov/youth/multimedia-gallery
- EEOC enforcement and litigation statistics. https://www.eeoc.gov/eeoc/statistics/enforcement/index.cfm

---

Employees who believe they are victims of employment discrimination have the option of filing a charge with the EEOC. Beyond filing suits, the EEOC investigates charges of alleged discrimination, reaches settlements with organizations, develops interpretive guidelines, issues regulations, and engages in prevention efforts (e.g., education and assistance programs). The laws enforced by the EEOC include Title VII, the Pregnancy Discrimination Act, Equal Pay Act, the Age Discrimination in Employment Act, and the Americans with Disabilities Act. The EEOC also enforces cases involving workplace retaliation and sexual harassment. For a review of how the EEOC has affected workplace practices, see Schlanger and Kim (2014).

Table 1.7 provides the number of discrimination charges filed with the EEOC over the past several years. Table 1.8 breaks down the 2020 charges filed by discrimination type. As shown, some types of lawsuits are more common than others, with the most common involving retaliation, race, disability, sex, and age. Figure 1.2 illustrates the phases that charges filed with EEOC go through. As shown, once filed, the charge is investigated by the EEOC (Landy, 2005). If the charge is determined to have merit, the

Table 1.7 Equal Employment Opportunity Commission (EEOC) charges by year 2013–2020

Year	2013	2014	2015	2016	2017	2018	2019	2020
Number of charges	93,727	88,778	89,385	91,503	84,254	76,418	72,765	67,448

Retrieved from https://www.eeoc.gov/statistics/charge-statistics-charges-filed-eeoc-fy-1997-through-fy-2020

EEOC will seek an amicable resolution between the parties (known as *conciliation*). If this is not successful, the EEOC issues a right-to-sue letter to the charging party (this must also be issued upon request even if the charge is determined to be without merit). At this point, the charging party may file a formal complaint with the court, naming the specific plaintiff and defendants. If the plaintiffs are a class of individuals, then the court must certify the class prior to the case going to trial. Both of these stages involve long and formal processes of discovery where evidence is collected, experts are deposed, and reports are filed with the court. At every stage

Table 1.8 Equal Employment Opportunity Commission (EEOC) charges by discrimination type (2020)

Discrimination type	Number of charges
Retaliation: All Statutes	37,632
Race	22,064
Disability	24,324
Sex	21,398
Age	14,183
National origin	6,377
Sexual harassment	6,587
Religion	2,404
Color	3,562
Pregnancy discrimination	2,698
LBGTQ	1,857
Equal Pay Act	980

Retrieved from https://www.eeoc.gov/statistics/charge-statistics-charges-filed-eeoc-fy-1997-through-fy-2020

Phases of EEO Litigation

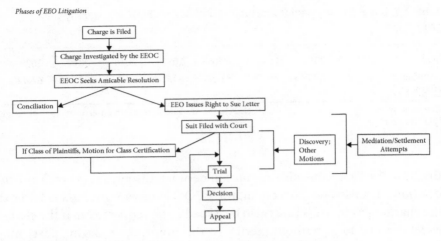

Figure 1.2 Phases of equal employment opportunity (EEO) litigation.
Adapted from Landy (2005).

there may be attempts to settle the case prior to trial and/or a formal decision by the court.

EEOC Settlements

It is fairly common for discrimination suits to end in settlements between the EEOC and organizations. Settlements are agreements between both parties (also known as *consent decrees*) that are mutually acceptable to each side (see EEOC Settlement Standards and Procedures).[35] These agreements can save time and money especially if they are reached early in the investigative process. Although settlements do not hold defendants liable and result in the dismissal of charges, they are legally enforceable and are often accompanied by monetary compensation to plaintiffs, as well as other forms of relief (e.g., mandatory training programs). Representative settlements will be summarized in each chapter and contain links to summaries of the settlements issued by the EEOC. As you will see, these settlements can result in significant monetary rewards to plaintiffs and contain other forms of relief that last for multiple years. Also, many claims contain multiple allegations of discrimination (e.g., sexual harassment and retaliation). To reduce redundancy, we organize settlements based on what we view to be the primary charge.

[35] https://www.eeoc.gov/eeoc/litigation/manual/3-4-a_settlement_standards.cfm

Office of Federal Contract Compliance Programs

Another relevant agency is the Office of Federal Contract Compliance Programs[36] (OFCCP). This agency is housed within the Department of Labor[37] and is responsible for the administration of Executive Order (EO) 11246,[38] as amended, for private, state, and municipal organizations. Federal contractors with contracts of $10,000 or more need to comply with OFCCP requirements. This figure represents the vast majority of organizations with government contracts. An informative site to keep abreast of OFCCP activity is provided by DCI Consulting.[39]

EO 11246 requires contractors with the federal government to implement affirmative action plans to help ensure that underrepresented individuals with protected status (e.g., women, persons of color) are not subject to adverse impact within employment decisions. We discuss the work of the OFCCP in greater detail within the affirmative action chapter.

A major difference between the EEOC and the OFCCP is that whereas the EEOC largely investigates claims filed by individuals, the OFCCP audits federal contractors to ensure compliance. The OFCCP investigative process is summarized in Table 1.9. The OFCCP has the power to inflict penalties on noncompliant organizations and can do so outside of the court system (i.e., *prior* to going to court).

Table 1.9 Overview of Office of Federal Contract Compliance Programs (OFCCP) Investigative Process

Step 1	OFFCP compliance review (e.g., desk audits using EEO-1 form; AAP data; onsite reviews)
Step 2	OFCCP tries to gain voluntary compliance if contractors are judged to be in violation
Step 3	If voluntary compliance is unsuccessful (e.g., no agreement), OFCCP can issue sanctions/fines
Step 4	Contractors may appeal OFCCP ruling; case goes to an Administrative Law Judge from the Department of Labor
Step 5	Contractors have to appeal to the Secretary of Labor (and lose) to have case forwarded to federal district court
Step 6	In federal district court, contractors must prove their innocence

Adapted from Dunleavy, E. M., & Gutman, A. (2010).

[36] https://www.dol.gov/ofccp/
[37] https://www.dol.gov
[38] https://www.dol.gov/ofccp/regs/statutes/eo11246.htm
[39] https://blog.dciconsult.com/

EEO in the Wild: Reducing Discrimination in the Interview: The Role of Artificial Intelligence

Furhat Robotics of Sweden has developed a robot (named Tengai) to interview job candidates. The approach is designed to eliminate common interview biases (e.g., first impressions) and discrimination based on such factors as race, sex, and age. Tengai can emit human-like expressions (e.g., smiling), to make the interactions more natural. The robot asks all candidates the same questions in the same voice tone. After the interview is completed, transcripts of the candidate's responses are reviewed by hiring officials to decide who will continue to the next step of the selection process.

   Test interviews were conducted to further refine the algorithms used to ensure Tengai emits as little bias as possible. An ultimate goal is to have the robot decide for itself which candidates are eligible to move to the next phase. A large recruitment firm in Sweden, TNG, started using the robot for interviews, and Tengai hired its first candidate, Anders Ornhed, for a job as digital coordinator at the municipality office. Such AI interventions are of particular interest in Sweden, given survey results suggesting that over 70% of candidates there believe to have been discriminated against when applying for jobs. What are your thoughts on this approach? Do you foresee any legal vulnerabilities from using robot interviewers? For more information, see Holloway (2019) and Savage (2019).

Recommendations/Best Practices

- Know the constitutional amendments that can be applied to employment discrimination.
- Know who qualifies as an "employee" under Title VII.
- Know the basic protections offered by Title VII, including the amended versions (e.g., 1972, 1978, 1991).
- Use bona fide occupational qualifications sparingly as a defense, and, when used, be sure to collect the evidence that is needed to support them.
- Regarding seniority systems, know when an illegal action occurs as stated in the Civil Rights Act of 1991.
- Know the requirements of the OFCCP and the investigative process that the agency uses.

Summary and Take-Aways

We began this chapter with a brief introduction to the court system for civil cases. Although the Supreme Court gets the most national attention, very few cases ever reach the Supreme Court. The vast majority of lawsuits end in the District Courts or Courts of Appeals. As one of the three co-equal branches of government, the Court has the ability to rule on the constitutionality of laws—sometimes ruling that certain laws violate the Constitution. On the other hand, Congress can amend laws in order to reverse decisions by the Supreme Court. As noted earlier, several Supreme Court decisions regarding employment discrimination were reversed by the Civil Rights Act of 1991.

As you can tell from the number and types of lawsuits listed in this chapter, employment discrimination continues to be a great concern from social, financial, and legal perspectives. Given this, sufficient knowledge of relevant constitutional amendments, laws, and key court cases related to employment discrimination is important for both employees and organizations alike. It is also beneficial to be cognizant of the functions of major agencies that regulate laws banning workplace discrimination. These include investigative procedures, regulations, enforcement and policy guidance, compliance manuals, and much more.

Glossary

Beyond a reasonable doubt: The strictest standard of proof that can be met. This standard is required to convict a criminal defendant of a crime.

Bona fide seniority systems: An established system in companies giving individuals with more years of tenure preference for a promotion, and/or terminating these individuals last when layoffs are implemented.

Case law: Judges use previous court decisions or precedents to create case law when deciding individual cases or disputes.

Clear and convincing: A higher standard than preponderance of evidence, this standard requires the trier of fact to conclude that there is highly probable evidence for the claim or defense.

Collective bargaining agreements: A contract or agreement between an employer and one or more unions that creates the terms of employment for the employees who belong to that labor union. The contract may include provisions regarding wages, paid time off, working hours and conditions, health insurance, and other benefits.

Consent decree: Agreement or settlement between two parties that concludes a lawsuit instead of resolving the case through a hearing and/ or trial. Consent decrees and consent judgments are the same.

Dissent: A disagreement or difference of opinion with the majority opinion among judges.

Precedent: Deference to a prior reported opinion (often of an appeals court) to form the basis of a legal argument in a subsequent case; the principle announced by a higher court that should be followed in later cases.

Preponderance of evidence: Evidence that indicates that a violation of law (e.g., discrimination) was more likely than not to be true. This is the type of evidence commonly used in civil trials, and is the least strict standard of evidence, as compared to beyond a reasonable doubt and clear and convincing evidence.

Glossary terms adapted from Gutman et al. (2011); https://uslegal.com/; merriamwebster.com/legal.

Cases Cited

Diaz v. Pan Am. World Airways, Inc., 442 F. 2d 385 (5th Cir. 1971).
Lorance v. AT&T Technologies, 490 U.S. 900, 911-12 (1989).
International Brotherhood of Teamsters v. United States, 431 U.S. 324 (1977).
Martin v. Wilks, 490 U.S. 755 (1989).
Patterson v. McLean Credit Union, 491 U.S. 164 (1989).
Price Waterhouse v. Hopkins, 490 U.S. 228 (1989).
Trans World Airlines, Inc. v. Hardison, 432 U.S. 63 (1977).
US Airways, Inc. v. Barnett, 535 U.S. 391 (2002).
Wards Cove Packing Co. v. Atonio, 490 U.S. 642 (1989).

References

Anderson, C. L. (2002). Neutral employer policies and the ADA: The implications of *US Airways, Inc. v. Barnett* beyond seniority systems. *Drake Law Review, 51,* 1–43.
Berry, L. M. (2003). *Employee selection*. Belmont, CA: Wadsworth.
Dunleavy, E. M., & Gutman, A. (2010). OFCCP settlement review: What was the burden on Bank of America? *The Industrial-Organizational Psychologist, 48,* 73–80.
Freeman, J. (1991). How sex got into Title VII: Persistent opportunism as a maker of public policy. *Law & Inequality: A Journal of Theory and Practice, 9,* 163–184.
Gold, M. E. (1980). A tale of two amendments: The reasons congress added sex to Title VII and their implication for the issue of comparable worth. *Duquesne Law Review, 19,* 453–477.

Guion, R. M. (1998). *Assessment, measurement, and prediction for personnel decisions.* Mahwah, NJ: Erlbaum.

Gutman, A., & Dunleavy, E. M. (2013). Contemporary Title VII enforcement: The song remains the same? *Journal of Business and Psychology, 28,* 487–503.

Highhouse, S., & Gutman, A. (2011). Was the addition of sex to Title VII a joke? Two viewpoints. *The Industrial-Organizational Psychologist, 48,* 102–107.

Holloway, H. (2019 September). Robot hires human being in world first as AI conducts job interview. Daily Star.https://www.dailystar.co.uk/news/world-news/robot-hires-human-being-world-19572551

Landy, F. J. (2005). Phases of employment litigation. In F. J. Landy (Ed.), *Employment discrimination litigation: Behavioral, quantitative, and legal perspectives* (pp. 3–19). San Francisco, CA: John Wiley & Sons.

Savage, M. (2019 March). Meet Tengai, the job interview robot who won't judge you. BBC News. https://www.bbc.com/news/amp/business-47442953

Schlanger, M., & Kim, P. (2014). The Equal Employment Opportunity Commission and structural reform of the American workplace. *Washington University Law Review, 91,* 1519–1590.

Vaas, F. J. (1966). Title VII: Legislative history. *Boston College Law Review, 7,* 431–458.

Zimmer, M. J. (1980). Title VII: Treatment of seniority systems. *Marquette Law Review, 64,* 79–102.

2

Basic Discrimination Scenarios

The objective of this chapter is to provide readers with a fundamental understanding of various forms of employment discrimination. Detailed information pertaining to these basic types of discrimination is contained in separate chapters that cover discrimination against various *protected classes*[1] such as race, sex, and age.

Proving discrimination in civil suits involves a three-step burden-shifting process. The initial phase consists of evidence provided by *plaintiffs* (those filing a suit) to establish a *prima facie* ("at first glance") case. The second phase allows the *defense* to justify its actions, which is then followed by the last phase in which plaintiffs counter the defense's arguments. The specific details involved in the phases vary by the type of case being filed and are described in the following sections.

Disparate Treatment

Disparate treatment involves *intentionally* treating individuals differently based on their membership in a protected group. In many respects,

---

[1] Italicized technical terms are defined in the glossary at the end of this chapter.

Employment Discrimination. Stephen J. Vodanovich and Deborah E. Rupp, Oxford University Press. © Oxford University Press 2022. DOI: 10.1093/oso/9780190085421.003.0003

this is the form of discrimination that Title VII of the Civil Rights Act of 1964 sought to outlaw. As stated in *International Brotherhood of Teamsters v. United States* (1977):

> Disparate treatment . . . is the most easily understood type of discrimination. The employer simply treats some people less favorably than others because of their race, color, religion, sex, or national origin. Proof of discriminatory motive is critical, although it can in some situations be inferred from the mere fact of differences in treatment.

Establishing a *prima facie* case for disparate treatment entails presenting sufficient *presumptive* (assumed to be true) direct or indirect evidence to support a claim of discrimination. Direct or "smoking gun" evidence of the intent to discriminate (e.g., policies that obviously prohibit hiring of protected group members; admitting guilt) is typically unavailable. Consequently, most employment discrimination claims, including those of disparate treatment, involve the presentation of indirect (or circumstantial) evidence by plaintiffs. If plaintiffs are successful in phase 1, the burden shifts to the defense to *articulate* (produce) a legal reason for their alleged discriminatory employment practice in phase 2. Finally, in phase 3, plaintiffs must counter the evidence offered by the defense by proving that the reason given by the organization is *pretext* for discriminatory behavior. The disparate treatment scenario is summarized in Table 2.1.

The criteria for establishing a *prima facie* case commonly involves presenting evidence that (1) plaintiffs belong to a protected class, (2) they were qualified for the position in question, (3) they received a negative employment decision despite being qualified, and (4) others *not* in the protected group were treated more favorably (e.g., hired, not terminated, received requested accommodation) or that the search process continued for similarly qualified individuals.

Table 2.1 Disparate treatment burden shifting process

Phase 1	The plaintiff must establish a *prima facie* case (presents *presumptive* evidence of discrimination).
Phase 2	The defense must *articulate* (*not prove*) that a legitimate reason exists for the alleged discriminatory practice.
Phase 3	The plaintiff must *prove* by direct or indirect evidence that the organization's reason(s) for its decision is a pretext for discrimination.

Pattern or Practice Discrimination

"Pattern or practice" is a form of discrimination that exists when organizations are alleged to have engaged in systemic, routine, intentional discrimination (e.g., discrimination is the standard operating procedure). Pattern or practice discrimination is outlawed in Section 707 of Title VII of the Civil Rights Act of 1964.[2] It states that civil actions can be taken by the Attorney General (such actions are now assigned to the Equal Employment Opportunity Commission [EEOC]) if there is "reasonable cause to believe that any person or group of persons is engaged in a pattern or practice of resistance to the full enjoyment of any of the rights secured by this subchapter."

Section 707 only allows for injunctive and declarative relief, but Section 706 can be used to pursue compensatory and punitive damages. *Injunctive relief* is a court-ordered remedy that requires a given party to do or not do an activity. The goal of an injunction is to stop and prevent future illegal acts. *Declarative relief* is a decision of the rights of those involved in a suit under a given law. No monetary awards are involved. *Compensatory damages* refer to paying plaintiffs for costs incurred, including pain and suffering, whereas *punitive damages* are used to reprimand organizations and prevent the reoccurrence of comparable discriminatory behavior.

The burden-shifting process in a pattern or practice case is generally the same as the more basic disparate treatment scenario (see Table 2.2). The exception is phase 1. The burden in this phase is met by using statistics that show (1) an underrepresentation of protected group members within the company compared to the relevant labor market (composition statistics) or (2) differences across jobs within the company, such as a relative lack

Table 2.2 Pattern or practice burden shifting process

Phase 1	Plaintiff offers statistical evidence that an underrepresentation of protected group members exists in the workforce or that an overrepresentation of protected group members are employed in less desirable positions.
Phase 2	Defendant articulates that a legitimate business reason exists to refute statistics presented by plaintiffs—uses the disparate treatment defense process against pattern or practice discrimination claims.
Phase 3	Plaintiff must prove that the reasons offered by the defense are a pretext for discrimination.

Adapted from Gutman, Koppes, & Vodanovich (2011).

[2] https://www.eeoc.gov/laws/statutes/titlevii.cfm

of underrepresented individuals in better, higher paying jobs (cross-job analysis).

Class Action Suits

Sometimes pattern or practice claims take the form of *class action* suits where a given plaintiff represents the group as a whole. An initial hurdle for plaintiffs in these suits is to be certified as a class. Basically, class certification must meet the following conditions under Rule 23(a) of the Rules of Civil Procedure:

1. The class is so numerous that claims by individuals are unrealistic (*numerosity clause*).
2. Questions of law or fact are common to the class (*commonality requirement*).
3. Claims of the plaintiff(s) are representative of those of the class parties (*typicality*).
4. The plaintiff(s) will sufficiently protect the interests of the class (*class protection*).

See Federal Rules of Civil Procedure (Rule 23).[3]

To be considered as a "class," *all* of the four conditions under Rule 23(a) must be met, followed by also meeting *one* of the stipulations under Rule 23(b)(1), 23b(2), or 23(b)(3):

Rule 23(b)(2) refers to *injunctive* and *declarative* relief and, if met, does not allow the defense to respond to claims by individual members of the class. Also, for 23(b)(2) to be met, claims for financial damages cannot outweigh those for injunctive and declarative relief. Finally, Rule 23(b)(3) contains a "predominance" and "superiority" requirement. That is, the interests of the class must be predominant over ones provided by individual members, and a class action challenge is shown to be better (superior) than other available mechanisms (for a more detailed summary of Rule 23 see Jackson, 2011;[4] Lesley, 2019).

---

[3] https://www.law.cornell.edu/rules/frcp/rule_23
[4] https://www.scotusblog.com/2011/09/class-actions-and-the-implications-of-rule-23/

Some have argued that after passage of the Civil Rights Act of 1991[5] (CRA-91), which allowed *compensatory* and *punitive damages* for charges of intentional discrimination, courts have applied greater scrutiny (and perhaps more reluctance) when deciding on whether to certify classes of plaintiffs (e.g., Hart, 2004).[6]

Mixed-Motive Scenarios

Cases involving *mixed motives* exist when both illegal *and* legal factors are used in making an employment decision. Plaintiffs can use *direct* or *indirect* evidence to prove the use of an illegal factor by organizations. Given the passage of CRA-91, it is illegal if protected group status (e.g., race, sex) *motivated* an employment decision in any way, even if the same decision would have otherwise been made had the illegal factor not been used. From CRA-91:

> Except as otherwise provided in this subchapter, an unlawful employment practice is established when the complaining party *demonstrates* that race, color, religion, sex, or national origin was a *motivating* factor for any employment practice, even though other factors also motivated the practice.[7]

So, CRA-91 makes the use of an illegal factor a violation of law. However, the CRA-91 stipulates that companies can *avoid* liability (e.g., damages) if they successfully demonstrate that the same decision would have been made even though they admittedly used an illegal factor. The burden-shifting process for mixed-motive cases is illustrated in Table 2.3. First, plaintiffs must *prove* that protected group status was used as a *motivating* factor in an adverse employment decision. Then, the defense must *prove* that the same decision would have been made despite the use of an illegal factor. Finally, as in the standard disparate treatment scenario, in phase 3, plaintiffs must *prove* that the phase 2 defense is pretext for discrimination.

---

[5] https://www.eeoc.gov/laws/statutes/cra-1991.cfm

[6] https://ideaexchange.uakron.edu/cgi/viewcontent.cgi?referer=https://scholar.google.com/scholar?hl=en&as_sdt=0%2C10&q=Hart%2C+M.+%282004%29.+Will+employment+discrimination+class+actions+survive%3F+Akron+Law+Review%2C+37%2C+813–846.&btnG=&httpsredir=1&article=1328&context=akronlawreview

[7] "Demonstrates" is defined in CRA-91 as the burden of production and persuasion (proof).

Table 2.3 Mixed-motive burden shifting process

Phase 1	Plaintiffs must *prove* by a preponderance of *direct or indirect* evidence that an illegal reason was a *motivating* factor in an adverse employment decision.
Phase 2	Defense must *prove* by a *preponderance of evidence* that they would have made the same employment decision even if they had not used an illegal factor.
Phase 3	Plaintiffs must *prove* by a *preponderance of evidence* that the stated, legal reasons offered by the defense are a *pretext* for discrimination.

Adverse Impact Discrimination

Another form of discrimination is referred to as *adverse impact*. Proving the existence of adverse impact can be quite complicated (Gutman, 2003, 2004; Morris, Dunleavy, & Howard, 2015; Outtz, 2010). In basic terms, it occurs when "neutral" employment practices, such as selection tests, disproportionally harm members of a protected group. In other words, the focus here is on the *consequences* of an organization's employment practices rather than their intentions. So, adverse impact suits do *not* require proof of the intent to discriminate.

The process of determining adverse impact also follows a three-step burden-shifting process (see Table 2.4). In phase 1, plaintiffs have the burden of *demonstrating* (producing and proving) that a *particular* employment practice *caused* the disproportionate exclusion of protected group members. This phase consists of the presentation of statistical evidence that the disproportionate exclusion is substantial enough to infer that illegal discrimination exists. This often involves the use of selection rate data for different subgroups (i.e., number hired relative to the number of applicants). However, data on *real* applicants are not always needed. This is because the requirements allegedly leading to discrimination, such as minimum educational requirements, may prevent individuals from seeking jobs. To quote the Supreme Court, "The application process might itself not adequately reflect the actual potential applicant pool, since otherwise qualified people might be discouraged because of a self-recognized inability to meet the very standards challenged as being discriminatory" (*Dothard v. Rawlinson*, 1977).[8,9]

---

[8] https://caselaw.findlaw.com/us-supreme-court/433/321.html
[9] https://www.oyez.org/cases/1976/76-422

Table 2.4 Adverse impact scenario

Phase 1	The challenger must demonstrate that a particular employment practice caused the discrimination in question (disproportionately excludes protected group members). "*Demonstrates*" means the burden of *both* production (articulation) and persuasion (proof). If plaintiffs demonstrate that the decision-making system *cannot be separated* for analytic purposes, the process can be evaluated as a whole.
Phase 2	The company must demonstrate (articulate and prove) that the challenged practice is job-related for the position in question and consistent with business necessity. (Data from a job analysis are very useful, but not required, to succeed in phase 2).
Phase 3	Plaintiffs must prove that an equally valid, job-related practice exists with less (or no) adverse impact.

If plaintiffs are successful, organizations in phase 2 can defend themselves by demonstrating that the challenged practice is job-related and consistent with business necessity. If organizations satisfy this burden, plaintiffs have one last option in phase 3. They are given the opportunity to prove that an equally valid, job-related alternative practice exists that causes less (or no) adverse impact.

Calculating and Mitigating Adverse Impact

Adverse impact is typically assessed using what is known as *applicant flow data*, which refers to the organization's actual data on individuals applying for jobs and who is and is not offered employment (or promotion, etc.).[10] Flow statistics are often contrasted with *stock statistics*, which refer to labor statistics about who comprises a particular *workforce* (e.g., within the organization, industry, a geographic region, etc.). We discuss the use of stock statistics in more detail in later chapters (e.g., Chapter 3).

Practical Significance
One of the statistical analyses that has commonly been used in phase 1 to illustrate the existence of adverse impact is the so-called *four-fifths rule*. With this approach, adverse impact is believed to exist if the selection rate for one group

---

[10] Determining who counts as an applicant is more complex than it may seem at first. This is particularly relevant for those who apply for work via the Internet. We discuss this issue in greater depth in the chapter on affirmative action.

Table 2.5 Calculating if the four-fifths rule has been violated

Group	Applicants	Hired	Selection ratio
Males	200	50	.25
Females	100	10	.10

(e.g., Black applicants) is less than 80% (four-fifths) of the contrasting (often majority) group (e.g., White applicants). This approach has been referred to as an assessment of *practical significance*, where the difference is meaningful in a pragmatic sense.[11] Table 2.5 shows an example where the four-fifths rule has been violated, thereby providing initial evidence for potential adverse impact.

In this instance, the selection process resulted in 25% of male applicants being hired versus 10% of female applicants. The difference in the selection ratio for women (.10) is much less than 80% of the selection radio for men (.25). Indeed, it is 40%. It is important to mention that although the four-fifths rule is mentioned in the *Uniform Guidelines of Employee Selection Procedures* (1978)[12] it is not a rigidly applied standard of adverse impact but is instead a rule-of-thumb that discrimination may have occurred (Dunleavy & Gutman, 2011; Siskin & Trippi, 2005; Zedeck, 2009). Importantly, adverse impact can exist even though the four-fifths rule is *not* violated. Conversely, adverse impact may be deemed as *not* being present even when the four-fifths rule has been violated. From the Uniform Guidelines, Section 4d:

> A selection rate for any race, sex, or ethnic group which is *less* than four-fifths (4/5) (or eighty percent) of the rate for the group with the highest rate will *generally* be regarded by the Federal enforcement agencies as *evidence of adverse impact*, while a *greater* than four-fifths rate will generally not be regarded by Federal enforcement agencies as evidence of adverse impact. *Smaller differences* in selection rate may nevertheless *constitute adverse impact*, where they are significant in both statistical and practical terms or where a user's actions have discouraged applicants disproportionately on grounds of race, sex, or ethnic group. *Greater differences* in selection rate *may not* constitute adverse impact where the differences are based on small numbers and are not statistically significant. (emphasis added)

[11] See Morris et al. (2015) for a detailed discussion of practical significance. Also, see Oswald, Dunleavy, and Shaw (2017) for a description of additional practical significance measures, including the phi coefficient, the odds ratio, the absolute difference in selection rates, the h statistic, and shortfall statistics.

[12] https://www.govinfo.gov/content/pkg/CFR-2014-title29-vol4/xml/CFR-2014-title29-vol4-part1607.xml

Statistical Significance

An alternative to using the four-fifths rule to assess adverse impact is statistical significance testing. This involves assessing whether or not the differences in selection rates for focal subgroups (e.g., women vs. men) are due to chance (Morris, 2015). Overall, it is more likely to find statistically significant differences as the number of people in the sample increases. Indeed, with very large samples, obtaining statistical significance is likely (e.g., Jacobs, Murphy, & Siva, 2012). Table 2.6 illustrates this. As shown, the selection rate of men and women is the same, as is the "impact ratio" (no evidence of adverse impact). However, as the number of applicants increases, so does the likelihood of statistically significant differences. This means that the choice of which method is used to determine adverse impact can yield different conclusions (see Murphy & Jacobs, 2017).

There are multiple tests for calculating statistical significance, including the Z-test for the difference between two proportions, the chi-square test of association, Fisher's exact test, and Landcaster's mid-p (LMP) test (Morris, 2017). These statistics often reach the same conclusion, but this is not always the case, and factors such as sample size can influence the results. Z- and chi-square tests should not be used with small samples. Fisher's exact test is more conservative—it will be less likely to yield significant results (which tends to favor defendants). The LMP tests seems to be more fairly suited for small samples.

Court decisions have varied as to which approach (practical or statistical significance) is best to use when determining adverse impact. Such decisions often depend on the specific facts (or context) of a given case. For instance, in both *Bew v. Chicago* (2001)[13] and *Isabel v. City of Memphis* (2003),[14] there were no four-fifths rule violations, but statistical evidence indicated the presence of significant differences. In *Bew*, the passing rate on a certification test for police officers was 99.9% for Whites and 98.2% for Blacks. Yet 32 of 33 people who failed the exam were Black. This resulted in a significant difference in proportions and a determination of adverse impact. In *Isabel*, there was also no difference in passing rates based on race. Still, adverse impact was found partly due to significant differences in average test scores between Whites and Blacks. Furthermore, in *Jones v. City of Boston* (2014),[15] only a 1% difference existed in positive drug test scores between Whites (.3%) and Blacks (1.3%). However, the frequency of positive drug test scores was much higher for Blacks versus Whites. Therefore, adverse impact was determined to exist.

---

[13] https://caselaw.findlaw.com/us-7th-circuit/1054230.html
[14] https://caselaw.findlaw.com/us-6th-circuit/1073540.html
[15] https://caselaw.findlaw.com/us-1st-circuit/1665635.html

Table 2.6 A demonstration of differing conclusions based on statistical significance and practical significance measures

Male applicants	Female applicants	Male selections	Female selections	Overall sel rate	Male sel rate	Female sel rate	Difference in rates	Impact ratio	Z test (in SDs)
100	100	99	98	0.985	0.99	0.98	0.01	0.99	0.58
1,000	1,000	990	980	0.985	0.99	0.98	0.01	0.99	1.84
1,200	1,200	1,188	1,176	0.985	0.99	0.98	0.01	0.99	2.02
10,000	10,000	9,900	9,800	0.985	0.99	0.98	0.01	0.99	5.82
100,000	100,000	99,000	98,000	0.985	0.99	0.98	0.01	0.99	18.40
1,000,000	1,000,000	990,000	980,000	0.985	0.99	0.98	0.01	0.99	58.17

Adapted from Dunleavy, E. M., & Gutman, A. (2011). An update on the statistical versus practical significance debate: A review of *Stagi v. Amtrak* (2010). *The Industrial-Organizational Psychologist, 48*, 121–130.

Contrary to the previous cases is *Apsley v. Boeing* (2012).[16] Here, a statistically significant difference in hiring rates was found to exist between younger and older workers. Nevertheless, since the hiring process only affected 60 out of approximately 9,000 employees within Boeing, the difference was judged to not be meaningful. See the articles by Dunleavy (2010); Dunleavy and Gutman (2011); Morris (2015); Murphy and Jacobs (2017); Oswald, Dunleavy, and Shaw (2017); Roth, Bobko, and Switzer (2006); and Tonowski (2014) that discuss issues regarding practical versus statistical significance testing.

Some have advocated using *both* practical and statistical significance testing to evaluate adverse impact (e.g., Murphy & Jacobs, 2012; Oswald, et al., 2017). As Oswald et al. stated,

> [S]ole reliance on statistical significance tests is clearly not an adverse impact strategy that is useful. . . . But sole reliance on practical significance is not helpful either . . . both statistical significance and practical significance metrics need to be examined together, which is consistent with contemporary social scientific methods, and the EEO [equal employment opportunity] context should develop decision rules consistent with this approach as well. (p. 100).

Alternative Selection Strategies Aimed at Reducing Adverse Impact

Organizations often grapple with how to choose and implement personnel selection procedures that are simultaneously viewed as fair, legally appropriate, and predictive of future job performance. For example, a physical ability test may effectively predict performance of future fire fighters, but such a test may disproportionally screen out women. Similarly, cognitive ability tests have both been shown to predict job performance but also have a long history of causing adverse impact against Black applicants (see Roth, BeVier, Bobko, Switzer, & Tyler, 2001).[17] Research has referred to this as the so-called *diversity-validity dilemma* (see Kravitz, 2008; Ployhart & Holtz, 2008; Pyburn, Ployhart, & Kravitz, 2008).[18] This has spurred many efforts to address such

---

[16] https://scholar.google.com/scholar_case?case=16840275944667175113&hl=en&as_sdt=6&as_vis=1&oi=scholarr

[17] We strongly recommend the chapter by Outtz and Newman (2010), who provide one of the only *theories* of adverse impact, which provides an in-depth review of the environmental and sociological influences on subgroup differences on cognitive ability test scores.

[18] We use the term "so-called" because we reject this as an actual dilemma as long as simply not using such tests is an option, and other, less discriminatory selection techniques are available that also predict job performance.

tradeoffs, which potentially allow organizations to reduce their risk of creating adverse impact against legally protected groups while simultaneously using tools to make selection and promotion decisions that effectively predict future job performance.

Recruitment

For example, one method involves placing increased effort on the recruitment of applicants from underrepresented groups—hoping that a more diverse applicant pool will increase diversity in who are ultimately offered positions (i.e., less adverse impact). Research has shown that this method is generally ineffective if selection tools continue to be used that systematically eliminate individuals from protected groups (Tam, Murphy, & Lyall, 2004). However, other research has shown preliminary evidence that more qualification-based recruitment of underrepresented applicants can be effective in reaching diversity and validity goals (Newman, Jones, Fraley, Lyon, & Mullaney, 2014; Newman & Lyon, 2009).

Choosing and Combining Predictors That Reduce Adverse Impact

Another method involves strategically selecting, weighting, and combining predictor scores in ways aimed at maximizing both diversity and the prediction of future job performance (Bobko, Roth, & Potosky, 1999; Finch, Edwards, & Wallace, 2009; Ployhart & Holtz, 2008; Sackett & Ellingson, 1997). This could include simply not using tools known to cause adverse impact (e.g., cognitive abilities tests) and/or using a wider variety of non-overlapping and valid predictors (in addition to widening the "criterion space" [i.e., what is considered effective job performance]; Hattrup, Rock, & Scalia, 1997). Although research has shown that such an approach can in some cases assist organizations in meeting their validity and diversity goals,[19] these are more approaches than methods and require quite a bit of trial and error and subjective judgment on the part of the organization. More systematic approaches that have been proposed are banding and Pareto-optimization.

Test Score Banding

Placing individuals into bands (or categories) that represent equivalent performance has been around for quite a long time. For instance, student test scores that fall within the range of 90–100 are often assigned the same grade, an "A." Therefore, students with a test score of 99 will receive the same grade as those

---

[19] Though we note that individual predictors as well as composite scores are vulnerable to legal challenge (e.g., *Connecticut v. Teal*, 1982). We discuss this in more depth in Chapter 3.

with scores of 90 despite the existence of a clear numerical difference in test performance. This same logic has been applied to reducing adverse impact in personnel selection, with the idea being that if applicants scoring within a band can be considered equally qualified, perhaps that could allow for more job offers to be made to members of protected underrepresented demographic subgroups. This is in contrast to "top-down selection," where every score difference is considered meaningful and therefore job candidates are rank ordered by their scores on selection tests and job offers are made in a top-down fashion.

Test score banding uses a statistic known as the standard error of the difference (SED) to create score bands. The SED is a statistic employed to determine the range of scores (bands) that are statistically equal to each other. An assumption behind this type of banding is that tests contain measurement error (e.g., imperfect reliability and validity), so that small differences in scores do not indicate real or true differences. The SED uses the standard deviation and reliability of test scores to create test score bands (Campion et al., 2001).

This metric can be used in conjunction with selection scores (e.g., a composite score of an applicant's ratings on a series of "tests" such as interviews, personality assessments, knowledge tests) to create bands of scores within which candidates are assumed to be equally qualified. For example, consider that the highest test score in a distribution of applicant scores is 98 out of 100 and the SED is 6. In this case, individuals with scores within 6 points of each other (e.g., 98 to 92) would be considered to be statistically equivalent and equally qualified for a favorable hiring and/or promotion decision. On the other hand, those with scores 91 and lower would be considered as having obtained a significantly lower score (and be less qualified) than those in the upper band (see Figure 2.1).

Since banding considers small differences in test scores not to be meaningful (e.g., due to measurement error),[20] making a job offer to applicants in protected underrepresented demographic subgroups (e.g., women, Blacks) with slightly lower test scores but within the same score band is considered legally justifiable. That is, such individuals are considered equally qualified to others in a given band despite their marginally lower scores. However, to be legally defensible, it is recommended that if banding is used, protected group status (e.g., race, sex) be used *in combination* with other factors in making employment decisions (Henle, 2004). For instance, two different circuit courts of appeals upheld the use

---

[20] To quote from a report published in *The Industrial-Organizational Psychologist* (TIP), "There is a legitimate scientific justification for the position that small differences in test scores might not imply meaningful differences in either the construct measured by the test or in future job performance" (Report of the Scientific Affairs Committee, 1994, p. 85).

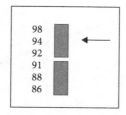

Figure 2.1 Illustration of basic banding process. All those within bands are considered statistically equal; anyone with a score from 92 to 98 can be selected. All individuals from the upper band are depleted before going to the next (lower) band.

of race in banding procedures (see *Bridgeport Guardians v. City of Bridgeport*, 1991,[21] and *Officers for Justice v. Civil Service Commission*, 1992).[22] In *Bridgeport*, race was one of nine factors used in selection decisions, while *Officers* employed race as one of four reasons to make promotion decisions.

The merits and shortcomings of banding have been discussed at length (e.g., Campion et al., 1991; Cascio, Outtz, Zedeck, & Goldstein, 1991, 1995; Henle, 2004; Murphy, Osten, & Myors, 1995; Schmidt, 1991). Proponents of test score banding assert that the approach can help reduce or avoid adverse impact and increase diversity in the workplace (e.g., Cascio et al., 1991). Others view banding as being incongruent with the goal of hiring the most qualified applicants and/or that it is logically or statistically unsound (e.g., Gasperson, Bowler, Wuensch, & Bowler, 2013; Schmidt, 1991). These divergent positions can be difficult to comprehend and can center on statistical and psychometric issues in addition to the consideration of social concerns (e.g., affirmative action, diversity).

Pareto-Optimization

A more recent method, which shows promise psychometrically but has yet to be vetted by the courts, is Pareto-optimization. This method involves statistically deriving weights to apply to predictors in creating composite scores for personnel selection (De Corte, Lievens, & Sackett, 2007). For example, an organization might use a knowledge test, an interview, and a personality inventory to select candidates for a particular job. Pareto-optimization allows the organization to come up with a weighting scheme for these three predictors that *simultaneously* maximizes both diversity and predictive validity. It is

[21] https://openjurist.org/180/f3d/42
[22] https://openjurist.org/934/f2d/1092/officers-v-civil

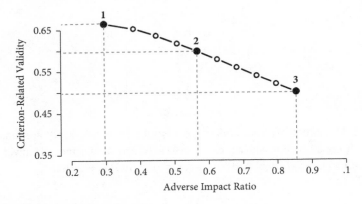

Figure 2.2 Pareto-optimal tradeoff curve.
Adapted from Rupp, Song, & Strah (2020).

similar to a regression approach, which derives weights that optimize one criterion (usually job performance), but differs by virtue of optimizing on more than one factor. The result is what is known as the Pareto curve, where a user can choose a set of weights at any point on the curve depending on desired thresholds for predictive validity and adverse impact.

An example Pareto curve is provided in Figure 2.2. As shown, predictive validity (the relationship between predictor scores and job performance) is crossed with the level of adverse impact likely to result from the use of the predictors if weighted in different ways. Each point on the curve is associated with a set of predictor weights. The weights associated with Point 1 represent the solution where predictive validity is maximized. In this example, this is likely to lead to adverse impact because the adverse impact ratio is well below the .80 cutoff needed to "pass" the four-fifths rule. The weights associated with Point 3 represent the solution where adverse impact is minimized (i.e., the selection rates of the subgroups being compared, such as Blacks vs. Whites, are as equal as possible). Here, the adverse impact ratio is greater than .80 and thus a finding of adverse impact would be less likely (though the predictive validity is lower). The weights associated with Point 2 represent the Pareto optimal solution where predictive validity and the reduction of adverse impact are considered equally important. Note that for this particular example, the weighting scheme associated with Point 2 may still cause adverse impact. In cases such as this, an organization might choose the weights that provide the highest possible validity where the adverse impact ratio is .80 or higher.

The research on Pareto-optimization has been promising, and it seems that the approach can be used to inform organizations about what various weighting schemes might do to increase or sacrifice predictive validity and adverse impact (e.g., De Corte, Lievens, & Sackett, 2008; Song, Wee & Newman, 2017; Wee, Newman, & Joseph, 2014). That being said, the approach has not yet been vetted in the court system in the way test score banding has, so it is unclear if the technique can and will stand up to legal challenges. Rupp, Song, and Strah (2020) offer an analysis of the ways in which the method could potentially be challenged, such as claims that (a) demographic information is used to determine the weights, (b) that the method advantages underrepresented groups, and (c) that the method does not stand up against the Daubert standard for admissible scientific evidence (see the "EEO in the Wild" boxed insert for more on this issue). They then provide evidence countering each of these challenges and provide recommendations for organizations implementing the technique. Only time will tell if organizations widely adopt this method for addressing the so-called diversity–validity dilemma and whether its use will be challenged legally.

EEO in the Wild: Industrial-Organizational Psychologists as Expert Witnesses

Prior to and throughout a potential trial, both plaintiff and defendant legal teams, as well as judges, rely on the consultation and testimony of expert witnesses who shed light on technical matters related to a complaint, claim, and/or court proceeding. The nature of what experts are asked to do can vary a great deal from case to case. They may be asked to analyze data and/or provide expert opinion as a retained and privileged consultant prior to a potential trial. The information they provide at this stage is often privileged, meaning it may not be available to the opposing side during the discovery period. This information may be useful to a legal team in deciding whether or not to recommend that their client settle outside of court (i.e., not go to trial).

Experts might also provide sworn testimony (under oath), which might be in the form of an expert report, a sworn deposition where the legal teams examine and cross-examine the expert ahead of trial, or testimony during trial. It is common for a legal team to seek a ruling from a judge that the opposing side's expert testimony is inadmissible. This is often done through the filing of a *Daubert* motion against the opposing side's expert witnesses, which seeks to persuade the judge to throw out the expert testimony by discrediting the witness or their methodology (or the methodology/research on which they rely in drawing conclusions). The criteria for admissible testimony were established in *Daubert v. Merrell Dow Pharmaceuticals Inc.* (1993). They include whether the expert's methods (a) have been tested previously, (b) have been published in peer-reviewed outlets, (c) have a known level of imprecision that is considered acceptable, (d) are generally supported by the scientific community, and

(e) can be judged based on their inherent characteristics rather than the conclusions based on their use.

As you can imagine, the deposing and discrediting of expert witnesses is a big part of litigation, and it is not uncommon in the EEO context to have "dueling experts," often university professors with impressive research records, sometimes from the same field, and other times from differing fields (such as industrial-organizational psychology and labor economics), which may offer different perspectives and apply different methodologies to determine if discrimination may or may not have occurred. Industrial-organizational psychologists are commonly used as expert witnesses in adverse impact cases, as because they have specialized expertise on personnel selection, job analysis, the development and validation of personnel selection tools, and the statistical analyses used to determine adverse impact (in addition to pay equity and other "data-heavy" EEO issues).

This type of work can be rewarding but is also high stress (imagine being deposed for eight hours straight by attorneys well-prepped to discredit all the work you've ever done!). It also requires the expert to (hopefully!) vigilantly adhere to the professional and ethical standards of their field. Whereas attorneys are ethically bound to support their clients (i.e., try to win each case), academic researchers are required to approach questions, data, and analyses with as much objectivity as possible. These differing ethical duties can create tensions that require a great deal of wisdom and integrity to manage. Finally, expert witnesses are not only required to analyze data and render a conclusion, they also have to explain their methods and findings (and potentially speak to the limitations of the opposing side's methods and findings) in a way that is understandable and persuasive to judges and jurors (i.e., non-experts). This can be especially challenging for academics whose day job is writing for highly technical audiences and outlets.

Would you like to be an expert witness? Why or why not? Interested readers might enjoy the following resources on the topic:

Several chapters in Landy (2005). *Employment Discrimination Litigation: Behavioral, Quantitative, and Legal Perspectives* (San Francisco: Jossey-Bass):

- Thornton, G. C. III, & Wingate, P. H. "Industrial and Organizational Psychologists as Expert Witnesses: Affecting Employment Discrimination Litigation Post Daubert."
- Copus, D., Ugelow, R. S., & Sohn, J. "A Lawyer's View."
- Copus, D. "Avoiding Junk Science."
- Ugelow, R. S. "I-O Psychology and the Department of Justice."
- Sohn, J. "Employment Discrimination Lawyers, the Doctor Will See You Now."
- Landy, F. J. "A Judge's View: Interviews with Federal Judges About Expert Witness Testimony."

Thornton, G. C. III, Eurich, T. L., & Johnson, R. M. (2009). Industrial/organizational psychologists as expert witnesses in employment discrimination litigation: Descriptions and prescriptions. *The Psychologist-Manager Journal, 12*, 187–203.
Sackett, P. R. (2011). The Uniform Guidelines is not a scientific document: Implications for expert testimony. *Industrial and Organizational Psychology, 4*(4), 545–546. doi: 10.1111/j.1754-9434.2011.01389.x.

Job Analysis and Legal Defensibility

A job analysis involves the systematic and thorough collection of information that describes work activities (tasks), the qualifications employees need to perform jobs, and the environmental conditions under which the work is performed. As such, job requirements and choice of selection devices should be based on the results of a systematic job analysis (Morgeson, Brannick, & Levine, 2019).

Besides helping select or promote the most qualified people, a job analysis can be an invaluable tool for organizations to legally defend themselves against charges of employment discrimination. That is, companies that conduct a job analysis are in a better position to support the legitimacy of job requirements, such as knowledge, skills, abilities, and other characteristics (KSAOs), as well as the choice of selection devices such as written tests, interviews, or work sample tests (see Table 2.7). As stated by Gutman, Outtz, and Dunleavy (2017), "Work analysis should establish the linkage between important functions/characteristics of the job and KSAOs, and it should form the basis for linking a selection procedure to those KSAOs . . ., thus linking the selection device to the job" (p. 638). Put another way, a job analysis provides organizations with data to help demonstrate that their personnel decisions are *job-related* for the position(s) in question and consistent with *business necessity*—both of which often must be evidenced when an organization's practices are challenged legally for being discriminatory.

There are a number of established methods for carrying out a job analysis. No single approach is inherently better than another. Rather, these approaches differ in several key respects, including (1) the type of data that are collected, (2) how the data are gathered, (3) where the data come from, and (4) what information is analyzed, including the degree of detail in the analysis. The selection of which method to use needs to be determined by the purpose of the job analysis; that is, how the information will eventually be used.

From a legal perspective, a job analysis approach that identifies key job *tasks*, the KSAOs required to successfully accomplish tasks, and gathers *ratings* of

Table 2.7 Pairing job qualifications with selection devices

Job requirements (e.g., KSAs)	Application form, resume	Job knowledge test	Interview	Situational exercises (e.g., assessment centers)	Work sample test
Knowledge of electrical principles, terms, and equipment	√	√	√		
Knowledge of appropriate safety and environmental guidelines		√			
Ability to perform arithmetic calculations and understand charts and tables	√	√			√
Ability to read blueprints, drawings, and schematics		√	√		√
Ability to use a variety of precision and non-precision measuring devices					√
Ability to assist and cooperate with others in a team-oriented work environment			√	√	
Ability to communicate effectively orally and in writing			√	√	

KSA, knowledge, skills, and ability.

Adapted from Gatewood et al. (2011, p. 290).

the relative *importance* of tasks and KSAOs can be quite beneficial (Gutman & Dunleavy, 2012; Levine, Ash, Hall, & Sistrunk, 1983; Thompson & Thompson, 1982). As stated in their summary of court decisions regarding job analysis for selection test validation, Thompson and Thompson note: "Knowledge, skills and abilities are mentioned with the greatest frequency and they are neces- sary, usually, for construction of a content valid exam . . . [and] . . . the courts stress the identification of tasks as prerequisite to an acceptable job analysis" (1982, p. 873).

As mentioned earlier, in addition to identifying job tasks and KSAOs, it is beneficial to assess (and differentiate) the importance of each. This is typically done by acquiring ratings from job experts on a variety of dimensions such as task criticality, difficulty, frequency/time spent, and consequences if tasks are performed poorly (e.g., Sanchez & Levine, 1989). Ratings of KSAOs often focus on how critical they are for successful job/task performance. To quote from an earlier key court case about test development, "Without such an analysis to single out the *critical* knowledge, skills and abilities required by the job, their importance *relative* to each other, and the level of *proficiency demanded* as to each attribute, a test constructor is aiming in the dark and can only hope to achieve job relatedness by blind luck" (*Kirkland v. Department of Correctional Services,* 1974; emphasis added).

Despite the importance of conducting a job analysis for selection purposes, organizations may not be fully utilizing this approach. For instance, Wang and Yancey (2012) reported survey results that indicated 64% of organizations used job analysis for selection. This finding is reasonably consistent with that of Drogan and Yancey (2011) who surveyed HR executives and concluded that 53% employed job analysis for selection purposes. Strah and Rupp (in press) discuss ways in which job analysis can be carried out such that a broader and more inclusive set of tasks and KSAOs are identified for recruiting more diverse applicant pools and identifying selection criteria and tools less likely to cause adverse impact.

Insights from Social Science: The Court's Opinion of Laboratory Research as the Basis of Expert Testimony

Readers with a social science background have likely taken a research methods course and been taught about the rigor and elegance of experimental research, where a researcher is interested in how one or more independent variables (e.g., leadership style) influence some outcome variable(s) (e.g., job satisfaction, work performance). For the research to be a true experiment, participants are randomly assigned to experimental conditions. The independent variable is manipulated and the dependent variable is carefully measured. This allows for true cause-and-effect relationships to be detected, which control for other extraneous variables (Campbell & Stanley, 1966; Cook & Campbell, 1979; Creswell & Creswell, 2018; Shadish, Cook, & Campbell, 2002). As such, we can have greater confidence in the research findings of experiments as compared to alternative designs, such as collecting data from employees on predictor and outcome variables at the same time and assessing the correlation between them. Such correlational designs cannot control for all possible extraneous variables affecting the relationships. Experimental research focused on the types of questions common to EEO litigation (e.g., gender stereotypes) often takes place in a psychological laboratory. This allows researchers to randomly assign participants to experimental conditions and create high levels of control, standardization, and measurement precision.

At first blush, you might think this would be the best sort of research to cite within EEO litigation (e.g., by an expert witness giving testimony). After all, it provides findings in which we can have the most confidence compared to alternative research designs. Despite this fact, the courts have found that evidence from laboratory research can be problematic within the legal context (Copus, Ugelow, & Sohn, 2005). For instance, although lab research allows for causal inference, it lacks ecological validity (Bronfenbrenner, 1977). That is, psychological laboratory research often relies on pools of undergraduate students (often freshman and sophomores in their late teens or early twenties enrolled in introductory psychology courses) to serve as research participants. The demographic make-up of such participant pools may be quite different from that of a defendant organization's workforce (or those in the particular position at issue in the case). Furthermore, the experimental conditions may be artificial and far removed from the context in which discrimination is alleged to have occurred.

Copus et al. (2005) provide the example of stereotype research being of questionable utility in cases where gender stereotypes are argued to have permeated an organization and led to widespread discrimination. This is because the majority of this research involves "stranger-to-stranger scenarios" where only a small piece of information about individuals is provided. The argument is that results stemming from these sterile and tightly controlled conditions cannot be generalized to the typical employment discrimination case, which involves information processing about non-strangers and a large number of other intervening variables.

The bottom line is that, in order for social science research to shed light on particular issues within EEO litigation, the research has to not only be pertinent to the question at hand (and carried out in a rigorous way so as to have confidence in the results), but it also has to be relevant to the context of the case in terms of the research participants and specific, pertinent variables. This may require doing research in the defendant's organization or potentially carrying out natural experiments in more generalizable settings (see Meyer, 1995), both of which present challenges of their own (e.g., access to usable data, temporal issues).

Recommendations/Best Practices

- Treat all job seekers the same when making personnel decisions (e.g., use same tests, procedures, requirements).
- Do not use protected group status (e.g., race, sex) as a motivating factor in making personnel decisions.
- Avoid using selection tests/job requirements that may lead to an underrepresentation of protected group members.
- Be aware that both actual and implied applicants can be used to demonstrate evidence of potential adverse impact.
- Consider using both statistical and practical significance tests in assessing the presence of adverse impact.
- If banding is used, be sure to use additional, job-related factors in conjunction with protected group status (e.g., race) in making personnel decisions.
- Consider alternatives/supplements to test score banding (e.g., measure non-cognitive factors, assess full range of KSAOs).
- Perform a systematic job analysis before deciding on which selection test and/or requirements to use.
- Ensure that all selection tests/requirements are appropriate (e.g., job-related) for the context in which they are being implemented.
- If the nature of work changes in certain jobs, reconsider the selection devices and job requirements that are being used (e.g., may need to measure new or different KSAOs).

Summary and Take-Aways

As we have discussed, several basic employment discrimination scenarios exist. These scenarios all follow the traditional three-phase burden-shifting process. However, the specific types of evidence required in certain phases vary. For instance, in disparate treatment cases, the burden for plaintiffs in phase 1 and organizations in phase 2 are relatively (and equally) light, with the proof of pretext being the ultimate burden for plaintiffs (phase 3). Importantly, proof of the intent to discriminate is required. One the other hand, in adverse impact scenarios, the consequences of otherwise neutral employment practices (e.g., selection tests) are paramount. There is no need to demonstrate intent to discriminate. Here, the burden for plaintiffs in phase 1 can be challenging to meet. Likewise, the defense burden in the second phase can also be rigorous (e.g., proof of job-relatedness of selection devices). In any event, it is important to be knowledgeable of the specific burdens required for both plaintiffs and organizations in each of these scenarios.

A number of methods can be used to test for the existence of adverse impact. Differences of opinion exist on the merits of using practical versus statistical significance tests. The pros and cons of each have been discussed at length. A noted earlier, a more recent approach is to use both to investigate the prevalence of adverse impact.

Finally, performing a detailed job analysis is a prerequisite for choosing selection tests or deciding on job requirements (e.g., educational degrees). Not only will the results of a job analysis help with the legal defensibility of selection components, it will likely increase the odds of hiring the best candidates by identifying job-relevant KSAOs.

Supplemental Readings on Basic Discrimination Scenarios

Beginner
SHRM: Avoiding adverse impact in employment practices. https://www.shrm.org/resourcesandtools/tools-and-samples/toolkits/pages/avoidingadverseimpact.aspx

Intermediate
EEOC. Adoption of questions and answers to clarify and provide a common interpretation of the Uniform Guidelines on Employee Selection Procedures. https://www.eeoc.gov/policy/docs/qanda_clarify_procedures.html

Gutman, A. (2017). Case law interpretations of statistical evidence regarding adverse impact. In S. Morris & E. Dunleavy (Eds.), *Adverse impact analysis: Understanding data, statistics, and risk* (pp. 349–362). New York: Routledge.

Sanchez, J. I., & Levine, E. L. (2009). What is (or should be) the difference between competency modeling and traditional job analysis? *Human Resource Management Review, 19,* 53–63.

Advanced
Klonoff, R. H. (2017). Class actions part II: A respite from the decline. *New York University Law Review, 92,* 971–997.

Morris, S. B., & Dunleavy, E. M. (Eds.). (2016). *Adverse impact analysis: Understanding data, statistics, and risk.* New York: Psychology Press.

Rupp, D. E., Song, Q. C., & Strah, N. (2020). Addressing the co-called validity-diversity trade-off: Exploring the practicalities and legal defensibility of Pareto-optimization for reducing adverse impact within personnel selection. *Industrial and Organizational Psychology: Perspectives on Science and Practice, 13,* 246–271.

Tobia, K. (2017). Disparate statistics. *Yale Law Journal, 126,* 2382–2420. https://philpapers.org/archive/TOBDS.pdf

Verstein, A. (2019). The failure of mixed-motives jurisprudence. *University of Chicago Law Review, 86,* 725–795. https://lawreview.uchicago.edu/sites/lawreview.uchicago.edu/files/Verstein_ART_POSTSA_OUT%20%28KT%29.pdf

Glossary

Adverse impact: When facially neutral selection criteria disproportionately exclude a higher percentage of one group relative to another. These differences are often assessed by using the four-fifths rule or statistical significance tests.

Applicant flow data: The number of people who apply to positions and are accepted from each demographic group.

Class action: One or more plaintiffs who represent a group of plaintiffs similarly affected by the defendant's actions, along with their counsel, bring a lawsuit against one or more defendants.

Class protection: The plaintiff(s) will sufficiently protect the interests of the class.

Commonality requirement: The requirement, applied in class action certification, that questions of law or fact are common to the entire class.

Compensatory damages: Awarding of payments for costs incurred (e.g., lost wages, bonuses, pain and suffering).

Daubert motion: A motion to exclude the presentation of unqualified evidence by questioning the expertise or methodology of an expert witness.

Declarative relief: A decision of the rights of those involved in a suit under a given law. No monetary awards are involved.

Defense: The arguments and evidence presented by the defendant in opposition to the allegations or charges brought against them by the plaintiff(s). Term is also used to refer to the party sued by a plaintiff.

Deposition: The written testimony of a sworn witness presented during discovery before the trial.

Direct evidence: Evidence which proves the existence of an alleged fact without needing inference or presumption. Direct evidence can not only suggest discrimination [or retaliation], or be subject to more than one interpretation.

Discovery: The fact-finding process that allows parties to prepare for settlement or trial that occurs after a lawsuit has been filed and before the trial takes place. During this period, evidence is obtained through formal requests between plaintiff(s) and the defense, or through subpoenas.

Disparate treatment: Intentionally treating an individual or group less favorably than another due to protected group status (e.g., race, religion, national origin, sex, disability).

Ecological validity: Research conducted in a naturalistic setting and involving materials and activities from everyday life.

Indirect evidence: Also referred to as circumstantial evidence, indirect evidence helps to establish the main fact by inference.

Injunctive relief: A court-ordered remedy that requires a given party to do, or not do, a given activity.

Mixed-motive cases: Cases where illegal and legal factors motivate an employment decision.

Natural experiments: Research that examines outcomes from observations of treatment and control groups that are not randomly assigned.

Numerosity clause: The class is so numerous that claims by individuals are unrealistic.

Plaintiff: The party who initiates a lawsuit.

Presumptive evidence: Evidence that the alleged discrimination was "more likely than not" to have transpired.

Prima facie: Latin for "at first glance." Consists of presenting evidence that is presumed to be true.

Privileged: Information that is not legally discoverable by the opposing party and is covered by statutory or common law protections.

Protected class: Groups protected by anti-discrimination laws; these groups include, including race, color, national origin, religion, sex (or gender), age (40 and older), and disability.

Punitive damages: Used to punish employers for discriminatory acts committed with malice or reckless indifference and to prevent the reoccurrence of comparable discriminatory behavior.

Typicality: Claims of the plaintiff(s) are representative of those of the class parties.

Glossary terms adapted from Bronfenbrenner (1977); Gutman et al. (2011); https://uslegal.com/; merriamwebster.com/legal; Mueller, Dunleavy, and Buonasera (2008).

Cases Cited

Apsley v. Boeing, 691 F.3d 1184 (10th Cir. 2012).
Bew v. City of Chicago, 252 F.3d 891 (7th Cir. 2001).
Bridgeport Guardians, Inc. v. City of Bridgeport, 933 F.2d 1140, 1149 (2nd Cir. 1991).
Connecticut v. Teal, 457 U.S. 440 (1982).
Daubert v. Merrell Dow Pharmaceuticals Inc., 509 U.S. 579 (1993).
Dothard v. Rawlinson, 433 U.S. 321 (1977).
International Brotherhood of Teamsters v. United States, 431 U.S. 324 (1977).
Isabel v. City of Memphis, 404 F. 3d 404 (6th Cir. 2005).
Jones v. City of Boston, 752 F.3d 38, 60 (1st Cir. 2014).

Kirkland v. New York St. Dept. of Correctional Services, 374 F.Supp. 1361 (S.D.N.Y. 1974).
Officers for Justice v. Civil Service Commission, 979 F.2d 721 (9th Cir. 1992).

References

Alliger (Eds.), *Handbook of work analysis Methods, systems, applications and science of work measurement in organizations* (pp. 139–167). New York: Routledge, Taylor & Francis Group.

Bobko, P., Roth, P. L., & Potosky, D. (1999). Derivation and implications of a meta-analytic matrix incorporating cognitive ability, alternative predictors, and job performance. *Personnel Psychology, 52,* 561–589.

Bronfenbrenner, U. (1977). Toward an experimental ecology of human development. *American Psychologist, 32,* 513–531.

Campbell, D. T., & Stanley, J. C. (1966). *Experimental and quasi-experimental designs for research.* Chicago: Rand McNally.

Campion, M. A., Outtz, J. L., Zedeck, S., Schmidt, F. L., Kehoe, J. F., Murphy, K. R., & Guion, R. M. (2001). The controversy over score banding in personnel selection: Answers to 10 key questions. *Personnel Psychology, 54,* 149–185.

Cascio, W. F., Outtz, J., Zedeck, S., Goldstein, I. L. (1991). Statistical implications of six methods of test score use in personnel selection. *Human Performance, 4,* 233–264.

Cascio, W. F., Outtz, J., Zedeck, S., & Goldstein, I. L. (1995). Selected science or selective interpretation? *American Psychologist, 50,* 881–882.

Cook, T. D., & Campbell, D. T. (1979). *Quasi-experimentation: Design & analysis for field studies.* Boston: Houghton Mifflin.

Copus, D., Ugelow, R. S., & Sohn, J. (2005). A lawyer's view. In F. J. Landy (Ed.), *Employment discrimination litigation: Behavioral, quantitative, and legal perspectives* (pp. 450–502). San Francisco: Jossey-Bass.

Creswell, J. W., & Creswell, J. D. (2018). *Research design: Qualitative, quantitative, and mixed methods approaches.* Thousand Oaks, CA: Sage Publications.

De Corte, W., Lievens, F., & Sackett, P. R. (2007). Combining predictors to achieve optimal trade-offs between selection quality and adverse impact. *Journal of Applied Psychology, 92,* 1380–1393.

De Corte, W., Lievens, F., & Sackett, P. R. (2008). Validity and adverse impact potential of predictor composite formation. *International Journal of Selection and Assessment, 16,* 183–194.

Drogan, O., & Yancey, G. B. (2011). Financial utility of best employee selection practices at organizational level of performance. *The Psychologist-Manager Journal, 14*(1), 52–69.

Dunleavy, E. M. (2010). A consideration of practical significance in adverse impact analysis. Washington, DC: DCI Consulting Group, July.

Dunleavy, E. M., & Gutman, A. (2011). An update on the statistical versus practical significance debate: A review of *Stagi v. Amtrak* (2010). *The Industrial-Organizational Psychologist, 48,* 121–130.

Finch, D. M., Edwards, B. D., & Wallace, J. C. (2009). Multistage selection strategies: Simulating the effects on adverse impact and expected performance for various predictor combinations. *Journal of Applied Psychology, 94,* 318–340.

Gasperson, S. M., Bowler, M. C., Wuensch, K. L., & Bowler, J. L. (2013). A statistical correction to 20 years of banding. *International Journal of Selection and Assessment, 21*(1), 46–56.

Gutman, A. (2003). Adverse impact: Why is it so difficult to understand? *The Industrial-Organizational Psychologist, 40,* 42–50.

Gutman, A. (2004). Ground rules for adverse impact. *The Industrial-Organizational Psychologist, 41*, 109–119.

Gutman, A., & Dunleavy, E. (2012). Documenting work analysis projects: A review of strategy and legal defensibility for personnel selection. In M. A. Wilson, W. Bennett Jr., S. G. Gibson, & G. M. Alliger (Eds.), The handbook of work analysis: Methods, systems, applications and science of work measurement in organizations (pp. 139–168). New York: Routledge/Taylor and Francis.

Gutman, A., Outtz, J. L., & Dunleavy, E. (2017). An updated sampler of legal principles in employment selection. In *Handbook of employee selection* (pp. 631–658). New York: Routledge, Taylor & Francis Group.

Hart, M. (2004). Will employment discrimination class actions survive? *Akron Law Review, 37*, 813–846.

Hattrup, K., Rock, J., & Scalia, C. (1997). The effects of varying conceptualizations of job performance on adverse impact, minority hiring, and predicted performance. *Journal of Applied Psychology, 82*, 656–664.

Henle, C. A. (2004). Case review of the legal status of banding. *Human Performance, 17*, 415–432.

Jackson, J. R. (2011, September 12). Class actions and the implications of Rule 23. SCOTUSBLOG. https://www.scotusblog.com/2011/09/class-actions-and-the-implications-of-rule-23/

Jacobs, R., Murphy, J., & Siva, J. (2012). Unintended consequences of EEO enforcement policies: Being big is worse than being bad. *Journal of Business and Psychology, 28*, 467–471. doi:10.1007/s10869-012-9268-3

Kravitz, D. A. (2008). The diversity-validity dilemma: Beyond selection—the role of affirmative action. *Personnel Psychology, 61*, 173–193.

Lesley, C. M. (2019). Making Rule 23 ideal: Using a multifactor test to evaluate the admissibility of evidence at class certification. *Michigan Law Review, 118*, 149–171.

Levine, E. L., Ash, R. A., Hall, H., & Sistrunk, F. (1983). Evaluation of job analysis methods by experienced job analysts. *Academy of Management Journal, 26*, 339–348.

Meyer, B. D. (1995). Natural and quasi-experiments in economics. *Journal of Business & Economic Statistics, 13*(2), 151–161.

Morgeson, F. P., Brannick, M. T., & Levine, E. L. (2019). *Job and work analysis: Methods, research, and applications for human resource management.* Thousand Oaks, CA: Sage Publications.

Morris, S. B. (2015). Statistical inference testing in adverse impact cases. In C. Hanvey & K. Sady (Eds.), *Practitioner's guide to legal issues in organizations* (pp. 71–91). New York: Springer.

Morris, S. B. (2017). Statistical significance testing in adverse impact analysis. In S. B. Morris & E. M. Dunleavy (Eds.), Adverse impact analysis: Understanding data, statistics, and risk (pp. 113–125). New York: Routledge. doi.org/10.4324/9781315301433

Morris, S., Dunleavy, E. M., & Howard, E. (2015). Measuring adverse impact in employee selection decisions. In C. Hanvey & K. Sady (Eds.), *Practitioner's guide to legal issues in organizations* (pp. 1–27). New York: Springer.

Mueller, L. M., Dunleavy, E. M., & Buonasera, A. K. (2008). Analyzing personnel selection decisions in employment discrimination litigation settings. *New Directions for Institutional Research, 138*, 67–83.

Murphy, K. R., & Jacobs, R. R. (2012). Using effect size measures to reform the determination of adverse impact in equal employment litigation. *Psychology, Public Policy, & Law, 18*, 477–499.

Murphy, K. R., & Jacobs, R. R. (2017). When and why do different indices lead to different conclusions about adverse impact. In S. B. Morris & E. M. Dunleavy (Eds.), *Adverse impact analysis: Understanding data, statistics, and risk* (pp. 113–125). New York: Routledge. doi. org/10.4324/9781315301433

Murphy, K. R., Osten, K., & Myors, B. (1995). Modeling the effects of banding in personnel selection. *Personnel Psychology, 48*, 61–84.

Newman, D. A., Jones, K. S., Fraley, R. C., Lyon, J. S., & Mullaney, K. M. (2014). Why minority recruiting doesn't often work, and what can be done about it: Applicant qualifications and the 4-group model of targeted recruiting. In K. Y. T. Yu & D. M. Cable (Eds.), *The Oxford handbook of recruitment* (pp. 492–526). New York: Oxford University Press.

Newman, D. A., & Lyon, J. S. (2009). Recruitment efforts to reduce adverse impact: Targeted recruiting for personality, cognitive ability, and diversity. *Journal of Applied Psychology, 94*, 298–317.

Oswald, F. L., Dunleavy, E. M., & Shaw, A. (2017). Measuring practical significance in adverse impact analysis. In S. B. Morris & E. M. Dunleavy (Eds.), *Adverse impact analysis: Understanding data, statistics, and risk.* (pp. 92–112). New York: Routledge. doi.org/10.4324/9781315301433

Outtz, J. L. (Ed.). (2010). *Adverse impact: Implications for organizational staffing and high-stakes selection.* New York: Routledge.

Outtz, J. L., & Newman, D. A. (2010). A theory of adverse impact. In J. L. Outtz (ed.), *Adverse impact: Implications for organizational staffing and high stakes selection* (pp. 80–121). New York: Routledge.

Ployhart, R. E., & Holtz, B. C. (2008). The diversity-validity dilemma: Strategies for reducing racioethnic and sex subgroup differences and adverse impact in selection. *Personnel Psychology, 61*, 153–172.

Pyburn, K. M., Ployhart, R. E., & Kravitz, D. A. (2008). The diversity-validity dilemma: Overview and legal content. *Personnel Psychology, 61*, 143–151.

Report of the Scientific Affairs Committee. (1994, July). An evaluation of banding methods in personnel selection. *The Industrial-Organizational Psychologist, 32*, 80–86.

Roth, P. L., BeVier, C. A., Bobko, P., Switzer III, F. S., & Tyler, P. (2001). Ethnic group differences in cognitive ability in employment and educational settings: A meta-analysis. *Personnel Psychology, 54*, 297–330.

Roth, P. L., Bobko, P., & Switzer, F. S. III. (2006). Modeling the behavior of the 4/5 rule for determining adverse impact: Reasons for caution. *Journal of Applied Psychology, 91*(3), 507–522.

Rupp, D. E., Song, Q. C., & Strah, N. (2020). Addressing the co-called validity-diversity trade-off: Exploring the practicalities and legal defensibility of Pareto-optimization for reducing adverse impact within personnel selection. *Industrial and Organizational Psychology: Perspectives on Science and Practice, 13*, 246–271.

Sackett, P. R., & Ellingson, J. E. (1997). The effects of forming multi-predictor composites on group differences and adverse impact. *Personnel Psychology, 50*, 707–721.

Sanchez, J. I., & Levine, E. L. (1989). Determining important tasks within jobs: A policy-capturing approach. *Journal of Applied Psychology, 74*, 336–342.

Schmidt, F. L. (1991). Why all banding procedures are logically flawed. *Human Performance, 4*, 265–278.

Shadish, W. R., Cook, T. D., & Campbell, D. T. (2002). *Experimental and quasi-experimental designs for generalized causal inference.* New York: Houghton Mifflin.

Siskin, B. R., & Trippi, J. (2005). Statistical issues in litigation. In F. J. Landy (Ed.), *Employment discrimination litigation: Behavioral, quantitative, and legal perspectives* (pp. 132–166). San Francisco: Jossey-Bass.

Song, Q., Wee, S., & Newman, D. A. (2017). Diversity shrinkage: Cross-validating pareto-optimal weights to enhance diversity via hiring practices. *Journal of Applied Psychology, 102*, 1636–1657.

Strah, N., & Rupp, D. E. (in press). Are there cracks in our foundation? An integrative review of diversity issues in job analysis. *Journal of Applied Psychology.*

Tam, A. P., Murphy, K. R., & Lyall, J. T. (2004). Can changes in differential dropout rates reduce adverse impact? A computer simulation study of a multi-wave selection system. *Personnel Psychology, 57*, 905–934.

Thompson, D. E., & Thompson, T. A. (1982). Court standards for job analysis in test validation. *Personnel Psychology, 35*, 865–874.

Tonowski, R. (2014). On the legal front. *The Industrial-Organizational Psychologist, 52*, 21–26.

Uniform guidelines on employee selection procedures. (1978). *Federal Register, 43*, 38, 290–238, 315.

Wang, X., & Yancey, G. G. (2012). The benefit of a degree in I-O psychology or human resources. *The Industrial-Organizational Psychologist, 50*, 45–50.

Wee, S., Newman, D. A., & Joseph, D. L. (2014). More than g: Selection quality and adverse impact implications of considering second-stratum cognitive abilities. *Journal of Applied Psychology, 99*, 547–563.

Zedeck, S. (2009). Adverse impact: History and evolution. In Outtz, J. L. (Ed.), *Adverse impact: Implications for organizational staffing and high stakes selection.* New York: Taylor & Francis.

3

Race, Color, and National Origin Discrimination

Basics of Race, Color, and National Origin Discrimination

Title VII of the Civil Rights Act of 1964[1] bans discrimination based on (among other factors) race (e.g., White, Black), color (e.g., skin tone), and national origin (e.g., place of birth). These forms of discrimination can occur across the spectrum of organizational practices from the collection of pre-employment information such as background checks and application form data, to personnel decisions (e.g., hiring, firing, pay), to workplace harassment and retaliation. This chapter focuses most heavily on issues of race discrimination, given that such claims are more frequent than cases based on color and national origin. Table 3.1 provides a summary of race, color, and national origin discrimination charges filed with the Equal Employment Opportunity Commission (EEOC) throughout the last several years.

---

[1] https://www.eeoc.gov/laws/statutes/titlevii.cfm

Employment Discrimination. Stephen J. Vodanovich and Deborah E. Rupp, Oxford University Press. © Oxford University Press 2022. DOI: 10.1093/oso/9780190085421.003.0004

Table 3.1 Race, color, and national origin discrimination charges filed with the Equal Employment Opportunity Commission (EEOC) 2013–2020

	2013	2014	2015	2016	2017	2018	2019	2020
	Race discrimination cases							
Number of charges	33,068	31,073	31,027	32,309	28,528	24,600	23,976	22,064
	Color discrimination cases							
Number of charges	10,642	9,579	9,438	9,840	8,299	3,166	3,415	3,562
	National origin discrimination cases							
Number of charges	10,642	9,579	9,438	9,840	8,299	7,106	7,009	6,377

Retrieved from https://www.eeoc.gov/statistics/charge-statistics-charges-filed-eeoc-fy-1997-through-fy-2020

Disparate Treatment Discrimination

Recall that disparate treatment involves *intentionally* treating individuals less favorably because of their membership in a protected group. The case of *McDonnell Douglas Corp. v. Green* (1977)[2,3] is a significant example of a disparate treatment claim based on race. Percy Green, a Black mechanic, was laid off as part of an overall workforce reduction. He subsequently participated in two illegal activities (a "stall-in" and a "lock-in") in protest of the organization's actions. When the company later advertised for jobs, Green reapplied for his previously held position. He was not hired, and the search continued for individuals with similar qualifications. In the end, Green sued for race discrimination.

Recall that disparate treatment cases follow a three-phase burden-shifting process:

1. The plaintiff establishes a *prima facie*[4] case (presents *presumptive* evidence of discrimination).
2. The defense articulates that a legitimate reason existed for the alleged discriminatory behavior.
3. The plaintiff proves (with *direct* or *indirect evidence*) that the organization's reason(s) were a pretext for discrimination.

---

[2] https://caselaw.findlaw.com/us-supreme-court/411/792.html
[3] https://www.oyez.org/cases/1972/72-490
[4] Italicized technical terms are defined in the glossary at the end of this chapter.

Table 3.2 *McDonnell Douglas v. Green* (1977) Summary

Sequence of events leading up to case	Events during case

1. Green laid off as part of a large downsizing effort.
2. Green participated in a "stall-in" and "lock-out" against the company—both illegal activities.
3. Company advertised for jobs. One of the jobs was for the position of "mechanic"—Green's former position with the company.
4. Green applied for his former job and was rejected.
5. Green filed race discrimination lawsuit.
	1. Green successfully formed a *prima facie* case:
	  a. He was a member of a protected group,
	  b. he applied for and was qualified to perform the job,
	  c. the company refused to hire Green,
	  d. and the organization continued to seek applications for the position.
	2. Company articulated a legitimate reason for their refusal to hire Green (e.g., illegal behavior).
	3. Green had the option to demonstrate that the company's reason was a pretext for discrimination (e.g., White workers were treated less harshly for similar behaviors as Green). Pretext was not proved.

The Supreme Court concluded that Green had successfully created a *prima facie* case under disparate treatment rules. The company then successfully met its burden by articulating a legitimate reason for not rehiring Green. They stated that he was not hired due to his participation in illegal acts. Green had the option to demonstrate that the company's reason for not hiring him was a pretext for discrimination (e.g., identifying White workers who were treated less harshly for behaviors similar to Green's), but this burden was not met. A summary of the case is presented in Table 3.2. The *McDonnell* decision was supported and extended a few years later in *Texas Department of Community Affairs v. Burdine*[5,6] (1981, a sex discrimination case). It is these two cases that established the burden-shifting process outlined earlier and in other chapters, and thus this has been termed the *McDonnell-Burdine* framework.

Another important disparate treatment case involving alleged race discrimination is *St. Mary's Honor Center v. Hicks* (1993).[7,8] Melvin Hicks was disciplined by his relatively new supervisor on a number of occasions and was eventually fired for purportedly violating several company rules. These included the failure to perform an acceptable investigation of a fight between inmates during his shift, failure to confirm that his subordinates recorded

---

[5] https://supreme.justia.com/cases/federal/us/450/248/
[6] https://www.oyez.org/cases/1980/79-1764
[7] https://www.law.cornell.edu/supct/html/92-602.ZO.html
[8] https://www.oyez.org/cases/1992/92-602

their use of a company vehicle in a logbook, and intimidating his boss during a verbal altercation. Hicks was fired after this last incident.

Interestingly, prior to getting his new supervisor, Hick's past job performance was judged to be acceptable. After being terminated, he filed a race discrimination suit. The Court of Appeals concluded that the reasons offered by the company for firing Hicks were not credible given substantial indirect evidence provided by Hicks. For instance, indirect evidence was presented that similar rule violations by coworkers did not result in disciplinary actions. Additional indirect evidence consisted of the fact that other coworkers' similar (or more egregious) abuses were either ignored or not taken seriously and that his supervisor initiated the verbal altercation to provoke Hicks. As such, the Court of Appeals ruled in favor of Hicks stating:

> Because all of defendants' proffered reasons were discredited, defendants were in a position of having offered no legitimate reason for their actions. In other words, defendants were in no better position than if they had remained silent, offering no rebuttal to an established inference that they had unlawfully discriminated against plaintiff on the basis of his race.

However, in an intensely debated decision by the Supreme Court, the majority of justices disagreed with the Court of Appeals' decision. They decided that Hicks needed to go beyond demonstrating that the defense's reasons for his firing (e.g., instances of poor performance) were not true. That is, Hicks had the additional burden of proving that the reasons were a *pretext for race discrimination*. This logic by the Court supported the earlier decision by the District Court judge in *Hicks* who stated that the actions taken by his supervisor were *personal* and not motivated by race.

Pattern or Practice Discrimination

A major pattern or practice case involving race is exemplified by *Teamsters v. United States* (1977).[9,10] As described in Chapter 2, pattern or practice discrimination occurs when organizations are alleged to have engaged in pervasive, intentional discrimination, where the discriminatory behavior is

[9] https://supreme.justia.com/cases/federal/us/431/324/
[10] https://www.oyez.org/cases/1976/75-636

a "standard operating procedure." In *Teamsters*, the government sued a trucking company for disproportionately hiring Black and Hispanic drivers into lower paying jobs (city drivers), while Whites were selected for the more desirable position (line drivers)—so-called cross-job comparisons. To quote from the Court:

> Negroes [*sic*] and Spanish-surnamed Americans who were hired were overwhelmingly excluded from line-driver jobs. Such employees were willing to work, had access to the terminal, were healthy and of working age, and often were at least sufficiently qualified to hold city-driver jobs. Yet they became line drivers with far less frequency than whites.

An important aspect of the case was that only 13 Black or Hispanic individuals were employed in the higher-paid line driver position, and these individuals were hired *after* the suit was filed (see Table 3.3).

The company, joined by the union (the International Brotherhood of Teamsters), countered that a *prima facie* case could not be based on statistics alone to show intentional discrimination and that the government failed to look at the percent of non-White individuals in the workplace relative to those in the labor market. This argument was favorable to the position advocated by the Teamsters. In the end, the Supreme Court decided that the major issue in this case involved cross-job comparisons, and these differences were quite large. As such, the Court ruled that the government proved that non-White individuals were overwhelmingly relegated to lower paid driver jobs. Regarding the role of statistics, the Court famously said that:

> fine tuning of the statistics could not have obscured the glaring absence of minority line drivers . . . the company's inability to rebut the inference of discrimination came not from a misuse of statistics but from "the inexorable zero."

Table 3.3 Cross-job comparisons in *Teamsters v. United States* (1971)

	White employees	Black and Hispanic employees
Line drivers	1,802	13
Local drivers	1,117	167

Retrieved from footnote 9 in *Teamsters v. United States*.

Table 3.4 Key numbers in *Hazelwood v. U.S.* (1977)

Black teachers hired by Hazelwood School District *before* 1972 (year public employers were covered by Title VII)	.06%
Black teachers hired by Hazelwood School District by 1972	1.8%
Black teachers in Saint Louis County *and* Saint Louis City School District	15.4%
Black teachers in Hazelwood School District at time suit was filed in 1973	3.7%
Black teachers in Saint Louis County alone, *excluding* Saint Louis City School District	5.7%

Another historic pattern or practice case is *Hazelwood School District v. United States* (1977).[11,12] In this case, the government's suit was based on an alleged underrepresentation of Black teachers in the Hazelwood School District. At the time of the suit, Black teachers comprised 3.7% of all teachers in the district. A key issue was determining what comparison (or relevant labor market) was proper to determine whether or not the 3.7% constituted an underrepresentation of Black teachers.

The government alleged that the proper comparison was between the 3.7% figure and the percent of Black teachers in Saint Louis County *and* the City of St. Louis School District,[13] which was 15.4%. However, the defense argued that the relevant labor market was the percent of Black teachers in the Hazelwood School District (3.7%) versus those in Saint Louis County alone, excluding the City of Saint Louis School District, which was 5.7%. The critical numbers are shown in Table 3.4.

The Supreme Court ruled that the percent of Black teachers in the Hazelwood school district (3.7%) and the percent of Black teachers in the county excluding Saint Louis (5.7%) was the relevant comparison (see percentages italicized in Table 3.4). Given this, the Court concluded that the difference in percentages was relatively minor and not sufficient to indicate the presence of discrimination. Consequently, they ruled that the government failed to make a *prima facie* case. The Court also added that even if a meaningful difference existed, Hazelwood had articulated a legitimate reason for the imbalance (e.g., competition from the City of St. Louis) and that the district's affirmative action plan raised hiring rates for non-White individuals after 1972, the year the Civil Rights act was applied to public entities.

[11] https://caselaw.findlaw.com/us-supreme-court/433/299.html
[12] https://www.oyez.org/cases/1976/76-255
[13] Interestingly, the city of Saint Louis is not located in Saint Louis County. It is a separate, independent entity.

Adverse Impact

As reviewed earlier, adverse impact occurs when "neutral" employment practices, such as selection tests and other criteria disproportionally harm members of a protected subgroup. Adverse impact cases consist of the following three phases: (1) plaintiffs must *demonstrate* (burden of production and proof) that a *particular* employment practice *caused* the discrimination in question (e.g., disproportionately excluded protected subgroup members), (2) the defense needs to *demonstrate* (articulate and prove) that the challenged practice is *job-related* for the position in question and consistent with *business necessity*, and (3) plaintiffs must *prove* that an equally valid, job-related practice exists with less (or no) adverse impact.

Discrimination in the form of adverse impact based on race is illustrated by the landmark Supreme Court case of *Griggs v. Duke Power Co.* (1972).[14,15] Before the Civil Rights Act of 1964 became effective, the company restricted Blacks to jobs in the Labor Department, the lowest paying positions in the plant. In the 1950s, the company began requiring a high school diploma to be eligible for jobs outside the Labor Department. Then, in the mid 1960s, the organization required the passing of two paper-and-pencil cognitive ability tests (the Wonderlic Personnel Test and Bennett Mechanical Aptitude Test) for individuals to be transferred or promoted. Curiously, the requirement to pass the tests was made on the exact date that Title VII became effective (July 2, 1965; see Garrow [2014] for a detailed legal history of the *Griggs* decision).

Duke Power contended that its requirements were legal. For instance, the high school diploma and passing the two tests were required of all employees, and there was no intent to discriminate based on race. In addition, the company stated that using "professionally developed" tests was justified by Title VII. For instance, section 703(h) of Title VII states that

> it shall not be an unlawful employment practice for an employer . . . to give and act upon the results of any professionally developed ability test provided that such test, its administration or action upon the results is not designed, intended or used to discriminate because of race, color, religion, sex or national origin.

However, it is important to mention that the EEOC's guidelines issued in 1966 interpreted "professionally developed tests" to be those that impartially assess the knowledge or skills required for jobs. The agency also noted that the

[14] https://caselaw.findlaw.com/us-supreme-court/401/424.html
[15] https://www.oyez.org/cases/1970/124

mere fact that tests were designed by a professional group is insufficient to pass muster under Title VII.

The educational requirement and cognitive ability tests were shown to be disadvantageous to Black applicants. For instance, only 12% of Black applicants possessed high school diplomas compared to 34% of White applicants in the state of North Carolina where the company was located. Furthermore, the two tests eliminated approximately 94% of Black applicants versus 43% of White applicants. Given these data, a race discrimination suit was filed. In the end, the Court unanimously ruled in favor of the plaintiffs. A key point in the ruling was that proof of intent to discriminate is *not* required if certain practices have an adverse impact on protected subgroups. As the Court noted, under the Civil Rights Act, "practices, procedures, or tests neutral on their face, and even neutral in terms of intent, cannot be maintained if they operate to 'freeze' the status quo of prior discriminatory practices." So, negative, disproportionate effects on protected subgroups are protected under Title VII. The Court went further in its ruling and memorably stated,

> The Act proscribes not only overt discrimination but also practices that are fair in form, but discriminatory in operation. The touchstone is business necessity. If an employment practice which operates to exclude Negroes [*sic*] cannot be shown to be related to job performance, the practice is prohibited.

Regarding the legitimacy of using professionally developed tests, the Court sided with the interpretation offered by the EEOC. While admitting the usefulness of employing tests for personnel decisions, the justices ruled that, to be consistent with Title VII, tests must measure abilities relevant to the job. Consequently, the *Griggs* decision set the precedent that all tests and requirements used for employment purposes must be (1) job-related and (2) consistent with business necessity. A summary of the Griggs decision is provided in Table 3.5.

The concept of job-relatedness was expanded on in *Albemarle Paper Company v. Moody* (1975).[16,17] Albemarle attempted to validate its tests by correlating test scores with supervisor assessments of performance. The rather hasty validation effort, performed a few months before trial (not prior to the suit being filed), had several flaws. The sample consisted of (1) only four Black

[16] https://supreme.justia.com/cases/federal/us/422/405/
[17] https://www.oyez.org/cases/1974/74-389

Table 3.5 Summary of *Griggs v. Duke Power*

Promotion requirements	• Pass the Wonderlic Personnel Test and Bennett • Mechanical Aptitude Test • Possess a high school diploma
Effects of these requirements	• Tests eliminated roughly 94% of Blacks as compared to 43% of Whites • 12% of Blacks possessed a high school diploma in North Carolina versus 34% of Whites
Race discrimination lawsuit filed	• Willie Griggs and 12 other Black employees who wanted promotion out of Labor department were part of the class in the class action lawsuit
Supreme Court ruling against the company	• All tests/requirements must be *job-related* • *Intent* to discriminate is not required for discrimination to exist • All tests must meet acceptable *professional guidelines* for psychometric worth • Employment discrimination can exist based on the *effects* of one's actions

employees, (2) mainly included individuals at the top of the organizational hierarchy, (3) the correlations (described as "patchwork" in nature) had no clear association with job performance, and (4) supervisors ranked employees against each other (i.e., a paired comparisons method) using unclear criteria. Part of the instructions to supervisors was to "determine which ones they felt, irrespective of the job that they were actually doing, but in their respective jobs, did a better job than the person they were rating against." In the end, the Court determined that Albemarle's efforts to justify its requirements were inadequate—their validation study was not acceptable.

In *Connecticut v. Teal* (1982),[18,19] the Court added more information regarding the scope by which adverse impact can be determined. The State of Connecticut used a multiple-hurdle approach for promotion decisions beginning with a written examination. That is, individuals needed to pass a written exam (hurdle 1) in order to be put on an eligibility list for future promotions where several other factors were used to make decisions (e.g., supervisor recommendations, tenure, work performance). Black employees who failed the written test and therefore were excluded from the promotion process sued for race discrimination. Their position was that the exam was not related to the job and resulted in adverse impact. Regarding the test, 79% of White employees passed versus 54% of Black employees.

[18] https://caselaw.findlaw.com/us-supreme-court/457/440.html
[19] https://www.oyez.org/cases/1981/80-2147

Connecticut did not deny the existence of adverse impact on the written test. Rather, they countered that the overall effect of their selection process, despite the results of the written exam, ended with a higher percent of Black employees (22.9%) being promoted as compared to White employees (13.5%).[20] This has been referred to as a "bottom line" defense.

The State of Connecticut added that the Uniform Guidelines indicate that when the *total* selection process does not result in adverse impact, individual aspects of the process would not be evaluated. However, the Supreme Court decided that every component of a multiple-hurdle approach must be related to the job (and be free of adverse impact) despite the fact that the selection process as a whole did not disadvantage Black employees. As the Court said, "It is clear that Congress never intended to give an employer license to discriminate against some employees on the basis of race or sex merely because he favorably treats other members of the employee's group." So, one important implication of the *Teal* decision is that organizations cannot "make up" for an initial discriminatory practice against Blacks by making more favorable decisions for different Black individuals later on in the process. That is, a discriminatory practice exists when a test adversely impacts legally protected job seekers and eliminates them from the rest of the selection process. Promoting other Black employees at the end of the entire procedure does not compensate for earlier discrimination. Another lesson to be learned from the *Teal* decision is that organizations need to examine each part of their selection system for job-relatedness and evidence of adverse impact when using a multiple-hurdle approach.

A controversial adverse impact case was *Wards Cove Packing Co. v. Atonio* (1989).[21,22] Wards Cove, a salmon cannery company, hired employees into two general classes of jobs (see Potter [1999] for a discussion of *Wards Cove*).[23] One job class consisted of cannery work, which offered lower pay and was occupied mostly by employees of color. The other category was non-cannery positions, which paid more, required greater skill, and was held primarily by White employees.

As a result of these disparities, a lawsuit was filed. The plaintiffs argued that the percent of non-White employees in the skilled/non-cannery positions was substantially lower than non-White employees in the cannery (low skilled) jobs. Plaintiffs also alleged that reasons for the cross-job racial discrepancies

---

[20] An interesting twist is that the promotion decisions by the state were made about a year *after* the suit was filed and about 30 days before the trial.

[21] https://caselaw.findlaw.com/us-supreme-court/490/642.html

[22] https://www.oyez.org/cases/1988/87-1387

[23] https://www.siop.org/Portals/84/TIP/Archives/271.pdf?ver=2019-08-19-115805-897

included separate hiring practices, nepotism, no objective criteria for selection, and a penchant for rehiring previous employees. However, the Supreme Court ruled that, unlike disparate treatment or pattern or practice scenarios, cross-job comparisons were not relevant in adverse impact cases. Instead, the Court stated that the appropriate comparison was between the racial makeup of qualified individuals in the relevant labor market and the percent of non-White and Whites employees *in the skilled/non-cannery jobs*. The Court also noted that there was evidence that most non-Whites did not possess the qualifications needed for the skilled positions and typically failed to apply for these jobs.

Another key issue was that the majority of justices in *Wards Cove* stated that the defense burden in adverse impact cases is to *articulate* (not prove) that a legitimate business reason existed for its decision, an easier standard to meet. The production/articulation standard decided in *Wards Cove* did not last very long. The Civil Rights Act of 1991 (CRA-91) stated that the defense burden in adverse impact cases is to "*demonstrate* that the challenged practice is job-related for the position in question and consistent with business necessity." The Act defined the word "demonstrate" as the burden of production and persuasion (proof). Also, one of the purposes of CRA-91 was to "codify the concepts of 'business necessity' and 'job-related' enunciated by the Supreme Court in *Griggs v. Duke Power Co.*, . . . and in the other Supreme Court decisions prior to *Wards Cove Packing Co. v. Atonio*."

Legal Commentary: *Wards Cove* as a Pattern or Practice Case (Not Adverse Impact)

The decision in *Wards Cove v. Atonio* has been discussed as having dismantled accepted law regarding adverse impact partly due to the lessening of the defense burden to that of articulation. However, it has been argued that *Wards Cove* should have been considered as a pattern or practice case rather than one of adverse impact (e.g., Gutman, 2004; Gutman et al., 2011).

The original suit filed in the district (trial) court alleged both adverse impact and pattern or practice discrimination given existing cross-job differences. The trial court rejected both claims. The Court of Appeals for the 9th Circuit also rejected the pattern or practice allegation but considered the adverse impact assertion. In doing so, it concluded that cross-job comparisons were legitimate for adverse impact suits and concluded that the defense burden was to show job-relatedness (an established defense for adverse impact cases). As we mentioned previously, the Supreme Court in *Wards Cove* rejected cross-job comparisons for adverse impact scenarios and also changed the defense burden from showing job-relatedness to that of articulation, a traditional disparate treatment defense. The articulation defense advocated by the Court was controversial and eventually overturned by CRA-91.

So, why did the Court consider *Wards Cove* to be an adverse impact case? As Gutman et al. (2011) state, "On its face, *Wards Cove* was *Teamsters* revisited. As in *Teamsters*, minorities were congregated in a less desirable job and whites in a more desirable job" (p. 56). Indeed, such cross-job comparisons were already judged to be legitimate in prior pattern or practice cases (see *Teamsters* and *Hazelwood*). Therefore, if *Wards Cove* was treated as a pattern or practice case, the Court could have ruled that cross-job data were acceptable and maintained the articulation defense for such scenarios. Thus, the job-relatedness defense for adverse impact cases could have remained intact.

To further muddy the waters, the Court in *Wards Cove* mentioned that *Hazelwood* was a classic adverse impact case. It wasn't. Recall that *Hazelwood* was a pattern or practice case. Indeed, as noted by Gutman et al. (2011), the concept of adverse impact was not discussed in *Hazelwood*, and not a single adverse impact case was cited.

Supplemental Readings on Race, Color, and National Origin Discrimination

Beginner

FindLaw. National origin and racial discrimination at work. https://employment.findlaw.com/employment-discrimination/national-origin-and-racial-discrimination-at-work.html

Smith, A. (2017 January). 7 myths about national origin discrimination: Armenian police officer awarded damages for discrimination. Society for Human Resource Management. https://www.shrm.org/resourcesandtools/legal-and-compliance/state-and-local-updates/pages/myths-national-origin-discrimination.aspx

Intermediate

EEOC. Compliance manual on race and color discrimination. https://www.eeoc.gov/policy/docs/race-color.html

EEOC. Enforcement guidelines for national origin discrimination. https://www.eeoc.gov/laws/guidance/national-origin-guidance.cfm

EEOC. Facts about race/color discrimination. https://www.eeoc.gov/eeoc/publications/fs-race.cfm

EEOC. Questions and answers about race and color discrimination. https://www.eeoc.gov/policy/docs/qanda_race_color.html

EEOC. Questions and answers regarding national origin discrimination. https://www.eeoc.gov/laws/guidance/national-origin-qa.cfm

Advanced

Outtz, J. L. (2005). Race discrimination cases: Common themes. In F. L. Landy (Ed.), *Employment discrimination litigation: Behavioral, quantitative, and legal perspectives* (pp. 201–228). San Francisco, CA: John Wiley & Sons.

Parliman, G. C., & Shoeman, R. J. (1994). National origin discrimination or employer prerogative? An analysis of language rights in the workplace. *Employee Relations Law Journal, 19*, 551–565.

Vuolo, M., Lageson, S., & Uggen, C. (2017). Record questions in the era of "ban the box." *Criminology & Public Policy, 16*, 139–165.

Altering or Discarding Test Results

Section 106 of the Civil Rights Act of 1991 states that it is against the law to alter test scores based on protected group status (e.g., race, sex). As the Act states,

> It shall be an unlawful employment practice for a respondent, in connection with the selection or referral of applicants or candidates for employment or promotion, to adjust the scores of, use different cutoff scores for, or otherwise alter the results of, employment related tests on the basis of race, color, religion, sex, or national origin.

In general, altering the content of tests, such as removing items, for the purpose of avoiding adverse impact will not ordinarily survive legal scrutiny given that such actions may lead to disparate treatment claims unless unusual circumstances exist. Such "unusual circumstances" were present in *Hayden v. Nassau County* (1999).[24] The county had a long history of using exams that had an adverse impact on Black, Latinx, and female applicants in the hiring of police officers.

After being sued by the Department of Justice (DOJ) in 1977, a consent decree was reached with Nassau County to develop a valid test with no adverse impact. Attempts to do so failed in both 1983 and 1987—adverse impact persisted. As a result, additional consent decrees followed in 1990, and an agreement was reached that the DOJ and Nassau County would jointly attempt to develop an exam that did not discriminate against non-Whites.

This work culminated in an exam that consisted of 25 factors. In 1994, the newly created exam was administered to more than 25,000 applicants.

---

[24] https://openjurist.org/180/f3d/42/hayden-v-county-of-nassau

A committee was established to analyze the test data and evaluate its validity. In doing so, many separate structures of the exam were investigated. In the end, the committee recommended eliminating 16 sections of the exam (e.g., cognitive sections) and using the remaining nine sections to make selection decisions. Importantly, both the scoring system and cutoff scores were identical for all applicants. This approach led to a reduction, but not elimination, of adverse impact. A suit was filed by a class of applicants alleging that the discarding of the test results was a violation of Title VII and the 14th Amendment. The Court of Appeals for the 2nd Circuit ruled in favor of Nassau County. The court stated that Nassau County

> sought to design a police officers' exam which would reduce or eliminate the prior exams' adverse impact on Black candidates. The 1994 exam was administered to all of the 25,000 candidates in identical fashion, regardless of race. The test was scored the same for all candidates, and no differential cutoffs were used. We conclude that the intent to remedy the disparate impact of the prior exams is not equivalent to an intent to discriminate against non-minority applicants.

What if an organization administers tests to applicants and has concerns about the *potential* of adverse impact given the distribution of test scores by race? Can they throw out the test scores and start over again? A highly debated case that fits this description is *Ricci v. DiStefano* (2009).[25,26] The City of New Haven sought to promote firefighters for the positions of captain and lieutenant. In doing so, the city followed a *collective bargaining agreement* between the fire department and the firefighters' labor union that required the use of a written test (weighted 60%) and an oral exam (weighted 40%). When the tests were scored, only two non-White members (both Hispanic) were eligible for promotion to captain, while no Blacks were eligible for promotion to either captain or lieutenant. A total of 17 Whites were deemed suitable for promotion—7 for captain and 10 for lieutenant (see Table 3.6).

Given the test results, New Haven feared that it would be sued for adverse impact by Black and Hispanic employees. So, the Civil Service Board (CSB) of New Haven decided after a prolonged process to discard (not use) the test results.[27] As a result of this decision, 17 White firefighters and one Hispanic firefighter (together) sued the city. The lower courts ruled in favor of the city.

---

[25] https://www.law.cornell.edu/supct/pdf/07-1428P.ZO
[26] https://www.oyez.org/cases/2008/07-1428
[27] The vote by the CSB was 2–2, with one person abstaining given a conflict of interest. Therefore, the test was not certified for use.

Table 3.6 Initial results for promotion exams in
Ricci v. DiStefano

	Whites	Blacks	Hispanics
Captain Exam (seven vacancies)			
Applicants	25	8	8
Passing score	16	3	3
Top nine scores	7	0	2
Lieutenant Exam (eight vacancies)			
Applicants	43	19	15
Passing score	25	6	3
Top 10 scores	10	0	0

One reason was that even though the city admittedly used race to conform to Title VII in denying the test results, the end result was deemed to be race-neutral: no one was promoted. This is somewhat analogous to the "no harm, no foul" reasoning in sports. As the District Court judge noted: "while the evidence shows that race was taken into account in the decision not to certify the test results, the result was race-neutral: all the test results were discarded, no one was promoted, and firefighters of every race will have to participate in another selection process to be considered for promotion."

The Supreme Court overruled the lower courts in a 5–4 decision.[28] As the Court stated, "The question is not whether that conduct was discriminatory but whether the city had a lawful justification for its race-based action." The majority of justices decided that the city was required to have a "strong basis in evidence" belief to justify using race in deciding to discard the test results (see Table 3.7). In the end, the Court concluded that this standard was not met by the city.[29]

The Court in *Ricci* also referred to Section 106 of the CRA-91 regarding the discriminatory use of test scores. The opinion noted that since it is illegal to alter test scores according to race, tossing out an entire test would be a greater violation. As the court said, "If an employer cannot rescore a test based on the candidates' race . . . then it follows . . . that it may not take the

---

[28] In a surprising move, the Court granted summary judgment to the plaintiffs rather than sending the case back to the Court of Appeals to interpret the strong basis-in-evidence standard stated in *Ricci*.

[29] The *Ricci* case has been categorized by some as an adverse impact case or an affirmative action suit. Fundamentally, *Ricci* was a *disparate treatment* case. That is, the plaintiffs articulated that race discrimination existed in the actions taken by the city. The normal and rather straightforward articulation defense in disparate treatment cases was supplanted by a "strong basis in evidence" standard, which the city failed to meet.

Table 3.7 Standards discussed in *Ricci v. DiStefano*

Good faith	*Trusting* or *believing* that the remedial action was necessary to avoid liability
Strong basis in evidence	Sufficient evidentiary data exist that demonstrate remedial action was warranted to avoid liability (standard applied in *Ricci* final decision)
Certainty	Evidence exists that liability would be inevitable if the remedial action were not taken; proof that an actual violation of law existed that merited a remedial action

Adapted from https://www.supremecourt.gov/opinions/08pdf/07-1428.pdf

greater step of discarding the test altogether to achieve a more even racial distribution."

An important lesson to be learned from *Ricci* is that organizations should take great care in choosing selection and/or promotion techniques, including getting expert input *before* they are administered for the purpose of selection/promotion decision-making (Gutman & Dunleavy, 2009).[30] This is especially the case for police and fire departments, many of which continue to use written tests despite their potential for adverse impact against non-White subgroups (e.g., Blacks, Hispanics; see Riccucci & Riccardelli, 2015).

As mentioned in *Ricci*, other alternatives could have been considered, such as the assessment center method. This method has been found to be job-related, valid, and produce less adverse impact than written tests and has seen increased usage by municipalities (see Jackson, Lance, & Hoffman, 2012; Thornton, Mueller-Hanson, & Rupp, 2017; Thornton & Potemra, 2010; Thornton & Rupp, 2005; Thornton, Rupp, & Hoffman, 2015). However, in a study of written test usage by police and fire departments, Riccucci and Riccardelli (2015) concluded that assessment centers "do not *replace* the use of written exams, rather they supplement them. In some cases, assessment centers are relied upon only when an applicant has passed the written exam. In effect, cities continue to place the greatest emphasis on written exams" (p. 362).

Criminal Background Checks

The gathering of information about the criminal history of job applicants is relatively common. For instance, a survey conducted by the Society for

---

[30] https://www.siop.org/Portals/84/TIP/Archives/472.pdf?ver=2019-08-20-115440-530

Human Resource Management (SHRM, 2012a)[31] found that almost 70% of organizations reported collecting these data on all of their applicants. This information is typically obtained via application forms and/or external organizations that specialize in such work. Concerns about the collection of criminal history data include the potential for adverse impact as well the use of non–job-related information for a particular position.

Making employment decisions based on criminal background information of job seekers has been used, and challenged legally, for quite some time. Two early cases found that strict prohibitions against employing individuals with a criminal record were a violation of the law (*Carter v. Gallagher*, 1971;[32] *Green v. Missouri Pacific Railroad Company*, 1975[33]). In *Carter*, applicants with criminal records were eliminated for fire department positions. The Court of Appeals for the 8th Circuit ruled that companies need to provide evidence that prior convictions are related to the inability to perform job tasks. In other words, the use of blanket disqualifications is not viewed as legally acceptable.

In *Green*, Buck Green (a Black male applicant) sued the railroad (MoPac) for its policy of refusing to hire job candidates with a previous criminal record. Essentially, Green asserted that the policy discriminated against Blacks and was not supported by evidence of business necessity. The railroad defended itself by providing several justifications for why its policy was needed, including theft concerns and increased chances of recidivism. However, the court agreed with Green. As the court stated, "MoPac has not empirically validated its policy with respect to conviction records, nor shown that a less restrictive alternative with a lesser racial impact would not serve as well. . . . Although the reasons MoPac advances for its absolute bar can serve as relevant considerations in making individual hiring decisions, they in no way justify an absolute policy which sweeps so broadly."

More recently, in *EEOC v. Freeman* (2015),[34] the company (Freeman), who offers services for conventions and various corporate occasions, was accused of race discrimination by using criminal and credit history information for personnel decisions. Criminal background checks were conducted for all applicants, while the use of credit history was limited to "positions involving money handling or access to sensitive financial information."[35]

---

[31] https://www.shrm.org/hr-today/trends-and-forecasting/research-and-surveys/pages/criminal backgroundcheck.aspx

[32] https://scholar.google.com/scholar_case?case=13249931782899875060&hl=en&as_sdt=6&as_vis=1&oi=scholarr

[33] https://scholar.google.com/scholar_case?case=10887957311026802385&hl=en&as_sdt=6&as_vis=1&oi=scholarr

[34] http://www.ca4.uscourts.gov/Opinions/Published/132365.P.pdf

[35] Freeman stopped conducting credit history checks in 2011.

The Court of Appeals for the 4th Circuit supported the District Court's decision and ruled in favor of Freeman. A primary reason for the decision was that the data submitted by the EEOC's statistical expert witness were deemed to be skewed and filled with omissions and errors (also see Copeland & Schmake, 2016). As the court stated in rather severe language, "The Commission's work of serving 'the public interest' is jeopardized by the kind of missteps that occurred here."

The EEOC has had some success in challenging the use of criminal background checks. For instance, a large settlement[36] ($3.1 million) was reached between the EEOC and Pepsi Bottling in 2012. Pepsi had a policy that excluded individuals who were arrested or convicted of crimes (even minor offenses). As a result, a disproportionate number of Black applicants from across the United States (more than 300) were denied employment. As the EEOC noted in its press release, "The use of arrest and conviction records to deny employment can be illegal under Title VII of the Civil Rights Act of 1964, when it is not relevant for the job, because it can limit the employment opportunities of applicants or workers based on their race or ethnicity."

In 2019, the EEOC reached another large settlement, this time with Dogencorp (Dollar General). The company made conditional job offers to candidates that were contingent on an investigation of criminal history data. This practice led to a race discrimination suit being filed by a class of Black applicants. The settlement required the company to pay $6 million in damages to Black applicants who were denied employment between 2014 and 2019.[37]

To address the potential of adverse impact, the EEOC has developed enforcement guidelines for arrest and conviction records[38] (see Table 3.8). Regarding conviction information, the guidelines stress that organizations should consider the

- *nature* and *severity* of the offense,
- amount of *time that has passed* since the conviction (or completion of one's sentence), and
- *nature* and *type* of job sought.

---

[36] https://www.eeoc.gov/eeoc/newsroom/release/1-11-12a.cfm
[37] https://www1.eeoc.gov/eeoc/newsroom/release/11-18-19b.cfm
[38] https://www.eeoc.gov/laws/guidance/arrest_conviction.cfm

Table 3.8 Best practices for employers: Equal Employment Opportunity Commission (EEOC) use of criminal records

General	• Eliminate policies or practices that exclude people from employment based on any criminal record. • Train managers, hiring officials, and decision-makers about Title VII and its prohibition on employment discrimination.
Developing a policy	• Develop a narrowly tailored written policy and procedure for screening applicants and employees for criminal conduct: • Identify essential job requirements and the actual circumstances under which the jobs are performed. • Determine the specific offenses that may demonstrate unfitness for performing such jobs. • Identify the criminal offenses based on all available evidence. • Determine the duration of exclusions for criminal conduct based on all available evidence. • Include an individualized assessment. • Record the justification for the policy and procedures. • Note and keep a record of consultations and research considered in crafting the policy and procedures. • Train managers, hiring officials, and decision-makers on how to implement the policy and procedures consistent with Title VII.
Questions about criminal records	• When asking questions about criminal records, limit inquiries to records for which exclusion would be job-related for the position in question and consistent with business necessity.
Confidentiality	• Keep information about applicants' and employees' criminal records confidential. Only use it for the purpose for which it was intended.

Adapted from http://www.eeoc.gov/laws/guidance/arrest_conviction.cfm#VIII

The Guidelines do *not* suggest prohibiting the collection of criminal background information. Rather, the EEOC proposes that conviction data should be obtained *later* in the selection process, preferably after an initial offer has been made, *and not collected earlier* in the decision-making procedure (e.g., on application forms). The value of this advice is bolstered by research showing that questions regarding prior criminal background information are routinely asked on application forms (e.g., Coady, 1986; Jolley & Frierson, 1989; Miller, 1980; Vodanovich & Lowe, 1992; Wallace, Tye, & Vodanovich, 2000; Wallace & Vodanovich, 2004).

The potential adverse effects of criminal background checks have led to the "Ban the Box" movement (BTB), which advocates making it illegal to require applicants to check whether they have a conviction record on application forms. The goal of this effort is to ensure that qualifications of

Table 3.9 List of all ban-the-box and fair-chance laws and policies by state

State laws	State polices	States with laws/policies *only* at city or county level
California	Arizona	Alabama
Colorado	Georgia	Arkansas
Connecticut	Indiana	Florida
Delaware	Kansas	Iowa
Hawaii	Kentucky	North Carolina
Illinois	Michigan	South Carolina
Louisiana	Missouri	Texas
Maryland	New York	
Maine	Oklahoma	
Massachusetts	Pennsylvania	
Minnesota	Virginia	
Nebraska		
Nevada		
New Jersey		
New Mexico		
North Dakota		
Ohio		
Oregon		
Rhode Island		
Tennessee		
Utah		
Vermont		
Washington		
Wisconsin		
District of Columbia (Washington, DC)		

Retrieved from https://www.nelp.org/publication/ban-the-box-fair-chance-hiring-state-and-local-guide/

applicants are evaluated before any criminal history is revealed. According to the National Employment Law Project, as of 2019, 35 states and approximately 150 municipalities have laws or policies that limit the collection of criminal history information on application forms for state-government jobs. In addition, 13 states have adopted such rules for private organizations[39] (see Table 3.9).

---

[39] https://www.nelp.org/publication/ban-the-box-fair-chance-hiring-state-and-local-guide/

It is noteworthy that a three-judge panel for the 5th Circuit ruled against the EEOC by barring the agency from enforcing its 2012 Guidelines against the state of Texas.[40] Texas argued that banning criminal background checks negated their ability to reject convicted felons for certain jobs or job categories, and the court agreed. This means that Texas can collect criminal background information (e.g., on application forms) for state-level jobs.

BTB has received its share of criticism (see Hyman, 2019).[41] One argument is that the process only delays the decision not to hire until later in the process and will have no real impact on hiring rates for those with criminal records. Furthermore, some have argued that BTB approaches can actually *harm* those that it intends to help (see Semuels, 2016,[42] for a concise review). For instance, Doleac and Hansen (2016)[43] examined the effects of BTB policies by examining job data for various demographic groups based on data from the Current Population Survey (2004–2014) before and after the implementation of BTB policies. The authors reported that "On average, young, low-skilled Black men are 3.4 percentage points (5.1%) less likely to be employed after BTB than before"—a statistically significant effect. A decrease in employment of 2.9% was also found for low-skilled, young Hispanic men, but this finding was not statistically significant.

In another study, Agan and Starr (2018)[44] sent fake resumes to approximately 15,000 organizations in New York City and New Jersey before and after BTB policies were enacted. A major finding by the authors was that "before BTB, White applicants to BTB-affected employers received 7% more callbacks than similar Black applicants, but after BTB this gap grew to 45%." One interpretation of such results is that eliminating criminal record data may lead organizations to assume that applicants with certain demographic characteristics (e.g., Black male applicants) are likely to have a greater likelihood of criminal offenses. So race is being used in lieu of criminal history information.

Given such results, some have suggested that a broader approach is needed to improve the employment opportunities of individuals with criminal histories (see Semuels, 2016). Such efforts include criminal justice reform to reduce the rate of incarceration (especially among Black men) and helping individuals with criminal records find a place to live and work to avoid recidivism.

[40] http://www.ca5.uscourts.gov/opinions/pub/18/18-10638-CV0.pdf
[41] https://www.workforce.com/news/a-pox-on-ban-the-box
[42] https://www.theatlantic.com/business/archive/2016/08/consequences-of-ban-the-box/494435/
[43] https://www.nber.org/papers/w22469.pdf
[44] https://papers.ssrn.com/sol3/papers.cfm?abstract_id=2795795

Credit History Information

Many organizations check credit scores or credit reports when making personnel decisions. For example, a SHRM survey in 2012 concluded that roughly 47% of companies reviewed credit information for at least some positions within their organizations. Most of these checks were performed for jobs that involve financial duties, executive positions, and ones that included access to confidential and/or sensitive information (SHRM, 2012b).

The validity of both criminal and credit history has not received much research attention, and the results have been mixed (e.g., Aamodt, 2015; see Table 3.10). Statistically significant associations have been found between results on such checks and job performance, but the relationships detected have been relatively small. One study found no relationship between credit ratings and performance scores or termination decisions with a sample of more than 170 employees in a financial organization (Bryan & Palmer, 2012). An investigation on the association between credit scores and both personality and job performance was conducted by Bernerth, Taylor, Walker, and Whitman (2012). They found that credit scores were significantly and positively related to conscientiousness and negatively to agreeableness. The authors also reported significant, positive associations between credit scores and both organizational citizenship behavior and supervisor ratings of task

Table 3.10 Correlations between criminal and credit history and work performance

Criterion	K	N	R	90% confidence interval		SE%
				Lower	Upper	
Criminal history	–	–	–	–	–	–
Work problems	13	19,844	0.071	0.05	0.09	40
Performance ratings	8	1,982	−0.208	−0.13	−0.29	20
Bad credit history						
Work problems	13	11,025	0.116	0.09	0.14	35
Discipline	8	9341	0.103	0.08	0.13	39
Absenteeism	6	1844	0.19	0.16	0.23	100
Performance ratings	4	674	−0.152	−0.32	0.02	13

Note. K number of studies, N total sample size, R sample-size-weighted uncorrected average correlation, $SE\%$ percent of variability that would have been expected by sampling error.

Adapted from Aamodt (2015).

performance. No connection was found between credit scores and workplace deviance.

Several studies have found that the use of credit information can lead to race-based adverse impact. Studies by the Board of Governors of the Federal Reserve System (2007)[45] and the Woodstock Institute (2010)[46] reported that Asian Americans and Whites have higher credit scores than do Hispanics and Blacks. In addition, Bernerth (2012) found that non-Whites had significantly lower credit scores than Whites.

In *EEOC v. Kaplan Higher Education Corporation* (2014),[47] the EEOC unsuccessfully alleged the existence of adverse impact against Black applicants through Kaplan's use of credit history data. The organization required credit history checks for those applying for certain positions, which included senior executives, accounting jobs, and those with access to student financial data. The case was partially marred by the fact that the EEOC used "race raters" to assess the race of applicants based on driver's license photographs. The court concluded that the "race rater" data presented by an expert witness were not admissible: it did not meet sufficient scientific rigor according to the *Daubert Standard* (see *Daubert v. Merrell Dow Pharmaceuticals, Inc.*, 1993).[48] Consequently, precedent regarding the issue of the legality of credit history requirements was not set in this case.

Supplemental Readings on Criminal and Credit Background Checks

Beginner
Nagele-Piazza, L. (2017 January). Do ban-the-box laws work? Society for Human Resource Management. https://www.shrm.org/resourcesandtools/legal-and-compliance/state-and-local-updates/pages/do-ban-the-box-laws-work.aspx

Natividad Rodriguez, M. (2015). Best practices and model fair-chance policies. National Employment Law Project (NELP). https://www.nelp.org/publication/best-practices-model-fair-chance-policies/

Intermediate
Dunleavy, E. & Gutman, A. (2013). The latest on EEO challenges to background checks. *The Industrial-Organizational Psychologist, 51*, 106–117.

---

[45] https://www.federalreserve.gov/boarddocs/rptcongress/creditscore/creditscore.pdf
[46] https://woodstockinst.org/wp-content/uploads/2013/05/bridgingthegapcreditscores_sept2010_smithduda.pdf
[47] http://www.opn.ca6.uscourts.gov/opinions.pdf/14a0071p-06.pdf
[48] https://caselaw.findlaw.com/us-supreme-court/509/579.html

Equal Employment Opportunity Commission and the Federal Trade Commission (n.d.). Background checks: What employers need to know. https://www.eeoc.gov/eeoc/publications/background_checks_employers.cfm

Advanced

Aamodt, M. G. (2015). Using background checks in the employee selection process. In C. Hanvey & K. Sady (Eds.), *Practitioner's guide to legal issues in organizations* (pp. 85–110). Cham: Springer International Publishing.

Vuolo, M., Lageson, S., & Uggen, C. (2017). Criminal record questions in the era of "ban the box." *Criminology and Public Policy, 16*, 139–165.

Insights from Social Science: Discrimination Based on Applicant Names

The names of job seekers are common on application forms and resumes. Can such information lead to discrimination in hiring? Research suggests that the answer is "yes." For instance, Bertrand and Mullainathan (2004) varied the qualification level (low vs. high) and names of applicants on fake resumes. Stereotypically White (Emily, Greg) and Black (Latisha, Jamal) -sounding names were randomly included on fake resumes in response to job advertisements. Almost 5,000 resumes were sent in response to more than 1,300 job openings advertised in the *Chicago Tribune* and *Boston Globe*. The types of jobs applied for were limited to sales, administrative, clerical, and customer services.

The authors identified the applicants who were contacted for follow-up job interviews. Generally, the authors found that resumes with Black-sounding names received 50% less actual "callbacks" for job interviews than those with White-sounding names—a statistically significant difference. Furthermore, high-qualification resumes with White-sounding names received significantly greater callbacks than low-qualification resumes. However, there was no difference in callback rates between high-versus low-quality resumes with Black-sounding names. Finally, the study found that the racial divide existed across job type (e.g., clerical, sales, administrative), organization size (average company size was about 2,000 employees), and industry. The most commonly represented industries in the sample were business/professional services, wholesale/retail trades, and health, educational, and social services. Similar evidence of this form of discrimination has been found in other studies based on national origin (Fibbi, Lerch, & Wanner, 2006; Widner & Chicoine, 2011).

It has also been suggested that companies may want to discourage applicants from submitting emails that can indicate the race, gender, age, etc. of applicants, which may include email addresses that contain names of individuals (e.g., Blackhurst, Congemi, Meyer, & Sachau, 2011; Wallace & Vodanovich, 2004). Given these findings, what can organizations do to reduce or eliminate such discrimination? One possibility is to have clerical personnel redact applicant names (and perhaps email addresses) before sending application forms and/or resumes to hiring managers.

Discrimination and English-Language Requirements

Requiring a certain level of fluency in the English language can lead to potential legal problems due partly to its relationship to national origin. When imposing certain language fluency standards, organizations need to certify that such criteria are related to the job and consistent with business necessity. Some examples of business necessity include situations where clear communication with others is paramount (e.g., customers, coworkers), emergency events (e.g., a "common" language is warranted), team-based work assignments, and when an English-speaking supervisor needs to assess job performance of subordinates where communication in English is required for the position. The requirement to speak English is best used in specific situations where speaking English is critical to performing essential job tasks safely and efficiently (see summary of English-only rules by Gevertz & Dowell, 2014).

Employees or applicants with foreign *accents* cannot be discriminated against unless (1) oral communication in English is a job requirement, and (2) their accents have a material, negative effect on their job performance (*Fragante v. City and County of Honolulu,* 1989).[49] Basically, fluency levels in English should be based on the nature of the job (e.g., degree to which oral communication is needed) and should not exceed that which is required by the work.

Requiring *English-only* rules on a permanent basis in the workplace is considered to be legally inappropriate. As the EEOC stated in its Guidelines regarding "speak English-only rules" (section 1606.7)[50]: "A rule requiring employees to speak only English at all times in the workplace is a burdensome term and condition of employment. . . . It may also create an atmosphere of inferiority, isolation and intimidation based on national origin which could result in a discriminatory working environment. Therefore, the Commission will presume that such a rule violates Title VII and will closely scrutinize it."

[49] https://openjurist.org/888/f2d/591/fragante-v-city-and-county-of-honolulu
[50] https://www.law.cornell.edu/cfr/text/29/1606.7

Although the courts have varied in their support of the EEOC's Guidelines,[51,52,53] the agency has succeeded in reaching settlements with companies that require English-only rules. Many of these settlements are large (i.e., costly to organizations) and involve claims of national origin discrimination. For instance, in 2003, Central Station Casino agreed to a $1.5 million settlement for verbally harassing Hispanic housekeepers and enforcing an English-only policy.[54] In another settlement occurring in 2012, Delano Regional Medical Center agreed to pay $975,000 to settle claims of workplace harassment and discrimination related to employee national origin. As the summary of the settlement stated, "Supervisors, staff, and even volunteers were allegedly encouraged to act as vigilantes, constantly berating and reprimanding Filipino-American employees for nearly six years," and that "staff constantly made fun of their accents, ordering them to speak English even when they were already speaking in English."[55] Finally, in 2019, the EEOC reached a settlement of $2,625,000 with La Cantera Resort and Spa.[56] The allegations were that supervisors had mistreated Hispanic banquet employees and did not allow them to speak Spanish while at work.

Recommendations/Best Practices

This chapter has discussed the ways in which race, color, and national origin discrimination can and have presented themselves within employment practices, as well as the precedent-setting case law that can aid organizations in proactively mitigating this form of bias. But it is not only court decisions that provide guidance on reducing this form of discrimination in the workplace. Table 3.11 lists a number of settlement agreements between organizations and the EEOC. It describes what was alleged and the outcomes of the settlements.

---

[51] The courts have not always supported the EEOC's Guideline on English-only rules. Some have rejected the commission's position (e.g., *Long v. First Union Corporation of Virginia*, 1996) while others have ruled in favor of the EEOC (e.g., *Maldonado v. City of Altus*, 2006).

[52] https://openjurist.org/86/f3d/1151/long-v-first-union-corporation-virginia

[53] https://scholar.google.com/scholar_case?case=5897598468161913903&q=Maldonado+v.+City+of+Altus,+433+F.3d+1294+(10th+Cir.+2006).+&hl=en&as_sdt=40006

[54] https://www.eeoc.gov/newsroom/central-station-casino-pay-15-million-eeoc-settlement-national-origin-bias

[55] https://www.eeoc.gov/newsroom/delano-regional-medical-center-pay-nearly-1-million-eeoc-national-origin-discrimination

[56] https://www.eeoc.gov/newsroom/la-cantera-resort-and-spa-pay-over-25-million-settle-eeoc-national-origin-discrimination

Table 3.11 Representative Equal Employment Opportunity Commission (EEOC) race, national origin, and/or color discrimination settlements (listed in descending chronological order by year)

Organization, year of settlement	Specific allegation(s)	Settlement and primary relief
Jackson National Life Insurance Company (2020)[1]	Permitted a hostile work environment toward Black and female workers.	• $20.5 million damage award • 4-year consent decree • Employee training • Use an Internal Compliance Monitor and hire external consultant to review EEO policies
Fidelity Home Energy, Inc. (2020)[2]	National origin suit. Employee of Afghan ancestry quit after being forced to refuse to hire applicants from the Middle East or India for sales jobs.	• $350,000 damage award • 3-year consent decree • Workforce training on equal employment opportunity (EEO) law • Remove information on race, ethnicity, or national origin from applicant database
Dollar General (2019)[3]	Class action suit—adverse impact against Black applicants by using criminal background checks.	• $6 million damage award • 3-year consent decree • Forbids discouraging those with criminal records from applying
Marquez Brothers International, Inc. (2019)[4]	Company refused to hire non-Hispanic applicants for unskilled jobs.	• $2 million damage award • EEO training • Maintain tracking system to document discrimination complaints
Breakthru Beverage Illinois, LLC (2019)[5]	Job segregation based on race or national origin.	• $950,000 damage award • EEO training • Refrain from using race or national origin in making job assignments • 3-year consent decree
Koch Industries (2018)[6]	Class action suit alleging sexual harassment (touching, sexual comments), race/national origin discrimination, and retaliation (Hispanic employees).	• $3,750,000 payment • Apply new policies, procedures • Anti-discrimination training
SLS Hotel (2018)[7]	Firing of black Haitian dishwashers because of their race, color, and national origin; referred to as "slaves" by supervisors (chefs).	• 3-year consent decree • $2.5 million payment • Training for all employees • Summary of training by independent monitor
Antonella's Restaurant & Pizzeria (2017)[8]	Creating a hostile work environment based on national origin (Hispanic employees) by using slurs, derogatory name calling, and required English-only rules at work.	• $50,000 payment • Anti-discrimination policies and training program • Problem-solving procedures

(continued)

Table 3.11 Continued

Organization, year of settlement	Specific allegation(s)	Settlement and primary relief
King-Lar Company (2017)[9]	Name calling (e.g., "wetback"), threats, and physical assault of Black employee from Puerto Rico	• $350,00 payment • Anonymous complaint hotline • Anti-harassment and discrimination training
J&R Baker Farms (2016)[10]	Disparate treatment regarding terms and conditions of employment (e.g., segregated transportation work crews, job assignments) based on national origin (White Americans, Black Americans); replacing fired White American and Black American employees with foreign workers.	• $205,000 payment • Change hiring procedures • EEO training • Develop anti-discrimination policy
Lawler Foods (2016)[11]	Pattern or practice discrimination based on race and national origin in hiring	• 4-year consent decree • $1,042,000 payment • Actively recruit and hire nonwhite applicants • Employee non-discrimination training • Choose internal leader to ensure compliance with consent decree
Signal International, LLC (2015)[12]	Pattern or practice discrimination based on race and national origin against Indian guest employees (e.g., poor work conditions, mandating rent of more than $1,000/month to live in crowded, dirty guarded camps)	• 5-million-dollar payment • Admission of misconduct and apology from CEO

[1] https://www.eeoc.gov/newsroom/jackson-national-life-insurance-pay-205-million-settle-eeoc-lawsuit

[2] https://www.eeoc.gov/newsroom/fidelity-home-energy-pay-350000-settle-eeoc-national-origin-discrimination-lawsuit

[3] https://www.eeoc.gov/newsroom/dollar-general-pay-6-million-settle-eeoc-class-race-discrimination-suit

[4] https://www.eeoc.gov/newsroom/marquez-brothers-pay-2-million-settle-eeoc-race-discrimination-suit

[5] https://www.eeoc.gov/newsroom/breakthru-beverage-illinois-pay-950000-settle-eeoc-class-employment-discrimination

[6] https://www.eeoc.gov/eeoc/newsroom/release/8-1-18b.cfm

[7] https://www.eeoc.gov/eeoc/newsroom/release/7-30-18.cfm

[8] https://www.eeoc.gov/eeoc/newsroom/release/6-22-17a.cfm

[9] https://www.eeoc.gov/eeoc/newsroom/release/3-30-17.cfm

[10] https://www.eeoc.gov/eeoc/newsroom/release/7-6-16.cfm

[11] https://www.eeoc.gov/eeoc/newsroom/release/4-26-16.cfm

[12] https://www.eeoc.gov/eeoc/newsroom/release/12-18-15.cfm

Retrieved from EEOC Press Releases: https://www.eeoc.gov/newsroom/search

This information, along with case law and EEOC guidance documents can point us toward best practices for preventing discrimination based on race, national origin, and color.

- Employ recruiting sources and techniques that will maximize the number of qualified applicants from underrepresented demographic groups.
- Regularly collect and analyze *applicant flow* and *stock statistics* for evidence of potential discrimination
- Ensure that selection tests and job qualifications are job-related and consistent with business necessity.
- Carefully choose valid selection/promotion devices that will reduce the likelihood of adverse impact *before* they are administered to applicants.
- Consider assessing evidence of both *practical* and *statistical significance* for possible adverse impact.
- Do *not* adjust test scores, use different cutoff scores, or alter the results of employment-related tests on the basis of race, color, religion, sex, or national origin.
- Define the relevant labor market for jobs and job categories.
- Clearly identify each part (component) of the selection system and specify how each is used to make personnel decisions.
- Ask about (or gather) criminal history information later in the selection process (and only when justified given the work required by the job).
- Eliminate, or sharply curtail, the use of credit history in making selection decisions (and only use when job-related and consistent with business necessity).
- Avoid collecting applicant data that can indicate protected demographic categories (treat names and email addresses with sensitivity).
- When evaluating criminal history data, consider the nature and severity of the offense, time that has passed since the conviction, and the nature and type of job sought by applicants.
- Avoid employing strict exclusionary policies (e.g., regarding criminal and credit information).
- Conduct regular diversity and inclusion training sessions for all personnel.
- Do not implement across-the-board English-only policies. Such policies ought to be limited to situations where speaking English is a business necessity and related to the work being performed.

Summary and Take-Aways

After reading this chapter, you will hopefully appreciate and understand the major cases that helped form the law regarding race, color, and national origin discrimination. Indeed, many of these cases defined the context in which employment discrimination cases, in general, are decided. That is, many of these cases were instrumental in setting the tone for how disparate treatment, pattern or practice, and adverse impact cases need to be resolved.

In this chapter we sought to illustrate the complexities involved in deciding employment law cases. In some instances, the evidence involves a rather detailed understanding of statistics and the proper comparisons that are required (e.g., stock vs. flow statistics, within- vs. across-job comparisons, differences in evidentiary requirements for adverse impact vs. pattern or practices cases). Court cases can succeed or fail depending on the choice of statistics and/or statistical comparisons.

We also introduced concerns about collecting criminal history data of applicants on application forms and performing credit history checks. These concerns center around the possibility of adverse impact if this information is used to make selection decisions, as well the job-relatedness of the data for some jobs. The legality and relevance of criminal history data was heightened by the EEOC's Guidelines in 2012 on arrest and conviction data along with several studies suggesting the possible discriminatory impact of credit information. There is disagreement on the legal and practical status of this information. But there is now an increased awareness and scrutiny of the effect that using criminal history and credit data can have on the fate of applicants and potential legal liability for organizations.

Glossary

Applicant flow statistics: Calculating and comparing the total number of applicants to the number of applicants selected/hired in each demographic group.

Applicant stock statistics: Statistics that compare organizational data (e.g., number of hires by demographic groups) with the number of qualified individuals in the relevant labor market.

Adverse impact: When facially neutral selection criteria disproportionately exclude a higher percentage of one group relative to another. These differences are often assessed by using the four-fifths rule or statistical significance tests.

Ban-the-box proposals: Laws that prohibit the use of criminal background data prior to making an initial job offer.

Collective bargaining agreement: A contract or agreement between an employer and one or more unions which creates the terms of employment for the employees who belong to that labor union. The contract may include provisions regarding wages, paid time off, working hours and conditions, health insurance, and other benefits.

Daubert standard: Rule of evidence used as a standard in determining the admissibility of expert witness testimony. The factors include if the technique or theory can be or has been tested, whether it has been subject to peer review and publication, the known or potential rate of error of the technique or theory, the existence and maintenance of standards and controls, and whether the technique or theory has been generally accepted within the scientific community.

Direct evidence: Evidence which proves the existence of an alleged fact without needing inference or presumption. Direct evidence cannot only suggest discrimination [or retaliation] or be subject to more than one interpretation.

Disparate treatment: Intentionally treating an individual or group less favorably than another due to protected group status (e.g., race, religion, national origin, sex, disability).

Indirect evidence: Also referred to as circumstantial evidence, indirect evidence helps to establish the main fact by inference.

Pattern or practice discrimination: A type of discrimination that occurs when organizations are alleged to have engaged in pervasive, intentional discrimination—where the discriminatory behavior is a "standard operation procedure."

Practical significance: Concerns whether a disparity is of a magnitude that is meaningful.

Prima facie: Latin phrase for "at first glance." Consists of presenting evidence that is presumed to be true.

Statistical significance: Evaluates the probability that group differences are due to chance, often using null hypothesis significance testing.

Glossary terms adapted from Gutman et al. (2011); Cohen and Aamodt (2010); https://uslegal.com/; and merriamwebster.com/legal.

Cases Cited

Albermarle Paper Company. v. Moody, 422 U.S. 405 (1975).
Carter v. Gallagher, 452 F. 2d 315 (8th Cir. 1971).
Connecticut v. Teal, 457 U.S. 440 (1982).
Daubert v. Merrell Dow Pharmaceuticals, Inc., 509 U.S. 579 (1993).
EEOC v. Freeman, 778 F. 3d 463 (4th Cir. 2015).
EEOC v. Kaplan Higher Education Corporation, 748 F. 3d 749 (6th Cir. 2014).
Fragante v. City and County of Honolulu, 888 F. 2d 591 (9th Cir. 1989).
Green v. Missouri Pacific Railroad Company, 523 F.2nd 1290 (8th Cir. 1975).
Griggs v. Duke Power Co., 401 U.S. 424 (1971).
Hayden v. Nassau County, 180 F.3d 42 (2nd Cir. 1999).
Hazelwood School District v. United States, 433 U.S. 299 (1977).
Long v. First Union Corporation of Virginia, 86 F.3rd (4th Cir. 1996).
Maldonado v. City of Altus, 433 F.3d 1294 (10th Cir. 2006).
McDonnell Douglas Corp v. Green, 411 U.S. 792 (1973).
Ricci v. DeStefano, 129 S. Ct. 2658 (2009).
St. Mary's Honor Center v. Hicks, 509 U.S. 502 (1993).
International Brotherhood of Teamsters vs. United States, 431 U.S. 324 (1977).
Texas Dept. of Community Affairs v. Burdine, 450 U.S. 248 (1981).
Wards Cove Packing Co. v. Atonio, 490 U.S. 642 (1989).

References

Agan, A., & Starr, S. (2018). Ban the box, criminal records, and racial discrimination: A field experiment. *The Quarterly Journal of Economics, 133*(1), 191–235.

Bernerth, J. B. (2012). Demographic variables and credit scores: An empirical study of a controversial selection tool. *International Journal of Selection and Assessment, 20,* 242–246.

Bernerth, J. B., Taylor, S. G., Walker, H. J. Walker, & Whitman, D. S. (2012). An empirical investigation of dispositional antecedents and performance-related outcomes of credit scores. *Journal of Applied Psychology, 97,* 469–478.

Bertrand, M., & Mullainathan, S. (2004). Are Emily and Greg more employable than Lakisha and Jamal? A field experiment on labor market discrimination. *American Economic Review, 94,* 991–1013.

Blackhurst, E., Congemi, P., Meyer, J., & Sachau, D. (2011). Should You Hire BlazinWeedClown@ Mail. Com?. *TIP: The Industrial-Organizational Psychologist, 49*(2), 27–37. https://cornerstone.lib.mnsu.edu/cgi/viewcontent.cgi?article=1185&context=psyc_fac_pubs

Bryan, L. K., & Palmer, J. K. (2012). Do job applicant credit histories predict performance appraisal ratings or termination decisions? *The Psychologist-Manager Journal, 15,* 106–127.

Board of Governors of the Federal Reserve System. (2007). Report to the Congress on credit scoring and its effects on the availability and affordability of credit. Washington, DC: US Federal Reserve. Retrieved from: https://www.federalreserve.gov/boarddocs/rptcongress/creditscore/creditscore.pdf

Coady, R. P. (1986). An analysis of state library job application forms for compliance with EEOC Guidelines. *Journal of Library Administration, 7*(1), 49–55.

Cohen, D. B., & Aamodt, M. G. (2010). *Technical advisory committee report on best practices in adverse impact analyses.* Washington, DC: Center for Corporate Equality.

Copeland, R. W., & Schmake, M. (2016). Protected classes, credit histories and criminal background checks: A new twist to old-fashioned disparate impact cases? *Journal of Business and Behavioral Sciences, 28*, 129–144.

Doleac, J. L., & Hansen, B. (2016). Does "ban the box" help or hurt low-skilled workers? Statistical discrimination and employment outcomes when criminal histories are hidden. (NBER Working Paper No. 22469). Cambridge, MA: National Bureau of Economic Research.

Fibbi, R., Lerch, M., & Wanner, P. (2006). Unemployment and discrimination against youth of immigrant origin in Switzerland: When the name makes the difference. *Journal of International Migration and Integration, 7*, 351–366.

Garrow, D. J. (2014). Toward a definitive history of *Griggs v. Duke Power Co. Vanderbilt University Law Review, 67*(1), 197–237.

Gevertz, D. E., & Dowell, A. C. (2014 March). Are English-only policies in the workplace discriminatory of national origin? American Bar Association. https://www.americanbar.org/groups/litigation/committees/civil-rights/articles/2014/are-english-only-policies-in-the-workplace-discriminatory-of-national-origin/

Gurchiek, K. (2011). Study: Some say email addresses a red flag to employers. *Society for Human Resource Management.* Available at: https://www.shrm.org/hr-today/news/hr-news/pages/emailredflags.aspx

Gutman, A. (2004). Ground rules for adverse impact. *The Industrial-Organizational Psychologist, 41*, 109–119.

Gutman, A., & Dunleavy, E. (2009). The Supreme Court ruling in *Ricci v. DeStefano. The Industrial-Organizational Psychologist, 47*, 57–71.

Gutman, A., Koppes, L. L., & Vodanovich, S. J. (2011). *EEO law and personnel practices* (3rd ed.). New York: Psychology Press/Routledge/Taylor & Francis Group.

Hyman, J. (2019). A pox on the box. Retrieved form Workforce.com at: https://workforce.com/news/a-pox-on-ban-the-box.

Jackson, D. J. R., Lance, C. E., & Hoffman, B. J. (2012). *The psychology of assessment centers.* New York: Routledge.

Jolley, J. P & Frierson, J. G. (1989). Playing it safe. *Personnel Administrator, 34*, 44–50.

Miller, E. (1980). An EEO examination of employment applications. *Personnel Administrator, 25*, 63–81.

Potter, E. E. (1999). Supreme Court's Wards Cove Packing decision redefines the adverse impact theory under Title VII. *The Industrial-Organizational Psychologist, 27*, 25–31.

Riccucci, N. M., & Riccardelli, M. (2015). The use of written exams in police and fire departments: Implications for social diversity. *Review of Public Personnel Administration, 35*(4), 352–366. doi:10.1177/0734371X14540689

Semuels, A. (2016, August 4). When banning one kind of discrimination results in another. The Atlantic https://www.theatlantic.com/business/archive/2016/08/consequences-of-ban-the-box/494435/.

SHRM. (2012a July). Background checking - The use of criminal background checks in hiring decisions. *Society for Human Resource Management.* https://www.shrm.org/hr-today/trends-and-forecasting/research-and-surveys/Pages/criminalbackgroundcheck.aspx

SHRM. (2012b July). Background checking: The use of credit background checks in hiring decisions. *Society for Human Resource Management.* https://www.shrm.org/hr-today/trends-and-forecasting/research-and-surveys/pages/creditbackgroundchecks.aspx

Smith, G., & Duda, S. (2010 September). Bridging the gap: Credit scores and economic opportunity in Illinois communities of color. *Woodstock Institute.* 1–25. https://woodstockinst.org/wp-content/uploads/2013/05/bridgingthegapcreditscores_sept2010_smithduda.pdf

Thornton, G., III, & Potemra, M. (2010). Utility of assessment center for promotion of police sergeants. *Public Personnel Management, 39*, 59–69.

Thornton, G. C., III, Mueller-Hanson, R. A., & Rupp, D. E. (2017). *Developing organizational simulations*. New York: Routledge.

Thornton, G. C., III, & Rupp, D. E. (2006). *Assessment centers in human resource management: Strategies for prediction, diagnosis, and development*. Mahwah, NJ: Lawrence Erlbaum.

Thornton, G. C., III, Rupp, D. E., & Hoffman, B. (2015). *Assessment center perspectives for talent management strategies*. New York: Routledge.

Vodanovich, S. J., & Lowe, R. H. (1992). They ought to know better: The incidence and correlates of inappropriate application blank inquiries. *Public Personnel Management, 21*, 363–370.

Wallace, J. C, Tye, M., & Vodanovich, S. J. (2000). Applying for jobs online: Examining the legality of Internet-based application forms. *Public Personnel Management, 29*, 497–504.

Wallace, J. C., & Vodanovich, S. J. (2004). Appropriateness of personnel application blanks: Persistence and knowledge of application blank items. *Public Personnel Management, 33*, 331–345.

Widner, D., & Chicoine, S. (2011). It's all in the name: Employment discrimination against Arab Americans. *Sociological Forum, 26*, 806–823.

4

Discrimination Based on Religion

Employment Discrimination. Stephen J. Vodanovich and Deborah E. Rupp, Oxford University Press. © Oxford University Press 2022. DOI: 10.1093/oso/9780190085421.003.0005

Congress shall make no law respecting an establishment of religion, or prohibiting the free exercise thereof.

From the 1st Amendment to the US Constitution

Overview of Discrimination Based on Religion

The protection against religious discrimination is guaranteed by the 1st Amendment, which is partly quoted here. [1] The initial part of the amendment, "Congress shall make no law respecting the establishment of religion," is referred to as the "Establishment clause." The second part "or prohibiting the free exercise thereof" is called the "Free Exercise clause" (for a legal review and critique of the establishment and free exercise clauses, see Beschle, 2018, and Simson, 2018). Although the religious protections contained in the 1st Amendment pertain to actions by the federal government, it has been interpreted to apply to states via the 14th Amendment. Guarantees against religious discrimination are also contained within the Religious Freedom Restoration Act (RFRA) of 1973.[2] Finally, employment discrimination based on religion is prohibited by Title VII of the Civil Rights Act of 1964 (along with discrimination based on race, color, sex, and national origin).

First Amendment and Religious Protections

The federal government is only allowed to affect an individual's free exercise of religion if it can demonstrate that a governmental action (1) advances a *compelling* government interest and (2) is the least restrictive method to achieve the compelling interest. These criteria create a high standard of review, known as *strict scrutiny*.[3] The strict scrutiny requirement has had an uneven legal history regarding religious discrimination.

Earlier cases employed a strict scrutiny analysis in cases involving the Free Exercise clause of the 1st Amendment. For example, in *Sherbert v. Verner* (1963),[4] Adeil Sherbert, a Seventh Day Adventist, was fired for refusing to work on Saturdays. When she applied for unemployment benefits with the State of South Carolina, her application was denied

---

[1] Sometimes charges of religious discrimination are combined with other allegations, such as those based on national origin.

[2] https://www.gpo.gov/fdsys/pkg/STATUTE-107/pdf/STATUTE-107-Pg1488.pdf

[3] Strict scrutiny will be discussed in more detail in Chapter 9, "Affirmative Action."

[4] https://www.law.cornell.edu/supremecourt/text/374/398

because she refused to accept work that required attendance on Saturdays. Sherbert alleged that the state's actions were a violation of the 1st and 14th Amendments. The Court noted that for the denial of benefits to be legitimate, it must not result in a violation of the free exercise rights of one's religion. The Court ruled in favor of Sherbert stating, "Our holding today is only that South Carolina may *not* constitutionally apply the eligibility provisions so as to constrain a worker to abandon his religious convictions respecting the day of rest."

Another case that applied strict scrutiny is *Wisconsin v. Yoder* (1972).[5] Here, Jonas Yoder et al. were Amish and challenged Wisconsin's requirement that children must attend school up to age 16. They alleged that such a requirement was against the Free Exercise clause of the 1st Amendment as applied to the States via the 14th Amendment. The State's position was that the education requirement was quite compelling, so much so that members of the Amish religion must comply. The Court disagreed with the State and ruled that the education requirement was *not* sufficiently compelling to justify its use in this case. As the Court noted, "Respondents have amply supported their claim that enforcement of the compulsory formal education requirement after the eighth grade would gravely endanger if not destroy the free exercise of their religious beliefs." The Court further commented that "the First and Fourteenth Amendments prevent the State from compelling respondents to cause their children to attend formal high school to age 16."

Strict scrutiny was *not* used by a majority of the justices in *Employment Division, Department of Human Resources of Oregon v. Smith* (1990).[6] Albert Smith et al. were fired from a drug rehabilitation company given their use of peyote (a hallucinogenic drug prepared from the peyote plant) for ceremonial purposes. They were also denied unemployment compensation since they were fired for misconduct related to work (drug use). Smith et al. sued, alleging that their denial of unemployment funds violated their 1st Amendment rights. The Supreme Court ruled in favor of Oregon stating, "Because respondents' ingestion of peyote was prohibited under Oregon law, and because that prohibition is constitutional, Oregon may, consistent with the Free Exercise clause, deny respondents unemployment compensation when their dismissal results from use of the drug." Aspects of the decision were overturned by the Religious Freedom Restoration Act of 1993 (RFRA),[7] which mandated strict scrutiny (see later discussion).

---

[5] https://scholar.google.com/scholar_case?case=5191879339794619665&q=Wisconsin+v.+Yoder,+1972&hl=en&as_sdt=40006

[6] https://www.law.cornell.edu/supremecourt/text/494/872

[7] https://www.gpo.gov/fdsys/pkg/STATUTE-107/pdf/STATUTE-107-Pg1488.pdf

For cases that involve challenges to the Establishment clause, the prevailing standard is that federal government laws are legitimate if they satisfy the following three-pronged test:

1. have a secular purpose (Purpose clause)
2. do not have the effect of advancing or inhibiting religion (Effect clause)
3. do not promote an excessive government entanglement with religion (Entanglement clause)

The preceding criteria emanated from *Lemon v. Kurtzman* (1971)[8,9] and has been referred to as the "Lemon Test." In *Lemon*, two states (Pennsylvania and Rhode Island) passed laws that provide financial support to non-secular, private elementary schools. The law was challenged by taxpayers and citizens who alleged that the law was in violation of the 1st Amendment's Establishment clause. The Court believed that the laws were secular in nature, satisfying Prong 1. But the majority ruled that the laws constituted an overbearing entanglement of government with religion, thus failing to pass Prong 3. As the Court noted, "Both statutes are unconstitutional under the Religion clauses of the First Amendment, as the cumulative impact of the entire relationship arising under the statutes involves excessive entanglement between government and religion." For a review and critique of the Lemon Test see Fallon (2017), Greenawalt (1995), and Ravishankar (2016).

Title VII and Religious Discrimination

Workplace religious discrimination continues to be an important legal and social concern. Table 4.1 illustrates the number of claims filed with the Equal Employment Opportunity Commission (EEOC) across the past several years.

Religious Beliefs and Practices

Title VII protects sincerely held religious beliefs and practices. A common question that people ask is what constitutes a religion and sincerely held

---

[8] https://www.law.cornell.edu/supremecourt/text/403/602#writing-USSC_CR_0403_0602_ZO
[9] https://www.oyez.org/cases/1972/71-1470

Table 4.1 Religious discrimination charges filed with the Equal Employment Opportunity Commission (EEOC) (2014–2020)

Year	2014	2015	2016	2017	2018	2019	2020
Number of Charges	3,549	3,502	3,825	3,436	2,859	2,725	2,404

Retrieved from https://www.eeoc.gov/statistics/charge-statistics-charges-filed-eeoc-fy-1997-through-fy-2020

religious beliefs/practices. The term "religion" within Title VII is defined quite broadly. As such, it is not confined to established, formal religions but can consist of new ones and those that are followed by just a few individuals (see Kelly, 2008). Quoting from Title VII: "The term 'religion' includes all aspects of religious observance and practice, as well as belief."

Whether or not religious beliefs are sincere is typically not challenged by businesses. It is generally recommended to assume that requests for religious accommodations are legitimate unless strong evidence to the contrary exists. For instance, sincerely held religious beliefs can be questioned if employees behave in a manner drastically at odds with their stated beliefs or if an accommodation results in benefits thought to be for secular purposes. Also, it is important to note that political and social views, as well as individual preferences, are not considered religious beliefs (see the National Institutes of Health [NIH] toolkit on religion and religious accommodation and EEOC Compliance Manual on religious discrimination).[10,11]

Religious Exemptions

There are some exemptions for religious institutions under Title VII. One involves religious organizations giving preference to personnel holding the same religion. Another involves the barring of the application of Title VII to issues involving "ministers."

[10] https://www.edi.nih.gov/sites/default/files/public/EDI_Public_files/guidance/toolkits/managers/manager-workplace-religious-accommodation03.pdf
[11] https://www.eeoc.gov/laws/guidance/section-12-religious-discrimination#_Toc203359487

Religious Organization Exemption

Title VII allows exemptions to religious institutions. From Title VII:

> [I]t shall not be an unlawful employment practice for a school, college, university, or other educational institution or institution of learning to hire and employ employees of a particular religion if such school, college, university, or other educational institution or institution of learning is, in whole or in substantial part, owned, supported, controlled, or managed by a particular religion or by a particular religious corporation, association, or society, or if the curriculum of such school, college, university, or other educational institution or institution of learning is directed toward the propagation of a particular religion.

So, under this exemption, religious organizations are allowed to give preferences when making employment decisions to members of their own faith. Unfortunately, Title VII does not offer specific criteria to determine what comprises a religious organization (see Dyer [2011][12] for a review of the religious organization exemption). To partly address this lack of specificity, the EEOC's Guidance on Religious Discrimination focuses on assessing if an organization's "purpose and character are primarily religious" and that this assessment should take into consideration all "significant religious and secular characteristics." According to the EEOC, factors to consider in deciding the extent to which an institution is primarily religious include whether its articles of incorporation state a religious purpose, whether its day-to-day operations are religious (e.g., in terms of services, products, curriculum), whether the organization is not-for-profit, and whether it is affiliated with or supported by a church or religious organization.[13]

It is important to note that the assessment of whether an entity is primarily religious should not be rigidly applied and that *not one specific factor* is determinative. Essentially, evidence is evaluated based on *all* relevant factors and weighted accordingly. Indeed, some factors may be more pertinent in some cases than others, with the weight or importance of each factor being established on a case-by-case basis. Finally, it is essential to mention that this exemption does *not* give religious organizations the right to discriminate on the basis of other protected groups (e.g., race, sex, age).

---

[12] https://scholarship.law.missouri.edu/cgi/viewcontent.cgi?article=3926&context=mlr

[13] As many as nine factors have been used by some courts in determining if the religious organization exemption has been met. See *LeBoon v. Lancaster Jewish Community Center Association* (2007).

Ministerial Exception

Another exemption is referred to as the "ministerial exception." Essentially, this prohibits clergy members (e.g., "ministers") from bringing claims for alleged violations of federal anti-discrimination laws (e.g., Title VII, Age Discrimination in Employment Act [ADEA], Equal Pay Act [EPA], Americans with Disabilities Act [ADA]). The ministerial exemption is gleaned from Section 702 of the Civil Rights Act, which states in part: "This subchapter shall not apply to . . . a religious corporation, association, educational institution, or society with respect to the employment of individuals of a particular religion to perform work connected with the carrying on by such corporation, association, educational institution, or society of its activities." The exception is also derived from the Religious clauses of the First Amendment. In this context, the Amendment prohibits government interference with employment decisions made by religious organizations regarding faith leaders (e.g., ministers).

A case that exemplifies the ministerial exception is *Hosanna-Tabor v. EEOC* (2012).[14],[15] The plaintiff (Cheryl Perich) was assigned the title of "Minister of Religion Commissioned" after completing the required training. Consistent with this job title, the plaintiff taught classes in religion, facilitated prayer/devotional exercises, and brought students to chapel services. One point of contention was the fact that the plaintiff's duties also overlapped with those of lay teachers.

The plaintiff went on disability leave in the fall and planned on returning to work the following January. However, the school principal told Perich that she had been replaced with a layperson and asked her to resign. She refused. In February, Perich went back to the school and would not leave until she received written documentation that she had shown up for work. Afterward, the principal contacted the plaintiff and mentioned that she would probably be fired, at which time the plaintiff said she intended to sue. After being fired for alleged insubordination and threatening to sue, Perich filed an ADA and retaliation lawsuit. In the end, the Supreme Court ruled the plaintiff's job title, duties, and training were congruent with that of a "minister" under Title VII and thereby decided in favor of the church.

The ministerial exception was expanded by the Supreme Court in *Our Lady of Guadalupe School v. Morrissey-Berru* (2020),[16],[17] a decision that was

---

[14] https://www.supremecourt.gov/opinions/11pdf/10-553.pdf
[15] https://www.oyez.org/cases/2011/10-553
[16] https://www.supremecourt.gov/opinions/19pdf/19-267_1an2.pdf
[17] https://www.oyez.org/cases/2019/19-267

consolidated with the case of *St. James School v. Biel*. Both suits involved teachers (Agnes Morrissey-Berru and Kristen Biel) who worked at Catholic elementary schools in Los Angeles County. Morrissey-Berru filed an age discrimination suit after being fired in favor of a younger teacher. Biel filed a disability discrimination suit alleging that she was terminated after requesting time off to be treated for breast cancer. At issue before the Court was whether both teachers were "ministers" and thus qualified for the "ministerial exception."

The Supreme Court ruled (7–2) that the ministerial exception was applicable in this case. As such, the schools could not be sued for employment discrimination. The Court concluded that the exception was available even though neither teacher had the word "minister" in their job titles and religious teaching was not their principal job duty. In addition, the Court considered the teachers to be ministers even though they had relatively less formal religious training when compared to Cheryl Perich in *Hosanna-Taber* (a case upon which the court relied heavily).

In making its decision, the Supreme Court stated that "What is important is what an employee does." In this context, the Court detailed that "Both were employed under nearly identical agreements that set out the schools' mission to develop and promote a Catholic School faith and community; imposed commitments regarding religious instruction, worship, and personal modeling of the faith; and explained that teaching performance would be reviewed on those bases." The Court further indicated that "There is abundant evidence that they both performed vital religious duties, such as educating their students in the Catholic faith and guiding their students to live their lives in accordance with that faith."

It is useful to note that several previous lower court decisions concluded that the ministerial exception is not limited to those officially ordained as ministers. Rather, the ministerial exception was pertinent if the work performed by employees was judged to be sufficiently religious in nature. This evaluation process has been referred to as the "primary duties test." Given this approach, various jobs have been deemed to be ministerial in nature, such as choir director (*Starkman v. Evans*, 1999),[18] parochial school teachers (*Coulee Catholic Schools v. Labor and Industry Review Commission*, 2009),[19] and press secretary (*Alicea-Hernandez v. Catholic Bishop of Chicago*, 2003).[20] For example, as the 7th Circuit stated in *Alicea-Hernandez*,

---

[18] https://casetext.com/case/starkman-v-evans-2
[19] https://caselaw.findlaw.com/wi-supreme-court/1265078.html
[20] https://scholar.google.com/scholar_case?case=17858354259037365049&hl=en&as_sdt=6&as_vis=1&oi=scholarr

The role of the press secretary is critical in message dissemination, and a church's message, of course, is of singular importance. . . . Indeed, the rationale for the ministerial exception is founded upon the principle that "perpetuation of a church's existence may depend upon those whom it selects to preach its values, teach its message, and interpret its doctrines both to its own membership and to the world at large."

For legal reviews of the ministerial exception see Coon (2001), Heller (2007), and Lund (2011).

Types of Religious Discrimination

Religious discrimination cases are not always easy to categorize. They can consist of a combination of allegations involving the failure to accommodate religious beliefs and practices, disparate treatment, harassment based on religion, and retaliation (see Ghumman, Ryan, Barclay, & Markel, 2013; Malos, 2010; Paludi, Ellens, & Paludi, 2011), which we review next.

Failure to Accommodate Religious Beliefs/Practices

Under Title VII, organizations must accommodate religious beliefs unless they are *unreasonable* or impose an *undue hardship* on the organization. Generally speaking, an undue hardship is an accommodation that is overly demanding or costly for a given organization when considering its resources, size, and nature of the business. Religious accommodations typically involve issues related to performing certain job tasks, physical appearance (e.g., hair style, clothing), religious observance (e.g., working on the Sabbath), and retaliation (e.g., Ghumman et al., 2013). As stated by the EEOC, "Religious observances or practices include, for example, attending worship services, praying, wearing religious garb or symbols, displaying religious objects, adhering to certain dietary rules, proselytizing or other forms of religious expression, or refraining from certain activities. Determining whether a practice is religious turns not on the nature of the activity, but on the employee's motivation." The religious accommodation scenario requires plaintiffs to establish a *prima facie* case, which begins with evidence that one's sincerely held religious beliefs are being negatively affected by an organizational policy. The organization then offers the defense

Table 4.2 Reasonable accommodation scenario for sincerely held religious beliefs

Prima facie case	1.	An employee possesses a sincerely held religious belief that is at odds with a requirement/policy of the organization.
	2.	The company must know of the existence of the religious belief and the conflict with the sincerely held religious beliefs of the employee.[1]
	3.	The employee is subjected to an adverse employment decision for not following the company's requirement/policy.
Company defense	1.	The employee's appeal for an accommodation is unreasonable.
	2.	The employee's request is reasonable, but it will create an undue hardship for the company.

[1] This knowledge requirement is altered by the Court's decision in *EEOC v. Abercrombie & Fitch* (2015), which concluded that having actual knowledge of the need for an accommodation is not required. Plaintiffs need to present evidence that the need for an accommodation was a *motivating* factor in an employer's decision.

Adapted from Gutman, Koppes, & Vodanovich (2011).

that the plaintiff's accommodation request is not reasonable or creates an undue hardship (see Table 4.2).

An earlier Supreme Court decision regarding the need to accommodate religious beliefs was *Trans World Airlines, Incorporated v. Hardison* (1977).[21,22] TWA and the International Association of Machinists & Aerospace Workers Union agreed to base personnel decisions (e.g., choice of jobs, shifts) on job seniority. Larry Hardison was Jewish, and his faith prohibited him from working on Saturdays. Given that Hardison had enough job seniority in his present job, he was able to arrange his schedule to avoid working on Saturdays.

But when he applied and was hired for a new position within the company, his seniority was low relative to other employees, and the new job required work on Saturdays. Several accommodations were considered but rejected, such as altering the seniority system (which was rejected by the union), allowing Hardison to work four days a week, or having someone else fill in on Saturdays. The latter two accommodations were deemed by the airline to create an undue hardship. After the accommodations were not provided, Hardison stopped working on Saturdays and was fired. He then filed a suit alleging a violation of Title VII based on religion.

The Supreme Court decided that TWA made reasonable efforts to accommodate Hardison's religious beliefs and that the accommodations that were considered posed an undue hardship to the airline. As the Court stated, "An

[21] https://scholar.google.com/scholar_case?case=15783181943891982721&hl=en&as_sdt=6&as_vis=1&oi=scholar
[22] https://www.oyez.org/cases/1976/75-1126

agreed-upon seniority system is not required to give way to accommodate religious observances." The Court further noted that, "To require TWA to bear more than a *de minimis* cost in order to give respondent Saturdays off would be an undue hardship . . . to require TWA to bear additional costs when no such costs are incurred to give other employees the days off that they want would involve unequal treatment of employees on the basis of their religion."

Another decision about the need to accommodate religious practices is provided by *Ansonia Board of Education v. Philbrook* (1986).[23],[24] Ronald Philbrook's religion required him not to work on various holy days, which led him to miss about six days of work annually. However, a collective bargaining agreement only permitted three days off for religious purposes. Philbrook requested that the School Board allow him to use personal leave to meet his religious obligations even though the agreement stated that personal leave did *not* include time off for religious reasons. The school board offered to grant Philbrook three days of *unpaid* leave to meet his religious practices. His use of personal, paid leave for religious reasons was denied. Consequently, Philbrook filed a Title VII case alleging religious discrimination.

The Court of Appeals for the 2nd Circuit ruled that an employer *must accept* an accommodation request unless the accommodation results in an undue hardship. But, in an 8–1 decision, the Supreme Court disagreed, concluding that offering a reasonable accommodation alone was sufficient. As the Court stated, "An employer has met its obligation . . . when it demonstrates that it has offered a reasonable accommodation to the employee. The employer need not further show that each of the employee's alternative accommodations would result in undue hardship. The extent of undue hardship on the employer's business is at issue only where the employer claims that it is unable to offer any reasonable accommodation without such hardship."

More recently, the EEOC was successful in a lawsuit against Star Transport for failure to accommodate religious beliefs. Two truck drivers who worked for the company asserted that transporting alcohol would violate their sincerely held religious beliefs under Islamic law. The drivers were not offered accommodations and were fired.[25] The company was found to have failed to accommodate the driver's religious beliefs, Therefore, the plaintiffs were granted a monetary award of $240,000.

---

[23] https://scholar.google.com/scholar_case?case=6664343332675261016&hl=en&as_sdt=6&as_vis=1&oi=scholar

[24] https://www.oyez.org/cases/1986/85-495

[25] https://www.eeoc.gov/newsroom/jury-awards-240000-muslim-truck-drivers-eeoc-religious-discrimination-suit

Dress and appearance codes developed by organizations can sometimes interfere with an individual's sincerely held religious beliefs or practices. On average, companies must accommodate religious-based attire (e.g., yarmulke, head scarf, dress/skirt length) and grooming practices (e.g., facial hair, hair length) unless they can prove (as before) that doing so will constitute an undue hardship. Companies may also deny religious-based dress and grooming practices if they offer evidence that such practices are a threat to workplace safety, health, or security. Such denials need to be made (a) on a case-by-case basis, (b) based on evidence that actual threats exist (not assumptions), and (c) show that no reasonable accommodations are available to offset the threats.

A number of charges of the failure to accommodate sincerely held religious beliefs have ended in settlements. For instance, in McDonalds Restaurants of California reached a settlement with the EEOC.[26] Here, the store did not allow a Muslim worker to grow a beard for religious reasons. Another settlement by the EEOC was reached with MGM Elegante Hotel (2013) after the company fired a Muslim housekeeper for refusing to remove a religious head scarf while working.[27]

Insights from Social Science: Religious Discrimination: Is There Prejudice Against Muslim Applicants?

Research has documented prejudice against Muslim job applicants. For example, Park, Malachi, Sternin and Tevet (2009) asked both students and working managers to review background and resume data regarding an alleged job applicant. The resumes were identical except that half of the applicants had a European American-sounding name (Jane Smith) and half had a Muslim-sounding name (Lyla Abdul). In addition, half of the participants were given supplementary, negative information about the applicant, while the other half did not receive any extra information.

The researchers reported that applicants with a Muslim-sounding name whose application was also accompanied by negative information were discriminated against. That is, they were offered lower salaries (particularly by managers), received poorer judgments of career progress (both samples), and managers judged them to have less work experience and be less qualified compared to applicants with European American sounding names. No discriminatory effects were found

---

[26] https://www.eeoc.gov/eeoc/newsroom/release/12-20-13a.cfm
[27] https://www.eeoc.gov/eeoc/newsroom/release/11-18-13.cfm

regarding the decision to hire. The authors suggest that the negative information provided was rather mild ("perceived to be a bit too assertive") and perhaps not adequate enough have a detrimental impact on a hiring decision. They also contend that "racial attitudes have changed from being blatant to being more subtle, such that racial prejudice is expressed in an indirect and justifiable manner." So, it may be that people are careful to avoid discriminatory behavior on very consequential decisions (e.g., hiring) but use derogatory information to defend less severe judgments.

Somewhat similar results were found by King and Ahmad (2010). Here, individuals expressed an interest in working at retail stores. When interacting with store personnel they either wore Muslim attire or neutral clothing. The individuals also expressed themselves in a way that was inconsistent or consistent with Muslim stereotypes. The authors found no differences in the rate of job offers or job interviews between Muslim and non-Muslim individuals. But the interpersonal interactions differed. For instance, the interactions with Muslim individuals were significantly shorter and rated as being more negative in nature (e.g., rude, hostile). Also, interactions were judged to be more negative when Muslim individuals did not display warmth.

A second study by the same authors investigated the effects of being a Muslim applicant (as indicated by the names on fake resumes and professional affiliations) versus a non-Muslim applicant. Participants rated the applicants on a variety of scale items such as reactions to the candidate, how they would interact with the applicant, characterization of the candidate, and an assessment of "formal" discrimination (e.g., likelihood of interviewing, hiring). Participants were found to rate Muslim applicants more negatively when they failed to provide warmth. Consistent with Study 1, the authors did not find significant differences in overt (formal) types of discrimination such as hiring. As the author stated, " there was no evidence of difference with regard to formal indicators of discrimination, suggesting that prejudice toward Muslims is manifested in subtle and interpersonal behaviors" (p. 901).

Disparate Treatment

In *EEOC v. Abercrombie & Fitch Stores, Inc.* (2015),[28],[29] a disparate treatment case was filed based on the alleged failure to accommodate a religious practice (see Dofner; 2016; Musa, 2016; Nasuti, 2017). Abercrombie & Fitch refused

[28] https://www.law.cornell.edu/supct/pdf/14-86.pdf
[29] https://www.oyez.org/cases/2014/14-86

to hire an otherwise qualified applicant because she wore a head scarf that violated its "Look Policy," which banned the wearing of caps. Abercrombie & Fitch contended that it did not know of the need for a religious accommodation. The Court ruled against the organization. In doing so, they ruled that there is no "knowledge requirement" for failure to accommodate disparate treatment claims based on religious practices. A plaintiff's burden is to show that the need for an accommodation was a *motivating* factor in a negative employment decision—a burden the plaintiff met. For instance, evidence was produced that the store's assistant manager informed her district manager that the plaintiff wore the scarf for religious reasons. The assistant manager was told not to hire the plaintiff. In this light, the Court reasoned that the failure to accommodate is synonymous with the refusal to hire based on one's religious practices. As the court stated, "To accuse the employer of the one is to accuse him of the other." It is important to note that the lack of a knowledge requirement is incongruent with other laws regarding accommodations. For instance, the ADA requires organizations to only accommodate "known" disabilities (see Flake [2019] who compares disability and religious accommodations).

Harassment Based on Religion

Cases involving harassment based on religion have generally followed the same process as other harassment cases (e.g., sexual harassment). That is, the alleged harassing behavior must be shown to be due to religion (and/or national origin) and must be shown to be unwelcome and create a hostile work environment. The EEOC sued National Tire and Battery in 2015 for allegedly harassing a mechanic on the job for being Muslim (religion) and Arab (national origin). Specifically, coworkers and managers were accused of calling the mechanic a variety of derogatory names (e.g., "Taliban," "terrorist") and alleged that he was developing bombs. Despite repeated protests to management, the organization did not end the harassing behavior. The suit was settled for $22,500.[30]

A similar suit was filed by the EEOC against Rizza Cadillac in 2014. Here, three Arab Muslim employees alleged workplace harassment based on their religion and national origin. They accused managers of making offensive comments toward them (e.g., "Hezbollah") and about the Qur'an and Muslim prayer practices. The organization eventually signed a consent decree[31] with

---

[30] https://www.eeoc.gov/eeoc/newsroom/release/10-20-15.cfm
[31] https://www.eeoc.gov/eeoc/newsroom/release/6-25-14a.cfm

the federal district court in Chicago for monetary damages ($100,000) and injunctive relief (e.g., employee training on employment discrimination law).[32]

In *EEOC v. United Health Programs of America, Inc.* (2018)[33] the EEOC filed a religious discrimination suit alleging that the company violated Title VII by creating a hostile work environment. Specifically, several employees alleged that they were forced to engage in religious activities while at work (e.g., workshops, prayer, cleansing rituals)—a practice described as "reverse religious discrimination." In the end, the jury awarded the plaintiffs $5,102,060 in compensatory and punitive damages, as well as injunctive relief. In its press release summarizing the case,[34] the EEOC stated, "Title VII of the Civil Rights Act of 1964 forbids employers from coercing employees to engage in religious practices at work."

Retaliation Based on Religion

The EEOC sued Wal-Mart Stores East for alleged claims of both national origin, religious discrimination, and retaliation. The EEOC asserted that a store manager made recurring negative comments about a Muslim employee who was from Gambia (e.g., "go back to Africa") and said that Muslims engage in violent behavior (e.g., they blow up buildings). In addition, when the employee protested against how he was being treated, he was allegedly retaliated against by his manager (e.g., warned about being fired, told coworkers to not help him in his job). The case was eventually settled in 2015.[35] Part of the settlement included paying damages ($75,000) and a requirement to engage in training for managers and HR personnel on federal workplace discrimination laws.

The Religious Freedom Restoration Act

The Religious Freedom Restoration Act of 1993 (RFRA)[36] was passed by Congress to counter the decision made in *Employment Division, Department*

---

[32] For more cases involving religious and national origin discrimination, see this EEOC site: https://www.eeoc.gov/eeoc/litigation/selected/religion_nationalorigin.cfm

[33] https://scholar.google.com/scholar_case?case=1243300210889432963&q=EEOC+v.+United+Health+Programs+of+America,+Inc.+(2018&hl=en&as_sdt=40006

[34] https://www.eeoc.gov/newsroom/jury-awards-51-million-workers-eeoc-religious-discrimination-case-against-united-health

[35] https://www.eeoc.gov/eeoc/newsroom/release/6-12-15.cfm

[36] https://www.gpo.gov/fdsys/pkg/STATUTE-107/pdf/STATUTE-107-Pg1488.pdf

of Human Resources of Oregon v. Smith (1990).[37] The Act made it illegal for the government to substantially burden a person's sincerely held religious beliefs by any governmental action (e.g., law, rule, policy), even if the law emanates from a rule of "general applicability." In this context, the concept of general applicability is reflected by laws that are considered to be neutral regarding religion (e.g., Shaman, 2012). The RFRA mandates that strict scrutiny be used to defend governmental actions (e.g., laws). So, as noted earlier, to be defensible, governmental actions must (1) advance a compelling government interest and (2) be the least restrictive method to achieve the compelling interest.

However, the RFRA was limited in scope by *City of Boerne v. Flores* (1997).[38,39] Flores, a Catholic Archbishop, challenged the city's denial of a permit to expand his church due to an existing historic preservation regulation. The Archbishop contended that the refusal to issue the permit was a violation of the RFRA. The Supreme Court ruled that Congress went beyond its powers by enforcing the RFRA on states and municipalities. Therefore, the Court upheld the city's refusal to issue the permit. As the Court stated, the RFRA "intruded into an area reserved by the Constitution to the States." The Court further concluded that "The stringent test RFRA demands of state laws reflects a lack of proportionality or congruence between the means adopted and the legitimate end to be achieved."

Consequently, the RFRA has been interpreted as applicable only to the federal government (see Kanda, 2002). As of this writing, 21 states have passed RFRA laws, which generally reflect the provisions included in the original RFRA of 1993 (see Table 4.3). So, a looming question surrounds the balance between the free exercise of religion and employment anti-discrimination laws. In other words, can the free exercise of religion be used as a defense against alleged violations of Title VII (e.g., sex discrimination) or other employment discrimination laws?

One extension of the RFRA was the Supreme Court's ruling in *Burwell v. Hobby Lobby* (2014)[40,41] where Hobby Lobby's position was supported by a ruling that the Affordable Care Act's contraception mandate was a violation of the RFRA. Generally, the mandate required organizations to provide health insurance that covered costs for birth control. The company objected to the mandate on the basis that it was a violation of the RFRA—it was contrary to their sincerely held religious beliefs to provide coverage for contraception. The Supreme Court ruled (5–4) that the RFRA allowed private, closely held

---

[37] https://www.law.cornell.edu/supremecourt/text/494/872
[38] https://supreme.justia.com/cases/federal/us/521/507/case.html
[39] https://www.oyez.org/cases/1996/95-2074
[40] https://www.law.cornell.edu/supct/pdf/13-354.pdf
[41] https://www.oyez.org/cases/2013/13-354

Table 4.3 States that have passed Religious Freedom
Restoration Act (RFRA) legislation

Existing RFRA legislation	No RFRA legislation
Alabama	Alaska
Arizona	California
Arkansas	Colorado
Connecticut	Delaware
Florida	Georgia
Idaho	Hawaii
Illinois	Maine
Indiana	Maryland
Kansas	Massachusetts
Kentucky	Michigan
Louisiana	Minnesota
Mississippi	Montana
Missouri	Nebraska
New Mexico	Nevada
Oklahoma	New Hampshire
Pennsylvania	New Jersey
Rhode Island	New York
South Carolina	North Carolina
Tennessee	North Dakota
Texas	Ohio
Virginia	Oregon
	South Dakota
	Utah
	Vermont
	Washington
	West Virginia
	Wisconsin
	Wyoming

corporations[42] (like Hobby Lobby) to be exempt from the mandate, given
provisions of the RFRA. Specifically, the Supreme Court concluded that the
contraception mandate posed a substantial burden to the free exercise of religion, and it was not the least restrictive/burdensome method of attaining a

---

[42] A closely held corporation is one in which greater than 50% of the stock is owned by five or fewer
people.

compelling governmental interest. Although not an employment discrimination case per se, the Court's decision has nurtured conflicts between religious freedom (e.g., the RFRA) and equal employment laws.

Other cases have not been employment-related but have rather pitted the religious beliefs of company owners against the customers they serve (or refuse to serve). Although not directly applicable to equal employment opportunity (EEO) issues, the decisions do offer some insight into the mindset of courts regarding the application of the RFRA. One illustrative case is *Craig v. Masterpiece Cakeshop, Inc.* (2015),[43] where the owner of the store refused to make a wedding cake for a same-sex couple based on his religious beliefs. This eventually became the Supreme Court decision rendered in *Masterpiece Cakeshop, Ltd. v. Colorado Civil Rights Commission* (2018),[44,45] wherein the Court rendered a (7–2) decision in favor of the baker (Jack Phillips). The justices' decision was largely based on the belief that the Colorado Civil Rights Commission demonstrated hostility toward Phillip's religious views. As the Court stated, "the record here demonstrates that the Commission's consideration of Phillips' case was neither tolerant nor respectful of Phillips' religious beliefs." In the end, the majority of justices ruled that Phillip's rights under the First Amendment's Free Exercise clause were violated. However, the decision did not address the larger question of whether one's religious opinions can be used to deny services to gay individuals, leaving this issue to be resolved via future case law. Quoting from the Court's decision:

> The outcome of cases like this in other circumstances must await further elaboration in the courts, all in the context of recognizing that these disputes must be resolved with tolerance, without undue disrespect to sincere religious beliefs, and without subjecting gay persons to indignities when they seek goods and services in an open market.

The case of *State of Washington v. Arlene's Flowers Inc.* (2017) involved a florist who refused to sell flowers to a gay couple for their wedding. A lawsuit was originally filed alleging discrimination based on sexual orientation. In 2017, the Washington State Supreme Court ruled that refusing to sell flowers to a gay couple violated state law (Washington Law Against Discrimination [WLAD]) that prohibits discrimination in public accommodation on the

---

[43] https://scholar.google.com/scholar_case?case=2695957032960182692&hl=en&as_sdt=6&as_vis=1&oi=scholarr

[44] https://www.law.cornell.edu/supct/pdf/16-111.pdf

[45] https://www.oyez.org/cases/2017/16-111

basis of sexual orientation.[46] However, after the *Masterpiece Cakeshop* decision, the United States Supreme Court sent the *Arlene's Flowers* case back to the State of Washington Supreme Court for further consideration.

In the end, the Supreme Court in Washington State affirmed its prior decision (see *State of Washington v. Arlene's Flowers, Inc.*, 2019). The company alleged, in part, that the WLAD was a violation of the 1st Amendment's guarantee of free speech (e.g., it coerced the endorsement of gay marriage) and that the state law violated the free exercise of religion. The court rejected both arguments and ruled against Arlene's Flowers. As the court stated, "We therefore hold that the conduct . . . cited and fined in this case . . . constitutes sexual orientation discrimination under the WLAD. We also hold that the WLAD may be enforced . . . because it does not infringe any constitutional protection . . . the WLAD does not compel speech or association." The court further noted that the WLAD did not violate the free exercise of religion protected under the First Amendment "because it is a neutral, generally applicable law that serves our state government's compelling interest in eradicating discrimination in public accommodations."

In the case of *EEOC v. R. G. & G. R. Harris Funeral Homes, Inc.* (2016),[47] the company had separate dress codes for men and women. Aimee Stephens, who was transitioning from man to woman, was fired for refusing to follow the company's dress code of wearing a traditionally male suit, preferring instead to wear female attire—a skirt suit (see case summary in the *Washington Post*).[48] Also, the organization apportioned clothing for male employees who interacted with the public, but not for female workers.

A sex discrimination case was subsequently filed. The company stated that abolishing its dress code would be a violation of RFRA—it would present a substantial burden to their sincerely held religious beliefs. The court agreed with the funeral home and ruled in favor of the organization, partly because the EEOC did not present the least restrictive (less burdensome) alternative as required by the RFRA (e.g., a sex-neutral dress code policy). However, in 2017, this decision was overturned by the 6th Circuit,[49] which held that the behavior of the funeral home was discriminatory, stating that " the funeral home fired Stephens because she refused to abide by her employer's stereotypical conception of sex." It also ruled that permitting Aimee Stephens to wear

[46] https://scholar.google.com/scholar_case?case=3597586148526886202&q=State+of+Washington+v.+Arlene's+Flowers+Inc.+&hl=en&as_sdt=40006

[47] https://casetext.com/case/equal-empt-opportunity-commn-v-rg-gr-harris-funeral-homes-inc-4

[48] https://www.washingtonpost.com/news/volokh-conspiracy/wp/2016/08/19/successful-religious-freedom-defense-in-title-vii-case-brought-by-transgender-employee/#comments

[49] https://www.opn.ca6.uscourts.gov/opinions.pdf/18a0045p-06.pdf

female attire does not substantially burden the sincerely held religious beliefs of the funeral home, therefore the company was not allowed to use a RFRA defense.[50]

As noted earlier in this chapter, many religious discrimination claims result in settlements with the EEOC. Table 4.4 provides a representative summary of such settlements.

Table 4.4 Representative Equal Employment Opportunity Commission (EEOC) religious discrimination settlements (listed in descending chronological order by year)

Organization (year of settlement)	Specific allegation(s)	Settlement and primary relief
Pediatrics 2000 (2020)1	Failure to accommodate a Jehovah's Witness worker; made negative comments about her religion. Employee eventually fired for missing a company party for religious reasons.	• $68,000 award • Develop anti-discrimination policies and procedures • Management and employee Title VII training
Service Caster Corporation (2020)2	Hostile work environment based on national origin and religion. Retaliation (fired) for opposing the harassment.	• $85,000 award • Title VII training • Enjoins company from discriminating against employees based on national origin or religious discrimination and retaliation
Versant Supply Chain, Inc. and AT&T Services, Inc. (2020)3	Not providing religious accommodations based on attire.	• $150,000 award • Two-year consent decree • Alter dress code policies • Management and employee training regarding religious discrimination and reasonable accommodation under Title VII
Halliburton Energy Services, Inc. (2019)4	Discrimination based on national origin and religion. Derogatory, degrading treatment of Muslim employees (e.g., name calling, taunts).	• $275,000 award • Three-year consent decree • Required company not to engage in national origin or religious discrimination or retaliation in the future • Provide training regarding national origin and religious discrimination to management and HR staff

---

[50] The *Harris Funeral Homes* case was consolidated with two other cases in by the Supreme Court in *Bostock v. Clayton County Georgia* (2020). The RFRA was omitted as a defense in the case before the Court. The issue was statutory in nature - whether the word "sex" in Title VII included gay and transgender individuals. The Supreme Court decided that such individuals are covered by Title VII. This decision is discussed in Chapter 6 in the section on LGBQT+protections.

Table 4.4 Continued

Organization (year of settlement)	Specific allegation(s)	Settlement and primary relief
United Parcel Service, Inc. (2018)5	Refused to hire or promote employees who didn't adhere to its appearance policy (e.g., no beards, hair length not below collar); failure to accommodate workers whose religious beliefs were inconsistent with its appearance policy; segregated workers into non-supervisory positions who didn't comply with appearance requirements.	• $4.9 million award • Five-year consent decree • Alter its appearance policy • Nationwide training to management and HR personnel • Send EEOC reports on religious accommodation requests regarding its appearance requirements
J. C. Witherspoon, Jr., Inc. (2018)6	Failure to accommodate religious belief of employee (to not work on Saturday); fired because of failure to work on the Sabbath.	• $53,000 award • Two-year consent decree • Develop policy to comply with Title VII protection regarding religious discrimination • Title VII training for managerial personnel
XPO Last Mile, Inc. (2018)7	Failure to accommodate religious belief. Rejected job offer to applicant after he couldn't start work on Rosh Hashanah.	• $94,541 award • Enjoined company from firing workers terminating employees based on religion or denying religious accommodations • Develop and distribute a policy regarding religious discrimination • Training on employment discrimination laws
U.S. Steel Tubular Products, Inc. (2017)8	Failure to accommodate applicant during a pre-employment hair follicle drug test. Applicant's religion did not allow cutting one's hair—he offered to have hair taken from his beard instead.	• $150,000 award • Two-year consent decree • Other undisclosed relief
Kasco, LLC. (2017)	Company sued for discrimination based on national origin, religion, and retaliation. Employee cited for poor performance during Ramadan. After she rebutted the performance issue, employee was accused of filing false time records and fired.	• $110,000 award • Three-year consent decree • Alter anti-discrimination policy • Management training

(continued)

Table 4.4 Continued

Organization (year of settlement)	Specific allegation(s)	Settlement and primary relief
Saint Vincent Health Center (2016)	Employees requested exemption for mandatory flu shot based on sincerely held religious beliefs. Denied religious accommodation requests but granted other employees accommodation requests based on medical reasons. Employees who refused to take flu shot for religious purposes subsequently fired.	• $300,000 award • Title VII training • Offers of reinstatement • Adopt definition of "religion" within Title VII when considering religious accommodation requests

[1] https://www.eeoc.gov/newsroom/pediatrics-2000-pay-68000-settle-religious-accommodation-lawsuit
[2] https://www.eeoc.gov/newsroom/service-caster-corp-will-pay-85000-settle-eeoc-suit-national-origin-and-religious-bias
[3] https://www.eeoc.gov/newsroom/versant-supplychain-and-att-pay-150000-settle-eeoc-religious-discrimination-suit
[4] https://www.eeoc.gov/newsroom/halliburton-pay-275000-settle-national-origin-and-religious-discrimination-suit
[5] https://www.eeoc.gov/newsroom/ups-pay-49-million-settle-eeoc-religious-discrimination-suit
[6] https://www.eeoc.gov/newsroom/jc-witherspoon-pay-53000-settle-eeoc-religious-discrimination-lawsuit
[7] https://www.eeoc.gov/newsroom/xpo-last-mile-will-pay-94541-settle-eeoc-religious-discrimination-suit
[8] https://www.eeoc.gov/newsroom/us-steel-subsidiary-pay-150000-settle-eeoc-religious-discrimination-and-retaliation-suit

Retrieved from EEOC Press Releases: https://www.eeoc.gov/newsroom/search

Supplemental Readings on Religious Discrimination

Beginner
FindLaw.com (December 4, 2018). Examples of religious discrimination in the workplace. https://employment.findlaw.com/employment-discrimination/facts-about-religious-discrimination.html
FindLaw.com (August 11, 2017). Federal laws against religious discrimination. https://civilrights.findlaw.com/discrimination/federal-laws-against-religious-discrimination.html

Intermediate
DOL. Religious exemption rule. https://www.dol.gov/agencies/ofccp/religious-exemption
EEOC. Best practices for eradicating workplace religious discrimination. https://www.eeoc.gov/policy/docs/best_practices_religion.html
EEOC. Compliance manual on religious discrimination. https://www.eeoc.gov/laws/guidance/section-12-religious-discrimination
EEOC. Questions and answers about workplace religious dress and grooming issues. https://www.eeoc.gov/eeoc/publications/qa_religious_garb_grooming.cfm
EEOC. Questions and answers on religious discrimination. https://www.eeoc.gov/policy/docs/qanda_religion.html
EEOC. Workplace religious accommodation. https://www.eeoc.gov/eeoc/newsroom/wysk/workplace_religious_accommodation.cfm

Advanced

Flake, D. F. (2016). Religious discrimination based on employer misperception. *Wisconsin Law Review, 87*, 88–133.

Ghumman, S., & Ryan, A. M. (2018). Religious group discrimination. In A. J. Colella & E. B. King (Eds.), *Oxford library of psychology: The Oxford handbook of workplace discrimination* (pp. 143–158). New York: Oxford University Press.

Smith, D. (2004). Workplace religious freedom: What is an employer's duty to accommodate? A review of recent cases. *The ALSP Journal of Employment and Labor Law, 10*, 49–65.

Recommendations/Best Practices

- Offer training programs to management and employees to eliminate religious discrimination (e.g., harassment, retaliation) and handle accommodation requests.
- Develop a comprehensive anti-discrimination policy that contains prohibitions against discrimination based on religious beliefs (e.g., what is banned, complaint procedures).
- For employees to qualify as "ministers," ensure that job duties contain relevant religious activities, especially if the word "minister" is absent from job titles.
- Interact with applicants/employees regarding their requests for religious accommodations.
- Document all religious accommodation requests and related communication between parties.
- Record precise reasons why any accommodations were considered to constitute an undue hardship.
- Be open to having flexible work and leave practices that can accommodate religious beliefs.
- Create a workplace climate that encourages acceptance of diverse religious beliefs.

Summary/Take-Aways

Protections against religious discrimination are deeply embedded in the law. Freedom from religious discrimination is covered by the 1st Amendment, and religion is one of the five original protected classes covered under Title VII. Further protections are provided by the religious exemptions under Title VII, such as those for religious organizations (e.g., hiring preference for those of a given religion) and for individuals whose jobs are defined as ministerial in nature. Indeed, the decisions in *Our Lady of Guadalupe v. Morrissey-Berru* (2020) expanded the criteria by which individuals can qualify for the ministerial exception.

Religious discrimination can occur in many forms, with the most common being the failure of organizations to accommodate sincerely held beliefs and practices. Other types of religious discrimination include disparate treatment, harassment, and retaliation.

It will be interesting to see the extent to which the RFRA will impact equal employment law. The Supreme Court decision in *Bostock v. Clayton County* (2020), which allowed legal protections for LGBTQ+ persons, did not rule on the RFRA. The decision was limited to whether the term "sex" in Title VII applied to gay and transgender individuals. Perhaps future court decisions may help shed light on this issue.

Glossary

De minimis: Something so small or trivial that it is not considered by the law; the term is often used to describe exemptions to legal rules and regulations.

Prima facie: Latin phrase for "at first glance." Consists of presenting evidence that is presumed to be true.

Strict scrutiny: A legal standard applied when fundamental rights are in question. Under strict scrutiny, governmental or organizational practices or policies (e.g., affirmative action programs) are legally defensible only if they (1) advance a compelling interest (i.e. a crucially important concern) and (2) are narrowly tailored, using the least restrictive method to achieve the compelling interest.

Undue hardship: An accommodation that is overly demanding or costly for a given organization (i.e., creates a disproportionate or unreasonable burden or obstacle) when considering its resources, size, and nature of the business. Can partially or fully exempt an organization from providing the accommodation.

Glossary terms adapted from https://uslegal.com/.

Cases Cited

Alicea-Hernandez v. Catholic Bishop of Chicago, 320 F. 3d 698 (7th Cir. 2003).
Ansonia Board of Education v. Philbrook, U.S. 41 EPD q 36,565 (1986).

Bostock v. Clayton County, Georgia, 140 S. Ct. 1731, 1739 (2020).
Burwell v. Hobby Lobby Stores, Inc., 134 S. Ct. 2751 (2014).
City of Boerne v. Flores, 521 U.S. 507 (1997).
Coulee Catholic Schools v. Labor and Industry Review Commission, 768 NW 2d 868 (Wis. 2009).
Craig v. Masterpiece Cakeshop, Inc., 370 P. 3d 272, Colo: Court of Appeals, 1st Div. (2015).
EEOC v. Abercrombie & Fitch Stores, Inc., 135 S. Ct. 2028 (2015).
EEOC v. R. G. & G. R. Harris Funeral Homes, Inc., 201 F. Supp. 3d 837 (E.D. Mich., 2016).
EEOC v. R. G. & G. R. Harris Funeral Homes, Inc., 884 F. 3d 560 (6th Cir. 2018).
EEOC v. Hosanna-Tabor Evangelical Lutheran Church and School, 597 F3d 769 (6th Cir. 2010).
EEOC v. United Health Programs of America, Inc., 350 F. Supp. 3d 199 (E.D.N.Y, 2018).
Employment Division, Department. of Human Resources of Oregon v. Smith, 494 US 872 (1990).
Hosanna-Tabor Evangelical v. EEOC, 565 U.S. 171 (2012).
Lemon v Kurtzman, 403 U.S. 602 (1971).
LeBoon v. Lancaster Jewish Community Center Association, 503 F. 3d 217 (3d Cir. 2007).
Masterpiece Cakeshop, Ltd. v. Colorado Civil Rights Commission, 138 S. Ct. 1719 (2018).
Our Lady of Guadalupe School v. Morrissey-Berru, 591 U.S. ___ (2020).
Sherbert v. Verner, 374 U.S. 398 (1963).
Starkman v. Evans, 198 F. 3d 173 (5th Cir. 1999).
State of Washington v. Arlene's Flowers, Inc., 389 P. 3d 543 (Wash: Supreme Court 2017).
State of Washington v. Arlene's Flowers, Inc., 441 P. 3d 1203 (Wash: Supreme Court 2019).
Trans World Airlines, Incorporated v. Hardison, 432 U.S. 63 (1977).
Wisconsin v. Yoder, 406 U.S. 205 (1972).

References

Beschle, D. L. (2018). Are two clauses really better than one: Rethinking the religion clause(s). *University of Pittsburgh Law Review, 80*(1), 1–32.

Coon, L. L. (2001). Employment discrimination by religious institutions: Limiting the sanctuary of the constitutional ministerial exception to religion-based employment decisions. *Vanderbilt Law Review, 54,* 481–546.

Dofner, E. K. (2016). The Supreme Court acknowledges Title VII's relaxed standard in favor of plaintiffs: *Equal Employment Opportunity Commission (EEOC) v. Abercrombie & Fitch Stores, Inc. Duquesne Business Law Journal, 18,* 81–102.

Dyer, R. W. (2011), Qualifying for the Title VII religious organization exemption: Federal circuits split over proper test. *Missouri, Law Review, 76.* 545–573.

Fallon, R. (2017). Tiers for the establishment clause. *University of Pennsylvania Law Review, 166*(1), 59–128.

Flake, D. F. (2019). Interactive religious accommodations. *Alabama Law Review, 71*(1), 67–114.

Ghumman, S., Ann Marie Ryan, A. M., Lizabeth A. Barclay, L. A., & Karen S. Markel, K. S. (2013). Religious discrimination in the workplace: A review and examination of current and future trends. *Journal of Business and Psychology, 28*(4), 439–454.

Greenawalt, K. (1995). Quo Vadis: The status and prospects of tests under the Religion Clauses. *Supreme Court Review, 8,* 323–392.

Heller, L. (2007). Modifying the ministerial exception: Providing ministers with a remedy for employment discrimination under Title VII while maintaining First Amendment protections of religious freedom. *St. John's Law Review, 81,* 663–699.

Kanda, K. S. (2002). Validity and application of the Religious Freedom Restoration Act in the Tenth Circuit after *City of Boerne v. Flores. Denver University Law Review, 79*(3), 295–330.

Kelly, E. (2008). Accommodating religious expression in the workplace. *Employee Responsibilities and Rights Journal, 20*, 45–56.

King, E. B., & Ahmad, A. S. (2010). An experimental field study of interpersonal discrimination toward Muslim job applicants. *Personnel Psychology, 63*, 881–906.

Lund, C. C. (2011). In defense of the ministerial exception. *North Carolina Law Review, 90*(1), 1–72.

Malos, S. (2010). Post-9/11 backlash in the workplace: Employer liability for discrimination against Arab- and Muslim-Americans based on religion or national origin. *Employee Responsibilities and Rights Journal, 22*, 297–310.

Musa, A. (2016). "A Motivating Factor"—The impact of *EEOC v. Abercrombie & Fitch Stores, Inc.* on Title VII religious discrimination claims. *Saint Louis University Law Journal, 61*, 143–164.

Nasuti, J. (2017). *E. E. O. C. v. Abercrombie & Fitch Stores, Inc.*: Reexamining the notice requirement in religious accommodation cases. *North East Journal of Legal Studies, 36*, 102–130.

Paludi, M. A., Ellens, J. H., & Paludi, C. A. (2011). Religious discrimination. In M. A. Paludi, C. A. Pauldi, & E. R. DeSouza (Eds.). *Praeger handbook on understanding and preventing workplace discrimination* (Vol. 1, pp. 157–182). Santa Barbara, CA: Praeger.

Park, J., Malachi, E., Sternin, O., & Tevet, R. (2009). Subtle bias against Muslim job applicants in personnel decisions. *Journal of Applied Social Psychology, 39*, 2174–2190.

Ravishankar, K. (2016). The establishment clause's hydra: The Lemon Test in the circuit courts. *University of Dayton Law Review, 41*(2), 261–302.

Shaman, J. M. (2012). Rules of general applicability. *First Amendment Law Review, 10*, 419–464.

Simson, G. J. (2018). Permissible accommodation or impermissible endorsement? A proposed approach to religious exemptions and the establishment clause. *Kentucky Law Journal, 106*(4), 535–601.

5

Title VII Legal Scenarios for Sex Discrimination and Sexual Harassment

---

General Legal Scenarios for Sex Discrimination Claims Under Title VII
Disparate Treatment
- Texas Department of Community Affairs v. Burdine (1981)

Adverse Impact
- Watson v. Fort Worth Bank and Trust (1988)

Class Action Suits
- Wal-Mart v. Dukes (2011)

Sex as a Bona Fide Occupational Qualification
- Dothard v. Rawlinson (1977)
- Automobile Workers v. Johnson Controls (1991)

Mixed-Motive Cases
- Price Waterhouse v. Hopkins (1989)
- Desert Palace Inc. v. Costa (2003)

Sexual Harassment
- Meritor Saving Bank v. Vinson (1986)

Vicarious Liability
- Burlington v. Ellerth (1998)
- Faragher v. Boca Raton (1998)
- Harris v. Forklift Systems (1993)

Definition of a Supervisor
- Vance v. Ball State University (2013)

Same-Sex Sexual Harassment
- Oncale v. Sundowner Offshore Services (1998)

Sexual Harassment and Constructive Discharge
- Pennsylvania State Police v. Suders (2004)

Recommendations/Best Practices
Summary and Take-Aways

Sex discrimination claims come in many forms. They have taken the form of *disparate treatment* (both traditional and *mixed-motive*)[1] and *adverse impact* cases, including *class action* cases (Gutek & Stockdale, 2005). Sex has also been employed, and challenged, as a *bona fide occupational qualification* (BFOQ). In this chapter we cover these specific scenarios as well as the topic of sexual harassment as it pertains to employment discrimination. In the next chapter we cover specific sex-related discrimination issues, including equal pay, pregnancy/family medical leave, dress-/appearance-related legal claims, and LGBTQ legal issues.

---

[1] Italicized technical terms are defined in the glossary at the end of this chapter.

Employment Discrimination. Stephen J. Vodanovich and Deborah E. Rupp, Oxford University Press. © Oxford University Press 2022. DOI: 10.1093/oso/9780190085421.003.0006

General Legal Scenarios for Sex Discrimination Claims Under Title VII

Disparate Treatment

Overall, sex discrimination suits are one of the more frequent cases filed with the Equal Employment Opportunity Commission (EEOC) (see Table 5.1). In this chapter, we cover various types of sex discrimination cases, beginning with the traditional disparate treatment scenario, followed by adverse impact, class action suits, cases where sex was alleged as a bona fide occupation, and mixed-motive cases.

As explained earlier, *Disparate treatment* cases based on sex refers to *intentionally* barring individuals from employment opportunities because of sex. There are three phases in disparate treatment cases, which are described again in Table 5.2. A well-known Supreme Court case of disparate treatment based on sex is *Texas Department of Community Affairs v. Burdine* (1981).[2,3] Joyce Burdine was fired and alleged that she was discriminated against because of her sex. She successfully met the criteria to form a *prima facie* case in phase 1. In *Burdine*, the Court reaffirmed its earlier decision in *McDonnell Douglas Corp. v. Green* (1973),[4,5] a race discrimination case, that the burden for the defense in disparate treatment scenarios was that of *production/articulation*.

> [T]he employer need only produce admissible evidence which would allow the trier of fact rationally to conclude that the employment decision had not been motivated by discriminatory animus.

As explained earlier, the *Burdine* decision also ruled that either *direct* or *indirect* evidence can be used by plaintiffs to prove pretext by organizations

Table 5.1 Sex discrimination charges filed with the Equal Employment Opportunity Commission (EEOC) 2013–2020

Year	2013	2014	2015	2016	2017	2018	2019	2020
Number of charges	27,687	26,027	26,396	26,934	25,605	24,655	23,532	21,398

Retrieved from https://www.eeoc.gov/eeoc/statistics/enforcement/charges.cfm

---

[2] https://www.oyez.org/cases/1980/79-1764
[3] https://supreme.justia.com/cases/federal/us/450/248/
[4] https://caselaw.findlaw.com/us-supreme-court/411/792.html
[5] https://www.oyez.org/cases/1972/72-490

Table 5.2 Disparate treatment scenario

Phase 1	The plaintiff must establish a *prima facie* case (present *presumptive evidence* of discrimination).
Phase 2	The defense must *articulate* (not prove) that a legitimate reason exists for the alleged discriminatory practice.
Phase 3	The plaintiff must *prove* by *direct* or *indirect* evidence that the organization's reason(s) for its decision is a pretext for discrimination.

in Phase 3 of the disparate treatment process. In this context, direct evidence provides, by itself, the existence of an intent to discriminate (e.g., a facially discriminatory policy; a statement such as "I terminated her because she was a woman"). It is sometimes referred to as "smoking gun" evidence. On the other hand, indirect (or circumstantial) evidence requires fact finders (judges, juries) to make inferences from information presented in a given case. Since the burden shifting requirements for disparate treatment cases in *Burdine* aligned with that of the previous *Green* decision (i.e., presentation of presumptive evidence by plaintiffs, articulation of non-discriminatory action by the defense, proof of pretext by plaintiffs), the disparate treatment scenario has been referred to as the *McDonnell-Burdine* framework.

Adverse Impact

A traditional *adverse impact* scenario pertaining to sex involves using "neutral" employment practices that disproportionally harm those of a particular sex relative to the opposite sex. No evidence of intent is necessary since the focus is on the effects or consequences of an employer's actions.

Early adverse impact cases involved the use of objective data (e.g., test scores) to make personnel decisions. In the Supreme Court Case *Watson v. Fort Worth Bank and Trust* (1988),[6,7] the plaintiff sued for sex discrimination after being denied a promotion on several occasions. The company countered that it used *subjective* performance assessments by supervisors. Consequently, the bank believed they did not have to comply with precedent (*Griggs v. Duke Power Co.*, 1971) that had only centered on objective test scores and educational requirements. In a unanimous decision, the Supreme

[6] https://caselaw.findlaw.com/us-supreme-court/487/977.html
[7] https://www.oyez.org/cases/1987/86-6139

Table 5.3 Adverse impact scenario

Phase 1	The plaintiff must *demonstrate* (prove) that a *particular* employment practice *caused* the disproportionate exclusion of protected group members. [This is true unless plaintiffs can demonstrate that an organization's decision-making process is not able to be separated for inspection. If so, the decision-making process can be analyzed as a whole].
Phase 2	The defense must *demonstrate* that its challenged practice(s) is(are) job-related for the position in question and consistent with business necessity.
Phase 3	The plaintiff must prove that an equally valid, job-related practice exists with less (or no) adverse impact.

Court decided that subjective data can be challenged using adverse impact rules. As the Court stated, "If an employer's undisciplined system of subjective decision-making has precisely the same effects as a system pervaded by impermissible intentional discrimination, it is difficult to see why Title VII's proscription against discriminatory actions should not apply . . . subjective or discretionary employment practices may be analyzed under the disparate impact approach in appropriate cases."

However, a *plurality* position (i.e., receiving support from the most justices, but not a majority) advocated a lower burden of proof in phase 2 of the adverse impact scenario to that of "production" (articulation) not "proof" (see Potter [1989] for a more detailed summary of the Watson case). In *Wards Cove Packing Co. v. Atonio* (1989; discussed in Chapter 3), a *majority* of Supreme Court justices agreed with the lower "production" standard advocated in *Watson* as the defense requirement in an adverse impact case. However, the Civil Rights Act of 1991 reversed this ruling by defining the word "demonstrates" as meeting the burden of both production and *persuasion* (proof). Table 5.3 again summarizes the phases of an adverse impact case.

Class Action Suits

When a plaintiff represents all the applicants or employees within the same protected group and who are alleged to have faced the same discrimination as the plaintiff, a class action suit may be filed. Importantly, such cases only proceed if a court certifies the group as a legitimate "class." One example of a large sex-based class action suit is *Wal-Mart v. Dukes* (2011),[8,9] which represented

---

[8] https://www.supremecourt.gov/opinions/10pdf/10-277.pdf
[9] https://www.oyez.org/cases/2010/10-277

more than 1.5 million women. Interpretation of the Federal Rules of Civil Procedure (Rule 23)[10] played a large role in the certification of the "class" in this case and ultimately had an impact on the final ruling. As explained in Chapter 2, to be certified as a class, *all* the following conditions must be met under Rule 23(a):

- The class is so numerous that claims by individuals are unrealistic (*numerosity clause*).
- Questions of law or fact are common to the class (*commonality requirement*).
- Claims of the plaintiff(s) are representative of those of the class parties (*typicality*).
- The plaintiff(s) will sufficiently protect the interests of the class (*class protection*).

If these conditions under Rule 23(a) are met, *one* of the following stipulations under Rule 23(b)(1), 23(b)(2), or 23(b)(3) must be proved for the class to be certified:

23(b)(1): The prosecuting of distinct actions by individual members of a class would create a risk of (a) incongruent decisions that would produce contrary principles for those contesting the class, or (b) decisions regarding individual class members "would be dispositive of the interests of the other members not parties to the individual adjudications or would substantially impair or impede their ability to protect their interests."

- 23(b)(2): Refers to *injunctive* and *declarative relief* and, if met, does not allow the defense to respond to claims by individual members of the class.

- 23(b)(3): "Predominance" and "superiority" requirement. That is, the interests of the class must be predominant over those of individual members, and a class action challenge must be shown to be better (superior) than other available mechanisms.

In the *Wal-Mart* case, the focus was on Rules 23(b)(2) and 23(b)(3). The basic allegation was that Wal-Mart routinely discriminated against women regarding pay and promotion decisions. The decision and facts of the case are complicated and involved expert testimony pertaining to a "social framework analysis" (e.g., evidence of Wal-Mart's culture) and a range of statistical analyses. However, the Supreme Court decision largely focused on whether

[10] https://www.law.cornell.edu/rules/frcp/rule_23

the plaintiffs met the commonality requirement to be certified as a class. The majority of justices ruled that the plaintiffs were treated too differently, there was no class-wide solution, and no common connection between the various charges. Consequently, the plaintiffs were *not* certified as a class. The overall ruling in favor of Wal-Mart was relatively complex and resulted in a divided decision (5–4) by the Court. Analysis of this case suggests that to be successful in certifying a large and broad class (as was attempted within the *Wal-Mart* case), there likely needs to be a common policy or practice that affects every member of the class in the same way (Gutman & Dunleavy, 2011).[11]

Sex as a Bona Fide Occupational Qualification

Other cases have positioned sex as a bona fide occupational qualification (BFOQ). BFOQs are exemptions to Title VII and can be used in defense of Title VII challenges. Examples of BFOQs include religion, sex, national origin, and age. As mentioned in Chapter 1, BFOQs are meant to be narrow exceptions under the law. To be used successfully, defendants must demonstrate that making personnel decisions based on protected group status (e.g., sex) is supported by actual evidence that a BFOQ is reasonably necessary for the operation of a business and that no viable alternatives exist. Privacy and safety concerns have also been used to justify BFOQs.

Sex has been argued to be a BFOQ in a number of cases. In *Dothard v. Rawlinson* (1977),[12,13] female correctional officers were not allowed to work alongside male inmates where close physical proximity was required. At the correctional facility in question, about one-fifth of the inmates were classified as sex offenders. In the end, the Supreme Court concluded that sex in this context was a BFOQ—being a woman was determined to pose a considerable risk to workplace safety.

A more recent decision supported the practice of only hiring female correctional officers in a women's correctional facility (*Teamsters Local Union No. 117 v. Washington Department of Corrections*, 2015).[14] The Court of Appeals for the 9th Circuit was convinced by the evidence offered by the state regarding concerns about preventing sexual assault, security, and privacy. Thus, limiting correctional officers to women was viewed as legitimate in this context. Similarly, limiting the hiring of female Transportation Security

[11] https://www.siop.org/Portals/84/TIP/Archives/492.pdf?ver=2019-08-20-115445-257
[12] https://supreme.justia.com/cases/federal/us/433/321/
[13] https://www.oyez.org/cases/1976/76-422
[14] https://cases.justia.com/federal/appellate-courts/ca9/13-35331/13-35331-2015-06-12.pdf

Authority (TSA) agents to physically check female passengers was upheld in *Wilson v. Chertoff* (2010).[15]

A contrary ruling occurred in the influential case of *United Automobile Workers v. Johnson Controls* (1991).[16,17] Johnson Controls made batteries. A result of this manufacturing process was exposure to lead, which the company feared could lead to fetal abnormalities in fertile women. As such, the company initially warned women of childbearing age of the dangers of lead exposure. This was followed by a strict ban on women working in jobs with high lead levels. A sex discrimination suit was subsequently filed. The company's position was that sex in this situation was a BFOQ. The Supreme Court ruled in favor of the women employees. One reason was that the ban was based on the potential for pregnancy, a violation of the Pregnancy Discrimination Act. Also, the policy only applied to women. Men were not banned from lead-exposure jobs even though their reproductive systems could also be negatively impacted by such exposure. The Court ultimately concluded that fetal protection policies based on sex are illegal under Title VII.

EEO in the Wild: BFOQs in the Restaurant Industry

The use of a BFOQ defense is meant to be a rather narrow exemption under the law. In the current context, organizations have to demonstrate that only hiring women is reasonably necessary for the operation of its business. For example, the restaurant Hooters has a policy of only hiring women as servers. Although Hooters has been sued for sex discrimination by male applicants for server positions on several occasions, the company has successfully fought off suits by settling out of court. For instance, following the filing of a class action suit, Hooters agreed to pay $3.75 million and open positions in their restaurants to men (though they only conceded to do this for non-server positions). Another settlement of an unknown amount occurred in 2009, after a suit was filed by a male applicant who was denied a server position. Currently, Hooters defines servers as "entertainers" and contends that limiting servers to women (known as "Hooters Girls") is a BFOQ.

Sex as a BFOQ in the restaurant industry is not limited to Hooters. Lawry's Restaurants settled a suit for more than $1 million for refusing to hire a male applicant for a server position. Soon after the suit was filed the restaurant began to hire men and women as servers. A similar case was filed against Twin Peaks restaurant

[15] https://scholar.google.com/scholar_case?case=943822378761032079&q=Wilson+v.+Chertoff+(2010)&hl=en&as_sdt=40006

[16] https://www.law.cornell.edu/supct/html/89-1215.ZO.html

[17] https://www.oyez.org/cases/1990/89-1215

(*Rafael Ortiz v. DMD Florida Restaurant Group*, 2016). Like past cases in this area, the suit ended in a settlement for an undisclosed amount later in the year. See Aamodt (2017) for a concise summary of BFOQs in the workplace, especially in the restaurant industry.

Mixed-Motive Cases

Cases tried under a mixed-motive scenario involve a situation where both illegal *and* legal factors are allegedly used in making an employment decision. A landmark mixed-motive Supreme Court case is illustrated by *Price Waterhouse v. Hopkins* (1989).[18,19] Ann Hopkins was denied a promotion on multiple occasions and subsequently sued for sex discrimination. She believed that her lack of promotion was due to the use of sex-based stereotypes (e.g., she was "macho" and "overcompensated for being a woman"). This was counter to the position of the company, which stated that her on-the-job behavior was the reason for their decisions. In the end, the Court ruled that discrimination based on sex stereotyping (e.g., a woman acting contrary to sex-based norms or social beliefs) is a form of sex discrimination and a violation of Title VII.

Another key decision in *Hopkins* was whether the use of an illegal factor (e.g., sex) was a "substantial" or "motivating" factor in the decision-making process. The *plurality* opinion among the Supreme Court justices was that an illegal reason only needs to be a "motivating factor" in an employment decision, as compared to a "substantial" factor, as advocated by other justices. However, since the "motivating factor" was not endorsed by a majority of justices, the decision on this point is not as powerful as a majority vote and offers less clarity to lower courts.

A separate point of contention was the proper standard needed by the defense to prove the use of a legal factor. That is, the question here was whether the defense must meet a "clear and convincing" or a "preponderance" evidentiary standard. The Court ruled that the correct defense standard in mixed-motive cases is a *preponderance of evidence*—a "more likely than not" standard, which is an easier standard to meet compared to a "clear and convincing" standard.

An additional issue in the case was whether plaintiffs are required to present *direct* or *indirect* evidence in mixed-motive cases. Justice O'Conner stated

---

[18] https://caselaw.findlaw.com/us-supreme-court/490/228.html
[19] https://www.oyez.org/cases/1988/87-1167

that Hopkins did what was required of her. That is, Hopkins provided *direct* evidence that the company "placed substantial negative reliance on an illegitimate criterion in reaching their decision." Importantly, O'Conner's position that direct evidence was required of plaintiffs was adopted by many lower courts after the *Hopkins* decision. This occurred even though O'Conner was the only justice to mention the direct evidence requirement. Finally, the Court decided that if a company could show that it would have made the same decision notwithstanding the use of an illegal factor, they could escape liability altogether. In the end, Hopkins won her case since the company could not prove that it would have made the same decision despite the use of an illegal factor (in this case, sex).

The Civil Rights Act of 1991 (CRA-91) clarified some issues the Court faced in *Hopkins*. An important provision was that the use of an illegal factor had to be a *motivating* (not substantial) factor in personnel decisions. From the CRA-91:

> Except as otherwise provided in this subchapter, an unlawful employment practice is established when the complaining party *demonstrates* that race, color, religion, sex, or national origin was a *motivating* factor for any employment practice, even though other factors also motivated the practice. (emphasis added)

So, CRA-91 made the use of an illegal factor a violation of law. However, the Act stipulates that companies can avoid some liability if they successfully demonstrate that the same decision would have been made even though they used an illegal factor. So, if an organization is found to have used race, color, religion, sex, or national origin in making an employment decision, it is guilty of violating the law and plaintiffs are eligible for various types of relief and having attorney fees covered. But if a company can prove that it would have made the same decision despite the use of an illegal factor, it can evade paying damages. CRA-91 did not address whether direct or indirect evidence is needed by plaintiffs in mixed-motive court cases. This was focused on in a Supreme Court case more than a decade later, which is discussed next.

In *Desert Palace, Inc., v. Costa* (2003),[20,21] Catharina Costa was fired for fighting with a coworker. However, she alleged that she had been treated more severely than her male counterparts in this regard. The defense asserted that Costa did not present *direct* evidence that sex was a motivating factor in the organization's decision to fire her. The Supreme Court ruled that direct

---

[20] https://www.law.cornell.edu/supct/html/02-679.ZO.html
[21] https://www.oyez.org/cases/2002/02-679

Table 5.4 Mixed-motive scenario

Phase 1	Plaintiffs must *prove* by a preponderance of *direct* or *indirect* evidence that an illegal motive was a motivating factor in an employment decision.
Phase 2	Defense must *prove* by a *preponderance* of evidence that the employment decision made would have been made anyway despite the illegal motive.
Phase 3	The plaintiff must *prove* by a preponderance of evidence that the reasons (evidence) offered by the defense are a pretext for discrimination.

evidence is *not* needed in mixed-motive cases; both *direct* and *indirect evidence* is admissible. Table 5.4 again summarizes the mixed-motive burden shifting process. In addition, sex discrimination settlements with the EEOC are summarized in Table 5.5.

Table 5.5 Selected sex discrimination settlements

Organization (year of settlement)	Specific allegation(s)	Settlement and primary relief
Performance Food Group (2020)[1]	Pattern or practice sex discrimination for refusing to hire females for "selector" and "driver" positions.	• $5,075,000 damage award • Five-year consent decree • Hire a Vice President of Diversity to comply with the settlement and guarantee that females are not discriminated against • Focus recruiting to attract qualified female applicants
Walmart, Inc. (2020)[2]	Physical ability test had an adverse disparate impact on women applying for grocery filler jobs.	• $20 million award • Eliminate use of the test
BHT Constructions LLC (2020)[3]	Failure to hire a qualified woman as a heavy machine operator. She was told by a supervisor that they "do not hire women."	• $38,000 damage award • Five-year consent decree • Construct and distribute policy against sex discrimination • Conduct in-person Title VII training
Burgers & Beer (2019)[4]	Did not consider men applicants and employees for server jobs.	• $150,000 damage award • Two-year consent decree • Review and alter job descriptions • Title VII training
Northern Arizona Orthopedics (2019)[5]	Company hired females over more qualified male applicants; retaliated against male applicant.	• $165,000 damage award • Four-year consent decree • Review and revise its hiring procedures • Title VII training • Three-year consent decree
AutoNation Chevrolet Coral Gables (2018)	Failed to allow a woman employee to apply for Parts Manager; hired a less-qualified man and required the denied woman employee to train him; stated that the "job needed a man."	• $150,000 damage award • Annual training for non-discrimination in hiring • Requires EEO language in job ads for Parts and Service department managerial positions[6]

Table 5.5 Continued

Organization (year of settlement)	Specific allegation(s)	Settlement and primary relief
CSX Transportation, Inc. (2018)	Class action adverse impact suit; use of physical ability tests (e.g., strength and endurance tests) for various positions discriminated against women.	• $3.2 million damage award • Refrain from using tests that discriminated against women • Hire an expert to study other tests of physical ability before use[7]
Estée Lauder Co. (2018)	Class action suit that men were given less paid parental leave than women; refused to give men "return-to-work" benefits (e.g., modified work schedules).	• $1.1 million damage award • Equalize parental leave benefits between males and females • EEOC monitoring of agreement[8]
The Children's Home, Inc. (2018)	Declined to consider a male applicant for a position in a maternity home program.	• $18,000 damage award • Place an EEO statement in job ads • Communicate for 2 years with the EEOC on hiring practices within the maternity home program • Yearly sex discrimination training[9]
DDZ CA, Inc. (2018)	Failure to employ women in boxer/packer jobs; creation of a hostile work environment based on sex.	• $625,400 damage award[10]
Candid Litho Printing, Ltd. (2018)	Sex discrimination, sexual harassment against female manager by a male general manager; retaliation (fired female manager after filing complaint; also fired her son and fiancée without cause).	• Three-year consent decree • $242,799 damage award • Alter sex discrimination, sexual harassment, and retaliation policies and complaints protocol • EEO training for employees[11]
First Tower Loan, LLC (2017)	Termination of a transgender employee; not following gender-based expectations.	• $53,000 damage award • 18-month consent decree with EEOC (alter policies prohibiting discrimination based on transgender status, training on sex discrimination)
Nevada Health Centers (2017)	Termination of a male ultrasound technician because of his sex.	• Two and a half-year consent decree • $15,000 damage award • Alter anti-discrimination policy and complaint procedure • Management non-discrimination training[12]
Special Education Associates, Inc. (2017)	Sex discrimination, sexual harassment, and retaliation suit. Hiring offer rescinded after female applicant refused to go on a date with CEO; hired a male instead	• $57,000 damage award • Develop new anti-discrimination policies/procedures • In-person anti-discrimination training[13]

(continued)

Table 5.5 Continued

Organization (year of settlement)	Specific allegation(s)	Settlement and primary relief
Automation Personnel Services, Inc. (2017)	Company recruiter refused to interview female applicant for shipping and receiving job based on her sex (e.g., position was "not suitable for women").	• $50,000 damage award • Anti-discrimination training for those responsible for hiring • Biannual training reports for several company locations[14]

[1] https://www.eeoc.gov/newsroom/performance-food-group-will-pay-over-5-million-resolve-eeoc-nationwide-sex-discrimination

[2] https://www.eeoc.gov/newsroom/walmart-inc-pay-20-million-settle-eeoc-nationwide-hiring-discrimination-case

[3] https://www.eeoc.gov/newsroom/bht-constructions-pay-38000-settle-eeoc-sex-discrimination-suit

[4] https://www.eeoc.gov/newsroom/burgers-beer-settles-eeoc-sex-discrimination-lawsuit-150000

[5] https://www.eeoc.gov/newsroom/northern-arizona-orthopedics-pay-165000-settle-eeoc-sex-discrimination-and-retaliation

[6] https://www.eeoc.gov/eeoc/newsroom/release/8-22-18.cfm

[7] https://www.eeoc.gov/eeoc/newsroom/release/6-13-18.cfm

[8] https://www.eeoc.gov/eeoc/newsroom/release/7-17-18c.cfm

[9] https://www.eeoc.gov/eeoc/newsroom/release/5-2-18.cfm

[10] https://www.eeoc.gov/eeoc/newsroom/release/4-16-18.cfm

[11] https://www.eeoc.gov/eeoc/newsroom/release/4-12-18a.cfm

[12] https://www.eeoc.gov/eeoc/newsroom/release/7-6-17b.cfm

[13] https://www.eeoc.gov/eeoc/newsroom/release/5-8-17.cfm

[14] https://www.eeoc.gov/eeoc/newsroom/release/5-5-17b.cfm

Retrieved from EEOC Press Releases: https://www.eeoc.gov/newsroom/search

Supplemental Readings on Sex Discrimination

Beginner

Barnes, R. (2011, June). Supreme Court blocks massive sex-discrimination suit against Wal-Mart. *The Washington Post*. https://www.washingtonpost.com/politics/supreme-court-blocks-massive-sex-discrimination-suit-against-wal-mart/2011/06/20/AGCQ81cH_story.html

Grimsley, K. D. (1995, December). Hooters plays hardball with the EEOC. *The Washington Post*. https://www.washingtonpost.com/archive/business/1995/12/10/hooters-plays-hardball-with-the-eeoc/ffec67d4-92fe-4a62-ad3b-e806e3f05f14/

Intermediate

Cavico, F. J., & Mujtaba, B. G. (2016). The bona fide occupational qualification (BFOQ) defense in employment discrimination: A narrow and limited justification exception. *Journal of Business Studies Quarterly, 7*, 15–29.

Dunleavy, E. M., & Gutman, A. (2011). A review of the Supreme Court ruling in Wal-Mart v. Dukes. *The Industrial-Organizational Psychologist, 49*(2), 75–80.

Advanced

Hopkins, A. (2005). *Price-Waterhouse v. Hopkins:* A personal account of a sexual discrimination plaintiff. *Hofstra Labor and Employment Law Journal, 22*, 357–416. https://scholarlycommons.law.hofstra.edu/cgi/viewcontent.cgi?article=1024&context=hlelj

Manley, K. (2009). The BFOQ defense: Title VII'S concession to gender discrimination. *Duke Journal of Gender Law and Policy, 16*, 169–210. https://scholarship.law.duke.edu/cgi/ viewcontent.cgi?article=1160&context=djglp#:~:text=The%20BFOQ%20defense%20 allows%20employers,normal%20operation%20of%20the%20business.

Sexual Harassment

Even with the development of legal protections, sexual harassment in the workplace continues to be prevalent (see Table 5.6). An important milestone occurred in 1980, when the EEOC issued its Guidelines on Sexual Harassment.[22] Prior to this time, the courts were slow to consider sexual harassment as being prohibited by Title VII. Since 1980, the guidelines have been updated and revised to incorporate evolving case law. Some of the basic elements of the EEOC Guidelines are that (1) evidence of alleged sexual harassment should be considered on a case-by-case basis, (2) facts ought to be evaluated based on the entire record of a case, and (3) consideration needs to be made of the totality of the situation (e.g., type and context of the sexual behavior). The guidelines state that organizations are accountable for the acts of its "agents" (e.g., supervisors) even if the acts are banned by the company and irrespective of whether the company "knew or should have known" of the sexual behavior.

Sexual harassment can occur in two forms: *quid pro quo* and hostile environment harassment. According to the EEOC, q*uid pro quo* ("something for something") sexual harassment occurs when "submission to or rejection of such conduct by an individual is used as the basis for employment decisions affecting such individual." Furthermore, the EEOC refers to *hostile environment* sexual harassment as consisting of *unwelcome* behaviors that create "an intimidating, hostile, or offensive working environment." To

Table 5.6 Sexual harassment charges filed with the Equal Employment Opportunity Commission (EEOC) 2013–2020

Year	2013	2014	2015	2016	2017	2018	2019	2020
Number of Charges	7,256	6,862	6,822	6,758	6,696	7,609	7,514	6,587

Retrieved from https://www.eeoc.gov/eeoc/statistics/enforcement/sexual_harassment_new.cfm

[22] https://www.eeoc.gov/policy/docs/currentissues.html

determine if behavior is unwelcome, a complaint by the victim at the time of the alleged offense is *not* required. Although such a complaint is helpful, many obstacles exist that prevent victims from doing so, such as fear of retaliation (e.g., Fitzgerald, Swan, & Fischer, 1995). A victim's nonverbal behavior (e.g., expression of disgust, anger) and collaboration by others can also be used to establish that a behavior was not welcome. In evaluating whether a hostile work environment exists, alleged sexually harassing behavior is typically determined from the perspective of a *reasonable person* (or a reasonable person from the point of view of the victim; see the EEOC's Policy Guidance on Current Issues of Sexual Harassment mentioned earlier).

Meritor Saving Bank v. Vinson (1986)[23,24] was the first time the Supreme Court ruled on sexual harassment. Michelle Vinson alleged that she was sexually harassed by her supervisor and vice president, Sidney Taylor, across a four-year timeframe. She ultimately filed a hostile environment claim of sexual harassment under Title VII. The bank asserted that Title VII only covered instances where concrete, economic damages occurred. In its view, negative psychological effects that were connected to the harassing behavior were not supported by the law. The Court disagreed. It ruled that sexual harassment can exist by creating a hostile work environment and therefore is a form of sex discrimination covered by Title VII. The existence of economic damages was not required. In this regard, the Court concluded that for sexual harassment to exist, the harassing behavior needs to be "sufficiently severe or pervasive" to create a hostile work environment. Trivial claims are not actionable.

In addition, Meritor Savings stated that it was unaware of the sexual harassment of Taylor and that Vinson did not adhere to the company's policy by not following its grievance procedure. However, the *Vinson* decision established that organizations could be held liable for sexually harassing behavior "whether or not the employer knew or should have known about it." The Court further stated that the existence of a policy and grievance procedure did not protect organizations from liability. Here, the policy of Meritor Savings failed to specifically mention sexual harassment, and the initial step in the grievance procedure was to contact one's immediate supervisor—in this case the person being accused of the illegal behavior. Another issue was that Vinson voluntarily engaged in sexual relations with her supervisor. The Court's decision stated that even though Vinson voluntarily engaged in sexual relations, the actions of her supervisor were *unwelcome* (e.g., she feared losing her job), an initial requirement for sexual harassment to exist.

---

[23] https://caselaw.findlaw.com/us-supreme-court/477/57.html
[24] https://www.oyez.org/cases/1985/84-1979

Although the *Meritor* decision was an important step forward for victims of sexual harassment, it was not completely "employee friendly." For instance, the Supreme Court ruled it was legitimate to admit evidence of a victim's provocative behavior and attire. Essentially, their reasoning was that such information was relevant in assessing the context of a case and assessing the entirety of the facts involved. Also, the Supreme Court stated that organizations are not automatically liable for the sexually harassing behaviors of their supervisors, a position advocated by the Court of Appeals. The Supreme Court left undecided the criteria for determining when organizations are responsible for the behavior of their supervisors or "agents" of the company (so-called *vicarious liability*). As a result, lower courts began using different standards for assessing vicarious liability. The standards for determining vicarious liability were eventually clarified by the Supreme Court in two important cases, summarized in the next section.

Vicarious Liability

Two fundamental Supreme Court cases that involved sexual harassment by supervisors/agents and the issue of vicarious liability are *Burlington Industries v. Ellerth* (1998)[25,26] and *Faragher v. City of Boca Raton* (1998).[27,28] In *Ellerth*, a female employee (Kimberly Ellerth) claimed that she was threatened with negative employment decisions if she failed to have sex with her male supervisor. None of the alleged threats were acted upon, so the Court considered the situation to be a hostile environment case. The justices ruled that the company was vicariously liable for its supervisory personnel since they function as agents of the organization.

In the *Faragher* case, two supervisors (lifeguards) were accused of verbal and physical sexual harassment toward female subordinates, one of whom was Beth Ann Faragher. The city countered that it had a policy against sexual harassment and was unaware of the actions of the supervisors. However, the policy was not widely distributed and the organization did not monitor the work performance of its supervisors. Consequently, the Court ruled in favor of Faragher, given that evidence indicated that the

[25] https://scholar.google.com/scholar_case?case=2707173104214869053&hl=en&as_sdt=6&as_vis=1&oi=scholarr
[26] https://www.oyez.org/cases/1997/97-569
[27] https://www.law.cornell.edu/supct/html/97-282.ZO.html
[28] https://www.oyez.org/cases/1997/97-282

company did not take reasonable care in preventing illegal behavior of its supervisory personnel.

In cases of vicarious liability, where supervisors have allegedly engaged in hostile environment sexual harassment, organizations can use an *affirmative defense*. That is, they can avoid liability by showing that (1) the company exercised reasonable care to *prevent* and *promptly correct* any sexually harassing behavior, and (2) the plaintiff *unreasonably* failed to take advantage of any *preventive or corrective* opportunities provided by the employer.

In *Harris v. Forklift Systems, Inc.* (1993),[29,30] Teresa Harris alleged that her supervisor had produced an abusive, hostile work environment. A key issue in the case was what criteria should be used to determine the existence of a hostile work environment. Some of the evidence offered by Harris included testimony that her supervisor tossed items on the floor and requested that female workers pick them up, asked female subordinates to take change out of his pockets, and proposed that Harris and he go to a motel to negotiate her raise. Upon informing her supervisor that his behaviors were unwelcome, he promised to stop behaving in such a manner. However, about a month later, after Harris arranged a deal with a customer, he asked her if she had promised the customer sex to get the contract. Harris quit and sued the organization.

The District Court in Tennessee believed this was "a close case." That is, the court concluded that although a "reasonable woman" would find the supervisor's behavior offensive, it was not "so severe as to be expected to seriously affect [Harris'] psychological well-being." The Supreme Court reversed this decision stating that it is sufficient if the environment is "perceived" to be hostile or abusive by the victim. Therefore, evidence of concrete psychological harm is not required. As the Court noted in *Harris*, "Title VII comes into play before the harassing conduct leads to a nervous breakdown." In essence, the Court in *Harris* took a middle ground approach (see Table 5.7) in assessing a hostile work environment by concluding that alleged sexually harassing behaviors do not need to cause *psychological harm* to victims to create a hostile work environment. The Supreme Court also elaborated on the reasonable person standard in *Harris*. Basically, the Court concluded that alleged sexually harassing behavior has to be *subjectively* perceived by victims as being hostile and *objectively* viewed as hostile by a reasonable person.

[29] https://www.law.cornell.edu/supct/html/92-1168.ZO.html
[30] https://www.oyez.org/cases/1993/92-1168

Table 5.7 Middle ground approach for hostile environment established in *Harris v. Forklift Systems*

Low	Merely offensive conduct; behavior that does not sufficiently affect conditions of employment and create a hostile work environment
Moderate	Supreme Court decision in *Harris*; no need for victims to demonstrate they experienced concrete psychological harm
High	Conduct causing psychological injury to victims [District Court decision in *Harris*]

Insights from Social Science: Reasonable Person or Reasonable Victim/Woman Standard for Determining a Hostile Work Environment?

There has been considerable debate within the legal community and social science researchers about the proper standard that courts should use in sexual harassment cases when assessing the existence of a hostile work environment. The reasonable person standard has been commonly employed in sexual harassment cases, with an early example being *Rabidue v. Osceola Refining Company* (1986).[a] As the court stated in *Rabidue*, factfinders should "adopt the perspective of a reasonable person's reaction to a similar environment under essentially like or similar circumstances." The reasonable person standard was endorsed in *Harris v. Forklift Systems, Inc.* (1993) and *Oncale v. Sundowner Offshore Services, Inc.* (1998). But, in the *Oncale* case, Justice Scalia focused on the context in which the alleged harassment occurred. He also stated that harassment "should be judged from the perspective of a reasonable person in the plaintiff's position."

The reasonable victim standard was endorsed by the 6th Circuit in *Ellison v. Brady* (1991). Consequently, other decisions in the 6th Circuit used the reasonable victim standard (e.g., *Davis v. Monsanto Chemical Company* [1988][b] and *Yates v. Avco Corporation* [1987]).[c] The reasonable victim standard has also been labeled as the "reasonable woman standard" partly because women are the majority of sexual harassment victims. In addition, the reasonable victim/woman standard was believed to be a fairer approach to assessing sexual harassment claims by incorporating the work experience of women.

For instance, research has indicated that women are more likely than men to judge behaviors as indicating sexual harassment (e.g., Burgess & Borgida, 1997; Popovich, Gehlauf, Jolton, & Somers, 1992; Shoenfelt, Maue, & Nelson, 2002). However, other researchers have found no, small, or moderate sex differences in defining behaviors as indicating sexual harassment (e.g., Blumenthal, 1998; Gutek, 1995; Katz, Hannon,

& Whitten, 1996; Rotundo, Nguyen, & Sackett, 2001) and that sex differences primarily exist when evidence is slight or ambiguous (Gutek, & O'Connor, 1995; O'Leary-Kelly, Bowes-Sperry, Bates, & Lean, 2009).

An important question is whether the use of a reasonable person versus a victim/woman standard makes a difference in inferring the existence of sexual harassment. The answer appears to be "no." For instance, Wiener et al. (1995) varied the standard (reasonable person vs. woman) for raters to use in assessing whether or not sexual harassment was present. The authors concluded that the different standards had no effect on the final judgments that were reached.

In another study, Shoenfelt et al. (2002) gave undergraduate students case scenarios to evaluate using each standard. In the end, the authors found that the standards failed to make a difference in sexual harassment determinations. In discussing whether the standard used is consequential, they stated, "The results of our study indicate the answer is 'No,' supporting our tenet that the argument over standards is moot."

[a] https://scholar.google.com/scholar_case?case=2052355767863111248&hl=en&as_sdt=6&as_vis=1&oi=scholarr

[b] https://casetext.com/case/davis-v-monsanto-chemical-co

[c] https://scholar.google.com/scholar_case?case=5819952823558801741&hl=en&as_sdt=6&as_vis=1&oi=scholarr

Definition of a Supervisor

Finally, an important decision regarding workplace harassment (including sexual harassment) is the case of *Vance v. Ball State University* (1993).[31,32] The fundamental issue in this case was what responsibilities are required for someone to be considered a "supervisor." Essentially, is a supervisor restricted to those who can take tangible employment actions against employees (e.g., hiring, demotion, discipline, termination), or could it also include someone who controls the daily work activities of others (e.g., job duties, schedules)? The latter position was adopted by the EEOC. Maetta Vance, a Black woman, sued the university claiming that a coworker created a hostile work environment for individuals of color. Consequently, she contended that the school was vicariously liable. Vance alleged that her coworker functioned as her supervisor since she directed her daily work activities. Whether or not this was

[31] https://www.law.cornell.edu/supct/pdf/11-556.pdf
[32] https://www.oyez.org/cases/2012/11-556

true was a point of disagreement in the case. In the end, the Supreme Court disagreed with the EEOC and ruled that a supervisor must be a person who is responsible for taking tangible employment actions, not one who only directs someone's work activities.

Although most often committed by supervisors, coworkers and clients can also commit sexual harassment. In these latter instances, the courts will often look at whether organizations took swift action to fix any existing problems, as well as the extent of control they possessed over a given situation. However, in these instances a plaintiff cannot claim vicarious liability.

Same-Sex Sexual Harassment

Protections for sexual harassment extend to both men and women. Moreover, given the Supreme Court's decision in *Oncale v. Sundowner Offshore Services, Inc.* (1998),[33,34] same-sex sexual harassment is also covered. In the *Oncale* case, supervisors allegedly subjected Joseph Oncale to verbal and physical sexual abuse, including a threat of rape. When his complaints were ignored, Oncale quit his job and sued for sexual harassment. The Supreme Court ruled in favor of Oncale, concluding that any type of discrimination "because of sex" was a violation of Title VII.

That being said, case law surrounding same-sex sexual harassment after the *Oncale* decision has not been as straightforward or as consistent as one would expect. For instance, the "because of sex" criterion in *Oncale* indicated that harassment due to one's *sexual orientation* was *not* protected under Title VII. This has resulted in some court decisions rejecting same-sex sexual harassment when the victim was gay—that the harassment was not "because of sex" but because of sexual orientation (see *Bibby v. Philadelphia Coca-Cola Bottling Co.*, 2001;[35] *Spearman v. Ford Motor Company*, 2000).[36] Interestingly, in *Bibby*, the court stated that "Harassment on the basis of sexual orientation has no place in our society." But the decision further noted that "Congress has not yet seen fit, however, to provide protection against such harassment. Because the evidence produced by Bibby—and, indeed, his very claim—indicated only that he was being harassed on the basis of his sexual orientation, rather than because of his sex, . . . there was no cause of action under Title VII." However, given the

---

[33] https://www.law.cornell.edu/supct/html/96-568.ZO.html
[34] https://www.oyez.org/cases/1997/96-568
[35] https://caselaw.findlaw.com/us-3rd-circuit/1302058.html
[36] https://caselaw.findlaw.com/us-7th-circuit/1203626.html

decision in *Bostock v. Clayton County, Georgia (2020)*,[37] where the Court found that if organizations fire someone for being gay or transgender it is a violation of Title VII, harassing an individual based on their sexual orientation or transgender status would also be against the law. As the EEOC has stated, "Discrimination also includes severe or pervasive harassment. It is unlawful for an employer to create or tolerate such harassment based on sexual orientation or gender identity." https://www.eeoc.gov/laws/guidance/protections-against-employment-discrimination-based-sexual-orientation-or-gender.

One defense used by companies is that the alleged behavior was not based on sex but was a form of "horseplay" (e.g., nonsexual playing around). This defense has often been employed when the alleged harassers were heterosexual. But inconsistent rulings exist on this point. For instance, in *McCown v. St. John's Health System* (2015),[38] the horseplay defense was successful, while in other cases the defense failed (*Martin v. Schwan's Sales Enterprises*, 1999; *Shepard v. Slater Steels Corporation*, 1999).[39]

Finally, there is the question of the legality of an "equal opportunity/bisexual harasser"—one who harasses both men and women in the workplace. For example, in *Holman v. Indiana* (2000),[40] the plaintiffs, Steven and Karen Holman, alleged that they were both sexually harassed by their supervisor. In the end, the Court of Appeals for the 7th Circuit ruled that such harassment was *not* a violation of law since the harassment was directed at a man and a woman. As the Court concluded, "Title VII does not cover the 'equal opportunity' or 'bisexual' harasser," then, because such a person is not *discriminating* on the basis of sex." However, some courts (e.g., *Steiner v. Showboat Operating Co.*, 1994) and the EEOC have rejected the legitimacy of this defense. One reason is the "belief that even a bisexual harasser is acting because of sex at the particular time he is propositioning either of the two genders" (Gutman, 2005, p. 73).

Sexual Harassment and Constructive Discharge

Pennsylvania State Police v. Suders (2004)[41,42] was a sexual harassment case that involved the issue of *constructive discharge*. Constructive discharge

---

[37] https://scholar.google.com/scholar_case?case=12024108937688553939&q=bostock+v+clayton+county+georgia&hl=en&as_sdt=40006
[38] https://caselaw.findlaw.com/us-8th-circuit/1173790.html
[39] https://caselaw.findlaw.com/us-7th-circuit/1078709.html
[40] https://caselaw.findlaw.com/us-7th-circuit/1348156.html
[41] https://www.law.cornell.edu/supct/pdf/03-95P.ZO
[42] https://www.oyez.org/cases/2003/03-95

basically refers to situations where the work environment becomes so unbearable that a *reasonable person* would be prompted or induced to quit. Nancy Drew Suders claimed that she had been sexually harassed by supervisors on a regular basis. Although she was told there would be negative consequences if she protested the harassment, she complained to the organization's equal employment opportunity (EEO) office, which largely ignored her complaint (Suders contended that she was incorrectly instructed by the EEO office on how to file her complaint). She was also charged with stealing and treated like a suspect (e.g., handcuffed, mug shots taken).

After working for only four months, Suders decided to quit. She filed a suit contending that she was a victim of sexual harassment and constructive discharge (being provoked to quit). The Supreme Court's ruling was restricted to the constructive discharge claim. The Court ruled in favor of Suders on constructive discharge, declaring the harassment she suffered constituted a working environment that a reasonable person would find unbearable. The Court also added that, under certain conditions, constructive discharge *may* constitute a tangible employment action and prompt "strict" employer liability, or *strict liability*.[43] Such liability depends on the extent to which specific, negative employment actions were authorized or sanctioned by organizations. So, if a negative change in an employee's job position was deemed to be an official company act, strict liability would likely apply. If so, similar to *quid pro quo* harassment, organizations would not have the opportunity to use an affirmative defense to contest liability. But if the role of organizations was less certain in this regard, companies may use the affirmative defense identified by the Court in the *Ellerth* and *Faragher* cases. As a reminder, an affirmative defense allows companies to demonstrate that they had an approach to *prevent* and *promptly correct* any sexually harassing behavior and that plaintiffs *unreasonably* failed to use *preventive or corrective* opportunities provided by the organization. A summary of sexual harassment settlements with the EEOC is provided in Table 5.8.

---

[43] Under strict liability, *no* affirmative defense is available to organizations, as is the case with *quid pro quo* cases. An affirmative defense consists of evidence presented by the defense which can limit or negate liability.

Table 5.8 Selected Equal Employment Opportunity Commission (EEOC) sexual harassment (SH) settlements

Organization (year of settlement)	Specific allegation(s)	Settlement and primary relief
Marelli Tennessee USA, LLC (2020)[1]	Women employees sexually harassed by supervisor (man); company failed to act after women complained of the harassing behavior.	• $335,000 damage award • Two-year consent decree • Alter sexual harassment policy • Yearly sexual harassment training
HM Solutions, Inc. (2020)[2]	Several women employees subjected to sexually hostile work environment; women subsequently fired for complaining after repeated complaints.	• $315,000 damage award • Two-year consent decree • Annual Title VII training • Revise anti-discrimination policy
Washington Resorts (2020)[3]	Women employees subjected to sexual harassment (offensive comments, groping); company failed to curtail harassment after complaints were made known.	• $570,000 damage award • Five-year consent decree • Develop policies and training regarding discrimination and harassment
Uber Technologies, Inc. (2019)[4]	Company alleged to have allowed a culture of sexual harassment and retaliation.	• $4.4 million damage award • Three-year consent decree • Identify employees alleging more than one instance of harassment • Identify managers who fail to respond to alleged sexual harassment
Waikiki Sports Bar (2019)[5]	Patrons and owners repeatedly sexually harassed workers (offensive comments, touching).	• $255,302 court ordered damage award (includes back pay and compensatory and punitive damages)
International House of Pancakes (2018)	Failed to take corrective action after complaints made. Retaliation and constructive discharge. Improper sexual comments, groping, physical threats by coworkers and managers.	• $975,000 damage award • Four-year consent decree • Changes to the sexual harassment policy and complaint procedures • Mandated sexual harassment training, improved records of sexual harassment complaints[6]
Las Trancas Restaurant (2018)[7]	Creation of hostile work environment (e.g., sexual grabbing/touching, sexual comments, intimidating behaviors); retaliation (e.g., firing, constructive discharge).	• $66,598 damage award • Posting of Title VII rights • Create anti-discrimination policy • Designate an EEO officer and hire third-party consultant to help with future claims
Alorica, Inc. (2018)	Creation of a hostile work environment by coworkers and managers affecting a class of plaintiffs and retaliation.	• Three-year consent decree • 3.5 million payment • SH training; revision of anti-discrimination policies • Establishing an EEO consultant and compliance officer[8]

Table 5.8 Continued

Organization (year of settlement)	Specific allegation(s)	Settlement and primary relief
Applebees, North Myrtle Beach, SC (2018)	Hostile work environment (e.g., groping, sexual comments); reported to several managers—harassment continued.	• Two-year consent decree • $75,000 award • Auditing process to identify and address sexual harassment complaints • SH training for director and managers[9]
Bornt & Sons, Inc. [dba Bornt Family Farms] (2018)	Sexual comments by a manager; grabbing private parts; unwelcome touching/kissing; retaliation for rejecting sexual advances (termination, refusal to hire).	• Three-year consent decree • $300,000 payment • Reinstatement for those retaliated against • Assignment of EEO compliance coordinator for compliance audits • Develop a policy manual on SH and reporting procedures • SH training for all employees[10]
Keller Paving and Landscaping (2018)[11]	Physical and verbal unwelcome sexual behaviors by coworkers.	• $59,000 award • Alter sexual harassment policy • Train non-managerial employees on rights under Title VII[12]
Discovering Hidden Hawaii Tours (2018)[13]	Man-on-man sexual harassment by company president against a class of male employees; retaliation.	• Three-year consent decree • $570,000 award • President relinquish control of company operations • Yearly sexual harassment and retaliation training
Goodwill Industries of the East Bay Area and Calidad Industries (affiliate) (2018)	Hostile work environment against several women employees (e.g., sexual-related touching); retaliation.	• $850,000 damage award • Alter EEO policies and complaint process • Workplace EEO training • Hire consultant to monitor reactions to future complaints[14]
Coral Gables Trust Company (2018)	Hostile work environment against women executive (physical and verbal sexually related behaviors); retaliation.	• $180,000 settlement • Disseminate revised sexual harassment policy • Company-wide sexual harassment training[15]
Scottsdale Wine Café, LLC (2018)	Sexual harassment (sexual comments, touching) based on sexual orientation, real or perceived; retaliation.	• $100,000 court ordered damage award • Refrain from engaging in future discriminatory behavior; disseminate SH and retaliation policies[16]

(continued)

Table 5.8 Continued

Organization (year of settlement)	Specific allegation(s)	Settlement and primary relief
Indi's Fast Food Restaurant, Inc. (2018)	Sexual harassment against 15 former women employees (asking for sexual favors, sexually inappropriate comments and touching).	• $340,000 damage award[17] • Develop new SH policies • Workforce anti-discrimination training • Letters of apology to victims
Rocky Mountain Casing Crews (2017)[18]	Harassment based on sex (toward men) and sexual orientation (e.g., pejorative sex-based comments, slurs).	• $70,000 damage award • Workforce harassment training • Construct SH policy
ABC Phones (2016)	Offensive touching by same-sex female coworker; sexually related remarks.	• $50,000 award • Employee training • Post notice of settlement[19]
Potato Packing Companies (2015)	Sexual harassment and retaliation charges. Inappropriate touching, gestures, and remarks by a supervisor; firing women employees after complaints were made.	• Three-year consent decree • $450,000 payment • Non-engagement in SH and retaliation • Workforce training • Letter of apology to victims • Firing of supervisor[20]

[1] https://www.eeoc.gov/newsroom/marelli-pays-335000-settle-eeoc-sexual-harassment-lawsuit
[2] https://www.eeoc.gov/newsroom/hm-solutions-pay-315000-settle-eeoc-sexual-harassment-and-retaliation-lawsuit
[3] https://www.eeoc.gov/newsroom/washington-resorts-pay-570000-settle-eeoc-sexual-harassment-lawsuit
[4] https://www.eeoc.gov/newsroom/uber-pay-44-million-resolve-eeoc-sexual-harassment-and-retaliation-charge
[5] https://www.eeoc.gov/newsroom/court-orders-waikiki-sports-bar-pay-over-250000-sexual-harassment
[6] https://www.eeoc.gov/eeoc/newsroom/release/7-19-18.cfm
[7] https://www.eeoc.gov/newsroom/las-trancas-restaurant-pay-66598-settle-eeoc-sexual-harassment-and-retaliation-lawsuit
[8] https://www.eeoc.gov/eeoc/newsroom/release/8-1-18.cfm
[9] https://www.eeoc.gov/eeoc/newsroom/release/7-17-18.cfm
[10] https://www.eeoc.gov/eeoc/newsroom/release/7-25-18.cfm
[11] https://www.eeoc.gov/newsroom/keller-paving-and-landscaping-pay-59000-settle-eeoc-sexual-harassment-lawsuit
[12] https://www.eeoc.gov/eeoc/newsroom/release/7-25-18.cfm
[13] https://www.eeoc.gov/newsroom/discovering-hidden-hawaii-tours-pay-570000-settle-eeoc-male-male-sexual-harassment-suit
[14] https://www.eeoc.gov/eeoc/newsroom/release/5-10-18.cfm
[15] https://www.eeoc.gov/eeoc/newsroom/release/4-4-18.cfm
[16] https://www.eeoc.gov/eeoc/newsroom/release/4-2-18a.cfm
[17] https://www.eeoc.gov/eeoc/newsroom/release/1-8-18.cfm
[18] https://www.eeoc.gov/newsroom/rocky-mountain-casing-crews-pay-70000-sexual-harassment
[19] https://www.eeoc.gov/eeoc/newsroom/release/10-31-16.cfm
[20] https://www.eeoc.gov/eeoc/newsroom/release/10-7-15.cfm

Retrieved from EEOC Press Releases: https://www.eeoc.gov/newsroom/search

Insights from Social Science: Using Organizational Justice Climate to Prevent Sexual Harassment

A number of approaches have been employed to prevent sexual harassment. For instance, organizations have developed policies that prohibit sexual harassment, which may include specific complaint procedures for alleged victims (e.g., Becton, Gilstrap, & Forsyth, 2017; Riger, 1991). Another common approach is to offer regular sexual harassment training programs for managers and employees (e.g., Antecol & Cobb-Clark, 2003; Meyer, 1992), which can be part of an overall approach to enhancing diversity (e.g., Bezrukova, Jehn, & Spell, 2012). However, the establishment of policies and training programs has had limited success in confronting sexual harassment[a] (Suddath, 2016), a conclusion supported by an EEOC taskforce.

A promising approach is to concentrate on organizational-level factors to prevent sexual harassment (Hulin, Fitzgerald, & Drasgow, 1996). In particular, researchers have stated that the establishment of a climate that focuses on emphasizing organizational justice (fairness) perceptions may enhance interpersonal interactions at work and help prevent sexual harassment (Liao & Rupp, 2005).

Rubino et al. (2018) conducted separate studies on two large military samples. They concluded that self-reported incidents of sexual harassment were lower when individuals perceived the climate of their organization as being fair and just. Higher justice perceptions also limited the role of other factors that have been shown to lead to sexual harassment, such as the gender representation of one's work team (e.g., few women relative to men) and perceived organizational tolerance for harassment.

As the authors concluded, "In addition to the sexual harassment policy guidelines put forth by the EEOC (EEOC, 2017)[b] organizations could more broadly focus on strategically promoting fairness in outcome decisions, processes, and treatment of employees rather than focusing on harassment specifically, which will not only yield similar results but can produce organizational environments that facilitate equity and reduce the likelihood of identity-based mistreatment in general" (p. 539).

[a] https://www.bloomberg.com/features/2016-sexual-harassment-policy/#/

[b] https://www.eeoc.gov/laws/types/sexual_harassment_guidance.cfm

Supplemental Readings on Sexual Harassment

Beginner

Meinert, D. (2018, February). How to investigate sexual harassment allegations. SHRM Puerto Rico Chapter. https://www.shrmpr.org/investigate-sexual-harassment-allegations/

Miller, C. C. (2017, December). Sexual harassment training doesn't work. But some things do. *The New York Times*. https://www.nytimes.com/2017/12/11/upshot/sexual-harassment-workplace-prevention-effective.html

Workplacefairmess.org. Sexual harassment—legal standards. https://www.workplacefairness.org/sexual-harassment-legal-rights

Intermediate

EEOC Enforcement Guidance on Vicarious Liability in Sexual Harassment Cases (1999). https://www.eeoc.gov/policy/docs/harassment.html

EEOC Policy Guidance on Current Issues of Sexual Harassment. Section 703(a)(1) of Title VII, 42 U.S.C. § 2000e-2(a) (2010). https://www.eeoc.gov/laws/guidance/policy-guidance-current-issues-sexual-harassment

Findlaw. (n.d.). Sexual harassment at work. https://employment.findlaw.com/employment-discrimination/sexual-harassment-at-work.html

McDonald, P. (2012). Workplace sexual harassment 30 years on: A review of the literature. *International Journal of Management Reviews, 14*(1), 1–17.

New York Times. Sexual harassment. [Times Topics archival site]. (n.d.). *The New York Times*. https://www.nytimes.com/topic/subject/sexual-harassment

Advanced

Feldblum, C. R., & Lipnic, V. A. (2016). Select task force on the study of harassment in the workplace. US Equal Employment Opportunity Commission. https://www.eeoc.gov/select-task-force-study-harassment-workplace

Fitzgerald, L. F., & Cortina, L. M. (2018). Sexual harassment in work organizations: A view from the 21st century. In C. B Travis, J. W. White, A. Rutherford, W. S. Williams, S. L. Cook, & K. F. Wyche (Eds.), APA handbooks in psychology series. *APA handbook of the psychology of women: Perspectives on women's private and public lives* (pp. 215–234). Washington, DC: American Psychological Association.

Quick, J. C., & McFadyen, M. A. (2017). Sexual harassment: Have we made any progress? *Journal of Occupational Health Psychology, 22,* 286–298.

Wiener, R. L., & Hurt, L. E. (1997). Social sexual conduct at work: How do workers know when it is harassment and when it is not? *California Western Law Review, 34,* 53–129. https://scholarlycommons.law.cwsl.edu/cwlr/vol34/iss1/4/

Recommendations/Best Practices

- Develop a detailed written policy against sexual harassment. The policy should include information such as a definition of sexual harassment, an outline of complaint/grievance procedures, and a description of the decision-making procedures for any disciplinary actions.

- Respond immediately to all sexual harassment complaints to negate further possible harm (e.g., paid leave for accused, physically separate parties involved).
- Employ trained investigators to process alleged sexual harassment complaints and gather information from both the alleged victim and perpetrator. The information-gathering process can be quite complex, but some basic data are important to gather. For example, the interview with the alleged victim ought to gather information about the nature of the incident and circumstances involved, the victim's response(s), the existence of any corroborating evidence, and consequences to the victim of the harassing behavior. For the accused, key questions to ask include:
  - Did the accused engage in any of the alleged sexual harassing behavior?
  - Did the accused know that their behavior was perceived as unwelcome?
  - What is the accused's explanation of the charges/evidence provided?
  - Were there any witnesses to the alleged behavior?
- Protect those who complain of sexual harassment (e.g., maintain confidentiality, protect from retaliation). It is important to note that retaliation is not limited to supervisory personnel but can be committed by others, such as coworkers.
- Document all complaints, the facts of investigations, and any resolution(s).
- Create work environments of fairness and mutual respect for all employees. This is useful if connected with organizational mission statements core values, etc. Using managers as models for appropriate behavior can be effective.
- Have regular sexual harassment training for *all* members of organizations (mandatory attendance is advisable). Options for training include the use of scenarios, vignettes, and videos of sexual harassment; role-playing exercises; group discussions. The use of external consultants can be helpful in this regard.

Summary and Take-Aways

This chapter covered legal scenarios for sex discrimination and sexual harassment. One important take-away for legal scenarios is that class action suits containing a sizeable number of plaintiffs will likely face difficulty meeting the commonality requirement (individuals treated in the same manner). Such a requirement can be challenging for plaintiffs within organizations where various decisions are made at different levels and by different people. As Justice Scalia stated in the *Wal-Mart* case,

> Here respondents wish to sue about literally millions of employment decisions at once. Without some glue holding the alleged reasons for all those decisions together, it will be impossible to say that examination of all the class members' claims for relief will produce a common answer to the crucial question *why was I disfavored*.

So, in the future, victims intending to be considered as a class must show they are homogeneous in suffering from the same specific employment practice.

Given the Bostock decision, sexual harassment based on one's sexual orientation or transgender status is a violation of Title VII.

Finally, the long-term implications of the Supreme Court's less expansive definition of a supervisor in the *Vance* case is unknown. In restricting supervisors to only those who are responsible for tangible employment decisions, the ruling arguably ignores the manner in which workplace supervision and organizational structures have changed (a point made by the dissent in *Vance*). For instance, many decentralized or team-based companies have individuals who manage the work duties of others but are not involved in hiring, suspension, demotion, or termination decisions (tangible employment actions). Given the Court's ruling in *Vance*, these individuals are *not* considered to be supervisors but more coworkers. As such, the motivation to prevent harassment by individuals in these types of roles may be lowered. One reason is that for instances of alleged coworker harassment, plaintiffs generally have to demonstrate that organizations failed to take corrective action—a more difficult burden than exists for supervisor harassment cases (see Vodanovich & Piotrowski, 2014). As Justice Ginsberg stated in her dissent in *Vance*, "The ball is once again in Congress' court to correct the error into which this Court has fallen, and to restore the robust protections against workplace harassment the Court weakens today." Time will tell if Congress accepts this challenge.

Glossary

Adverse impact: When facially neutral selection criteria disproportionately exclude a higher percentage of one group relative to another. These differences are often assessed by using the four-fifths rule or statistical significance tests.

Affirmative defense: A defense raised that contains facts contrary to those stated by the plaintiff and which justifies the challenged actions.

Bona fide occupational qualification: Defense applies to facial discrimination (i.e., "need not apply" rules) based on sex, national origin, religion, and age but only if the defendant can prove it is reasonably necessary for the essence of the business to exclude all or most members of these protected classes.

Class action: One or more plaintiffs who represent a group of plaintiffs similarly affected by the defendant's actions, along with their counsel, bring a lawsuit against one or more defendants.

Commonality requirement: The requirement, applied in class action certification, that questions of law or fact are common to the entire class.

Consent decree: Agreement or settlement between two parties that concludes a lawsuit instead of resolving the case through a hearing and/or trial. Consent decrees and consent judgments are the same.

Constructive discharge: Discrimination or harassment so egregious that would compel a reasonable person in the same position to resign.

Declarative relief: A decision of the rights of those involved in a suit under a given law. No monetary awards are involved.

Direct evidence: Evidence which proves the existence of an alleged fact without needing inference or presumption. Direct evidence can not only suggest discrimination [or retaliation], or be subject to more than one interpretation.

Disparate treatment: Intentionally treating an individual or group less favorably than another due to protected group status (e.g., race, religion, national origin, sex, disability).

Hostile work environment: An environment that is intimidating, offensive, or unreasonably interferes with an employee's work performance.

Indirect evidence: Also referred to as circumstantial evidence, indirect evidence helps to establish the main fact by inference.

Injunctive relief: A court-ordered remedy that requires a given party to do, or not do, a given activity.

Mixed-motive cases: Cases where illegal and legal factors motivate an employment decision.

Monetary damages/relief: Compensation given to an injured party by a liable party (e.g., back pay, lost salary, fringe benefits, bonuses, compensation for pain and suffering).

Numerosity clause: The class is so numerous that claims by individuals are unrealistic.

Plaintiff: The party who initiates a lawsuit.

Plurality: Receiving the greatest number, but not a majority, of the votes.

Precedent: Deference to a prior reported opinion (often of an appeals court) to form the basis of a legal argument in a subsequent case; the principle announced by a higher court that should be followed in later cases.

Preponderance of evidence: Evidence that indicates that a violation of law (e.g., discrimination) was more likely than not to be true. This is the type of evidence commonly used in civil trials and is the least strict standard of evidence as compared to beyond a reasonable doubt and clear and convincing evidence.

Presumptive evidence: Evidence that the alleged discrimination was "more likely than not" to have transpired.

Prima facie: Latin phrase for "at first glance." Consists of presenting evidence that is presumed to be true.

Quid pro quo: Latin phrase literally meaning "something for something." Getting something of value in exchange for giving something of value. Often seen in sexual harassment cases.

Reasonable person standard: Standard often used to determine whether a hostile work environment exists in sexual harassment cases. Consists of assessing whether behavior would be considered as hostile from the perspective of a reasonable person (or a reasonable person from the point of view of the victim).

Strict liability: Cases where no affirmative defense is available to organizations to limit or negate liability, as is the case with quid pro quo cases.

Vicarious liability: Cases where organizations are responsible for the behavior of their supervisors or "agents" of the company.

Glossary terms adapted from Gutman et al. (2011); https://uslegal.com/, and merriamwebster.com/legal.

Cases Cited

Bibby v. Philadelphia Coca-Cola Bottling Co., 260 F.3d 257, 260-61 (3rd Cir. 2001).

Bostock v. Clayton County, 140 S. Ct. 1731, 1739 (2020).

Burlington Industries v. Ellerth, 524 U.S. 742 (1998).

Davis v. Monsanto Chemical Company, 858 F.2d 345 (6th Cir. 1988).

Desert Palace, Inc. v. Costa, 539 U.S. 90 (2003).

Dothard v. Rawlinson, 433 U.S. 321 (1977).

Ellison v. Brady, 924 F.2d 872 (9th Cir. 1991).

Faragher v. City of Boca Raton, 524 U.S. 775 (1998) (No. 97-282).

Griggs v. Duke Power Co., 401 U.S. 424 (1971).

Harris v. Forklift Sys. Inc., 510 U.S. 17 (1993).

Holman v. Indiana, 211 F.3d 399 (7th Cir. 2000).

Martin v. Schwan's Sales Enterprises, App. Lexis 31975 (6th Cir 1999).

McCown v. St. John's Health System, 349 F.3d 540, 543-44 (8th Cir. 2003).

McDonnell Douglas Corp. v. Green, 411 U.S. 792 (1973).

Meritor Savings Bank v. Vinson, 477 U.S. 57 (1986).

Oncale v. Sundowner Offshore Services, Inc., 523 U.S. 75 (1998).

Pennsylvania State Police v. Suders, 542 U.S. 129 (2004).

Price Waterhouse v. Hopkins, 490 U.S. 228 (1989).

Rabidue v. Osceola Refining Company, 805 F. 2d 611 (6th Cir. 1986).

Rafael Ortiz v. DMD Florida Restaurant Group, Southern District of Florida, Case number 0:16-cv-61375. (2016).

Shepherd v. Slater Steels Corporation, 168 F.3d 998, (7th Cir. 1999)

Spearman v. Ford Motor Company, 231 F.3d 1080, (7th Cir. 2000).

Steiner v. Showboat Operating Co., 25 F.3d 1459, 1463 (9th Cir. 1994).

Teamsters Local Union No. 117 v. Washington Department of Corrections, 789, F.3rd, 979 (9th Cir., 2015)

Texas Dept. of Community Affairs v. Burdine, 450 U.S. 248 (1981).

United Automobile Workers v. Johnson Controls, Inc., 499 U.S. 187 (1991).

Vance v. Ball State University, 570 U.S. 421 (2013).

Wal-Mart v. Dukes, 564 U.S. 338, 350 (2011).

Wards Cove Packing Co. v. Atonio, 490 U.S. 642 (1989).

Watson v. Fort Worth Bank & Trust, 487 U.S. 977 (1988).

Wilson v. Chertoff, 699 F.Supp.2d 364 (D. Mass. 2010).

Yates v. Avco Corporation, 819 F. 2d 630 (6th Cir. 1987).

References

Aamodt, M. (2017). Really, I come here for the food: Sex as a BFOQ for restaurant servers. *The Industrial-Organizational Psychologist, 54*(3). https://www.siop.org/Research-Publications/TIP/TIP-Back-Issues/2017/January/ArtMID/20301/ArticleID/1624/Really-I-Come-Here-for-The-Food-Sex-as-a-BFOQ-for-Restaurant-Servers

Antecol, H., & Cobb-Clark, D. (2003). Does sexual harassment training change attitudes? A view from the federal level. *Social Science Quarterly, 84,* 826–842.

Becton, J. B., Gilstrap, J. B., & Forsyth, M. (2017). Preventing and correcting workplace harassment: Guidelines for employers. *Business Horizons, 60,* 101–111.

Bezrukova, K., Jehn, K. A., & Spell, C. S. (2012). Reviewing diversity training: Where we have been and where we should go. *Academy of Management Learning & Education, 11,* 207–227.

Blumenthal, J. A. (1998). The reasonable woman standard: A meta-analytic review of gender differences in perceptions of sexual harassment. *Law and Human Behavior, 22,* 33–57.

Burgess, D., & Borgida, E. (1997). Sexual harassment: An experimental test of sex-role spillover theory. *Personality and Social Psychology Bulletin 23,* 63–75.

Dunleavy, E. M., & Gutman, A. (2008). *Ledbetter v. Goodyear Tire Co.*: A divided Supreme Court causes quite a stir. *The Industrial-Organizational Psychologist, 45,* 55–63.

Equal Employment Opportunity Commission (EEOC). (2017). *Policy guidance documents related to sexual harassment.* Retrieved from https://www.eeoc.gov/laws/types/sexual_harassment_guidance.cfm

Fitzgerald, L. F., Swan, S. C., & Fischer, K. (1995). Why didn't she just report him? The psychological and legal implications of women's responses to sexual harassment. *Journal of Social Issues, 51,* 117–138.

Gutek, B. A. (1995). How subjective is sexual harassment? An examination of rater effects. *Basic and Applied Social Psychology, 17*(4), 447–467.

Gutek, B. A., & O'Connor, M. (1995). The empirical basis for the reasonable woman standard. *Journal of Social Issues, 51*(1), 151–166.

Gutek, B. A., & Stockdale, M. S. (2005). In F. Landy (Ed.), *Employment discrimination litigation: Behavioral, quantitative, and legal perspectives.* (pp. 229–254). San Francisco: Jossey-Bass.

Gutman, A. (2005). Unresolved issues in same-sex harassment. *The Industrial-Organizational Psychologist, 42,* 67–75.

Gutman, A., & Dunleavy, E. (2011). A review of the Supreme Court ruling *Wal-Mart v. Dukes*: Too big to succeed? *The Industrial-Organizational Psychologist, 49*(2), 75–80.

Hulin, C. L., Fitzgerald, L. F., & Drasgow, F. (1996). Organizational influences on sexual harassment. In M. S. Stockdale & M. S. Stockdale (Eds.), *Sexual harassment in the workplace: Perspectives, frontiers, and response strategies* (pp. 127–150). Thousand Oaks, CA: Sage Publications.

Katz, R. C., Hannon, R., & Whitten, L. (1996). Effects of gender and situation on the perception of sexual harassment. *Sex Roles, 34*(1-2), 35–42.

Liao, H., & Rupp, D. E. (2005). The impact of justice climate and justice orientation on work outcomes: Across-level multifoci framework. *Journal of Applied Psychology, 90,* 242–256.

McDonald, P. (2012). Workplace sexual harassment 30 years on: A review of the literature. *International Journal of Management Reviews, 14*(1), 1–17.

Meyer, A. (1992). Getting to the heart of sexual harassment. *HR Magazine, 37*(7), 82–84.

O'Leary-Kelly, A., Bowes-Sperry, L., Bates, C., & Lean, E. (2009). Sexual harassment at work: A decade (plus) of progress. *Journal of Management, 35,* 503–536.

Popovich, P. M., Gehlauf, D. N., Jolton, J. A., & Somers, J. M. (1992). Perceptions of sexual harassment as a function of sex of rater and incident form and consequence. *Sex Roles, 27,* 609–625.

Potter, E. E. (1989). Employer's burden of proof may be reduced in testing cases. *The Industrial-Organizational Psychologist, 26,* 43–47.

Riger, S. (1991). Gender dilemmas in sexual harassment policies and procedures. *American Psychologist, 46,* 497–505.

Rotundo, M., Nguyen, D.-H., & Sackett, P. R. (2001). A meta-analytic review of gender differences in perceptions of sexual harassment. *Journal of Applied Psychology, 86,* 914–922.

Rubino, C., Avery, D. R., McKay, P. F., Moore, B. L., Wilson, D. C., Van Driel, M. S., . . . McDonald, D. P. (2018). And justice for all: How organizational justice climate deters sexual harassment. *Personnel Psychology, 71,* 519–544.

Shoenfelt, E. L., Maue, A. E., Nelson, J. (2002). Reasonable person versus reasonable woman: Does it matter? *Journal of Gender, Social Policy and Law, 10,* 633–672.

Suddath, C. (2016). Why can't we stop sexual harassment at work? *Bloomberg Business Week.* Retrieved from https://www.bloomberg.com/features/2016-sexual-harassment-policy//

Vodanovich, S. J., & Piotrowski, C. (2014). What constitutes the definition of supervisor in workplace harassment cases? *Journal of Instructional Psychology, 41,* 97–99.

Wiener, R. L., Watts, B. A., Goldkamp, K. H., & Gaspar, C. (1995). Social analytic investigation of hostile work environments: A test of the reasonable woman standard. *Law and Human Behavior, 19,* 263–281.

6

Sex-Specific Workplace Discrimination

Equal Pay, Pregnancy/FMLA, Dress/Appearance, LGBTQ+ Issues

In Chapter 5), we discussed sex discrimination/sexual harassment more generally. In this chapter we take on more specific forms of sex discrimination, including equal pay, pregnancy, dress/appearance, and LGBTQ+ issues. We begin this chapter with a discussion of some of the earliest sex-based discrimination law—that which pertains to (un)equal pay.

Employment Discrimination. Stephen J. Vodanovich and Deborah E. Rupp, Oxford University Press. © Oxford University Press 2022. DOI: 10.1093/oso/9780190085421.003.0007

Equal Pay

Equal Pay Act (EPA) of 1963

Introduction

The mandating of equal pay for equal work has been a lengthy battle. Attempts to authorize equal pay were made during the late 19th century and specific bills failed in Congress from 1945 to 1962 (see Claussen, 1996). Unsuccessful bills to guarantee equal pay used the phrase *comparable*[1] work. The current version of the Equal Pay Act (EPA) eventually passed only after the word "comparable" was replaced with the word "equal." The EPA,[2] which was passed the year before Title VII of the Civil Rights Act, makes it illegal to pay men and women different rates of pay for jobs consisting of *equal* work within the same establishment (e.g., Cooper & Barrett, 1984; Crampton, Hodge, & Mishra, 1997). Even though equal pay has been a social and political issue for quite some time, suits filed with the Equal Employment Opportunity Commission (EEOC) are relatively infrequent (see Table 6.1). For instance, since 2014, EPA claims have averaged about 1,000 claims annually while those for race, sex, and retaliation have averaged approximately 29,000, 26,000, and 40,000 per year, respectively.[3]

The EPA is contained within the Fair Labor Standards Act[4] and is a very specific law. It protects pay discrimination solely on the basis of sex. Under the Act, jobs are considered to be equal if they require the same (a) skill, (b) effort, (c) responsibility, and (d) work conditions.

Table 6.1 Equal pay act charges filed with the Equal Employment Opportunity Commission (EEOC) 2013–2020

Year	2013	2014	2015	2016	2017	2018	2019	2020
Number of Charges	1,019	938	973	1,075	996	1,066	1,117	980

Retrieved from https://www.eeoc.gov/eeoc/statistics/enforcement/charges.cfm

---

[1] Italicized technical terms are defined in the glossary at the end of this chapter.
[2] https://www.eeoc.gov/laws/statutes/epa.cfm
[3] https://www.eeoc.gov/eeoc/statistics/enforcement/charges.cfm
[4] https://www.dol.gov/whd/regs/statutes/FairLaborStandAct.pdf

Table 6.2 Process for Equal Pay Act (EPA) claims

Phase 1	Plaintiffs must show that differences in rates of pay exist between males and females in a given establishment and that jobs are equal regarding *skill, effort, responsibility, and work conditions* (jobs do NOT have to be identical but be substantially equal).
Phase 2	Defendants can use any of four affirmative statutory defenses to prove that pay differences are due to either seniority, merit, quantity or quality of work, or any factor other than sex (FOS). Minor differences in any category are insufficient to justify a claim.
Phase 3	Plaintiffs offer proof that the defendant's reasons are a *pretext* for pay differences *based on sex.*

Process

Table 6.2 lays out the process by which an EPA case unfolds. Under the EPA, *plaintiffs* (i.e., those who are accusing the defendant of wrongdoing), must first (phase 1) establish that their rate of pay is less than someone of the opposite sex who performs equal work in the same establishment. Unlike Title VII, even organizations with *fewer* than 15 employees are required to comply with the EPA. That is, only one opposite-sex individual (or comparator) is needed to pursue an EPA claim.

An *establishment* is often a physical location. However, a key aspect in determining the establishment involves where central administration occurs. For instance, in *Brennan v. Goose Creek Consolidated Independent School District* (1975),[5] the average salary of female janitors was lower than male janitors at different schools. A pay discrimination suit was filed, and the defense countered that the janitors worked at different establishments/locations. However, it was concluded that the school district, rather than the individual schools, controlled the work of janitors (e.g., pay, hiring, schedules, location of work). Consequently, the suit was successful.

If plaintiffs satisfy that equal jobs are differentially paid as a function of employee sex, organizations can defend themselves (in phase 2) by providing evidence that the pay differences are not based on sex but on *any* of the following:

1. a seniority system,
2. a merit system,
3. a system based on quantity or quality of production, or
4. any *factor other than sex* (FOS).

[5] https://scholar.google.com/scholar_case?case=6420261444999942261&hl=en&as_sdt=6&as_vis=1&oi=scholarr

Although the EPA literally states that the use of "any" factor other than sex is legal, a defense is more powerful when the use of factors other than sex are viewed as reasonable and can be justified for legitimate business reasons. For instance, in *Kouba v. Allstate* (1982)[6] the court required a legitimate business rationale to justify the use of previous salary as a FOS. If the company's defense is accepted, plaintiffs have the opportunity to show that the company's stated reason for pay disparities was a pretext for sex discrimination (phase 3).

Organizations have lost many cases for failing to show that the pay disparities alleged by plaintiffs in phase 1 are justified by meaningful differences in job duties. For instance, the use of separate job titles for men and women to defend greater pay for men have not fared well in the courts. Calling male employees "orderlies," "tailors," "bookbinders," and "pursers" and female workers "nurse aides," "seamstresses," "bindery employees," and "stewardesses," respectively, has not been found to justify lower pay for women and is a losing defense (see *Hodgson v. Brookhaven General Hospital*, 1970[7]; *Brennan v. City Stores, Inc.*, 1973[8]; *Laffey v. Northwest Airlines*, 1984[9]; *Thompson v. Sawyer*, 1982[10]). This is true *unless* more evidence is introduced that shows meaningful disparities exist in the work performed.

In addition, paying women less because they work different shifts despite having the same job titles and duties as men is generally not legitimate. In both *Corning Glass Works v. Brennan* (1974)[11,12] and *Schultz v. American Can Co.* (1970),[13] men worked the night shift received greater salaries than women. However, the jobs were found to be substantially equal and the differences in "effort" (*Schultz*) and "working conditions" (*Corning*) were not sufficient to justify pay gaps.

Factors Other Than Sex

One of the defenses that organizations can use to confront an EPA claim is to prove that pay disparities are based on "any factor other than sex." The FOS defense was at issue in the case of *City of Los Angeles Department of Water*

---

[6] https://openjurist.org/691/f2d/873/kouba-v-allstate-insurance-company

[7] https://openjurist.org/436/f2d/719/hodgson-v-brookhaven-general-hospital

[8] https://scholar.google.com/scholar_case?case=15192309171101056 57&hl=en&as_sdt=6&as_vis=1&oi=scholarr

[9] https://openjurist.org/740/f2d/1071/laffey-v-northwest-airlines-inc-laffey

[10] https://scholar.google.com/scholar_case?case=8046493753160085793&hl=en&as_sdt=6&as_vis=1&oi=scholarr

[11] https://scholar.google.com/scholar_case?case=7542299068311812851&hl=en&as_sdt=6&as_vis=1&oi=scholarr

[12] https://www.oyez.org/cases/1973/73-29

[13] https://law.justia.com/cases/federal/appellate-courts/F2/424/356/385127/

& Power v. Manhart (1978).[14],[15] The Department mandated that women had to pay more into the pension program (almost 15% more) than their male counterparts since women, on average, lived longer. This policy was adopted because the cost to the city was greater for women, as a group, compared to men.

After a sex discrimination suit was filed, a key defense by the Department was that their policy was based on longevity (an alleged FOS) and therefore was allowed by the EPA and the Bennett Amendment (discussed later). In reaching its decision, the Court decided that the pension program violated the EPA. That is, the justices found that forcing women to pay more into the pension fund, using actuarial data, was based on a solitary factor: sex.

Past Salary

Another FOS that has been presented by organizations is *past salary*. The previous salary (or salary history) of applicants has been used by companies to justify starting salaries as well as existing pay differences between men and women. Also, employer requests for past salary data (e.g., on job application forms) are quite common (e.g., Jolly & Frierson, 1989; Lax, 2007; Vodanovich & Lowe, 1992; Wallace, Tye, & Vodanovich, 2000; Wallace & Vodanovich, 2004). Consistent with the decision in *Kouba v. Allstate* (1982), organizations are in a better legal position if past salary is one of several factors being considered and/or when a legitimate business reason is proposed to justify its use. However, at present, it is unclear whether prior salary constitutes a lawful FOS in determining pay rates in that the courts have differed on this matter (Hamburg, 1989).

However, a decision by the Court of Appeals for the 9th Circuit determined that the use of past salary is illegal (*Rizo v. Yovino,* 2018).[16] Specifically, the court stated that "prior salary alone or in combination with other factors cannot justify a wage differential." Furthermore, the majority of justices concluded that prior salary does not qualify as an FOS. Essentially, the *Rizo* decision overruled *Kouba v. Allstate* (1982). As stated in the *Rizo* decision:

> Because *Kouba,* however construed, is inconsistent with the rule that we have announced in this opinion, it must be overruled. First, a factor other than sex *must* be one that is job-related, rather than one that "effectuates some business policy." Second, it is impermissible to rely on prior salary to set initial wages. Prior salary

---

[14] https://www.law.cornell.edu/supremecourt/text/435/702
[15] https://www.oyez.org/cases/1977/76-1810
[16] http://cdn.ca9.uscourts.gov/datastore/opinions/2018/04/09/16-15372.pdf

is not job related and it perpetuates the very gender-based assumptions about the value of work that the Equal Pay Act was designed to end. This is true whether prior salary is the sole factor or one of several factors considered in establishing employees' wages.

The *Rizo* decision was vacated by the Supreme Court in February 2019. That is, the Court ruled that the 9th Circuit erred in counting the vote of Judge Stephen Reinhardt, who died 11 days before the decision was released. So, the *Rizo* case was sent back to the 9th Circuit for reconsideration. In 2020, the 9th Circuit affirmed its previous ruling that past salary is not job-related and does not qualify as an FOS.[17] As the court stated,

> Applying the rule that only job-related factors qualify under the EPA's fourth affirmative defense and that prior pay is not one of them, resolution of Rizo's case is straightforward.... Fresno County relied on Rizo's prior pay to justify paying her less than male colleagues who performed the same work.... Rizo's prior wages do not qualify as "any other factor other than sex," and the County cannot use this factor to defeat Rizo's prima facie case. The County cites no other reason for paying Rizo less.

Additionally, there has been a recent push by various states, cities, and counties to make it illegal to ask for salary history information. Currently, several states, Puerto Rico, and various municipalities have passed laws that disallow salary inquiries as a condition of employment (see Table 6.3). Some bans apply to all employers while others are restricted to state and city agencies. See HRDive.com[18] for more detailed information on states regarding who is covered and what actions are prohibited. In contrast, the state of Wisconsin has adopted an opposite approach by making salary history bans illegal. That is, local government agencies are prohibited from implementing bans regarding asking about applicant salary history.

Market Forces
Another FOS that the courts have considered to be illegal in defending pay differences between men and women is *market forces* (see Gutman, Koppes, & Vodanovich, 2011). In several EPA cases mentioned earlier (*Corning Glass*

---

[17] https://scholar.google.com/scholar_case?case=5032995281488089914&q=Rizo+v.+Yovino&hl=en&as_sdt=40006
[18] https://www.hrdive.com/news/salary-history-ban-states-list/516662/

Table 6.3 States and cities banning past salary inquiries

State/Territory bans	Local bans
Alabama	Atlanta
California	San Francisco
Colorado	New Orleans
Connecticut	Montgomery County, MD
Delaware	Chicago
Hawaii	Louisville, KY
Illinois	Chicago, IL
Maine	Jackson, MS
Massachusetts	Kansas City, MO
Michigan	New York City
New Jersey	Albany County, NY
New York	Suffolk County, NY
North Carolina	Cincinnati, OH
Oregon	Westchester County, NY
Pennsylvania	Philadelphia, PA
Puerto Rico	Richland County, SC
Utah	Salt Lake City, UT
Vermont	Pittsburgh, PA
Washington State	

Retrieved from https://www.hrdive.com/news/salary-history-ban-states-list/516662/

Works v. Brennan, 1974; *Hodgson v. Brookhaven General Hospital*, 1970; *Brennan v. City Stores, Inc.*, 1973) the market forces defense (e.g., that men can command greater pay than women) was found to be illegitimate. In other words, paying women less just because other organizations do so is a violation of the EPA.

Bennett Amendment, Title VII, and the EPA

Given that the EPA was passed prior to Title VII of the Civil Rights Act and that sex as a protected group was inserted late into the writing of Title VII, there was concern that the two laws would potentially clash. So, to guarantee that a plaintiff who won an EPA suit would also be victorious with a Title VII claim, the Bennett Amendment was written into Title VII. The Amendment states that

> [i]t shall not be an unlawful employment practice under this sub-chapter for any employer to differentiate upon the basis of sex in determining the amount of the wages or compensation paid or to be paid to employees of such employer if such differentiation is authorized by the provisions of [the Equal Pay Act].

However, on average, the courts have ruled that a victorious EPA suit does not guarantee a Title VII victory and vice versa. One reason for this is that most courts have used the EPA framework for deciding EPA pay discrimination suits while using Title VII rules to decide Title VII pay discrimination cases. That is, a different legal process (e.g., phases, evidence required) is followed depending on which law is claimed to be violated in the suit filed.

Since the burdens of proof are different for the two laws, it has been argued that they are not interchangeable. For instance, under the EPA, sex-based wage differences for jobs of substantially equal work are illegal unless they can be accounted for by one of the four affirmative defenses (i.e., seniority, merit, quality/quantity, FOS). No evidence of intent is needed. Title VII disparate treatment suits (unlike the EPA) demand proof of intentional discrimination; that is, that the pay differential was intentionally sex-based. Another distinction is that Title VII offers wider coverage for sex discrimination, which covers sex-based pay discrimination as well as various terms and conditions of employment, such as hiring, promotions, and termination.

Other key differences between the EPA and Title VII regarding pay discrimination suits include damage awards, time frame for filing suits, and the minimum number of employees a company must have to trigger compliance requirements. These are outlined in Table 6.4.

Given the preceding differences, some pay discrimination challenges are filed under *either* or *both* the EPA and Title VII. As Gutman, Koppes, and Vodanovich (2011) stated, it is most common to use the EPA "for back pay and liquidated damages, and to use Title VII for injunctions (and other Title VII remedies not permitted in the EPA)." *Liquidated damages* are typically included within contracts and specify a given monetary award if contracts are broken. An *injunction* is a court-ordered remedy that requires a party to do or not do a given activity. Thus, filing under both laws can allow plaintiffs to maximize outcomes if successful.

A key question is whether jobs must meet the equal work criteria to be covered by Title VII in pay discrimination suits. Legal opinions have varied on this point. Some have argued that the entire EPA is assimilated within Title

Table 6.4 Distinctions between the Equal Pay Act (EPA) and Title VII pay discrimination claims

EPA	Title VII
Claim must be filed within 2 years (3 years if a willful violation exists)	Claims must be files within 180 days or 300 days, depending on the state
Plaintiffs must prove that jobs are substantially equal	No requirement for jobs to be substantially equal
Opt-in requirement for *class action* suits	Opt-out requirement for class action suits
No *compensatory* or *punitive* damages allowed (*liquidated* damages allowed)	Compensatory and punitive damage awards allowed
Employees must work in the same establishment (e.g., where centralized decisions are made)	No requirement that employees work in the same establishment
No minimum number of employees required; only another "comparator" is required	Only companies with 15 or more employees must comply

VII, thus mandating that equal work be established under Title VII pay discrimination suits. Others maintain that only the four affirmative defenses of the EPA are integrated into Title VII, and, consequently, no proof of equal work is necessary (Miller, 1980). For example, in the case of *Lemons v. City & County of Denver* (1980),[19] the 10th Circuit stated that jobs must be substantially equal for plaintiffs to pursue a Title VII claim. Nurses (mostly women) sued because they were underpaid compared to employees in the "General Administrative Series" classification. Since the jobs being compared were admittedly different, the plaintiffs lost.

The Supreme Court reached a different conclusion in *County of Washington v. Gunther* (1982).[20,21] In this case, correctional officers only worked with inmates of the same sex. An internal job evaluation study determined that female officers should be paid 95% of the salary given to male officers. But the salary of female officers was only approximately 70% compared to men. Given this discrepancy, the female officers filed a Title VII disparate treatment suit contending that the failure of the county to follow its own job evaluation study was evidence of intentional sex discrimination. Importantly, the two jobs were not substantially equal (e.g., male officers oversaw more inmates). As such, the county argued that the Bennett Amendment required that jobs meet the equal

[19] https://scholar.google.com/scholar_case?case=4549575398605606167&hl=en&as_sdt=6&as_vis=1&oi=scholarr
[20] https://scholar.google.com/scholar_case?case=5084465081971356796&hl=en&as_sdt=6&as_vis=1&oi=scholarr
[21] https://www.oyez.org/cases/1980/80-429

work standard for Title VII suits to proceed. The Supreme Court disagreed. They concluded that plaintiffs are *not* limited to the equal work requirement to form a *prima facie* case of pay discrimination. Plaintiffs establish a *prima facie* case by presenting evidence that is presumed to be true (presumptive evidence). Their reasoning was that only the four affirmative EPA defenses (i.e., seniority, merit, quantity or quality of work, any FOS) were merged into Title VII—not proof of equal work. So, plaintiffs had the opportunity form a *prima facie* case of pay discrimination without jobs being substantially equal.

This view gave false hope to proponents of *comparable worth*, a theoretically, practically, and legally complicated concept. At its heart, it is an effort to reduce the traditionally lower pay of women versus men in different jobs/occupations that have arisen due to a myriad of factors including job segregation and market forces. It emphasizes the utility of conducting job evaluation studies to assess the value (or worth) of *dissimilar* but comparable jobs and adjust pay scales accordingly.

But, in *Gunther*, the Supreme Court went out of its way to state that its decision was *not* about comparable worth and that its decision was a narrow one, focusing on the county's refusal to abide by its job evaluation study. The *Gunther* case was decided based on a disparate treatment analysis, so proof of intentional pay discrimination was required to establish a *prima facie* case under Title VII. Ultimately, the decision was restricted in that it merely allowed plaintiffs to *pursue* a claim of sex discrimination under Title VII without proving equal work. As the Court stated, "We do not decide in this case the precise contours of law-suits challenging sex discrimination in compensation under Title VII. It is sufficient to note that respondents' claims of discriminatory undercompensation are not barred by § 703(h) of Title VII merely because respondents do not perform work equal to that of male jail guards." In the end, the county was not required to raise the salary of female officers given that intent to discriminate was not proved.

After *Gunther*, so-called comparable worth suits have been unsuccessful. That is, Title VII and EPA claims applying adverse impact and disparate treatment theory to argue that *different* jobs can involve the same amount of skill, effort, and responsibility under similar working conditions have not been successful (Gutman et al., 2011). Plaintiffs filing under Title VII have contended that "market forces" was the reason why women in comparable (but different) jobs were paid less than men (see *American Federation etc. (AFSCME) v. State of Washington*, 1985[22]; *Spaulding v. University of Washington*, 1984). However,

---

[22] The American Federation of State, County and Municipal Employees (AFSCME) and the State of Washington reached a settlement of almost $5 million to reduce the pay inequities based on gender of roughly 35,000 employees (mostly women), to be distributed across several years.

market forces have not been found to be a "specific employment practice" (a Title VII adverse impact requirement), and statistical data *alone* have not been shown to be sufficient for establishing "intent" (a disparate treatment requirement). Comparable worth suits under the EPA have been unsuccessful as a matter of law (see *Alexander v. Chattahoochee Valley Community College*, 2004; *Little v. Cobb County*, 2006). This is because, under the EPA, jobs must be substantially equal. Jobs alleging to be of comparable worth or value are not viable under the EPA. That being said, the legal landscape is shifting on this issue at the state level, as some states are passing equal pay laws where "similar/comparable" as opposed to "equal" is the standard (see Strah, Rupp, & Morris, in press, for a full discussion of this issue).

The Lily Ledbetter Fair Pay Restoration Act of 2009

One issue that has come into play in pay discrimination cases involves *when* a claim is filed with the EEOC (i.e., the length of time since the pay event in question occurred). This issue was highlighted in the contentious 5–4 Supreme Court decision of *Ledbetter v. Goodyear Tire & Rubber Co., Inc.* (2007).[23],[24] Although Lily Ledbetter filed both EPA and Title VII suits, only the Title VII suit was allowed to continue.

Ledbetter asserted that she was the victim of pay discrimination (see footnote for video of Ledbetter's testimony before Congress).[25] Near the end of her career, Ledbetter provided evidence that her salary was much lower compared to men who performed equal work within the company.[26] She worked at Goodyear from 1979 to 1998, but waited until 1998 to file an EPA and Title VII sex discrimination suit. Goodyear claimed that Ledbetter had waited too long to file her suit since it was filed beyond the 180-day time frame required by the EEOC. Therefore, the company contended that her discrimination suit was time-barred (see Barkacs & Barkacs, 2009; Dunleavy & Gutman, 2009).

The Supreme Court only ruled on Ledbetter's Title VII claim since her EPA suit was eliminated by the district court. The Court decided in favor of Goodyear in a 5–4 vote. As the majority stated in the decision, "Because the later effects of past discrimination do not restart the clock for filing an EEOC charge, Ledbetter's claim is untimely." A main finding by the Court was that

---

[23] https://www.law.cornell.edu/supct/html/05-1074.ZS.html
[24] https://www.oyez.org/cases/2006/05-1074
[25] https://www.youtube.com/watch?v=jRpYoUu5XH0
[26] When Ledbetter left Goodyear, her salary was about $3,700/month. Similarly situated men earned monthly salaries of between $4,200 and $5,200.

pay decisions are discrete, separate acts. Each pay decision was ruled as being independent of previous and future payments. Given this view, Ledbetter was required to file a claim within 180 days of each pay decision. Quoting from the majority, "The EEOC charging period is triggered when a discrete unlawful practice takes place." The Court further ruled that, "Ledbetter should have filed an EEOC charge within 180 days after each allegedly discriminatory pay decision was made and communicated to her. She did not do so." The Court also decided that Ledbetter failed to prove that Goodyear intentionally discriminated against her, a requirement in a disparate treatment suit.

Justice Ginsburg wrote a biting dissent in the *Ledbetter* case. She believed that pay decisions are distinct from discrete acts such as issuing a promotion or terminating an employee. As Ginsburg wrote, "The Court's insistence . . . overlooks common characteristics of pay discrimination. Pay disparities often occur, as they did in Ledbetter's case, in small increments; cause to suspect that discrimination is at work develops only over time." In such a scenario, initial pay disparities may be too small to suspect discrimination and/or not sufficiently large enough to file a successful suit. Furthermore, Ginsburg emphasized that organizations often treat salary data as private, so it is difficult to know if one employee is underpaid relative to others. Ginsburg differed from the majority in that she believed that pay decisions *and* payment of wages that are affected by discrimination are unlawful acts. So, consistent with a continuing violations approach, the issuance of each paycheck resulting from discrimination would start a new EEOC filing period (see Cimpl-Wiemer, 2008). In the end, Justice Ginsburg concluded that Ledbetter's case was not time-barred. She called on the legislative branch to act, stating, "Once again, the ball is in Congress' court. As in 1991, the Legislature may act to correct this Court's parsimonious reading of Title VII."

As it turned out, Congress responded by passing the Lily Ledbetter Fair Pay Restoration Act in 2009,[27] with the intent to overturn the Supreme Court's ruling in the *Ledbetter* case. As stated in the act, "The Ledbetter decision undermines those statutory protections by unduly restricting the time period in which victims of discrimination can challenge and recover for discriminatory compensation decisions or other practices, contrary to the intent of Congress." Specifically, the Ledbetter Act stipulates that an unlawful compensation decision takes place when (1) it is implemented, (2) an individual becomes subject to it, or (3) one is impacted by its application (this includes each time a paycheck is issued resulting from pay discrimination). The third stipulation is relevant to the *Ledbetter* case.

---

[27] https://www.govtrack.us/congress/bills/111/hr11/text

The Paycheck Fairness Act

The Paycheck Fairness Act (PFA) has been introduced into the House of Representatives every legislative session since 1997–1998. The House has passed the Act in three separate sessions: in 2007–2008, 2009–2010, and 2019–2020. As of this writing, it has never been passed by the Senate (although the 2009–2010 version failed by two votes).

The purpose of the PFA is to bolster the protections of the EPA (see Dunleavy & Gutman, 2009). The current bill contains several key provisions, including changing the FOS EPA defense to "a bona fide factor other than sex" (e.g., educational attainment, job experience). Furthermore, these bona fide factors must be job-related and consistent with business necessity. The definition of an "establishment" was also expanded. As the Act states, "employees shall be deemed to work in the same establishment if the employees work for the same employer at workplaces located in the same county or similar political subdivision of a State."

Recall that, under the EPA, an establishment is defined as where central decision-making (or administration) occurs. But in some organizations various types of pay decisions may not be centralized and may be made at different levels. This can complicate the determination of where a given pay-related decision (central administration) occurs. For instance, salary decisions may be made at the corporate level, promotions may be decided within smaller divisions within a company, and bonuses may be determined by local supervisors. As stated by Gutman et al. (2011), "organizations (particularly large ones) should document which pay decisions are made at its various locations. This is particularly important if the Paycheck Fairness Act is enacted with its broader definition of an 'establishment' " (p. 242).

Another key feature of the PFA is that it allows for compensatory and punitive damages, which are not currently available under the EPA. *Compensatory damages* are used to cover actual costs (e.g., lost salary) and can also include money for the pain and suffering of plaintiffs. *Punitive damages* are designed to reprimand a defendant and serve to discourage other organizations from engaging in comparable discriminatory activity. Consequently, the PFA would allow broader damage awards than the EPA, which may result in larger payments to plaintiffs. This applies to many settlement agreements as well. Table 6.5 summarizes the settlement awards and primary relief for a number of recent EPA challenges.

Finally, the Act contains a non-retaliation section that protects employees who engage in protected activities (e.g., complaining about a company, participating in an investigation, filing a claim) under or associated with the PFA. Importantly, the Act prohibits retaliation for discussing pay information.

Table 6.5 Selected Equal Pay Act settlement agreements

Organization (year of settlement)	Specific allegation(s)	Settlement and primary relief
Bryce Corporation (2020)[1]	Paid a male senior business analyst $18,000 more than a woman in the same position; company refused to raise her pay when requested to do so.	$50,000 damage award Title VII and EPA training.
Snobear USA (2020)[2]	Company paid a woman welder a lower salary than a male welder with the same skill and experience.	$20,000 damage award; four-year consent decree; Title VII and EPA training; track pay data by gender and job title.
Covenant Medical Center, Inc. (2020)[3]	Company paid a woman employee less salary than men in the same position who performed the same job tasks.	$104,707 damage award; two-year consent decree; alter pay policies; managerial training on the EPA.
Fastenal Company (2019)[4]	Paid woman sales employees lower hourly rate than men performing equal work.	$50,000 damage award; two-year consent decree; EPA training; Post a notice of the settlement and worker rights regarding EPA and Title VII.
Cummins, Inc. (2019)[5]	Paid former woman employee less than a man doing the same work; company failed to correct salary discrepancy when they determined she was paid less.	$77,500 damage award; five-year consent decree; workforce training on the EPA and Title VII.
National Association for the Education of Young Children (2018)[6]	Lower pay for woman Associate Editor compared to male counterpart with less experience.	$41,777 in back pay and liquidated damages.
TrueCore Behavioral Solutions (2018)[7]	Paid substantially less to a woman employee who replaced a man working in same job (EPA and Title VII violation).	$38,000 damage award.
The University of Denver (2018)[8]	Pay for female full professors was significantly lower ($19,781 lower on average) compared to male full professors; failure to correct salary disparities after acknowledging the discrepancies.	$2.66 million damage award; raise salaries of the female professors; provide salary data to faculty on a yearly basis; hire labor economist to perform yearly compensation equity study.
Spec Formliners, Inc. (2018)[9]	Base pay of female sales representative was less than male counterpart; company made woman employee acquire more sales to get same commission.	$105,000 damage award; hire EEO consultant to assist in developing policies that comply with EPA and Title VII; perform anti-discrimination training and disseminate policies to employees.
Denton County (2018)[10]	Paid a male physician $34,000 higher salary for identical job duties.	$115,000 damage award; develop a compensation policy for physicians; provide EPA training.

Table 6.5 Continued

Organization (year of settlement)	Specific allegation(s)	Settlement and primary relief
Community Pharmacy (2017)[11]	Woman pharmacy technician was paid more than $4.00 less per hour than a male counterpart; terminated her after she complained about her salary.	$60,000 damage award; hire an EEO monitor to help with altering policies to comply with the EPA, Title VII, and retaliation; annual anti-discrimination training for employees.
Kevothermal, LLC (2017)[12]	Paid woman supervisor less than male counterpart for equal work; not allowed to speak Spanish at work even though doing so (translation duties) was part of her job (national origin discrimination).	$60,000 damage award; offer workforce training on the EPA, national origin discrimination and retaliation; develop a policy that prohibits sex discrimination (e.g., EPA violations) and national origin discrimination; ongoing compliance review with the EPA; revise employee pay for any violations found.
Prince George's County, MD. (2017)[13]	Paid a male employee a higher starting salary than a woman (Joanna Smith) for substantially equal work (Engineer III job); promoted a man to the Engineer III position and paid him more than Smith; paid a man in the Engineering II job more than Smith despite having less experience and the job had less complex work duties.	$145,402 damage award; three-year consent decree; hire a consultant to train personnel (e.g., county's position review board members, managers, supervisors) on anti-discrimination law; post notice of the settlement.

[1] https://www.eeoc.gov/newsroom/bryce-corporation-pay-50000-settle-eeoc-equal-pay-lawsuit
[2] https://www.eeoc.gov/newsroom/snobear-usa-pay-20000-settle-eeoc-equal-pay-lawsuit
[3] https://www.eeoc.gov/newsroom/covenant-healthcare-will-pay-104707-settle-eeoc-wage-discrimination-lawsuit
[4] https://www.eeoc.gov/newsroom/fastenal-company-pay-50000-settle-eeoc-pay-discrimination-lawsuit
[5] https://www.eeoc.gov/newsroom/cummins-inc-pay-77500-settle-eeoc-pay-discrimination-lawsuit
[6] https://www.eeoc.gov/newsroom/national-association-education-young-children-pay-41777-settle-eeoc-equal-pay-lawsuit
[7] https://www.eeoc.gov/newsroom/truecore-behavioral-solutions-pay-38000-settle-eeoc-equal-pay-and-title-vii-lawsuit
[8] https://www.eeoc.gov/newsroom/university-denver-pay-266-million-and-increase-salaries-settle-eeoc-equal-pay-lawsuit
[9] https://www.eeoc.gov/newsroom/spec-formliners-pay-105000-settle-eeoc-equal-pay-lawsuit
[10] https://www.eeoc.gov/newsroom/denton-county-pay-115000-after-judgment-eeoc-equal-pay-lawsuit
[11] https://www.eeoc.gov/newsroom/community-pharmacy-pay-60000-settle-equal-pay-discrimination-suit
[12] https://www.eeoc.gov/newsroom/kevothermal-llc-pay-60000-settle-eeoc-equal-pay-and-national-origin-discrimination-lawsuit
[13] https://www.eeoc.gov/newsroom/prince-georges-pay-145402-and-increase-woman-engineers-salary-settle-eeoc-pay-bias-suit

Retrieved from EEOC Press Releases: https://www.eeoc.gov/newsroom/search

For instance, the PFA states that retaliation is not allowed if an employee has "inquired about, discussed, or disclosed the wages of the employee or another employee." This latter protection may allow women to better recognize if their salaries are lower than men who perform substantially equal work.

Supplemental Readings on Equal Pay Act

Beginner

Ledbetter, L., & L. S. Isom (2012). *Grace and grit: My fight for equal pay and fairness at Goodyear and beyond.* New York: Three Rivers Press.

Miller, L. (1981). Comparable worth and the limitations of the Bennett Amendment. *Chicago-Kent Law Review, 57*, 735–764. https://scholarship.kentlaw.iit.edu/cgi/viewcontent.cgi?article=2419&context=cklawreview

Sadin, S. (2019, 19 August). Schneider panel: Gender pay gap hurts individuals, this country's economy. *Chicago Tribune.* https://www.chicagotribune.com/suburbs/lincolnshire/ct-lsr-schneider-wage-gap-roundtable-tl-0822-20190819-vqb6y73tzzez5juh5btwij5zsu-story.html

Intermediate

Dunleavy, E., & Gutman, A. (2008). Ledbetter v. Goodyear Tire Co.: A divided Supreme Court causes quite a stir. *The Industrial-Organizational Psychologist, 45*, 55–63. https://www.siop.org/Portals/84/TIP/Archives/453.pdf?ver=2019-08-20-115133-897

US Equal Employment Opportunity Commission. The Equal Pay Act of 1963. https://www.eeoc.gov/eeoc/publications/fs-epa.cfm

Advanced

Bible, J. (2007). Ledbetter v. Goodyear Tire & Rubber Co.: Supreme Court places roadblock in front of Title VII pay discrimination plaintiffs. *Labor Law Journal, 58*, 170–182.

Lax, J. (2007). Do employer requests for salary history discriminate against women? *Labor Law Journal, 58*, 47–52.

Linsted, J. L. (2006). The Seventh Circuit's erosion of the Equal Pay Act. *Seventh Circuit Review, 1*, 129. https://www.kentlaw.iit.edu/sites/ck/files/public/academics/jd/7cr/v1-1/lindsted.pdf

Strah, N., Rupp, D. E., & Morris, S. (in press). Job analysis and job classification for addressing pay inequality in organizations: Adjusting our methods within a shifting legal landscape. *Industrial and Organizational Psychology: Perspectives in Science and Practice.*

Sex-Based Dress and Appearance Requirements

Are different dress and appearance requirements for men and women legal? The answer to these questions has historically been "yes," though contrary legal opinions exist. Traditionally, the law in this area has reflected a "separate but equal" mindset. In this regard, courts have upheld the establishment of separate dress/appearance codes for men and women as long as such standards placed equivalent burdens on each sex (e.g., Findley, Fretwell, Wheatley, & Ingram, 2006; Levi, 2007; Zalesne, 2007).

Separate dress codes are typically seen as acceptable because they are often viewed as practical manifestations of social norms regarding suitable attire for men and women. Furthermore, dress and appearance requirements are particularly acceptable if they affect mutable (changeable) features such as hair length and are not based on immutable characteristics (e.g., sex). For instance, courts have ruled in favor of organizational policies that restrict men from wearing long hair, beards, dresses, or "female" jewelry and requiring women to wear makeup or dresses at work (e.g., *Barker v. Taft Broadcasting Co.,* 1977[28]; *Harper v. Blockbuster Entertainment Corporation,* 1998[29]; *Jespersen v. Harrah's Operating Co.,* 2006[30]; *Lanigan v. Bartlett and Company Grain,* 1979[31]; *Tavora v. New York Mercantile Exchange,* 1996[32]). As the court stated in *Jespersen,* "Under established equal burdens analysis, when an employer's grooming and appearance policy does not unreasonably burden one gender more than the other, that policy will not violate Title VII."

Dress code and appearance policies that affect only one sex (or are stricter for one sex) have generally shown to be legally problematic (e.g., *Carroll v. Talman Federal Savings and Loan Association of Chicago,* 1979[33]; *Frank v. United Airlines, Inc.,* 2000[34]; *Laffey v. Northwest Airlines, Inc.,* 1976[35]). For instance, in *Carroll,* the 7th Circuit ruled that a requirement that women wear uniforms while men could wear "business attire" was an illegal practice under Title VII. However, the equal burdens perspective regarding dress and appearance codes has been questioned by many legal scholars who have stressed that having equivalent burdens for men and women does not consider their perpetuation of sex-based stereotypes (e.g., Bartlett, 1994; Levi, 2007; Miller, 2006; Zalesne, 2007). Similar concerns have been expressed by the courts. For instance, in *Smith v. City of Salem, Ohio* (2004),[36] the 6th Circuit stated

---

[28] https://scholar.google.com/scholar_case?case=844240737817773747

[29] https://caselaw.findlaw.com/us-11th-circuit/1396708.html

[30] https://scholar.google.com/scholar_case?case=13073805400077839878

[31] https://scholar.google.com/scholar_case?case=9441253095426261881&q=Lanigan+v.+Bartlett,+1979&hl=en&as_sdt=40006

[32] https://scholar.google.com/scholar_case?case=3059935682009147588&q=Tavora+v.+New+York+Mercantile+Exchange&hl=en&as_sdt=6,47

[33] https://scholar.google.com/scholar_case?case=5141482442200943804&q=Carroll+v.+Talman+Federal+Savings+and+Loan+Association&hl=en&as_sdt=6,47

[34] https://scholar.google.com/scholar_case?case=11325921737388906173&q=Frank+v.+United+Airlines,+2000&hl=en&as_sdt=6,47

[35] https://scholar.google.com/scholar_case?case=6793560658137202776&q=Laffey+v.+Northwest+Airlines,+Inc.,1979&hl=en&as_sdt=6,47

[36] https://scholar.google.com/scholar_case?case=9882340233444471066&q=Smith+v.+City+of+Salem,+Ohio+378+F.3d+566+(6th+Cir.+2004)+&hl=en&as_sdt=6,47

that compelling women to wear attire such as dresses, makeup, and jewelry was sex discrimination since these requirements would not endure "*but for*" someone's sex. As the court noted in *Smith*, "After *Price Waterhouse*, an employer who discriminates against women because, for instance, they do not wear dresses or makeup, is engaging in sex discrimination because the discrimination would not occur but for the victim's sex."

In a case described in detail later in this chapter (*EEOC v. R. G. & G. R. Harris Funeral Homes, Inc.*, 2016),[37] the court ruled that the organization engaged in sex discrimination by firing a transgender employee for refusing to wear the attire required of men at work. Technically, the decision in *Harris* was not about the legality of having separate dress codes for men and women. Rather, the issue was whether the organization was guilty of sex discrimination by engaging in sex stereotyping. But the court went further and stated that "even if we would permit certain sex-specific dress codes in a case where the issue was properly raised, we would not rely on either *Jespersen* or *Barker* to do so." As the court reasoned, the *Barker* decision (where different hair lengths were required for men and women) was not applicable given it was decided *before* sex stereotyping was banned by *Price Waterhouse v. Hopkins* (1987).[38] The justices also concluded that the *Jespersen* decision (where women were required to wear makeup while men were not allowed to do so) was contrary to the *Smith* decision, where the court noted that "requiring women to wear makeup does, in fact, constitute improper sex stereotyping."[39]

Pregnancy Discrimination Act of 1978

Prior to 1978, female employees were often penalized for becoming pregnant. In addition to losing benefits, pregnant women were frequently denied the opportunity to apply for work and lost their jobs due to pregnancy. As an example, in *General Electric Co. v. Gilbert* (1976),[40,41] the Supreme Court allowed the company to omit pregnancy for coverage under its disability plan. In response to this and similar rulings that failed to consider pregnancy discrimination as a form of sex discrimination (e.g., *Geduldig v. Aiello*, 1974[42]), the Pregnancy Discrimination Act[43] (PDA) amended Title VII to offer protections for pregnancy and related

---

[37] https://casetext.com/case/equal-empt-opportunity-commn-v-rg-gr-harris-funeral-homes-inc-5
[38] https://www.law.cornell.edu/supremecourt/text/490/228#writing-USSC_CR_0490_0228_ZO
[39] The Court of Appeals for the 6th Circuit issued rulings in the *Smith* and *Harris* cases.
[40] https://caselaw.findlaw.com/us-supreme-court/429/125.html
[41] https://www.oyez.org/cases/1975/74-1589
[42] https://caselaw.findlaw.com/us-supreme-court/417/484.html
[43] https://www.eeoc.gov/laws/statutes/pregnancy.cfm

Table 6.6 Pregnancy discrimination charges filed with the Equal Employment Opportunity (EEOC) 2013–2020

Year	2013	2014	2015	2016	2017	2018	2019	2020
Number of Charges	3,541	3,400	3,543	3,486	3,174	2,790	2,753	2,698

Retrieved from https://www.eeoc.gov/eeoc/statistics/enforcement/pregnancy_new.cfm

medical conditions. The Act states that pregnant women must be treated the same for employment purposes as other persons not so affected, but who are similar in their ability or inability to work. The Act also provides job protections for women who become pregnant and made it illegal to reject female applicants because of pregnancy. A summary of pregnancy discrimination cases filed with the EEOC over the past several years is provided in Table 6.6.

Another early case that set the tone for legal protections for sex discrimination in this context was not about pregnancy per se, but involved women with pre-school aged children. In *Phillips v. Martin Marietta* (1971),[44,45] the company refused to allow women with pre-school aged children to apply for jobs but did not ban applications from similarly situated men. The Supreme Court decided that the presence of separate policies for men and women was a violation of Title VII. The *Phillips* case has been referred to as a "sex-plus" decision. For instance, this occurs when a protected group characteristic (sex) is combined with another factor (having pre-school children) that leads to discrimination. Other sex-plus cases have involved banning married women from working as flight attendants while no such policy applied to men (e.g., *Sprogis v. United Airlines*, 1971[46]; *Laffey v. Northwest Airlines, Inc.,* 1973[47]).

A recent case involved sex-plus-age discrimination (*Frappied v. Affinity Gaming Black Hawk. LLC,* 2020[48]). In this case, eight women older than 40 were terminated versus one similarly situated man. The plaintiffs filed a sex-plus-age discrimination charges—that they were fired because of their sex and age. Specifically, the plaintiffs filed Title VII and Age Discrimination in Employment Act (ADEA) claims of both adverse impact and disparate treatment. The company's defense centered on its contention that sex-plus-age

[44] https://scholar.google.com/scholar_case?case=14318546533206023249&hl=en&as_sdt=6&as_vis=1&oi=scholarr
[45] https://www.oyez.org/cases/1970/73
[46] https://scholar.google.com/scholar_case?case=6414446781408942176&q=Sprogis+v.+United+Airlines,+1971&hl=en&as_sdt=40006
[47] https://scholar.google.com/scholar_case?case=4794888029493000221&q=Laffey+v.+Northwest+Airlines,+1973&hl=en&as_sdt=40006
[48] https://law.justia.com/cases/federal/appellate-courts/ca10/19-1063/19-1063-2020-07-21.html

cases are not available under Title VII. United Airlines asserted that age is not covered under Title VII and that ADEA and Title VII are configured differently, have distinctive burdens of proof, as well as unique remedies and relief.

The Court of Appeals for the 10th Circuit ruled that sex-plus-age discrimination suits are viable under Title VII. As the court reasoned,

> We hold that sex-plus-age claims are cognizable under Title VII. There is no material distinction between a sex-plus-age claim and the other sex-plus claims we have previously recognized for which the "plus-" characteristic is not protected under Title VII. Like claims for which the "plus-" factor is marital status or having preschool-age children, a sex-plus-age claim alleges discrimination against an employee because of sex and some other characteristic. It is thus a sex discrimination claim, albeit one that alleges that the discrimination was based only in part on sex.

The 10th Circuit also affirmed the ADEA disparate treatment and adverse impact claims but rejected the Title VII disparate treatment suit. The court noted that their decision on the sex-plus-age claim was the first to be sustained by a circuit court, although several district courts and the EEOC have supported the feasibility of such suits.

In *California Federal Savings & Loan v. Guerra* (1987),[49] state law was pitted against the PDA, a federal law. The company provided two months of leave for *all* employees who had the same ability or inability to work, a policy that was consistent with the PDA. However, California had passed a law (the Fair Employment and Housing Act [FEHA]) that granted pregnant women up to four months of leave time. So, Lillian Garland, an employee at California Federal Savings and Loan, took more than two months leave following the birth of her child. After she informed her employer of her ability to return to work, she was told her job had been filled. Garland subsequently filed a formal complaint with Department of Fair Employment and Housing[50] (DFEH). She asserted that California Federal Savings and Loan's actions violated the state's FEHA, which allowed for the amount of maternity leave she took. In response, California Federal Savings and Loan filed a suit against DFEH. The company contended that the state's FEHA was unlawful, claiming it was contrary to Title VII and that Title VII trumped state law.

The Supreme Court ruled against California Federal. The majority of justices decided that California's law, by allowing more leave time for pregnancy, was congruent with the goals of the PDA. As the Court noted, the state law "is not

---

[49] https://caselaw.findlaw.com/us-supreme-court/479/272.html
[50] Mark Guerra was the Director of the Department of Fair Employment and Housing and the respondent (party being sued) in this case.

preempted by Title VII, as amended by the PDA, because it is not inconsistent with the purposes of Title VII, nor does it require the doing of an act that is unlawful under Title VII." The Court rejected the claim made by California Federal that the state law afforded women "special treatment" status with regard to leave. As the Court said, California law "does not compel employers to treat pregnant employees better than other disabled employees; it merely establishes benefits that employers must, at a minimum, provide to pregnant workers" and that the goal of Congress was for the PDA to be "a *floor* beneath which pregnancy disability rights may not drop—not a ceiling above which they may not rise."

Insights from Social Science: Supervisor Reactions to Pregnancy Disclosure and Perceived Supervisor Support

Some research has indicated that the manner in which supervisors react to women's disclosure of their pregnancy can have long-term effects for the women disclosing (Little, Hinojosa, & Lynch, 2017). For instance, longitudinal and experimental research on this topic has shown that when supervisors react in a positive and excited manner to a pregnancy disclosure (e.g., "My supervisor brought joy to me by his/her reaction to my pregnancy"), female employees feel more supported both in the short and long term. That is, in addition to experiencing positive emotions following the encounter, research has detected positive effects on women's well-being even a full year following the interaction!

In addition, when supervisors initiated a discussion about needed accommodations due to being pregnant, female employees felt more support (compared to when this was not discussed). Indeed, expressing positive excitement about pregnancy and discussing accommodations for pregnancy had the most beneficial effects on female employees' perceived supervisor support.

The authors of this research emphasize the importance of creating positive emotional experiences during the course of disclosure and accommodations discussions and how such encounters can enhance the quality of the relationships between pregnant employees and supervisors. This can further result in greater organizational commitment, less turnover, and better job performance among these individuals. Given the results of their study, the authors stress the need to train supervisors on how to treat pregnancy disclosures by employees (beyond the legal training that is often done).

An important PDA case, *Young v. United Parcel Service* [UPS] (2015),[51] involved a pregnant employee whose doctor stipulated that she should not lift

---

[51] https://www.law.cornell.edu/supremecourt/text/12-1226#writing-12-1226_OPINION_3

more than 20 pounds. Peggy Young was a truck driver for UPS, and one key job requirement was the ability to lift 70 pounds. So she asked to be transferred to a job that required less heavy lifting (i.e., "light duty work"). Her request was denied. Instead, UPS offered her unpaid leave for her pregnancy (see interview with Peggy Young[52]). Consequently, Young filed a disparate treatment suit alleging a violation of the PDA. In doing so, she pointed out that UPS regularly accommodated other employees (e.g., granted light duty assignments) who experienced on-the-job injuries.[53] Both lower courts ruled against Young. Generally, they concluded that she failed to make a *prima facie* case under disparate treatment rules given that she was not a member of a group that had received accommodations, such as employees with on-the-job injuries, something pregnancy was not.

The Supreme Court reversed the lower courts and ruled in favor of Young given that she introduced evidence that "UPS provided more favorable treatment to at least some employees whose situation cannot reasonably be distinguished from hers." As the majority stated, "An individual pregnant worker who seeks to show disparate treatment may make out a *prima facie* case under the *McDonnell Douglas* framework by showing that she belongs to the protected class, that she sought accommodation, that the employer did not accommodate her, and that the employer did accommodate others similar in their ability or inability to work." See the disparate treatment scenario for pregnancy discrimination in Table 6.7.

Table 6.7 Pregnancy discrimination under a disparate treatment scenario

Phase 1	Plaintiff forms a *prima facie* case of pregnancy discrimination: • She belongs to the protected class. • She sought accommodation. • The employer did not accommodate her. • The employer did accommodate others "similar in their ability or inability to work."
Phase 2	The organization articulates a "legitimate, nondiscriminatory" reason(s) for denying accommodation for pregnancy (reasons such as greater expense or inconvenience for not accommodating pregnant workers are insufficient).
Phase 3	Plaintiff shows the company's reasons are a pretext for illegal discrimination. Examples: • The employer's policies impose a *significant burden* on pregnant workers and the employer's "legitimate, nondiscriminatory" reasons are *not sufficiently strong* to justify the burden. • The employer accommodates a large percentage of non-pregnant workers while failing to accommodate a large percentage of pregnant workers.

[52] http://www.msnbc.com/andrea-mitchell-reports/watch/pregnancy-discrimination-case-heard-by-scotus-367233603839
[53] Prior to the Supreme Court decision, UPS changed its policy and began offering temporary, light-duty work duty to pregnant employees.

In the end, the decision was largely viewed as a victory for pregnant employees.[54] An important feature of the disparate treatment process for pregnancy is that defenses of greater costs and/or inconvenience are not acceptable. Later in 2015, a settlement was reached between Young and UPS, the details of which were not provided. Selected pregnancy discrimination settlements are contained within Table 6.8.

Table 6.8 Selected pregnancy discrimination settlement agreements

Organization (year of settlement)	Specific allegation(s)	Settlement and primary relief
Life Care Centers of America, Inc. (2020)[1]	Refused to pregnancy accommodation request (15-pound lifting requirement).	$170,000 damage award; three-year consent decree; employee training on Title VII and PDA.
Ralphs Grocery Co. (2020)[2]	Denied schedule change request due to pregnancy.	$30,000 damage award; two-year consent decree; revise policies and procedures; training focused on PDA and pregnancy; accommodation requests
United Parcel Service, Inc. (2019)[3]	Failed to accommodate pregnant employees by providing them with light duty assignments or other accommodations.	$2.25 million damage award; human resource and managerial training on revised PDA policy; report to EEOC on pregnancy accommodation requests.
Friedman Realty Group (2019)[4]	Treated individual more strictly after she told company of her pregnancy; fired her due to being pregnant.	$60,000 settlement; five-year consent decree to refrain from future pregnancy discrimination and retaliation; pregnancy discrimination training to personnel; distribute pregnancy discrimination policy[5]
Family HealthCare Network (2018)[6]	Company leave policies denied reasonable accommodations to pregnant and disabled workers; fired employees when they could not return to their jobs after their leave and fired some before approved leave had expired.	$1.75 million settlement; three-year consent decree; hire an EEO monitor to check and revise company policies; train employees on the prevention of disability and/or pregnancy discrimination; construct a tracking process for accommodation requests and discrimination charges.[7]
Absolut Care LLC (2018)[8]	Pregnancy and disability *discrimination*; failed to accommodate those with disabilities (e.g., denied leave); did not accommodate and fired pregnant employees.	$465,000 settlement; three-year consent decree; revise leave policies; employee training on the ADA and PDA.[9]

(continued)

[54] https://blog.dciconsult.com/blog/supreme-court-ruling-young-v-ups-major-victory-pregnant-employees

Table 6.8 Continued

Organization (year of settlement)	Specific allegation(s)	Settlement and primary relief
Bendinelli Law Firm (2018)[10]	Fired employee after 10 days on the job after learning she was pregnant.	$30,000 settlement; two-year consent decree; develop policies to prevent pregnancy discrimination; employee PDA training.[11]
LA Louisanne, Inc. (2018)[12]	Decreased hours of a server and ultimately removed her from work schedule; refused to rehire her after she had her baby (other female workers experienced the same treatment due to pregnancy).	$82,500 settlement; three-year consent decree; have an EEO monitor to revise company discrimination policies; employee training on discrimination and harassment.[13]
Silverado Company (2018)[14]	Failed to accommodate a pregnant employee (e.g., give light-duty work).	$80,000 settlement; revise anti-discrimination policies; report requests for light duty to EEOC; managerial training regarding compliance with discrimination laws.[15]
Trinity Hospital (2017)[16]	Denied light-duty work assignment to a pregnant nurse and then fired her (light duty given to nurses injured on the job).	$95,000 settlement; three-year consent decree; revamp policies to comply with ADA and PDA (e.g., accommodation requests) and make policies available to workforce; HR training.[17]

[1] https://www.eeoc.gov/newsroom/life-care-centers-america-pay-170000-settle-eeoc-discrimination-lawsuit

[2] https://www.eeoc.gov/newsroom/ralphs-settles-eeoc-pregnancy-discrimination-lawsuit-30000

[3] https://www.eeoc.gov/newsroom/ups-pay-225-million-settle-eeoc-pregnancy-discrimination-charge

[4] https://www.eeoc.gov/newsroom/friedman-realty-group-pay-60000-settle-eeoc-pregnancy-discrimination-suit

[5] https://www.eeoc.gov/eeoc/newsroom/release/03-15-19.cfm

[6] https://www.eeoc.gov/newsroom/family healthcare-network-settles-eeoc-disability-and-pregnancy-discrimination-suit-175

[7] https://www.eeoc.gov/eeoc/newsroom/release/12-06-18.cfm

[8] https://www.eeoc.gov/newsroom/absolut-care-pay-465000-settle-eeoc-pregnancy-and-disability-discrimination-suit

[9] https://www.eeoc.gov/eeoc/newsroom/release/10-22-18a.cfm

[10] https://www.eeoc.gov/newsroom/bendinelli-law-firm-pay-30000-settle-eeoc-pregnancy-discrimination-lawsuit

[11] https://www.eeoc.gov/eeoc/newsroom/release/9-20-18.cfm

[12] https://www.eeoc.gov/newsroom/la-louisanne-restaurant-settles-eeoc-pregnancy-discrimination-lawsuit-82500

[13] https://www.eeoc.gov/eeoc/newsroom/release/7-2-18.cfm

[14] https://www.eeoc.gov/newsroom/silverado-pay-80000-settle-eeoc-pregnancy-discrimination-lawsuit

[15] https://www.eeoc.gov/eeoc/newsroom/release/1-29-18.cfm

[16] https://www.eeoc.gov/newsroom/trinity-hospital-pay-95000-settle-eeoc-pregnancy-discrimination-suit

[17] https://www.eeoc.gov/eeoc/newsroom/release/12-20-17a.cfm

Retrieved from EEOC Press Releases: https://www.eeoc.gov/newsroom/search

---

Supplemental Readings on Pregnancy Discrimination

Beginner

Cunha, D. (2014, September 24). When bosses discriminate against pregnant women. *The Atlantic.* https://www.theatlantic.com/business/archive/2014/09/when-bosses-discriminate-against-pregnant-women/380623/

Kitroeff, N., & Silver-Greenberg, J. (2019, February 6). Pregnancy discrimination is rampant inside America's biggest companies. *New York Times.* https://www.nytimes.com/interactive/2018/06/15/business/pregnancy-discrimination.html

Lithwick, D. (2015, March 25). A pregnant worker's right to sue: The Supreme Court compromises a smart new rule into existence. *Slate.* https://slate.com/news-and-politics/2015/03/young-v-ups-supreme-court-decision-a-victory-for-pregnant-women-facing-discrimination-in-the-workplace.html

Pregnancy discrimination. Workplacefairness.org. https://www.workplacefairness.org/pregnancy-discrimination

Intermediate

US Equal Employment Opportunity Commission. (1997). Pregnancy discrimination. https://www.eeoc.gov/eeoc/publications/fs-preg.cfm

US Equal Employment Opportunity Commission. (2015). EEOC Enforcement Guidance on Pregnancy Discrimination and Related Issues. https://www.eeoc.gov/laws/guidance/pregnancy_guidance.cfm

Advanced

Grossman, J. L. (2009). Pregnancy, work, and the promise of equal citizenship. *Georgetown Law Journal, 98,* 567–628. https://scholarlycommons.law.hofstra.edu/cgi/viewcontent.cgi?article=1335&context=faculty_scholarship

Grossman, J. L. (2016). Expanding the core: Pregnancy discrimination law as it approaches full term. *Idaho Law Review, 52,* 825–866. https://scholar.smu.edu/law_faculty/11/

Widiss, D. A. (2017). The interaction of the Pregnancy Discrimination Act and the Americans with Disabilities Act after Young v. UPS. *U. C. Davis Law Review, 50,* 1423–1453. https://www.repository.law.indiana.edu/facpub/2546/

Family and Medical Leave Act of 1993

Another important piece of legislation related to family issues is the Family and Medical Leave Act of 1993 (FMLA).[55] The general purpose of the Act was to provide time away from work to have or adopt a child or to care for

---

[55] https://www.dol.gov/whd/fmla/fmlaAmended.htm

oneself or an immediate family member with a serious health condition. Getting this Act passed was a lengthy and difficult process. Formal bills began in Congress in 1985[56] and ended with the passage of the FMLA in 1993. In the initial version, the amount of leave was set at 26 weeks for medical purposes and 18 weeks for family/parental leave and required organizations with five or more employees to comply. In the next version of the bill, organizations with 15 or more workers (a number consistent with Title VII) were required to comply, and the bill capped family or medical leave to a total of 26 weeks across a two-year time frame. In the final version passed in 1993, the FMLA requires companies with 50 or more employees to provide a total of 12 weeks of *unpaid* leave for childbirth, adoption of a child, and caring for oneself or immediate family members with serious medical conditions (Guerin & England, 2018).[57] This version of the FMLA was approved by Congress on two earlier occasions (1991, 1992) but was vetoed each time by President George H. W. Bush.

To qualify for FMLA leave, employees must have worked for their organization a minimum of 12 months and worked a minimum of 1,250 hours during the previous 12-month period. FMLA leave applies to men as well as women. The United States is rather unique in that, compared to many other nations, it does not offer *paid* leave for having a child (see Figure 6.1). However, in December 2019, the National Defense Authorization Act of 2020[58] was passed, which in part allows Federal civilian workers 12 weeks of paid family leave "for the birth, adoption, or foster placement of a child."

The FMLA is a fairly complex law with numerous definitions and requirements. To begin with, a "serious health condition" is a physical or mental impairment that requires inpatient care or ongoing treatment by a healthcare provider (e.g., pregnancy, chronic diseases, dialysis, stroke). Organizations are allowed to request certification for FMLA leave that contains information such as

(a) the date when the serious health condition happened;
(b) the duration of the condition;
(c) relevant facts about the impairment;

---

[56] The name of the bill changed a few times beginning with the Parental and Disability Leave Act, followed by the Parental and Medical Leave Act, before culminating in the Family and Medical Leave Act (see this site for a short history of family leave in the United States: https://tah.oah.org/november-2016/the-history-of-family leave-policies-in-the-united-states/).

[57] If a husband and wife work for the same organization, they are entitled to a total of 12 weeks unpaid leave.

[58] https://www.chcoc.gov/content/paid-parental-leave-federal-employees

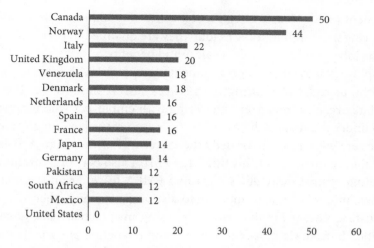

Figure 6.1 Weeks of paid maternity leave by country.
Adapted from https://www.nationmaster.com.

(d) if applicable, verification that a worker must care for an immediate family member; and

(e) a statement that an employee is unable to perform job tasks.

Organizations do have the right to request a second opinion regarding the need for FMLA leave if they have reason to question the legitimacy of the medical information provided. Such second opinions must be paid for by the company and be generated by someone who does not work for the organization. If the two views differ, a third opinion by a mutually agreed upon provider can be obtained at the company's expense. If acquired, the third opinion is final. If foreseeable, employees must notify their employer of their need for leave within an acceptable timeframe. For instance, in cases where the birth of a child is used for FMLA leave, employees should provide no less than 30 days' notice. In addition, when medical treatments are known in advance, employees are required to "make a reasonable effort to schedule the treatment so as not to disrupt unduly the operations of an employer."

During FMLA leave, employees retain their healthcare coverage. However, organizations are not required to apply FMLA leave time for seniority purposes. If it is a better option, intermittent leave is allowable as long as both the company and employee agree to such an arrangement. When employees return from FMLA leave, they must be given their same or equivalent job.[59] Also, it is legitimate to transfer employees to an alternate job during intermittent leave as long they are qualified to perform the work and the job provides equivalent salary and benefits.

Employees may choose, or a company can *require*, the use of vacation, personal, or sick leave during the 12-week FMLA time frame. The FMLA prohibits organizations from interfering with employees who exercise their rights under the Act. As the Act states, it is against the law "for any employer to interfere with, restrain, or deny the exercise of or the attempt to exercise, any right provided under this title." The FMLA also bars organizations from retaliating against individuals regarding FMLA leave. From the text of the Act, it is "unlawful for any employer to discharge or in any other manner discriminate against any individual for opposing any practice made unlawful by this title." Indeed, claims of interference and retaliation are usually the focus of legal cases under the FMLA.

One example is the Supreme Court case *Nevada Department of Human Resources v. Hibbs* (2003).[60,61] Walter Hibbs was given FMLA leave to care for his wife who had neck surgery resulting from a car accident. After taking his 12 weeks of unpaid leave, Hibbs alleged that the organization interfered with his FMLA rights by requiring him to return to work on a specified date. Hibbs was terminated after he did not return to his job on the stated date. As a result, Hibbs sued his former employer in the Nevada federal district court for *monetary damages* (financial awards such as lost wages and benefits). A key issue in this case was whether individuals can sue states that breach the FMLA. The state used the 11th Amendment (state sovereign immunity) as its defense. Essentially, this amendment limits the power of individuals to sue states in federal court. An important question was whether Hibbs could sue for monetary damages in federal court. In the end, the Supreme Court ruled in favor of Hibbs. The Court concluded that he was eligible for monetary damages in federal court given that Nevada was deemed to be in violation of the FMLA. Here, the Court found that the state had a record of discrimination in the administration of leave benefits.

Another FLMA case was *Escriba v. Foster Poultry Farms, Inc.* (2014).[62] Here, Maria Escriba asked for two weeks off to take care of her father. Her leave was approved, and Escriba was granted two weeks of paid vacation, not FMLA leave. But Escriba failed to return to her job after the two-week time frame

---

[59] The Department of Labor will ask for comments on ideas to improve FMLA regulations by April of 2020.

[60] https://supreme.justia.com/cases/federal/us/538/721/#tab-opinion-1961257

[61] https://www.oyez.org/cases/2002/01-1368

[62] https://cdn.ca9.uscourts.gov/datastore/opinions/2014/02/25/11-17608.pdf

(she needed more time to care for her father). Indeed, she waited for 16 days after her expected return date to contact a representative of her union. Given that she had violated company policy by missing three straight days without giving notice, Escriba was terminated. She filed a lawsuit accusing the company of violating her FMLA rights. Escriba argued that the company knew she qualified for FMLA leave although she officially declined to use it. The 9th Circuit ruled that since Escriba decided *not* to use her FMLA leave in order to save it for future use, her FMLA rights were not interfered with and therefore ruled in favor of the organization.

However, the *Escriba* decision included an interesting reading of the FMLA. For instance, the court concluded that the FMLA is vague about whether employees can opt to delay FMLA leave. Furthermore, the court believed that organizations have the responsibility to ascertain if employees are seeking FMLA leave. As the court noted, "The employee need not expressly assert rights under the FMLA or even mention the FMLA, . . . but the employer 'should inquire further of the employee if it is necessary to have more information about whether FMLA leave is being sought by the employee, and to obtain the necessary details of the leave to be taken.'"

One interpretation of this decision is that employees may be able to choose to delay their FMLA leave versus being required to do so. As noted by Miller (2016), the *Escriba* decision "opens the door for employee liability suits if employers involuntarily place employees on FMLA leave in the future" (p. 16). As Miller further states, the ruling in *Escriba* may be consistent with the purpose of the FMLA (e.g., more flexible leave policies), but it differs from *Wysong* and other circuit courts. For example, in *Strickland v. Water Works and Sewer Board of the City of Birmingham* (2001),[63] the 11th Circuit ruled that "an employer who is subject to the FMLA and also offers a paid sick leave policy has two options when an employee's leave qualifies both under the FMLA and under the employer's paid leave policy: the employer may either permit the employee to use his FMLA leave and paid sick leave sequentially, or the employer may require that the employee use his FMLA leave entitlement and his paid sick leave concurrently."

In *Hogancamp v. County of Volusia* (2018),[64] Wanda Hogancamp was given FMLA leave to deal with pronounced depression and anxiety after her son died in a car accident. After being on leave for nine weeks, the county told Hogancamp that she had to return to work on an adjusted schedule and then

---

[63] https://openjurist.org/239/f3d/1199/russell-strickland-v-water-works-and-sewer-board-of-the-city-of-birmingham

[64] https://scholar.google.com/scholar_case?case=14713623234474418240&hl=en&as_sdt=6&as_vis=1&oi=scholarr

subsequently denied her the previously offered modified work schedule. After stating that the county deterred her from pursuing an Americans with Disabilities Act (ADA) suit, she sued for retaliation and interference under the FMLA. The county asked the court to dismiss both charges since they contended that Hogancamp was actually challenging the county with lack of compliance with the ADA. But the circuit court did not accept the county's position. Their reasoning was that Hogancamp's failure to file an ADA claim was not germane to her FMLA retaliation allegation. Also, the court concluded that the county interfered with her FMLA leave by requiring Hogancamp to return to work after only nine weeks of leave. When the case reached the 11th Circuit on appeal, it was dismissed since Hogancamp failed to file the mandatory paperwork within the required time period.

Finally, in *Guzman v. Brown County* (2018),[65] Caroline Guzman, an emergency dispatcher, filed an FMLA claim of interference and retaliation after being fired from her job. Here, both the district court and the 11th Circuit issued *summary judgments* in favor of Brown County. One reason for the rulings was that Guzman did not offer documentation that she had a serious medical condition. Although Guzman suffered from sleep apnea several years earlier, she was not currently receiving treatment for the condition. Also, the court denied the interference and retaliation claims since she was terminated *before* requesting FMLA leave. Finally, Guzman did not give sufficient notice (30 days) of her need for leave.

Recommendations/Best Practices

Organizations need to be diligent to avoid lawsuits related to the FMLA. As with other suits, they can be time-consuming and costly. Consequently, a number of suggestions have been proposed to help organizations comply with the FMLA. Several of these are summarized here.

- Develop and disseminate a detailed, written FMLA policy.
- Train supervisors (and employees) on how to comply with the provisions of the FMLA.
- Keep accurate records of FMLA leave, especially intermittent leave.
- Ensure that all FMLA forms and notices are submitted on time.
- Guarantee confidentiality of FMLA leave requests.

[65] https://scholar.google.com/scholar_case?case=8427884283991965629&hl=en&as_sdt=6&as_vis=1&oi=scholarr

- Be careful not to interfere with FMLA leave and avoid retaliation.
- Preserve records of all employee requests for FMLA leave and responses to requests by the organization.

Supplemental Readings About the FMLA

Beginner

FMLA forms from the Department of Labor. https://www.dol.gov/whd/fmla/forms.htm

Length of medical & family leave allowed under the FMLA & covered employers' number of employees: Development of statutory text (1985–1993) (2005). Georgetown University Law Center. https://scholarship.law.georgetown.edu/cgi/viewcontent.cgi?article=1015&context=regulations

Schulte, B. (2013, 10 February). Landmark family leave law doesn't help millions of workers. *The Washington Post.* https://www.washingtonpost.com/local/landmark-family leave-law-doesnt-help-millions-of-workers/2013/02/10/aa1cd468-720f-11e2-8b8d-e0b59a1b8e2a_story.html?noredirect=on

Thorbecke, C. (2019, 17 December). 2.1 million federal employees to get paid parental leave for 1st time. ABC News. https://abcnews.go.com/US/21-million-federal-employees-paid-parental-leave-1st/story?id=67777014

Intermediate

FMLA forms. US Department of Labor Wage and Hour Division. https://www.dol.gov/agencies/whd/fmla/law

US Department of Labor Wage and Hour Division. (2012). Fact sheet #28: The Family and Medical Leave Act. https://www.dol.gov/whd/regs/compliance/whdfs28.pdf

Advanced

Clabault, D. M. (2016). The Family and Medical Leave Act: Changes and challenges. In M. Foegen Karsten (Ed.), *Emerging issues and enduring challenges* (pp. 281–300), Santa Barbara, CA: Praeger.

MaGill, N.L. (2015). Balancing career and parenthood: The Family and Medical Leave Act and maternity leave. *Widener Law Review, 20,* 279–300. http://widenerlawreview.org/files/2015/02/9-Magill.pdf

Tighe, M. F. (2015). Family and medical leave act. *Georgetown Journal of Gender and the Law, 16,* 141–162.

LGBTQ+ Issues

Sex Discrimination

The EEOC has concluded that discrimination based on LGBTQ+ status is a form of sex discrimination and has filed numerous suits on this issue (see

Table 6.9 LBGTQ discrimination charges filed with the Equal Employment Opportunity Commission (EEOC) 2014–2020

Year	2014	2015	2016	2017	2018	2019	2020
Number of Charges	1,100	1,412	1,768	1,762	1,811	1,868	1,857

Retrieved from https://www.eeoc.gov/eeoc/statistics/enforcement/lgbt_sex_based.cfm

Table 6.9). One example is the case of *Macy v. Holder* (2012).[66] After being offered a job with a crime lab (contingent on passing a background check), Mia Macy informed the staffing agency in charge of filling the position that she was "in the process of transitioning from male to female." After being informed of this transition, the staffing company told Macy that the position was no longer open due to budget issues. However, the position was subsequently filled with another individual. Consequently, Macy sued for sex discrimination. The EEOC concluded, "Claims of discrimination based on *transgender status*, also referred to as claims of discrimination based on gender identity, are *cognizable* under Title VII's sex discrimination prohibition (emphasis added)." The EEOC further stated that "we conclude that intentional discrimination against a transgender individual because that person is transgender is, by definition, discrimination based on . . . sex, and such discrimination therefore violates Title VII". Despite the EEOC's position that transgender individuals are covered by Title VII, opinions by the EEOC are not law. As such, courts are free to make decisions independent of the agency.

Hostile Work Environment

Hostile work environment claims based on *sex stereotyping* (e.g., *Price Waterhouse v. Hopkins*, 1989) are covered by Title VII. Such a claim occurred in *EEOC v. Pallet Companies, Inc.* (2016), where a lesbian employee complained to management alleging harassment by her supervisor due to her noncompliance with female gender norms as well as her sexual orientation. After complaining, she was fired. A settlement[67] was reached between the EEOC and the organization. The agreement awarded the employee more than

---

[66] https://www.eeoc.gov/decisions/0120120821%20Macy%20v%20DOJ%20ATF.txt
[67] https://www1.eeoc.gov/eeoc/newsroom/release/6-28-16.cfm

$180,000 in damages and required the organization to stop sex discrimination and retaliation, mandating that they hire an expert to help establish a training program on sexual orientation, gender identity, and transgender inclusion in the workplace.

Moreover, in *EEOC v. Scott Medical Health Center* (2016),[68] a federal district court judge ruled in favor of a gay male employee. Dale Massaro claimed that he was the victim of pejorative comments by his supervisor because he was gay. Massaro reported the harassment to the organization's CEO but the harassing behavior continued. As a result of the harassment, Massaro eventually quit his job. In supporting the EEOC's charge that the organization violated Title VII, Massaro was awarded back pay as well compensatory and punitive damages.

A similar conclusion was reached in *Hively v. Ivy Tech Community College* (2017).[69] Kimberly Hively was a lesbian who was working as a part-time teacher for Ivy Tech. She had repeatedly applied for a full-time position but was never granted one. After the school denied to renew her contract, she filed suit with the EEOC alleging that she was discriminated against due to her sexual orientation. Initially, a three-judge panel of the 7th Circuit concluded that discrimination based on sexual orientation was not a violation of Title VII.[70] As the panel stated, "Congress has time and time again said 'no,' to every attempt to add sexual orientation to the list of categories protected from discrimination by Title VII." However, a *full panel* of judges on the 7th Circuit reversed the three-judge panel decision and ruled that sexual orientation was a form of sex discrimination. As the court noted "It would require considerable calisthenics to remove the 'sex' from 'sexual orientation.'"

An inconsistent ruling is illustrated by an earlier 3rd Circuit decision in *Bibby v. Philadelphia Coca-Cola Bottling Co.* (2001).[71] John Bibby, a gay man, claimed that he was the victim of same-sex harassment at work. The 3rd Circuit ruled that Bibby failed to prove a violation of Title VII given that he was harassed because of his sexual orientation (not his sex) and that discrimination based on sexual orientation was not protected under the law. Although the 3rd Circuit was sympathetic to Bibby's claim, they felt they were restricted by Title VII's protections. That is, at that time, Title VII did not protect sexual orientation.

[68] http://hr.cch.com/eld/EEOCScott111617.pdf
[69] https://harvardlawreview.org/2018/03/hively-v-ivy-tech-community-college/
[70] https://law.justia.com/cases/federal/appellate-courts/ca7/15-1720/15-1720-2016-07-28.html
[71] https://law.justia.com/cases/federal/appellate-courts/F3/260/257/494844/

The issue of whether sexual orientation and gender identity are covered by Title VII was resolved by the Supreme Court in the landmark decision of *Bostock v. Clayton County, Georgia* (2020).[72,73] The Court ruled (6–3) that the inclusion of "sex" in Title VII protects gay and transgender individuals from employment discrimination. Three separate cases were consolidated into the decision. All involved charges that employees were fired for being either transgender or gay. Before addressing the Supreme Court's decision, it is beneficial to provide a brief summary of the three individual decisions that were made at the circuit court level.

As described in Chapter 4, in *EEOC v. R. G. & G. R. Harris Funeral Homes, Inc.* (2018),[74] Aimee Stephens, a transgender employee who identified as a woman, filed a sex discrimination suit because she was subsequently fired after refusing to wear a traditional male suit (required of men). The company stated that abolishing its dress code would be a violation of the Religious Freedom Restoration Act (RFRA)[75]—it would present a substantial burden to their sincerely held religious beliefs. The 6th Circuit held that the behavior of the funeral home was discriminatory, stating that "the funeral home fired Stephens because she refused to abide by her employer's stereotypical conception of sex." It also ruled that permitting Aimee Stephens to wear female attire would not substantially burden the sincerely held religious beliefs of the funeral home, so the RFRA was not a viable defense.

In *Zarda v. Altitude Express, Inc.* (2018),[76] an employee, Donald Zarda, sometimes told female clients with whom he was tandem diving that he was gay to reduce potential concerns from being in close proximity to a man during a dive. Zarda was accused of fondling a female client during a drive and was subsequently fired. He denied the accusation and sued the company for firing him because of his sexual orientation. The company countered that sexual orientation is not protected under Title VII. However, the 2nd Circuit ruled in favor of Zarda, concluding that sexual orientation is a form of sex discrimination. As the court stated, "We now conclude that sexual orientation discrimination is motivated, at least in part, by sex and

---

[72] https://www.supremecourt.gov/opinions/19pdf/17-1618_hfci.pdf
[73] https://www.oyez.org/cases/2019/17-1618
[74] https://www.opn.ca6.uscourts.gov/opinions.pdf/18a0045p-06.pdf
[75] https://www.law.cornell.edu/uscode/text/42/chapter-21B
[76] https://scholar.google.com/scholar_case?case=15064059163678779713&q=Altitude+Express+Inc.+v.+Zarda&hl=en&as_sdt=40006

is thus a subset of sex discrimination. Looking first to the text of Title VII, the most natural reading of the statute's prohibition on discrimination 'because of . . . sex' is that it extends to sexual orientation discrimination because sex is necessarily a factor in sexual orientation."

In another circuit court decision, *Bostock v. Clayton County Board of Commissioners* (2018),[77] Gerald Bostock also alleged that he was terminated from his job as a child welfare services coordinator for being gay. He was terminated after playing in a gay softball league for behavior "unbecoming" an employee of the county. The 11th Circuit ruled in favor of Clayton County based its own previous decisions that Title VII did not protect sexual orientation.

The issue before the Supreme Court was whether sexual orientation or transgender status is a form of sex discrimination and therefore covered under Title VII's "because of . . . sex" provision. In the consolidated case, *Bostock v. Clayton County* (2020), the defense was primarily that organizations who fire employees for being transgender or gay are not guilty of violating Title VII—such individuals are not covered by the Act. In addition, the defense contended that Congress did not foresee that "sex" would cover gay or transgender people.

As noted earlier, the Supreme Court concluded otherwise. As stated by the majority, "When an employer fires an employee for being homosexual or transgender, it necessarily intentionally discriminates against that individual in part because of sex. Second, the plaintiff's sex need not be the sole or primary cause of the employer's adverse action." The Court further commented that, "We agree that homosexuality and transgender status are distinct concepts from sex. But, as we've seen, discrimination based on homosexuality or transgender status necessarily entails discrimination based on sex; the first cannot happen without the second."

It is important to note that *Bostock* (2020) did not consider the extent to which sincerely held religious beliefs (e.g., the RFRA) can be used to defend actions against gay or transgender individuals. This defense was not used in the case. Whether or not such a defense can be viable (and under which conditions) may be fodder for future employment discrimination cases.

[77] https://www.scotusblog.com/wp-content/uploads/2018/06/17-1618-opinion-below.pdf

Table 6.10 LGBT employment protection laws by state

Employment discrimination protection for orientation *and* gender identity	Employment discrimination protection for orientation *and/or* gender identity	Employment discrimination protection for orientation *only*	No employment nondiscrimination laws
Hawaii	Michigan	Wisconsin	Idaho
Washington	Pennsylvania		Montana
Oregon			Alaska
California			Wyoming
Nevada			North Dakota
Utah			South Dakota
Colorado			Nebraska
New Mexico			Kansas
Minnesota			Oklahoma
Iowa			Texas
Illinois			Arizona
Maryland			Missouri
New Jersey			Arkansas
Maine			Louisiana
Massachusetts			Mississippi
Vermont			Tennessee
Delaware			Kentucky
Rhode Island			West Virginia
Connecticut			North Carolina
Washington DC			South Carolina
New Hampshire			Georgia
New York			Florida
Virginia			Ohio
			Indiana
			Alabama

Retrieved from Movement Advancement Project, https://www.lgbtmap.org/equality-maps/non_discrimination_laws

Supplemental Readings on LGBTQ+ Issues

Beginner

Miller, S. (2019, 8 October). "Shocking" numbers: Half of LGBTQ adults live in states where no laws ban job discrimination. *USA Today*. https://www.usatoday.com/story/news/nation/2019/10/08/lgbt-employment-discrimination-half-of-states-offer-no-protections/3837244002/

Sopelsa, B. (2019, 23 August). Gay workers not covered by civil rights law, Trump admin tells Supreme Court. NBC News. https://www.nbcnews.com/feature/nbc-out/gay-workers-not-covered-civil-rights-law-trump-admin-tells-n1045971

Teeman, T. (2019, 3 September). Inside the Supreme Court discrimination cases that could change LGBTQ rights. The Daily Beast. https://www.thedailybeast.com/inside-the-supreme-court-discrimination-cases-that-could-change-lgbtq-rights

Intermediate

EEOC: What you should know about EEOC and the enforcement protections for LGBT workers. https://www.utsystem.edu/sites/default/files/offices/police/files/annual-promotional-exams/facts-about-lgbt-discrimination.pdf

Munoz, C. S., & Thomas, K. M. (2006). LGBTQ issues in organizational settings: What HRD professionals need to know and do. In R. Hill (Ed.), *Challenging homophobia and heterosexism* (pp. 85–95). Hoboken, NJ: John Wiley & Sons.

Advanced

Employment Law—Title VII—EEOC Affirms Protections for Transgender Employees—*Macy v. Holder*. (2013). *Harvard Law Review, 126*, 1731–1738. http://cdn.harvardlawreview.org/wp-content/uploads/pdfs/vol126_macy_v_holder.pdf

Parrington, T. (2019). Title VII & LGBTQ employment discrimination: An argument for a modern updated approach to Title VII claims. *Washington University Journal of Law and Policy, 60*, 293–315. https://openscholarship.wustl.edu/law_journal_law_policy/vol60/iss1/17/

Sanders, L. (2016). Effects of EEOC recognition of Title VII as prohibiting discrimination based on transgender identity. *Duke Journal of Gender Law and Policy, 23*, 263–281. https://scholarship.law.duke.edu/cgi/viewcontent.cgi?referer=&httpsredir=1&article=1309&context=djglp

Recommendations/Best Practices

- Establish the means to determine if jobs are equal (or not) in terms of skill, effort, responsibility, and work conditions.
- Use the same pay rates for jobs that are equal regarding skill, effort, responsibility, and work conditions.
- Do not use market forces to determine employee salaries.

- Refrain from using salary history in setting wages. If past salary is used, ensure that other job-related factors are employed to determine pay.
- Know and abide by all applicable state-level legislation and case law pertinent to equal pay.
- Use sex-neutral dress and appearance requirements. If different requirements are employed, ensure that they place equivalent burdens on men and women.
- Do not make personnel decisions using sex-based stereotypes.
- Do not ask female applicants or employees if they plan to have a family.
- Treat pregnant individuals the same for employment purposes as other persons who are similar in their ability or inability to work (e.g., workplace accommodations).

Summary and Take-Aways

As this chapter illustrates, sex discrimination cases are wide-ranging (e.g., equal pay, pregnancy, sex-role stereotyping) and relatively common. The legal protections for sex discrimination are still being affected by the late introduction of "sex" as a protected group within Title VII and emerging issues surrounding pay equity, sexual harassment, protections for LGBTQ+ individuals, and the like. However, in 2020, the Supreme Court decided that employment discrimination against gay and transgender individuals is illegal under Title VII, thus clarifying a previously unresolved legal issue.

A budding issue is the increasing number of bans on the use of wage history to establish starting salaries. As noted, increasing numbers of states, counties, and cities have passed laws that bar the use of such information. Whether or not this practice will continue is an open question. If so, it will be important to assess if these bans help minimize pay disparities between men and women.

The PFA has been in limbo for quite a while, but shifts in political orientations within the congressional and executive branches of government may open the door for potential passage. If so, it will offer more protections and damage awards for EPA plaintiffs.

There appears to be growing interest for offering *paid* FMLA leave in the United States. Although a number of proposals have been put forth in Congress, none have passed. But federal civilian workers are eligible for paid family leave, beginning October 1, 2020. At present, paid leave exists in a handful of states,[78] while many other states are contemplating it. In other cases,

---

[78] California, Rhode Island, New York, Washington, and New Jersey.

certain organizations have opted to offer some form of paid leave. It appears safe to say that there is more to come on this issue that bears monitoring.

Glossary

Bennett Amendment: An amendment inserted into Title VII to ensure that violations of the Equal Pay Act would also violate Title VII.

"But for" analysis: Frequently used to assess causation. It is often referred to as the actual or factual cause. For instance, but for sex, different dress codes would not exist. Also known as but for causation.

Cognizable: A viable claim or a claim that is capable of being judicially heard and determined.

Comparable worth: The concept that women and men should receive equal pay for jobs requiring comparable (not equal) work.

Compensatory damages: Awarding of payments for costs incurred (e.g., lost wages, bonuses, pain and suffering).

Defense: The arguments and evidence presented by the defendant in opposition to the allegations or charges brought against them by the plaintiff(s). Term is also used to refer to the party sued by a plaintiff.

Equal work: Under the Equal Pay Act, this is defined as jobs that are substantially equal with respect to effort, skill, responsibility, and work conditions.

Establishment: Often, but not limited to, a physical location. According to the Equal Pay Act, a place where central decisions are made.

Factor other than sex (FOS): A defense available to organizations that their decision(s) were based on any factor other than sex in Equal Pay Act cases.

Injunction: A court order which prevents or commands an action from the defense. To receive an injunction, the plaintiff must show that monetary damages will not suffice and that an irreparable injury will result unless the injunction is issued.

Liquidated damages: Typically included within contracts; specifies a given monetary award if contracts are broken. Often used when actual damages are difficult to determine.

McDonnell Douglas framework: A three-step burden-shifting process used for cases of intentional discrimination.

Monetary damages/relief: Compensation given to an injured party by a liable party (e.g., back pay, lost salary, fringe benefits, bonuses, pain and suffering).

Plaintiff: The party who initiates a lawsuit.

Prima facie: Latin phrase for "at first glance." Consists of presenting evidence that is presumed to be true.

Punitive damages: Used to punish employers for discriminatory acts committed with malice or reckless indifference and to prevent the reoccurrence of comparable discriminatory behavior.

Summary judgments: Decisions by a judge that resolves lawsuits in favor of a given party.

Glossary terms adapted from Gutman et al. (2011); https://uslegal.com/, and merriamwebster.com/legal.

Cases Cited

Alexander v. Chattahoochee Valley Community College, 345 F. Supp. 2d 1306 (M.D. Ala. 2004).
American Federation etc. (AFSCME) v. State of Washington, 770 F.2d 1401 (9th Cir. 1985).
Barker v. Taft Broadcasting Co., 549 F.2d 400 (6th Cir. 1977).
Bibby v. Philadelphia Coca-Cola Bottling Co., 260 F.3d 257, 260-61 (3rd Cir. 2001).
Bostock v. Clayton County Board of Commissioners, 894 F.3d 1335 (11th Cir. 2018).
Bostock v. Clayton County, Georgia, 590 U.S., 140 S. Ct. 1731 (2020).
Brennan v. City Stores, Inc., 479 F.2d 235 (5th Cir. 1973).
Brennan v. Goose Creek Consolidated Independent School District, 519 F.2d 53 (5th Cir. 1975).
California Federal Savings & Loan Association v. Guerra, 479 U.S. 272 (1987).
Carroll v. Talman Federal Savings & Loan Association of Chicago, 604 F. 2d 1028 (7th Cir. 1979).
City of Los Angeles, Dept. of Water & Power v. Manhart, 435 U.S. 702 (1978).
Corning Glass Works v. Brennan, 417 U.S. 188 (1974).
County of Washington et al. v. Gunther, 452 U.S. 161 (1981).
EEOC v. Pallet Companies d/b/a IFCO, Inc., Case No. 1:16-CV-00595 (D. Md. 2016).
EEOC v. R. G. & G. R. Harris Funeral Homes, Inc., 884 F. 3d 560 (6th Cir. 2018).
EEOC v. Scott Medical Health Center, 217 F. Supp. 3d 834. (W. D. Pa. 2016).
Escriba v. Foster Poultry Farms, Incorporated, 743 F. 3d 1236 (9th Cir. 2014).
Frank v. United Airlines, Inc., 216 F. 3d 845 (9th Cir. 2000).
Frappied v. Affinity Gaming Black Hawk, LLC. (10th Cir. 2020).
Geduldig v. Aiello, 417 U.S. 484 (1974).
General Electric Co. v. Gilbert, 429 U.S. 125 (1976).
Guzman v. Brown County, 884 F.3d 633, 641 (7th Cir. 2018).
Harper v. Blockbuster Entertainment Corporation, 139 F.3d 1385 (11th Cir. 1998).
Hively v. Ivy Tech Community College, South Bend, 830 F.3d 698 (7th Cir. 2016).
Hodgson v. Brookhaven General Hospital, 423 F.2d 719; 470 F.2d 729 (5th Cir. 1970).
Hogancamp v. County of Volusia, 316 F. Supp. 3d 1354 (M. D. Fla. 2018).
Jespersen v. Harrah's Operating Co., 280 F. Supp. 2d 1189 (D. Nev. 2002).
Kouba v. Allstate, 691 F.2d 873 (9th Cir. 1982).
Laffey v. Northwest Airlines, Inc., 366 F. Supp. 763 (D.D.C. 1973).
Laffey v. Northwest Airlines, Inc., 567 F.2d 429 (D.C. Cir. 1976).
Laffey v. Northwest Airlines, Inc., 740 F.2d 1071 (D.C. Cir. 1984).
Lanigan v. Bartlett and Company Grain, 466 F. Supp. 1388 (W.D. Mo. 1979).
Ledbetter v. Goodyear Tire & Rubber Co., Inc., 550 U.S. 618 (2007).

Lemons v. City & County of Denver, 620 F.2d 228, 229-30 (10th Cir. 1980).

Little v. Cobb County, 203 Fed. Appx. 993 (11th Cir. 2006).

Macy v. Holder, No. 0120120821, 2012 WL 1435995 (E.E.O.C. Apr. 20, 2012).

Nevada Department of Human Resources v. Hibbs, 538 U.S. 721 (2003).

Phillips v. Martin Marietta, 400 U.S. 542 (1971).

Price Waterhouse v. Hopkins, 490 U.S. 228 (1989).

Rizo v. Yovino, 887 F.3d 453 (9th Cir. 2018).

Schultz v. American Can Co., 424 F.2d 356 (8th Cir. 1970).

Strickland v. Water Works and Sewer Board of the City of Birmingham, 239 F.3d 1199 (11th Cir. 2001).

Smith v. City of Salem, Ohio, 378 F.3d 566 (6th Cir. 2004)

Spaulding v. University of Washington, 740 F.2d 686, 692 (9th Cir. 1984).

Sprogis v. United Airlines Inc. 444 F.2d 1194 (7th Cir., 1971).

Tavora v. New York Mercantile Exchange, 101 F.3rd 907 (2nd Cir. 1996).

Thompson v. Sawyer, 678 F.2d 257, 264 (D.C. Cir. 1982).

Wysong v. Dow Chemical Company, 503 F. 3d 441 (6th Cir. 2007).

Young v. United Parcel Service, 135 U.S. 338 (2015).

Zarda v. Altitude Express, Inc., 883 F. 3d 100 (2nd Cir. 2018).

References

Barkacs, L. L., & Barkacs, C. B. (2009). The time is right—or is it? The Supreme Court speaks in *Ledbetter v. Goodyear Tire & Rubber Co. Journal of Legal, Ethical and Regulatory Issues, 12,* 1–7.

Bartlett, K. T. (1994). Only girls wear barrettes: Dress and appearance standards, community norms, and workplace equality. *Michigan Law Review, 92,* 2541–2582. https://repository.law.umich.edu/mlr/vol92/iss8/7/

Bible, J. (2007). *Ledbetter v. Goodyear Tire & Rubber Co.*: Supreme Court places roadblock in front of title VII pay discrimination plaintiffs. *Labor Law Journal, 58,* 170–182.

Cimpl-Wiemer, A. (2008). *Ledbetter v. Goodyear*: Letting the air out of the continuing violations doctrine? *Marquette Law Review, 92*(2), 355–382.

Claussen, C. L. (1996). Gendered merit: Women and the merit concept in federal employment, 1864–1944. *The American Journal of Legal History, 40,* 229–252.

Cooper, E. A., & Barrett, G. A. (1984). Equal pay and gender: Implications of court cases for personnel practices. *Academy of Management Journal, 9,* 84–94.

Crampton, S. M., Hodge, J. W., & Mishra, J. M. (1997). The Equal Pay Act: The first 30 years. *Public Personnel Management, 26,* 335–344.

Dunleavy, E., & Gutman, A. (2008). Ledbetter v. Goodyear Tire Co.: A divided Supreme Court causes quite a stir. *The Industrial-Organizational Psychologist, 45,* 55–63.

Dunleavy, E., & Gutman, A. (2009). What's new in compensation discrimination enforcement: A review of the Ledbetter Fair Pay Act and Paycheck Fairness Act. *The Industrial-Organizational Psychologist, 47,* 49–57.

Employment Law—Title VII—EEOC Affirms Protections for Transgender Employees—Macy v. Holder. (2013). *Harvard Law Review, 126,* 1731–1738.

Findley, H., Fretwell, C., Wheatley, R., & Ingram, E. (2006). Dress and grooming standards: How legal are they? *Journal of Individual Employment Rights, 12,* 165–182.

Grossman, J. L. (2016). Expanding the core: Pregnancy discrimination law as it approaches full term. *Idaho Law Review, 52,* 825–866.

Grossman, J. L. (2009). Pregnancy, work, and the promise of equal citizenship. *Georgetown Law Journal, 98*, 567–628.

Guerin, L., & England, D. D. (2018). *The essential guide to family & medical leave.* Berkeley, CA: Nolo.

Gutman, A., Koppes, L. L., & Vodanovich, S. J. (2011). *EEO law and personnel practices* (3rd ed.). New York: Psychology Press/Routledge/Taylor & Francis Group.

Hamburg, J. (1989). When prior pay isn't equal pay: A proposed standard for the identification of "factors other than sex" under the Equal Pay Act. *Columbia Law Review, 89*, 1085–1110.

Jolly, J. P., & Frierson, J. G. (1989). Playing it safe. *Personnel Administrator, 34*, 44–50.

Lax, J. (2007). Do employer requests for salary history discriminate against women? *Labor Law Journal, 58*, 47–52.

Ledbetter, L., & Isom, L. S. (2012). *Grace and grit: My fight for equal pay and fairness at Goodyear and beyond.* New York: Three Rivers Press.

Levi, J. L. (2007). Some modest proposals for challenging established dress code jurisprudence. *Duke Journal of Gender Law and Policy, 14*, 243–255. https://scholarship.law.duke.edu/djglp/vol14/iss1/8/

Linsted, J. L. (2006). The Seventh Circuit's erosion of the Equal Pay Act. *Seventh Circuit Review, 1*, 129–151.

Little, L., Hinojosa, A., & Lynch, J. (2017). Make them feel: How the disclosure of pregnancy to a supervisor leads to changes in perceived supervisor support. *Organization Science, 28*, 618–635.

Miller, E. (1980). An EEO examination of employment applications. *Personnel Administrator, 25*, 63–81.

Miller, K. R. (2016). The Ninth Circuit's decision in *Escriba v. Foster Poultry Farms, Inc.* may limit the use of involuntary leave and why that is okay. *University of Cincinnati Law Review, 84*, 307–326.

Miller, M. (2006). Lost in the balance: A critique of the Ninth Circuit's unequal burdens approach to evaluating sex-differential grooming standards under Title VII. *North Carolina Law Review, 84*, 1357–1372. https://scholarship.law.unc.edu/nclr/vol84/iss4/8/

Strah, N., Rupp, D. E., & Morris, S. (in press). Job analysis and job classification for addressing pay inequality in organizations: Adjusting our methods within a shifting legal landscape. *Industrial and Organizational Psychology: Perspectives in Science and Practice.*

Vodanovich, S. J., & Lowe, R. H. (1992). They ought to know better: The incidence and correlates of inappropriate application blank inquiries. *Public Personnel Management, 21*, 363–370.

Wallace, J. C., Tye, M. G., & Vodanovich, S. J. (2000). Applying for jobs online: Examining the legality of Internet-based application forms. *Public Personnel Management, 29*, 497–504.

Wallace, J. C., & Vodanovich, S. J. (2004). Appropriateness of personnel application blanks: Persistence and knowledge of application blank items. *Public Personnel Management, 33*, 331–345.

Zalesne, D. (2007). Lessons from equal opportunity harasser doctrine: Challenging sex-specific appearance and dress codes. *Duke Journal of Gender Law and Policy, 14*, 535–560. https://scholarship.law.duke.edu/djglp/vol14/iss1/18/

7

Age Discrimination

Employment Discrimination. Stephen J. Vodanovich and Deborah E. Rupp, Oxford University Press. © Oxford University Press 2022. DOI: 10.1093/oso/9780190085421.003.0008

Introduction to Basic Protections Under the ADEA

During the crafting of Title VII, discussions occurred about whether to incorporate age as a protected group. However, Congress decided to wait and collect more information on the impact of age discrimination. In the end, Congress concluded that older individuals had a difficult time acquiring jobs and were victims of capricious age limits (e.g., mandatory retirement age requirements). A few years later, in 1967, Congress passed the Age Discrimination in Employment Act (ADEA).[1,2] As stated in the Act, the ADEA sought "to promote employment of older persons based on their ability rather than age; to prohibit arbitrary age discrimination in employment; to help employers and workers find ways of meeting problems arising from the impact of age on employment."

The ADEA prohibits discrimination against individuals aged 40 years and older. There is no upper age limit.[3] However, some exemptions exist, such as retirement at age 65 for bona fide executives (those in upper-level management positions with policy-making duties), firefighters and police officers (e.g., legitimate to not hire after age 35; compulsory retirement at age 55), and mandatory retirement at age 70 for elected officials with policy-making responsibilities. Despite the requirements put forth by the ADEA, age discrimination is one of the more common charges filed with the Equal Employment Opportunity Commission (EEOC)[4] (see Table 7.1).

The Bureau of Labor Statistics has projected the percent of older workers to increase over the next several years (see Figure 7.1). Several factors have fueled this increase, such as the need for income, people living longer,

Table 7.1 Age-related charges filed with the Equal Employment Opportunity Commission (EEOC) 2014–2020

Year	2014	2015	2016	2017	2018	2019	2020
Number of Charges	20,588	20,144	20,857	18,376	16,911	15,573	14,183

Retrieved from https://www.eeoc.gov/eeoc/statistics/enforcement/charges.cfm

[1] https://www.eeoc.gov/laws/statutes/adea.cfm
[2] The ADEA was originally managed by the Department of Labor. In 1978, this responsibility was given to the Equal Employment Opportunity Commission (EEOC). Also, remedies under the ADEA stem from the Fair Labor and Standards Act (FLSA).
[3] The original Act placed an upper age limit on ADEA protections at 65 (i.e., those 65 and older were not covered). In 1978, the upper limit was raised to 70 (those aged 70 years and older were not covered). The upper age limit was removed in 1987. Those aged 40 years and older are protected.
[4] https://www.eeoc.gov/eeoc/statistics/enforcement/charges.cfm

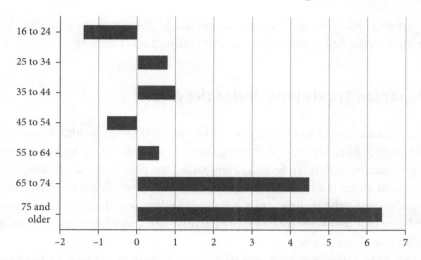

Figure 7.1 Annual growth in labor force by age, projected 2014–2024 (percent).
Source: Bureau of Labor Statistics.

overall higher education levels, and the changing nature of work. Also, the median age of employees is projected to be 42.5 years by 2024.[5] This highlights the large percentage of the workforce with legal protections under the ADEA.

The ADEA includes some unique provisions in comparison to Title VII. First, it is "one-sided." Unlike the protected demographic categories under Title VII, such as race and sex, where all subgroups are protected (e.g., both men and women), only one subgroup is protected by the ADEA: those aged 40 and older. Discrimination claims against younger individuals (i.e., those younger than 40) are not available under the ADEA. Also, age is considered as a continuous (i.e., there exists a range of ages from 40 years onward) rather than a categorical variable (e.g., man vs. woman).[6] We discuss the implications of this later in the chapter. Furthermore, the ADEA requires companies with *20 or more* employees to comply with the Act, versus those with a minimum of 15 workers under Title VII. The ADEA applies to municipalities and federal organizations as well as the private sector. However, the Supreme Court concluded that private individuals cannot sue states under the ADEA in *Kimel v. Florida Board of Regents* (2000),[7] although the EEOC may file suits on behalf

---

[5] https://www.bls.gov/emp/tables/median-age-labor-force.htm
[6] Opinions and court decisions have differed as to whether age groups can be established among those 40 years and older. This is discussed later in the chapter.
[7] https://www.law.cornell.edu/supct/pdf/98-791P.ZO

of private parties. Finally, damages under the ADEA are congruent with those set forth in the Fair Labor Standards Act[8] rather than Title VII.

Disparate Treatment Under the ADEA

The disparate treatment process under the ADEA generally follows the McDonnell-Burdine burden shifting scenario adapted to the specific aspects of age discrimination. To form a *prima facie* case, plaintiffs must belong to the protected group (i.e., be 40 years of age or older), be qualified for the position in question, be the recipient of a negative employment decision, and provide evidence that they were treated more harshly than a *similarly situated substantially younger* employee.

The ADEA also provides special features within the disparate treatment scenario, which we will review in turn, such as the same actor defense (or inference), small age differences, reduction in force (RIF) strategies, and re-organization efforts. Five *affirmative defenses* are also available under the ADEA.[9] These are (1) bona fide seniority systems (BFSS), (2) bona fide occupational qualifications (BFOQs), (3) reasonable factor other than age (RFOA), (4) "good cause" (considered to be a subset of the RFOA defense), and (5) bona fide benefit plans (BFBPs). We review each of these later in the chapter. Table 7.2 illustrates the burden shifting process for ADEA disparate treatment claims.

Table 7.2 Age discrimination disparate treatment scenario

Phase 1	Plaintiffs must establish a *prima facie* case by providing evidence of age discrimination by showing that 1. They are age 40 or older 2. They were qualified for the position in question 3. They were victims of an unfavorable employment decision (e.g., not hired, not promoted, fired, laid off) 4. The organization disfavored an older worker versus a *similarly situated substantially younger employee*
Phase 2	Company must *articulate* that a legitimate, nondiscriminatory reason exists for its decision. Age-specific factors also exist (small age differences, the same actor defense, reduction in force efforts, and reorganization plans).
Phase 3	The plaintiff *proves* that the organization's reason for their rejection is a pretext for discrimination.

[8] https://www.dol.gov/agencies/whd/flsa
[9] An affirmative defense consists of facts proved by a defendant that defeats (or lowers) legal penalties for illegal behavior committed by the defense.

As noted earlier, for plaintiffs to successfully form a *prima facie* case under the ADEA, they must produce evidence that they were disadvantaged as compared to a similarly situated *and* substantially younger individual. Although these two requirements are linked together in ADEA cases, we present them separately. One reason is that different standards exist to determine if someone is a valid comparator (i.e., similarly situated) as opposed to being considered substantially younger. As you will see, there is no consensus on how to specifically define either term, but case law has provided some useful parameters.

Similarly Situated Employee

Importantly, the factors that determine whether someone is "similarly situated"[10] to another individual can vary based on case-specific factors as well as the court in which suits are filed. Essentially, at issue is how much similarity must exist for someone to be considered a valid comparator. For instance, in *Andujar v. General Nutrition Corporation* (2019),[11] an ADEA case, the 3rd Circuit stated that "Comparators must be similarly situated, not identical." But the courts have not provided specific criteria to determine similarly situated status. Instead, they have applied various criteria in determining "similarly situated," including requirements that the comparator be (a) "nearly identical," (b) similar in "all material aspects," (c) similar in "all relevant aspects," and (d) similar "in all respects." Some factors courts have used to assess whether individuals are similarly situated include having the same supervisor, job tasks, and workplace standards, as well as a match in the type and frequency of a comparator's job behavior (see Beckles, 2008; Lidge, 2002). In certain ADEA cases, such as those involving a RIF, it is not easy to find a specific younger employee who was retained for comparison purposes. In these situations, plaintiffs may present facts that similarly situated younger employees, on average, were treated better than their older counterparts.

In *Reeves v. Sanderson Plumbing Products Inc.* (2000),[12,13] Roger Reeves was fired for alleged poor performance. In turn, Reeves presented compelling *indirect evidence* that his so-called poor performance (careless recordkeeping) was a pretext for age discrimination. Reeves successfully proved that the company treated him more severely than a similarly situated employee (Joe

---

[10] The "similarly situated" requirement is not limited to ADEA cases and is a common element in Title VII disparate treatment cases.

[11] https://www2.ca3.uscourts.gov/opinarch/181715np.pdf

[12] https://www.law.cornell.edu/supct/pdf/99-536P.ZO

[13] https://www.oyez.org/cases/1999/99-536

Oswalt). Both Reeves and Oswalt were supervisors in the same department and had similar job duties. Although Oswalt was perceived to have comparable recordkeeping problems and was about 24 years younger than Reeves, he was not fired. Reeves also introduced evidence that someone with the capacity to fire him made derogatory remarks about his age. In the end, a jury ruled in favor of Reeves. As the Court stated,

> Given that petitioner established a prima facie case of discrimination, introduced enough evidence for the jury to reject respondent's explanation, and produced *additional* evidence of age-based animus, there was *sufficient evidence* for the jury to find that respondent had intentionally discriminated (emphasis added).

In *Earl v. Nielsen Media Research, Inc.* (2011),[14] Christine Earl was fired from her job for poor job performance (e.g., policy violations) when she was age 57. Although her performance problems were an issue, Earl presented evidence that younger employees, who ranged in age from 36 to 42, had committed similar policy violations but were not fired. Earl and the other employees worked as recruiters for the organization and had to adhere to the same procedures and policies. The defense maintained that to be considered as being similarly situated all employees must have the same immediate supervisor. The court disagreed and ruled in favor of Earl. To quote from the Circuit Court's decision, "Earl has provided specific and substantial evidence that significantly younger recruiters who repeatedly violated similar policies received more lenient treatment from the company. She has thereby raised a triable issue that Nielsen's proffered reason was pretext for age discrimination."

In *Barnett v. PA Consulting Group, Inc.* (2013), Judith Barnett (age 57) was fired while George Gao (age 41) was retained during an organizational restructuring, leading Barnett to file an ADEA suit. The defense indicated that a primary reason for terminating Barnett was that she was not a "good fit" with the "new" organization. Barnett and Gao were considered to be similarly situated, and the favored employee (Gao) was 16 years younger than the plaintiff. As the court noted, "Different outcomes for Barnett and Gao matter because in nearly all respects material to PA's explanation, Gao was similarly situated to Barnett. The most significant differences between the two are that Gao is male and younger than Barnett." So, a key question was whether or not age was a factor in the layoff decision. To this point, evidence was produced that the company used a spreadsheet to inform their decision, which included the

---

[14] https://scholar.google.com/scholar_case?case=12558978316422668544&q=Earl+v.+Nielsen+Media+Research,+Inc.+(2011)&hl=en&as_sdt=40006

age of employees along with other performance-related data. The 3rd Circuit ruled in favor of Barnett. In doing so, they stated, "A reasonable jury could find the spreadsheet to be probative of discrimination, because the jury might infer that PA's leadership included age as a factor in its personnel decisions."

In *McDaniel v. Progress Rail Locomotive Inc.* (2020),[15] David McDaniel (age 55), who held a material handler position, was terminated for violating safety rules. McDaniel contended that he was fired due to his age and filed an ADEA suit. He contended that eight other material handlers, whom he *believed* to be younger and qualified as being similarly situated, were treated more favorably. However, the 7th Circuit ruled that McDaniel failed to produce evidence that the supposedly younger employees were similarly situated. The court stated that McDaniel did not "provide any information that would allow a finder of fact to determine that these individuals are indeed similarly situated: he did not submit the employees' names, work history, performance reviews, or—most importantly—their ages. In fact, he provided no information at all about the eight individual employees who he alleges are similarly situated." Furthermore, McDaniel did not present information that the "similarly situated" employees also violated safety rules and were treated better. The court subsequently ruled in favor of the organization.

Substantially Younger Employee and Age Differences

The *substantially younger* criteria for forming a *prima facie* ADEA case was illustrated in *O'Conner v. Consolidated Coin Caterers Corporation* (1996).[16] This case involved the firing of James O'Conner (age 67) and replacing him with a younger individual (age 40). The organization stated that since *both* people were in the protected age group, there was no violation of the ADEA. The Supreme Court disagreed with this defense. They concluded that the rather large age difference (27 years) was sufficient evidence that the termination of O'Conner was made because of his age—something that is outlawed by the ADEA (see EEOC enforcement guidance on the *O'Conner* decision).[17] Quoting from the Court's decision:

> The fact that one person in the protected class has lost out to another person in the protected class is thus irrelevant, so long as he has lost out *because of his age* . . . the

---

[15] https://scholar.google.com/scholar_case?case=7611249652098709576&q=McDaniel+v.+Progress+Rail+Locomotive,+Inc.&hl=en&as_sdt=40006
[16] https://www.law.cornell.edu/supct/html/95-354.ZO.html
[17] https://www.eeoc.gov/policy/docs/oconnor.html

fact that a replacement is substantially younger than the plaintiff is a far more reliable indicator of age discrimination than is the fact that the plaintiff was replaced by someone outside the protected class.

In general, when age differences are comparatively *small* between a plaintiff and the person who replaced them (or was treated better), the advantage is with the defense. However, there is no definitive age difference that is considered to be "small." On average, if the age difference is less than 8–10 years, plaintiffs will have a difficult time making a *prima facie* case of age discrimination.

For instance, in *Barber v. CSX Distribution Services* (1995),[18] Kathy Ball (age 44) was hired over Simon Barber (age 52) for the job of territorial account executive despite the fact the Barber had 14 more years of railroad experience. Barber wrote a letter asking why he was not chosen for the position. Several months later, Barber was also informed that his job was being eliminated due to a RIF. As a result, Barber filed an ADEA and a retaliation suit. The topic of workplace retaliation will be discussed at length in Chapter 10. Regarding the ADEA claim, the 3rd Circuit concluded that the difference of eight years in age was sufficient to form a *prima facie* case of age discrimination. To quote the court, "It is clear that here, the eight-year difference between Barber and the successful candidate, Kathy Ball, could support a finding that Ball was 'sufficiently younger' than Barber to permit an inference of age discrimination." The 3rd Circuit also ruled that a nine-year difference in age was enough to form a *prima facie* ADEA case in *Healy v. New York Life Insurance Company* (1988).[19]

On the other hand, in *Grosjean v. First Energy* (2003)[20] William Grosjean (age 54) was replaced by someone 48 years of age. The court ruled that this difference was not substantial enough to establish a *prima facie* case of age discrimination. As the court stated, "Grosjean failed to make his prima facie case of age discrimination because he was not replaced by a person significantly younger than himself."

However, additional evidence, such as pejorative age-related comments expressed by someone with decision-making capacity (e.g., supervisors), can signify age discrimination. One example is the 9th Circuit case of

---

[18] https://scholar.google.com/scholar_case?case=18153248697600202022&q=Barber+v.+CSX+Distribution+Services+(1995),+&hl=en&as_sdt=40006

[19] https://scholar.google.com/scholar_case?case=4623657805474120303&q=Barber+v.+CSX+Distribution+Servs&hl=en&as_sdt=40006

[20] https://caselaw.findlaw.com/us-6th-circuit/1173765.html

France v. Johnson (2015),[21] where John France (age 54) was not promoted to a border patrol position while four younger candidates were hired. Interestingly, all four successful candidates were older than 40 (i.e., ages 44, 45, 47, and 48). The average age difference between France and the younger candidates who were promoted was eight years. As the court stated, "Were the eight-year age difference all the evidence before us, it would not be sufficient to satisfy the fourth prong." The court further noted that: "We hold that an average age difference of ten years or more between the plaintiff and the replacements will be presumptively substantial, whereas an age difference of less than ten years will be presumptively insubstantial." In this case, France presented evidence of age bias on the part of a key decision-maker (e.g., being partial to "young, dynamic agents"; having recurring retirement conversations with the plaintiff). Consequently, the court ruled that a *prima facie* case was made since age was shown to be "significant in making its promotion decisions."

Finally, in *Abnet v. Unifab Corporation* (2006),[22] Jerry Abnet (age 68) was fired from his job as a purchasing agent and eventually replaced by Robert Payne (age 23). Abnet filed an ADEA suit asserting that he was terminated because of his age and replaced with a much younger individual. The District Court ruled that Abnet failed to form a *prima facie* case of age discrimination in that he failed to meet the fourth prong of the ADEA burden shifting process—that he was supplanted by a substantially younger person. In essence, the Court determined that Payne did not actually *replace* Abnet since Payne performed many additional duties beyond that previously performed by the plaintiff.

EEO in the Wild: Derogatory Age-Based Comments

Some evidence exist that derogatory age comments are relatively common. A survey[a] of 3,900 individuals aged 45 and older administered by the American Association of Retired Persons (AARP) indicated that 24% of respondents reported receiving negative age-related comments. The majority of the comments were made by coworkers (15%), while 9% were reported as emanating from supervisors.

---

[21] https://caselaw.findlaw.com/us-9th-circuit/1709789.html
[22] https://scholar.google.com/scholar_case?case=16536518360512240661&q=Abnet+v.+Unifab+Corp.,&hl=en&as_sdt=40006

Age-based remarks do not always indicate discriminatory intent. The specificity of the comments, who made them, and their frequency of occurrence matter. For instance, general or vaguely negative comments about older individuals, comments made by those in non–decision-making roles, infrequent (e.g., one time) comments, and a long time frame between comments and a negative employment decision are generally not sufficient to demonstrate age discrimination (see Hunter & Shannon, 2019). As Mariani and Robertson (1997) stated, "To constitute probative evidence, age-related comments must have a temporal nexus to the employer's decision and generally must be attributable to a person involved in the decision-making process" (p. 96).

Some criteria have been offered to distinguish between stray remarks and those indicative of potential age discrimination. One example comes from *Brown v. CSC Logic Inc.* (1996),[b] a RIF case. Here, the court outlined four important criteria for whether age-related comments would be considered as evidence of an ADEA violation. Essentially, for such comments to be probative, they need to be (a) related to age, (b) occur close in time to a negative employment decision, (c) be uttered by an individual with decision-making authority, and (d) connected to the specific employment decision being contested.

Finally, the EEOC has issued guidelines on how age-based derogatory remarks can create a hostile work environment for older employees. As the EEOC has stated,[c]

"Harassment can include . . . offensive or derogatory remarks about a person's age. Although the law doesn't prohibit simple teasing, offhand comments, or isolated incidents that aren't very serious, harassment is illegal when it is so frequent or severe that it creates a hostile or offensive work environment or when it results in an adverse employment decision."

[a] https://www.aarp.org/content/dam/aarp/research/surveys_statistics/econ/2018/value-of-experience-age-discrimination-highlights.doi.10.26419-2Fres.00177.002.pdf
[b] https://caselaw.findlaw.com/us-5th-circuit/1339806.html
[c] https://www1.eeoc.gov/laws/types/age.cfm

Mixed-Motives and the ADEA

Previously, we mentioned that the Civil Rights Act of 1991 (CRA-91) made it illegal if "race, color, religion, sex, or national origin was a *motivating* factor for any employment practice, even though other factors also motivated the practice." As you may have noticed, the word "age" is *not* included here. This omission created uncertainty around whether ADEA cases were covered by CRA-91. For instance, in a Court of Appeals case (*Mereish v. Walker*, 2004),[23] the 4th Circuit stated that age discrimination is *not* protected under the mixed-motive section of CRA-91 by stating that "when Congress enacted the Civil Rights Act of 1991 in response to *Price Waterhouse*, it amended only Title VII and did not pass a corresponding amendment to the ADEA."

The Supreme Court later supported this logic in *Gross v. FBL Financial Services* (2009).[24,25] Jack Gross sued FBL for age discrimination after being demoted. However, the Court agreed that the CRA-91 did not amend the ADEA, only Title VII. The Court opined that CRA-91's omission of age/ADEA in its language about motivating factors was intentional. To quote from the decision,

> Because Title VII is materially different with respect to the relevant burden of persuasion, this Court's interpretation of the ADEA is not governed by Title VII decisions. . . . Unlike Title VII, which has been amended to explicitly authorize discrimination claims where an improper consideration was 'a motivating factor' for the adverse action . . . the ADEA does not provide that a plaintiff may establish discrimination by showing that age was simply a motivating factor.

So the Court decided that plaintiffs in ADEA cases that involve mixed motives must prove that age was the *but for* (or actual) reason for the alleged discriminatory action (see Harper, 2010; Van Ostrand, 2009). This is a much more onerous burden for plaintiffs to meet versus proving that age was a "motivating" factor.

After the *Gross* decision, some members of Congress made regular attempts to make it illegal to use age as a *motivating factor* in employment decisions. These efforts have not succeeded. But, in June of 2021, a bill called the Protecting Older Workers against Discrimination Act (POWADA) was passed by the House of Representatives that would make it illegal to use age as a motivating factor in employment decisions. As of this writing, it has been sent to the Senate for consideration.

[23] https://caselaw.findlaw.com/us-4th-circuit/1241938.html
[24] https://www.law.cornell.edu/supct/pdf/08-441P.ZO
[25] https://www.oyez.org/cases/2008/08-441

ADEA and the Federal Sector

In the case of *Babb v. Wilkie* (2020),[26,27] the Supreme Court decided that the criteria to demonstrate age discrimination differs for federal-sector employees versus those in private entities. Noris Babb (age 54) filed a gender-plus-age discrimination and retaliation claim against the Veterans Administration (VA) Medical Center (Robert Wilkie was the Secretary of the VA at the time). The Supreme Court decision only dealt with the ADEA claim.

Babb alleged that she was the recipient of several negative personnel decisions that were based on her age. These included (a) removing a designation she possessed, the removal of which made her ineligible for promotions; (b) being overlooked for specific jobs, (c) refusing to grant her training opportunities, and (d) transferring her to a new job where her holiday pay was decreased.

The defense contended that proof that age was a *but for* cause of an employment decision was needed under the ADEA, while the plaintiff disagreed, stating that *any* use of age in personnel decisions is illegal. A key to the Court's decision was the interpretation of the ADEA's Section 633a(a), which pertains to individuals employed in the federal sector. This section states that, "All personnel actions affecting employees or applicants for employment who are at least 40 years of age . . . shall be made free from any discrimination based on age." In the end, the Court ruled (8–1) that under Section 633a(a) of the ADEA, plaintiffs do not have to show that age was a but for cause of personnel actions being challenged. As the Court stated, "the plain meaning of the statutory text shows that age need not be a but for cause of an employment decision in order for there to be a violation of §633a(a)." Furthermore, the opinion stated that the "statute does not require proof that an employment decision would have turned out differently if age had not been taken into account. Instead, if age is a factor in an employment decision, the statute has been violated."

Finally, the Court concluded that Congress purposely inserted a separate section specifically aimed toward the federal sector rather than adding the federal government to entities counted as an "employer," as it did with state and local government agencies. In this regard, the Court wrote that the wording in §633a(a) is quite distinct from the ADEA's private-sector provisions and that it is not atypical for the federal government to be held to a more stringent standard than those within private industry.

---

[26] https://www.supremecourt.gov/opinions/19pdf/18-882_3ebh.pdf
[27] https://www.oyez.org/cases/2019/18-882

Insights from Social Science: Does Job Performance Decline with Age?

The increasing average age of the workforce gives salience to the question of whether job performance declines with age. However, it is important to distinguish age-related stereotypes from actual age-related performance decrements. Research has shown significant evidence of age-related stereotypes, indicating that older workers are often viewed as less capable and less productive compared to younger workers (e.g., Finkelstein, Burke, & Raju, 1995; Issacharoff & Harris, 1997; Perry, Kulik, & Bourhis, 1996), though results are nuanced. Posthuma, Wagstaff, and Campion (2012) provided six facets on which older workers may be judged in comparison to younger workers: (1) job performance, (2) ability to learn, (3) job tenure, (4) costs, (5) resistance to change, and (6) dependability. Whereas stereotypes around many of these facets may be negative for older workers (e.g., resistance to change, ability to learn), some may be positive (e.g., dependability). For example, Finkelstein, Ryan, and King (2013) found that 60% of young (18–30) and 85% of middle-aged (31–50) employees gave positive descriptions of older workers (aged 51 and older), though negative perceptions about older worker's inability to learn and resistance to change still existed. Other research has found age bias even when the performance of an older versus younger worker was held constant (see Rupp, Vodanovich, & Crede, 2006; Waldman & Avolio, 1986).

Despite evidence that older workers are often assumed to have performance declines, a comprehensive meta-analysis of the age–job performance relationship does not support stereotypical beliefs and assessments about older employees. Ng and Feldman (2008) analyzed data from 380 studies on ten performance criteria. The findings indicated that older workers are more likely to exhibit:

- Safety behaviors
- Organizational citizenship behaviors

Older employees were less likely to:
- Perform counterproductive work behaviors
- Be aggressive
- Engage in on-the-job substance use
- Be late for work
- Miss work voluntarily

Age was not significantly related to task performance and creativity. A small negative association was found between age and training performance, much of which involved technology-based training programs. This suggests that care be taken when making assumptions about older workers who very well may serve the workforce in positive ways.

Hostile Environment Based on Age

The courts did not recognize ADEA hostile environment claims until recently. Generally, the formation of a *prima facie* case follows that of hostile environment claims under Title VII (e.g., sexual harassment). In the first age-based hostile environment case to reach the circuit court level (*Crawford v. Medina General Hospital* (1996),[28] the 5th Circuit listed the criteria needed to form a *prima facie* case of age-based harassment. These criteria were that individuals must (1) be in a protected group (i.e., aged 40 years or older), (2) be recipients of either physical or verbal harassment due to age, (3) show that the alleged harassment "had the effect of unreasonably interfering with the employee's work performance and creating an objectively intimidating, hostile, or offensive work environment," and (4) some employer liability is present.

Given this framework, the court ruled that Mary Ann Crawford (age 55) failed to meet the second and third prongs required of a *prima facie* case. That is, she failed to show that the harassment was based on her age and that a hostile environment was created. Specifically, Crawford presented two comments by one of her supervisors as evidence of age bias. One was that old people "should be seen and not heard." The other negative comment attributed to her supervisor was "I don't think women over 55 should be working."

The court concluded that such comments, while rude, were *not* severe enough to form a hostile environment. In addition, the court decided that Crawford failed to offer evidence that the alleged harassment interfered with her work performance (in fact, Crawford admitted to liking her job). As the court noted, "even apart from the fact that only two comments were actually discernibly age-based, there is simply no question that the hostility at Medina, while not insubstantial, was not particularly severe or degrading. Crawford's

---

[28] https://scholar.google.com/scholar_case?case=12262906048492807771&q=crawford+v+medina+general+hosp&hl=en&as_sdt=40006

complaints are of 'mere offensive utterance[s],' as opposed to physically threatening or humiliating conduct."

In general, it has been difficult for plaintiffs to succeed in age harassment claims. In the case of *Snyder v. Pierre's French Ice Cream Co.* (2014),[29] Donald Snyder (age 59) was laid off along with ten other employees. When business increased, the company began recalling employees (based on seniority) who had been previously laid off, several of which were ten years younger than Snyder. When Snyder was eligible for an open position, the organization decided to hire a temporary worker instead, something that was allowed under an existing collective bargaining agreement. Snyder filed a disparate treatment and hostile environment claim.

Regarding the hostile environment charge, Snyder presented evidence that he was the recipient of consistent negative age-related remarks by his supervisor across three years. Examples of age-based comments included, "old man"; "Don, nothing against you personally, but if I was in charge, I would never have hired you, you're too old"; and "Can you handle that, old man?" The 6th Circuit ruled in favor of the organization. Part of their reasoning was that the age-based comments were not sufficient to establish a hostile work environment. The court stated that, "The record shows that there was a culture of 'shop talk' in the warehouse, and Snyder himself participated in the banter." They also believed that his supervisor's comments did not have a negative effect on the plaintiff's job performance. So, given the record as a whole, the 6th Circuit concluded that "Snyder cannot demonstrate that the harassment he alleges was sufficiently severe or pervasive that it created an objectively hostile work environment."

Other failed hostile work environment suits based on age include *Bennis v. Minnesota Hockey Ventures Group* (2013)[30] and *Fletcher v. Gulfside Casino, Inc.* (2012).[31] Both cases involved derogatory age-related comments. In *Bennis*, the plaintiff (William Bennis) was fired for alleged poor job performance. Bennis filed an ADEA hostile environment suit largely based on negative age-based comments by supervisory personnel that included being labeled as "old fashioned," being told "your eyes get worse as you get older," and that he liked so-called classic rock music since it was "from your era," and being told that "times have changed." The suit also contended that he was treated poorly compared to younger employees. The district court in Minnesota ruled that Bennis

---

[29] https://scholar.google.com/scholar_case?case=5852625053157318485&q=snyder+v.+Pierre%27s+french+ice+cream&hl=en&as_sdt=40006
[30] https://scholar.google.com/scholar_case?case=3595049677580548362&q=Bennis+v.+Minnesota+Hockey+&hl=en&as_sdt=40006
[31] https://scholar.google.com/scholar_case?case=11383318138490900372&q=Fletcher+v.+Gulfside+Casino++&hl=en&as_sdt=40006

did not show that he was treated negatively versus a similarly situated younger employee and that the age comments were mild in nature and did not occur very often. From the court's opinion, "These comments were mild, reflecting little if any age-discriminatory animus. At best, they were teasing comments, and at worst, they were unkind or insensitive. Such offhand comments and isolated incidents do not constitute a hostile work environment."

In the *Fletcher* case, Debra Fletcher (age 58) was terminated for poor performance and violating company rules. According to the plaintiff, she was the recipient of age-based remarks that were "offensive" and "humiliating" (e.g., "you got your hearing aids on?"; "maybe you all need to get a walker. . . "; "did you take your Geritol today?"). In ruling for the casino, the court stated, "This Court is of the opinion that no reasonable factfinder could construe the evidence that has been presented on this claim to be of a level serious enough to constitute age harassment."

All is not lost, however, for hostile work environment claims based on age. For instance, in *Dediol v. Best Chevrolet, Inc.* (2011),[32] Milan Dediol (age 65) alleged that he was subjected to both age-based physical and verbal harassment by his supervisor on a regular basis for about two months. The verbal remarks included calling him "old man," "pops," and other more derogatory terms. His supervisor also physically threatened Dediol (e.g., stating that he was going to beat him up, charging at him in front of several other employees). The plaintiff also contended that his supervisor guided certain jobs away from him in favor of younger workers. In the end, Dediol stated that he could not work in such an environment and decided to not show up for work. He was subsequently fired and filed ADEA, religious discrimination, and constructive discharge suits. In terms of the ADEA claim, the 5th Circuit ruled that Dediol had made a *prima facie* case of an age-related hostile work environment. As the court noted, "the record supports Dediol's assertion that he endured a pattern of name calling of a half-dozen times daily and that it may have interfered with his pecuniary interests." The court also stated that these events, combined with the physically threatening behavior by his supervisor "underscore our conclusion that at the very least, there is a genuine issue of material fact on this claim."

Another successful hostile environment case for plaintiffs is *Worden v. Interbake Foods LLC* (2012).[33] Mary Worden (age 54) was fired for allegedly violating company rules. After her termination, the plaintiff filed a suit

---

[32] https://scholar.google.com/scholar_case?case=5555043418652493543&q=Dediol+v.+Best+Chevrolet+2011&hl=en&as_sdt=40006
[33] https://scholar.google.com/scholar_case?case=14272473651428296663&q=Worden+v.+Interbake+Foods+(2012).&hl=en&as_sdt=40006#[10

that included a hostile work environment claim alleging ongoing (daily) age-based comments by her supervisor (e.g., that she ought to retire, was forgetful, old, ought to be caring for her husband, her "brain needs a lot of rest"). Furthermore, Worden stated that these remarks were delivered while other workers were present and that she voiced objections to her supervisor about the comments. Finally, Worden stated that the age-related comments began soon after her supervisor learned of her age. The District Court in South Dakota ruled in favor of Worden. In doing so, the court stated, "The proximity of these remarks in relation to the date of her termination, the frequency of the remarks, and the substance of the remarks are sufficient to establish a specific link between the discriminatory animus and Worden's termination." The court further noted that "Based on the totality of the circumstances, the evidence in the record shows that the harassment directed at Worden rose to a level sufficient enough to support a hostile work environment claim."

Adverse Impact and the ADEA

The viability of adverse impact claims under the ADEA has had an uneven history. Earlier cases allowed adverse impact suits for age discrimination and used the burden shifting scenario within Title VII (see *Geller v. Markham*, 1980[34]; *Leftwich v. Harris-Stowe State College*, 1983[35]). Recall that the burden shifting process under Title VII requires that (1) plaintiffs demonstrate that an identified employment practice disproportionately omits individuals in a protected group, (2) the defense proves the job-relatedness and business necessity of its challenged practices, and (3) plaintiffs prove that an equal alternative exists that leads to less or no adverse impact.

In *Geller v. Markham*, Geller (age 55) was replaced by another teacher who was 25 years of age. The defense used a policy that gave preference to recruiting and hiring those below the sixth step in the salary scale. In *Leftwich v. Harris-Stowe*, Leftwich (age 47 with tenure status) was let go in a RIF plan while an untenured teacher (age 33) was not terminated. The school had a plan that reserved certain jobs for untenured faculty. The defense included the fact that tenured personnel were paid more, that tenure (not age) was a factor in their decision, and that the *average* age of tenured faculty was the same as those without tenure.

[34] https://scholar.google.com/scholar_case?case=11473547471713631348&hl=en&as_sdt=6&as_vis=1&oi=scholarr
[35] https://casetext.com/case/leftwich-v-harris-stowe-state-college

In both cases, the alleged legitimate factors of salary steps (*Geller*) and tenure status (*Leftwich*) were shown to correlate with age and found *not* to be a legitimate defense. Also, reducing costs was judged to be an impermissible defense under Title VII. Finally, the lack of significant age differences between the tenured and untenured faculty in *Leftwich* was judged to be an illegitimate defense. Essentially, the Court considered it a so-called bottom line defense that was prohibited by the Supreme Court in *Connecticut v. Teal* (1982).[36,37]

The legal scene began to change in the 1990s, when court decisions slowly questioned the legitimacy of adverse impact suits under the ADEA. A key case in this regard was *Hazen v. Biggens* (1993).[38,39] Walter Biggens was age 62 when he was terminated. He had been employed by the company for more than nine years and was a few weeks away from being vested in the company's pension plan. Biggins filed an ADEA claim stating that age was a key factor in the decision to fire him. The defense countered that Biggins was fired for doing business with its competitors.

The Court rejected the claim that Biggins was a victim of age discrimination. In doing so, the decision stated that a legitimate business reason can be defensible despite being *correlated* with age (e.g., years of service, pension status). As the Court stated: "Because age and years of service are analytically distinct, an employer can take account of one while ignoring the other, and thus it is incorrect to say that a decision based on years of service is necessarily 'age based.'"

The justices also cast doubt on the applicability of adverse impact claims under the ADEA, favoring the disparate treatment framework instead. Although the Court did not explicitly rule that adverse impact was unavailable under the ADEA, several lower courts started to ban adverse impact suits of age discrimination in light of this ruling.

All was not lost for Biggens, however. The organization was found to have violated the Employment Retirement Income Security Act (ERISA).[40] The criteria for forming a *prima facie* case under ERISA requires plaintiffs to show, with direct or indirect evidence, that they were covered under an organizations' plan, were the recipient of an adverse employment action, met the company's reasonable expectations, and showed that the denial of benefits by

---

[36] Recall that in *Teal* the Court ruled that Title VII protects *individual* victims of discrimination. The fact that Blacks, as a whole, did not suffer adverse impact at the end of the promotion process did not justify discriminating against certain Black individuals at the beginning (first hurdle) of the process.

[37] https://caselaw.findlaw.com/us-supreme-court/457/440.html

[38] https://caselaw.findlaw.com/us-supreme-court/507/604.html

[39] https://www.oyez.org/cases/1992/91-1600

[40] https://www.dol.gov/sites/dolgov/files/EBSA/about-ebsa/our-activities/resource-center/faqs/retirement-plans-and-erisa-compliance.pdf

the organization was a motivating factor in making an adverse employment decision (e.g., termination).

Many years later, the Supreme Court affirmed and added to its decision in *Hazen v. Biggens.* In 2005, the Court ruled on the case of *Smith v. City of Jackson* (2005).[41,42] The city of Jackson, Mississippi, decided to give larger raises (on a percentage basis) to officers and dispatchers in the police department who had fewer than five years of job tenure. By doing so, a significant difference in age (four standard deviations) was found to exist between those with fewer than five years of job tenure compared to employees with five or more years on the job. Consequently, an ADEA suit was filed by Azel Smith and other police employees included in the protected age group. The lower courts in this case decided that adverse impact suits were prohibited under the ADEA. However, the Supreme Court reversed these rulings and concluded that adverse impact suits were a legitimate option for age discrimination cases. But, consistent with *Hazen,* the Court stated that it was appropriate to use factors that are cor-related with age (job tenure in this case), further signaling that the use of such factors was *not* a violation of the ADEA.

Critically, in *Smith,* the Court also altered the burden of proof in phases 2 and 3 for ADEA adverse impact claims as compared to Title VII (see Table 7.3). That is, in phase 2, use of a reasonable factor other than age (RFOA) is required by the defense to justify its alleged discriminatory beha-vior. Recall that in Title VII adverse impact scenarios, the defense burden is to demonstrate job-relatedness and business necessity. In phase 3 of ADEA suits, plaintiffs are required to prove that the RFOA generated by the de-fense is *not reasonable* or is a *pretext* for the use of an illegal factor. This is in contrast to Title VII requirements that plaintiffs prove that an equally valid alternative with less (or no) adverse impact was available (see Gutman, 2005).[43] The EEOC has stated that the determination of "reasonable" can be based on the *degree* of impact that a practice has on older individuals in adverse impact cases (see EEOC questions and answers regarding disparate treatment and RFOA under the ADEA.)[44]

In *Meacham v. KAPL* (2008),[45,46] the Supreme Court added some clarity to the *Jackson* decision. Prior to the Supreme Court's decision in 2008, the Court of Appeals for the 2nd Circuit ruled in (*Meacham v. Knolls Atomic Power*

[41] https://www.law.cornell.edu/supct/pdf/03-1160P.ZO
[42] https://www.oyez.org/cases/2004/03-1160
[43] https://www.siop.org/Portals/84/TIP/Archives/431.pdf?ver=2019-08-20-115130-747
[44] https://www.eeoc.gov/laws/regulations/adea_rfoa_qa_final_rule.cfm
[45] https://www.law.cornell.edu/supct/pdf/06-1505P.ZO
[46] https://www.oyez.org/cases/2007/06-1505

Table 7.3 Comparison of adverse impact scenarios under Title VII and the Age Discrimination in Employment Act (ADEA)

	Title VII adverse impact scenario	ADEA adverse impact scenario
Phase 1	Plaintiffs present statistical evidence that a particular employment practice causes a disproportionate exclusion of protected group members.	Plaintiffs present statistical evidence that a particular employment practice disproportionally excludes individuals age 40 and older.
Phase 2	Defendants offer proof that the challenged employment practice is job-related for the position in question and consistent with business necessity.	Defendants offer proof that the alleged discriminatory employment action is based on a reasonable factor other than age (RFOA).
Phase 3	Plaintiffs offer proof that an equally valid, alternate job-related practice with less or no adverse impact is available.	Plaintiffs offer proof that the reason offered by the defense is either unreasonable or a pretext for age discrimination.

Adapted from Gutman, Koppes, & Vodanovich (2011).

Laboratory, 2006)[47] that the RFOA defense in an ADEA adverse impact scenario required organizations to produce (or articulate) a reasonable, non-age factor for its actions. But the Supreme Court reversed the 2nd Circuit. That is, the majority of justices on the Court concluded that organizations need to *prove* (not simply articulate) the existence of an RFOA. Their reasoning was that an RFOA is an *affirmative defense* under the ADEA, and, like all affirmative defenses (e.g., BFOQ, BFBP, BFSS), the burden of proof (persuasion) is required. As the Court stated, "The ADEA's text and structure indicate that the RFOA exemption creates an affirmative defense, for which the burden of *persuasion* falls on the employer" (emphasis added).

The end result of these decisions is that adverse impact is actionable for ADEA claims. Nevertheless, the burden shifting process differs from adverse impact suits under Title VII. This distinction arguably makes it more difficult for plaintiffs to win ADEA adverse impact cases, particularly given the need for plaintiffs to prove that an organization's use of a RFOA was "unreasonable." Table 7.3 illustrates the differences between the adverse impact scenario under Title VII versus the ADEA.

In adverse impact cases under the ADEA, the courts have disagreed on *who* is covered. In *Villarreal v. RJ Reynolds Tobacco Co.* (2015),[48] the 11th Circuit concluded that ADEA adverse impact suits can only be filed by employees. A similar conclusion was reached by the 7th Circuit in *Kleber v. Carefusion*

---

[47] https://scholar.google.com/scholar_case?case=2563047757974732437&q=Meacham+v.+KAPL+2nd+circuit&hl=en&as_sdt=40006
[48] https://caselaw.findlaw.com/us-11th-circuit/1750280.html

Incorporated (2019). These decisions are at odds with a district court ruling that stated *applicants* may also pursue such claims (*Rabin v. Price Waterhouse Coopers LLP*, 2017).[49] The cases centered on the interpretation of Section 4(a)(2) of the ADEA which makes it unlawful for an organization to

> limit, segregate, or classify his employees in any way which would deprive or tend to deprive *any individual* of employment opportunities or otherwise adversely affect his status *as an employee*, because of such individual's age (emphasis added).

Basically, the difference between the decisions is whether ADEA protections are constrained to employees or to individuals as a whole (i.e., both applicants *and* employees). The *Rubin* decision adopted a more comprehensive viewpoint regarding who is covered. In doing so, *Rubin* is consistent with previous Supreme Court decisions regarding coverage in Title VII cases (e.g., both applicants and employees are covered). The EEOC's position also advocates the coverage of *individuals*, thereby including *both* applicants and employees.

Adverse Impact and Age Subgroups

In adverse impact cases, the courts have differed as to whether age *categories* (or subgroups) among those within the protected group can be established for data analysis purposes (see McAllister, 2019[50]; Weber, 2018). For instance, in *Karlo v. Pittsburg Glass Works, LLC* (2017)[51] the court allowed age groups to be established within the protected age group to determine the existence of adverse impact. In *Karlo*, a RIF effort was challenged under the ADEA. Adverse impact was *not* suggested to exist for those between 40 and 49 years of age, but rather for those age 50 and older. The 3rd Circuit ruled that subgroups within the protected age group (40 and older) were legitimate to use as comparators in determining adverse impact (see also Gutman, 2012; Vilella, 2018).[52]

The 3rd Circuit used two Supreme Court decisions to support its verdict. One was the previously mentioned case of *O'Connor v. Consolidated Coin Caterers* (1996), where a substantially younger employee (age 40) was favored over an older one (age 67). The Court decided that the ADEA prohibited discrimination because of age even if both individuals belonged to the protected

---

[49] https://scholar.google.com/scholar_case?case=18312586460117514102&q=Rabin+v.+Price+Waterhouse+Coopers,+2017&hl=en&as_sdt=40006&as_vis=1
[50] https://pdfs.semanticscholar.org/8d6a/c6d1744c2a89f0ecf8ac293079b4a2395f5e.pdf
[51] https://scholar.google.com/scholar_case?case=6619428715888806063&hl=en&as_sdt=6&as_vis=1&oi=scholarr
[52] https://digitalcommons.wcl.american.edu/cgi/viewcontent.cgi?article=1103&context=aublr

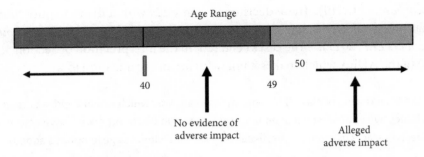

Figure 7.2 Age subgroup comparisons in *Karlo v. Pittsburg Glass Works* (2017).

group. In *O'Conner*, the large difference in ages of the two individuals ("substantially younger" criteria) was sufficient to infer that the decision was a violation of the ADEA.

The other case that the court used to back its ruling in *Karlo* was *Connecticut v. Teal* (1982). Recall that in *Teal*, the Court decided that it was illegal to discriminate against certain Black individuals while also treating other Blacks favorably—invalidating the so-called bottom line defense. The judge in *Karlo* suggested that, if the data were combined (i.e., using *everyone* aged 40 years and older), organizations could hide adverse impact for employees age 50 and older by simply not discriminating against individuals age 40–49 years. In other words, such an analysis could minimize the detection of any adverse impact of those in the upper age range. This was thought to be a clear violation of the precedent set in *Teal*. The primary issue in *Karlo* is illustrated in Figure 7.2.

Contrary opinions occurred in *Lowe v. Commack Union Free School District* (1989)[53]; *EEOC v. McDonnell Douglas Corporation* (1999)[54]; and *Smith v. Tennessee Valley Authority* (1991). In these cases, the formation of age subgroups was *not* permitted for adverse impact cases. For instance, in *Lowe*, statistical analysis was used to indicate adverse impact in the hiring of older workers. Consequently, the plaintiffs, Annemarie Lowe and Marie Delisi, filed an ADEA suit. They alleged that the subjective hiring practice used by the school district adversely impacted individuals older than 50 versus those younger than 50. Importantly, the court concluded that the formation of subgroups within the protected age group (40 and older) was not legitimate. As the 2nd Circuit noted, the plaintiffs "ask us to expand the disparate impact approach so as to include recognition of 'sub-groups' in the analysis of

---

[53] https://openjurist.org/886/f2d/1364/lowe-v-commack-union-free-school-district-l
[54] https://openjurist.org/191/f3d/948/equal-employment-opportunity-commission-v-mcdonnell-douglas-corporation

the impact a hiring process . . . under the ADEA . . . they seek to define the protected group as those 50 or older. . . . If appellants' approach were to be followed, an 85-year-old plaintiff could seek to prove a discrimination claim by showing that a hiring practice caused a disparate impact on the 'sub-group' of those age 85 and above. . . . We find no support in the case law or in the ADEA for the approach to disparate impact analysis appellants advocate." Another ruling by the court was that the plaintiffs failed to identify a specific employment practice that caused the alleged adverse impact (see Dee [1991] for a review of the *Lowe* case).[55]

Particular ADEA Defenses

The ADEA contains a few defenses for organizations that are unique to the law. As such, these defenses can lead to changes in the traditional disparate treatment scenario. These defenses often make it more difficult for plaintiffs to succeed given that extra information is required.[56]

Same Actor Defense

The same actor defense (also known as the *same actor inference*) occurs when the *same* actor (e.g., supervisor) makes a positive employment decision (e.g., hiring) that is followed by a negative action (e.g., firing) regarding the *same person*.[57] As an example, in *Proud v. Stone* (1991),[58] the supervisor who hired Warren Proud subsequently fired him for poor performance several months later after offering to help Proud increase his skills as a supervisor. In this context, the implication of the same actor defense is that age is not likely to be a factor in the decision-making process. The same actor defense has been supported in other ADEA cases (see *Brown v. CSC Logic*, 1996[59]; *Buhrmaster v. Overnite Transportation Co.*, 1995[60]; *Houk v. Peopleoungers*, 2007; *Rand v. CF Industries, Inc.*, 1994[61]).

---

[55] https://openscholarship.wustl.edu/cgi/viewcontent.cgi?article=1891&context=law_lawreview

[56] The issue of age differences has been considered as a particular ADEA defense. However, we included it earlier in the section discussing the substantially younger criteria, given the amount of overlap between the two.

[57] The same actor defense is not limited to ADEA claims. For instance, it can be used for groups protected by Title VII and those with disabilities.

[58] https://scholar.google.com/scholar_case?case=4830269821409352102&hl=en&as_sdt=6&as_vis=1&oi=scholarr

[59] https://caselaw.findlaw.com/us-5th-circuit/1339806.html

[60] https://caselaw.findlaw.com/us-6th-circuit/1300733.html

[61] https://casetext.com/case/rand-v-cf-industries-inc

However, the same actor defense is not bulletproof. It can be offset if plaintiffs present evidence of age discrimination, which can include disparaging age-related comments by decision-makers. In *Madel v. FCI Marketing, Inc.* (1997),[62] two employees, Robert Madel (age 55) and Frank Brennen (age 62) were terminated. Poor performance was given as the reason for the firings. The same person who hired Madel, Allen Carlson, recommended to the President of the company that both employees should be fired. But evidence was presented that negative age-based comments were made by Carlson soon before the firing decisions were made. The District Court issued a summary judgment in favor of FCI, concluding that age was not a factor in the termination decisions. The Court of Appeals for the 8th Circuit disagreed. As the appeals court noted,

> Plaintiffs have presented evidence in response to Defendant's justifications from which a jury could conclude that age was a determinative factor in Defendant's decision to terminate them. We are primarily concerned with the allegedly pervasive use of age-based epithets by Carlson. . . . Plaintiffs have satisfied their burden of presenting sufficient evidence to create a genuine issue of fact as to whether FCI intentionally discriminated against Plaintiffs because of their age.

Another example is *Wexler v. White's Fine Furniture, Inc.* (2003).[63] Donald Wexler was hired, promoted (at age 57), and then demoted in less than two years' time by the President and CEO of the organization (Gordon Schiffman). Wexler was replaced by someone in his mid-30s, which led to Wexler filing an ADEA suit. At trial, evidence was presented that disparaging remarks (e.g., "pops," "old man") were made by two individuals with decision-making ability, including Schiffman. Indeed, Schiffman told Wexler on a phone call that he would tell the employees that the reason for Wexler's demotion was due to his "getting older." As with the Madel case, the district court issued a summary judgment in favor of White's Fine Furniture based on the same-actor defense. However, the 6th Circuit refuted the summary judgment and sent the case back for trial by a jury. As the Court of Appeals stated,

> We therefore specifically hold that where, as in this case, the factfinder decides to draw the same-actor inference, it is insufficient to warrant summary judgment for the defendant if the employee has otherwise raised a genuine issue of material

---

[62] https://caselaw.findlaw.com/us-8th-circuit/1188451.html
[63] https://caselaw.findlaw.com/us-6th-circuit/1361717.html

fact.... Thus, the district court erred when it invoked the same-group inference at the summary judgment stage.

This was not the first time a court has questioned the weight of presumptive evidence[64] given to the same-actor defense. For instance, in the ADEA case *Williams v. Vitro Services Corporation* (1998),[65] the 11th Circuit overturned a lower court decision that ruled in favor of the organization's use of the same actor inference (As the *Williams* court stated, it is the role of a jury "to determine whether the inference generated by 'same actor' evidence is strong enough to outweigh a plaintiff's evidence of pretext." Similar logic was used in *Waldron v. SL Industries, Inc.* (1995)[66]—another ADEA case where a summary judgment for the defense issued by a district court was reversed. Here, the 3rd Circuit noted that the same actor defense "is simply evidence like any other and should not be accorded any presumptive value" and that the importance of the same actor defense is best determined by a jury (see Goldman [2007] for a critical review of the same-actor inference).[67]

Finally, arguments have been made that the same actor can make both positive and negative employment decisions and nonetheless be driven by discriminatory intent (e.g., Northup, 1998[68]; Quintanilla & Kaiser, 2016[69]) and that the same actor defense is inconsistent with social science research regarding how bias and discrimination operate (see Ventrell-Monsees, 2019).

Reduction in Force Defense

The majority of ADEA claims involving RIFs have centered around disparate treatment claims that older workers were treated more severely in comparison to their younger counterparts. In *Williams v. General Motors Corporation* (1981),[70] the company engaged in a large reduction in force that affected almost 400 salaried workers who were terminated or dropped to hourly jobs. An ADEA suit was filed stating that GM's RIF favored younger employees with less job tenure and was part of an overall approach to keep younger workers (e.g., college graduates). Here it was alleged that the organization, in

---

[64] Presumptive evidence is evidence that is believed to be true until proved otherwise.

[65] https://caselaw.findlaw.com/us-11th-circuit/1365085.html

[66] https://caselaw.findlaw.com/us-3rd-circuit/1336832.html

[67] https://www.virginialawreview.org/articles/putting-pretext-context-employment-discrimination-same-actor-inference-and-proper/

[68] https://digitalcommons.law.uw.edu/wlr/vol73/iss1/9/

[69] https://www.californialawreview.org/print/01same-actor-inference-nondiscrimination/

[70] https://scholar.google.com/scholar_case?case=8447940149510329496&q=Williams+v.+Gen.+Motors+Corp.,+656+F.2d+120,&hl=en&as_sdt=40006

an effort to retain younger employees, rotated younger individuals between jobs, put them in the personnel department, or placed them on training budgets. After such rotations, the younger employees would return to service or manufacturing jobs. After a long and complicated trial at the district court level, the 5th Circuit decided on appeal that the plaintiff failed to make a *prima facie* case under the ADEA. General Motors argued that the plaintiffs needed to provide evidence that the company intentionally failed to retain them in the RIF because of their age—a requirement that was not met. Consequently, the court ruled in favor of General Motors.

In *EEOC v. Borden's, Inc.* (1984),[71] Borden's closed one of its plants and terminated all employees working there. According to a recent organization policy, employees who were eligible for retirement (those age 55 and older and with 10 years of service) did *not* qualify for severance pay. However, other workers not suitable for retirement were given a severance. Consequently, the EEOC filed a suit alleging that the policy violated the ADEA, alleging that older workers were denied severance pay because of their age. The Court of Appeals for the 9th Circuit ruled that Borden's severance policy discriminated against older employees, concluding that the severance policy discriminated against employees age 55 and older, and that this was true under either disparate treatment or disparate impact. Regarding disparate treatment, the court noted, "Borden's severance pay policy denied a benefit to certain employees because they were age 55 or older. The discrimination was intentional in the sense that Borden's purposefully drafted its severance pay policy to have this effect." In terms of disparate impact, the court disagreed with the defense that such suits are not available under the ADEA. Specifically, the court stated that "While it is true that the disparate impact theory first arose in cases under Title VII of the Civil Rights Act of 1964, the similar language, structure, and purpose of Title VII and the ADEA, as well as the similarity of the analytic problems posed in interpreting the two statutes, has led us to adopt disparate impact in cases under the ADEA."

Another RIF case is *Benson et al. v. Tocco, Incorporated* (1997).[72] Four mechanical designers (Fredrick Benson, Frank Dollar, Robert Brown, Rolan Archambault) were terminated in a RIF. The organization articulated that the RIF was for economic reasons and that the plaintiffs were identified for layoffs due to performance deficits (e.g., insufficient computer skills). However, some of the plaintiffs (Benson, Archambault) were not informed

[71] https://scholar.google.com/scholar_case?case=68149960287917 19222&q=EEOC+v.+Bordens,+1984&hl=en&as_sdt=40006
[72] https://scholar.google.com/scholar_case?case=8367136057133697005&q=benson+et+al.+v.+tocco+1997&hl=en&as_sdt=40006

at the time of the RIF that their terminations were related to poor performance. In addition, evidence was introduced that younger employees were hired or retained with respect to three of the plaintiffs (Archambault, Dollar, Brown).

Plaintiffs were also able to show that they were qualified for their "restructured" job or other available positions within the company at the time of the RIF. Finally, an expert witness presented evidence that individuals in the protected age group were five times more likely to be laid off during the RIF than those younger than 40. Importantly, the statistical evidence was considered relevant in conjunction with other information. To quote from the court, "We view the evidence submitted by the appellants regarding the rate of termination of older employees to be statistically significant and, accordingly, consider it, where relevant, in tandem with the other evidence adduced in the record."

The 11th Circuit reversed the District Court's summary judgment for the defense and ruled in favor of three of the four plaintiffs. As the court stated, "We conclude that Archambault, Brown, and Benson have produced sufficient evidence to permit a rational trier of fact to infer that the defendants acted with discriminatory intent in choosing to discharge them." The court decided that Dollar failed to prove that the reasons for firing him were a pretext for age discrimination.

Meacham v. KAPL (2008),[73,74] an adverse impact case mentioned earlier, involved a RIF that required laying off employees who had worked for the organization for 20 years or longer. To determine who to terminate, the company asked supervisors to rate employees on several factors including job performance, "flexibility," "critical skills," and job tenure. Ratings on flexibility and critical skills carried the most weight in the decision-making process. In the end, 30 out of 31 employees who were laid off were age 40 or older—a statistically unlikely outcome. Given this outcome, the plaintiffs filed an ADEA adverse impact case. As noted earlier, the Supreme Court ruled that KAPL had to prove, rather than articulate, the presence of a RFOA.[75] As Gutman (2012) noted about the decision, "The moral is clear—if employers establish layoff criteria that disproportionately affect older workers, they must be prepared to prove that these are legitimate reasons that can be backed with factual evidence " (p. 618).

---

[73] https://www.law.cornell.edu/supct/pdf/06-1505P.ZO
[74] https://www.oyez.org/cases/2007/06-1505
[75] Interestingly, the type of proof eventually required of KAPL is unclear. That is, in *Meacham v. KAPL* (2009) a district court ruled that the RFOA defense was not available to KAPL since the company knew of the defense and failed to pursue it.

Hartman and Homer (1990) provided a set of recommendations for organizations involved in RIF efforts. These include (a) a policy that indicates how RIFs are handled and an analysis to defend the reasons for the layoffs and the number of employees affected, (b) records showing that alternative RIF approaches were considered and found not to be doable, (c) use organizational tenure to decide who to terminate, and (d) employ a committee of employees (rather than a single individual) to decide who to terminate.

Wingate, Thornton, McIntyre, and Frame (2003), after reviewing relevant case law, concluded that the vast majority (73%) of district court cases involving RIFs resulted in decisions favorable to organizations (i.e., summary judgments for the defense). These rulings were partly due to organizations following sound personnel practices in their RIFs such as organizational justifications for their decisions, employing performance appraisals, and having an explicit layoff strategy.

Reorganization Defense

Efforts by organizations to restructure their operations and personnel can be a useful defense against age discrimination allegations. On the other hand, depending on how they are developed and utilized, they may have negative implications for older employees and lead to ADEA claims. In the case of *Tomassi v. Insignia Financial Group Inc.* (2007),[76] Patricia McCarthy Tomassi (age 63) was informed that her position was being abolished and replaced with a novel one and that the new job was being filled by someone else (age 25). The decision to hire the younger employee was partly based on her technical expertise, which Tomassi was not thought to possess. Tomassi countered that she was able to perform the functions of the new job and had already been performing some of the job's tasks (e.g., assisting website maintenance). In addition, a few years earlier, the company began an effort to hire "younger, energetic, . . . attractive" employees.

Tomassi filed an ADEA suit. In addition to evidence that she was replaced by a much younger individual, Tomassi provided information that her supervisor (Steve Stadmeyer) made age-related comments to her on a regular basis (e.g., asking if she had considered retiring, was tired of working and the commute, stating that she was well-equipped to work with seniors, often starting conversations by using the phrase "In your day and age . . . "). The

[76] https://scholar.google.com/scholar_case?case=3474169835339558675&q=Tomassi+v.+Insignia+(2007),+&hl=en&as_sdt=40006

Court of Appeals for the 2nd Circuit ruled in favor of Tomassi. The age-related statements made by her supervisor and the hiring of younger employees played a role in the court's decision. As the court noted,

> The remarks were made by the person who decided to terminate Tomassi. They could reasonably be construed, furthermore, as explaining why that decision was taken. A jury could reasonably construe Stadmeyer's remarks, in all the circumstances, as persuasive evidence that Stadmeyer believed a younger person would be better suited to attract a young clientele ... and that he replaced Tomassi for that reason.

In *Waters v. Logistics Management Institute* (2018),[77] the organization eliminated a supervisory position held by Craig Waters (age 52) as part of a reorganization of the Corporate Information Systems department. Waters subsequently filed ADEA and retaliation suits. Regarding his ADEA claim, the plaintiff stated that at a town hall meeting, the company's CEO remarked that "people with gray hair are probably not the future" of the organization. In addition, Waters said that workers with more than 15 years on the job had their benefits reduced (e.g., annual leave, retirement contributions).

The 4th Circuit concluded that Waters failed to form a *prima facie* case and ruled in favor of the organization. A key reason for their decision was that Logistics Management did not keep Waters's position open (it was abolished), and Waters failed to present evidence that he was replaced by a substantially younger worker. Also, the age-related comment made by the CEO was *not* thought to be indicative of age discrimination. That is, the CEO was not involved in the decision to terminate Waters's position, and there was no evidence that he affected the decision about Waters in any way. Essentially, the CEO's comment was judged to be harmless and not reflective of a company-wide policy. Pertaining to the reduction of benefits, these decisions about benefits were applied to both younger and older employees. As the court mentioned, "The retirement contribution limits affected young and older workers alike, and the limitations on annual leave accruals were based on tenure, not age." Finally, the court concluded that Waters would have lost even if he had successfully formed a *prima facie* case. They believed that the organization had a legitimate business reason for eliminating Waters's job, stating that "A decision to reorganize or restructure management responsibilities constitutes a non-discriminatory business decision."

[77] https://scholar.google.com/scholar_case?case=15067826316375030136&q=Waters+v.+Logistics+Mgmt.+Inst.,+&hl=en&as_sdt=40006

BFSS, BFOQ, and BFBP Defenses

BFSS Defense

Under the ADEA, the BFSS defense is uncommon. This is because seniority is typically related to age. Therefore, seniority systems are often *advantageous* to older employees. A caveat is that the seniority systems must not have been designed to discriminate against older workers, which is a violation of the ADEA.

BFOQ Defense

Regarding the BFOQ defense, in this context, companies must show that using age is

- *reasonably necessary* to the essence of the business,
- supported by facts that all or substantially all persons within the protected age group would be unable to perform the duties of the job(s) *safely and efficiently*,
- that it is *impossible* or *impractical* to assess those in the protected age group on an *individual basis*, and
- that the use of age furthers a stated objective (e.g., public safety) and *no viable alternative* exists with equal or less discriminatory effect.

Examples of successful BFOQ defenses include those that require a maximum starting age for certain jobs (e.g., 30–40) based on concerns for public safety, such as bus drivers and airline pilots (*EEOC v. American Airlines, 1995*[78]; *Hodgson v. Greyhound Lines (1974)*[79]; *Usery v. Tamiami Trail Tours, Inc., 1976*[80]). Another legitimate BFOQ has involved a mandatory retirement age of 60 for pilots (*Coupe v. Federal Express, 1997*[81]; *EEOC v. Exxon Mobil, Corp., 2014*[82]). The successful evidence in these cases largely centered around an existing (and since revised) Federal Aviation Association (FAA) rule that required pilots to retire when they reached the age of 60.[83]

---

[78] https://casetext.com/case/eeoc-v-american-airlines-inc
[79] https://openjurist.org/499/f2d/859/hodgson-v-greyhound-lines-inc
[80] https://scholar.google.com/scholar_case?case=927929649985281002&hl=en&as_sdt=6&as_vis=1&oi=scholarr
[81] https://caselaw.findlaw.com/us-6th-circuit/1296980.html
[82] https://law.justia.com/cases/federal/appellate-courts/ca5/13-10164/13-10164-2014-03-25.html
[83] In 2007, Congress passed the "Fair Treatment for Experienced Pilots Act." This law allows individuals to operate as pilots in multicrew operations until they reach 65 years of age. In addition, the Act, also referred to as the "Age 65 Law," disallows more frequent or difficult medical exams or higher medical standards because of age unless such requirements are deemed necessary for flight safety.

An instructive case of age as a BFOQ is *Western Airlines v. Criswell* (1985),[84,85] where flight engineers were forced to retire when they reached the age of 60. Based on this policy, Criswell was forced to retire and subsequently filed an ADEA claim. The company contended that age was a BFOQ based on the following reasons:

- The airline's primary business was the safe transportation of passengers.
- The company had a *rational basis* for believing those age 60 and older were unqualified.
- That *individually testing* the ability levels of all flight engineers age 60 or older was *unworkable*.

The Supreme Court ruled that a BFOQ defense was intended to be used sparingly and that "employers are to evaluate employees . . . on their merits and not their age." Furthermore, the decision stated that organizations must present facts to justify the reason(s) for their use of age instead of relying on a "rationale basis" for their decisions. The airline's defense was not helped by the fact that (a) its retirement age was inconsistent with (lower than) other airlines, (b) the airline employed individualized assessments for similar jobs, and (c) the FAA thought that individualized testing was doable for flight engineers.

BFBP Defense and the Older Workers Benefits Protection Act of 1990

The BFBP defense is contained in the Older Workers Benefit Protection Act (OWBPA).[86] The Act makes it illegal to discriminate against older workers in terms of retirement benefits and outlines the specific requirements associated with early retirement and severance packages. The OWBPA states that early retirement packages are legitimate as long as they are voluntary in nature. Also, such packages are especially defensible if they offer more benefits to older workers beyond that for which they are already eligible (see Padilla [2018] for a discussion of OWBPA waiver requirements).[87] Finally, under the Act, companies can offer more generous benefits to older versus younger workers, as well as to older employees *within* the protected age group.

---

[84] https://caselaw.findlaw.com/us-supreme-court/472/400.html
[85] https://www.oyez.org/cases/1984/83-1545
[86] https://www.congress.gov/bill/101st-congress/senate-bill/1511/text
[87] https://ir.lawnet.fordham.edu/ulj/vol45/iss3/6/

To comply with the OWBPA, businesses must adhere to eight provisions specified in the Act. That is, organizations must ensure that waivers

1. Are in writing and easy to understand by the average person
2. Include rights or claims resulting from the ADEA
3. Do not contain claims that can occur after the agreement is signed
4. Offer "new" incentives, such as additional benefits or compensation
5. Notify employees in writing to contact a lawyer before signing the agreement
6. Allow individual employees 21 days to consider waivers and groups 45 days to review waivers
7. Give employees seven days to rescind a signed agreement
8. (For groups) inform workers of the:
   - ages of all those who are eligible
   - time frame for making a decision
   - job titles of others accepting voluntary retirement
   - similarly situated individuals working in the same organizational unit

It is critical that organizations follow the provisions for voluntary waivers under the OWBPA. Failure to do so can result in the filing of lawsuits despite the fact that to be eligible for such packages, employees must often waive their rights to sue under the ADEA (see EEOC document, section IV, on waivers in severance agreements under the ADEA).[88]. An example is the Supreme Court's decision in *Oubre v. Entergy Operations* (1998).[89,90] The plaintiff, Dolores Oubre, filed an ADEA suit after signing a voluntary termination agreement that included a release to waive all claims against the company. However, the organization failed to comply with three waiver requirements under the OWBPA. That is, she was given only 14 days to consider the waiver instead of the necessary 21 days, she was not allowed the mandated seven days to rescind the offer, and the release failed to include claims under the ADEA. As the court noted, "Since Oubre's release did not comply with the OWBPA's stringent safeguards, it is unenforceable against her insofar as it purports to waive or release her ADEA claim."

Under the OWBPA, benefit plans based on an individual's age are legal if organizations can prove that benefits are *more costly* for older employees. However, the defense of increased costs is not always a "winning hand" for companies. For instance, in *Carras v. MGS* (2008)[91] the plaintiff (George

[88] https://www.eeoc.gov/policy/docs/qanda_severance-agreements.html
[89] https://www.law.cornell.edu/supct/pdf/96-1291P.ZO
[90] https://www.oyez.org/cases/1997/96-1291
[91] https://casetext.com/case/carras-v-mgs-728-lex-inc

Carras, aged 62 years) was employed at MGS as Chief Financial Officer (CFO) for about two years. He was fired and replaced as CFO by someone age 26, and Carras subsequently filed an ADEA lawsuit. The company contended that it was having financial issues and was attempting to reduce costs. Therefore, it stated that age was not a factor in its decision. But Carras had told the company that he would accept less salary than his younger replacement to keep his job. The Court of Appeals for the 2nd Circuit believed that there was enough evidence to conclude that the organization's defense was pretext, stating, "the employer's motivation for firing him was not cost cutting but was rather discrimination against his age."

Retirement plans are also legitimate if they are developed using factors that are related to, but distinct from, age. In the case of *Kentucky Retirement Systems v. EEOC* (2008),[92,93] a pension plan for employees with disabilities added years of service based on the age at which individuals took on their disability. The goal was to add years of service so that employees with disabilities could receive retirement benefits by reaching 20 years of employment (or the number of years they would have been employed had they worked to age 55). As an example, under the plan, an employee age 40 with a disability who has 10 years of service would be granted an additional 10 years, while those age 50 with disabilities would only receive five extra years. Individuals age 55 and older received no additional years of service to account for a disability.

In the *Kentucky Retirement Systems* case, Charles Lickteig took on a disability at age 61 and therefore received no additional years of service for his pension. He subsequently filed an ADEA suit. As in prior cases, the Court concluded that age and pension status were rationally different. As the Court stated, "one can easily conceive of decisions that are actually made 'because of' pension status and not age, even where pension status is itself based on age."

EEO in the Wild: Age Discrimination in Social Media Job Advertisements

Stories by ProPublica and the *New York Times*[a,b,c] have uncovered a fairly pervasive practice of posting job advertisements on Facebook using recruitment efforts that could exclude older individuals. Indeed, a host of organizations have been shown to employ these practices, including Verizon, Amazon, State Farm, and UPS. For

[92] https://www.law.cornell.edu/supct/pdf/06-1037P.ZO
[93] https://www.oyez.org/cases/2007/06-1037

instance, one ad stated that individuals might be seeing the job posting because the company wants to reach "people age 25 to 36 " while another stated that it sought "people age 27 to 40." Other ads were intended to attract individuals from different age groups, such as between 25 and 60, and 18 and 50. These ads were only be sent to applicants of interest, so older individuals would have no way of viewing them. Initially, Facebook rejected the allegations[d] that targeting ads to certain audiences (e.g., younger people) was a discriminatory practice stating that, " responsibly, age-based targeting for employment purposes is an accepted industry practice and for good reason: it helps employers recruit people of all ages find work." Following the filing of several lawsuits, Facebook announced that it will not allow ads for housing, credit, and employment to target their audiences according to protected demographic status such as race, gender, and age; and that it would investigate how its algorithms can lead to bias.[e]

[a] https://www.propublica.org/article/facebook-ads-age-discrimination-targeting
[b] https://projects.propublica.org/graphics/facebook-job-ads
[c] https://www.propublica.org/article/facebook-lets-advertisers-exclude-users-by-race
[d] https://newsroom.fb.com/news/h/addressing-targeting-in-recruitment-ads/
[e] https://www.propublica.org/article/facebook-ads-discrimination-settlement-housing-employment-credit?utm_campaign=dailynewsletter&utm_content=&utm_medium=email&utm_name=&utm_source=govdelivery&utm_term=

Representative EEOC Age Discrimination Settlements

Table 7.4 provides a sample of EEOC age discrimination settlements since 2015. As shown, these settlements often pertain to organizations that refuse to hire or that terminate older individuals. They also involve various forms of discrimination including class action and pattern or practice claims, which can involve substantial monetary penalties. Given this, it is important that organizations evaluate their personnel decision-making processes to avoid making judgments because of age.

Recommendations/Best Practices

- Develop and disseminate a policy that covers age discrimination (e.g., definitions, examples, complaint procedures, consequences for policy abuses).
- Do not indicate a preference for younger applicants in job advertisements (e.g., avoid qualifications or descriptors such as "youthful").

Table 7.4 Representative Equal Employment Opportunity Commission (EEOC) age discrimination settlements (listed in descending chronological order by year)

Organization (year of settlement)	Specific allegation(s)	Settlement and primary relief
CBS Stations Group of Texas (2020)[1]	Failure to hire female traffic reporter because of her age; hired younger and less-qualified applicant.	• $215,000 penalty • ADEA training • Publish employee rights notice
Capital City Dental Care (2020)[2]	Terminated dental hygienists who were older than 40 and replaced them almost exclusively employees younger than 40.	• $100,000 penalty • 4-year consent decree • Update discrimination policy focusing on the ADEA
Baltimore County (2020)[3]	Retirement contributions were based on age and required older employees to pay more for the same benefits as younger workers.	• $5.4 million penalty (including back pay)
Haynes International, Inc. (2020)[4]	Refusal to hire applicants for the position of general assistant operator who were older than 40.	• $180,000 penalty • ADEA training for decision makers
Norfolk Southern Corporation (2020)[5]	Refused to hire qualified individuals older than 51 for a railway security position.	• $350,000 penalty • Three-year consent decree • Annual ADEA training • Periodic reports to EEOC regarding adherence to consent decree
Tucoemas Federal Credit Union (2019)[6]	Failed to hire female applicants older than 50; hired younger male candidate with no relevant experience.	• $450,000 penalty • Three-year consent decree • Evaluate and revise policies regarding Title VII and ADEA • Employee training regarding age and sex discrimination
Atlas Energy Group LLC (2019)[7]	Employee (age 52) pushed out of his job by a new superintendent.	• $85,000 penalty • ADEA training to management and HR personnel • Report future ADEA claims to EEOC
Seasons 52 (2018)[8]	Class action suit of age discrimination in hiring (e.g., significantly fewer applicants hired who were age 40 and older; age-related questions and comments during interviews).	• $2.85 million penalty • Alteration of recruitment and hiring procedures • Injunctive relief stopping age discrimination • Hiring a compliance monitor to ensure conditions of the consent decree
Professional Endodontics (2018)[9]	Fired employee based on company policy when she turned 65.	• $47,000 damage award • Injunctive relief prohibiting future discrimination • Anti-discrimination training (e.g., ADEA training)

(continued)

Table 7.4 Continued

Organization (year of settlement)	Specific allegation(s)	Settlement and primary relief
Montrose Memorial Hospital (2018)[10]	Older workers terminated or forced to quit (poor performance as pretext for age-based decisions); derogatory age-related comments.	• Three-year consent decree • $400,000 damage award • Yearly company-wide training • Circulate anti-discrimination policy
Texas Roadhouse (2017)[11]	Pattern or practice class action claim of failing to hire older applicants for "front of the house" positions.	• Three and a half-year consent decree • $12 million damage award • Hire a "Diversity Director" and compliance monitor • Alter recruitment and hiring procedures
Ruby Tuesday (2016)[12]	Refusing to hired older applicant for managerial position (company wanted to "maximize longevity" of hires).	• Three-year consent decree • $45,000 damage award • Appoint a Diversity Director • Educate and training of employees on the ADEA
Seymore Midwest (2016)[13]	Not hiring applicant who was older than the "ideal" age range of 45–52 years.	• $100,000 payment • Prevents collecting age-related information • Training for HR personnel
City of Milpitas (2016)[14]	Refusal to hire older applicants (older than 50) in favor of a younger applicant with lower scores.	• $140,000 penalty • Distribute ADEA policy • Establish procedure for handling complaints • Annual anti-discrimination training

[1] https://www.eeoc.gov/newsroom/cbs-broadcast-affiliate-texas-pay-215000-settle-eeoc-age-suit-female-reporter

[2] https://www.eeoc.gov/newsroom/capital-city-dental-care-pay-100000-settle-eeoc-age-discrimination-suit

[3] https://www.eeoc.gov/newsroom/baltimore-county-will-pay-54-million-settle-long-running-eeoc-age-discrimination-lawsuit

[4] https://www.eeoc.gov/newsroom/haynes-international-pay-180000-resolve-eeoc-age-discrimination-allegation

[5] https://www.eeoc.gov/newsroom/norfolk-southern-pay-350000-settle-eeoc-age-discrimination-lawsuit

[6] https://www.eeoc.gov/newsroom/tucoemas-federal-credit-union-settles-eeoc-discrimination-lawsuit-450000

[7] https://www.eeoc.gov/newsroom/atlas-energy-group-pay-85000-settle-eeoc-age-discrimination-suit

[8] https://www.eeoc.gov/newsroom/seasons-52-pay-285-million-settle-eeoc-age-discrimination-lawsuit

[9] https://www.eeoc.gov/newsroom/professional-endodontics-pay-47000-settle-eeoc-age-discrimination-suit

[10] https://www.eeoc.gov/newsroom/montrose-memorial-hospital-pay-400000-settle-eeoc-age-discrimination-lawsuit

[11] https://www.eeoc.gov/newsroom/texas-roadhouse-pay-12-million-settle-eeoc-age-discrimination-lawsuit

[12] https://www.eeoc.gov/newsroom/ruby-tuesday-pay-45000-settle-eeoc-age-discrimination-suit

[13] https://www.eeoc.gov/newsroom/seymour-midwest-pay-100000-resolve-eeoc-age-discrimination-lawsuit

[14] https://www.eeoc.gov/newsroom/milpitas-pay-140000-settle-eeoc-age-discrimination-suit

Retrieved from EEOC Press Releases, https://www.eeoc.gov/newsroom/search

- Avoid questions on application blanks and during interviews that can reveal an individual's age (e.g., graduation dates).
- Train supervisors in ways to measure job performance that do not violate the ADEA (the use of structured, behaviorally anchored rating techniques is advisable here).
- Ensure that individuals avoid making pejorative age-related comments, especially those in decision-making positions.
- Educate employees and supervisors about age-related stereotypes and prejudice.
- Construct a process that allows older workers to speak up about alleged age-based discriminatory behavior(s).
- Develop, document, and carefully follow plans for RIFs and reorganization efforts.
- Clearly communicate and document the reasons that employees were negatively affected by RIFs and reorganization plans (supervisor training can be useful in this regard).
- Evaluate age differences when replacing older workers with younger ones (e.g., RIFs).
- Carefully follow voluntary waiver rules under the OWBPA.

Summary and Take-Aways

Age discrimination claims continue to be relatively common despite the ADEA. With the number of older workers projected to increase in the future, the frequency of age-based suits may rise accordingly.

Although the ADEA shares many characteristics with Title VII, many notable distinctions exist. For instance, organizations with at least 20 employees must comply with the Act (versus 15 under Title VII) and ADEA damages are closely aligned with principles within the FLSA.

Furthermore, the decision in *Gross v. FBL* (2009) does not allow age discrimination claims under mixed-motive scenarios. Despite repeated attempts to include age in such cases, legislation has not been successful. Time will tell if Congress will rectify this situation.

Recall also that the burden shifting processes for adverse impact suits between the ADEA and Title VII are distinct. The defense burden under Title VII is to show that practices are job-related and consistent with business necessity, while the ADEA requires proof that a reasonable factor other than age was used. Plaintiffs under Title VII must show that an alternative, nondiscriminatory practice was available compared to demonstrating that the organization's practice was either unreasonable or pretext for discrimination.

As mentioned earlier in this chapter, different criteria have been used to determine what constitutes a similarly situated individual. More clarity on this issue (from the courts or Congress) would be helpful. Finally, the viability of age subgroups (e.g., those age 50 and older) remains an open question and could have important implications for future adverse impact suits.

Supplemental Readings on Age Discrimination

Beginner
Age discrimination: Workplacefairness.org. https://www.workplacefairness.org/age-discrimination

Kleiman, L. S., & Denton, D. (2000). Downsizing: Nine steps to ADEA compliance. *Employment Relations Today, 27*, 37–45.

Palmer, K. (2017). AARP: 10 things you should know about age discrimination. https://www.aarp.org/work/on-the-job/info-2017/age-discrimination-facts.html

Wilkie, D. (2019). SHRM: 50 years after age discrimination became illegal, it persists. https://www.shrm.org/resourcesandtools/hr-topics/employee-relations/pages/age-discrimination-in-the-workplace-.aspx

Intermediate
FindLaw.com: Same-Actor Inference. https://corporate.findlaw.com/litigation-disputes/the-same-actor-inference.html

Feder, J. (2010). The Age Discrimination in Employment Act (ADEA): A legal overview. Congressional Research Service. Retrieved March 26, 2020, from https://www.llsdc.org/assets/sourcebook/crs-rl34652.pdf

Gutman, A. (2012). Age-related laws, rules, and regulations in the United States. In J. W. Hedge & W. C. Borman (Eds.), *The Oxford handbook of work and aging* (pp. 606–628). New York: Oxford University Press.

Questions and answers on EEOC final rule on disparate impact and "Reasonable Factors Other Than Age" under the Age Discrimination in Employment Act of 1967. https://www.eeoc.gov/laws/regulations/adea_rfoa_qa_final_rule.cfm

Tonowski, R. (2017). Happy 50th anniversary ADEA! *The Industrial-Organizational Psychologist, 55*(1). Retrieved November 6, 2019, https://www.siop.org/Research-Publications/TIP/TIP-Back-Issues/2017/July/ArtMID/20297/ArticleID/1577/On-the-Legal-Front-Happy-50th-Anniversary-ADEA

Advanced
Cavico, F. J., Mujtaba, B. G., & Samuel, M. (2016). Code words and covert employment discrimination: Legal analysis and consequences for management. *International Journal of Organizational Leadership, 5*, 231–253.

Federal Register. Disparate impact and reasonable factors other than age under the Age Discrimination in Employment Act (EEOC rule). https://www.federalregister.gov/documents/2012/03/30/2012-5896/disparate-impact-and-reasonable-factors-other-than-age-under-the-age-discrimination-in-employment

Lipnic, V. A. (EEOC, 2018). The state of age discrimination and older workers in the U.S. 50 years after the Age Discrimination in Employment Act (ADEA). https://www.eeoc.gov/reports/state-age-discrimination-and-older-workers-us-50-years-after-age-discrimination-employment

Manning, K. L., Carroll, B. A., & Carp, R. A. (2004). Does age matter? Judicial decision making in age discrimination cases. *Social Science Quarterly, 85*(1), 1–18. http://www.umassd.edu/media/umassdartmouth/politicalscience/facultydocs/klmssq04.pdf

McCann, L. A. (2018). The Age Discrimination in Employment Act at 50: When will it become a "real" civil rights statute? *ABA Journal of Labor and Employment Law, 89,* 89–104. https://www.aarp.org/content/dam/aarp/aarp_foundation/litigation/pdf-beg-02-01-2016/aba-journal-article-mccann.pdf

Glossary

Affirmative defense: A defense raised that contains facts contrary to those stated by the plaintiff and which justifies the challenged actions.

But for analysis: Frequently used to assess causation. It is often referred to as the actual or factual cause. For instance, but for sex, different dress codes would not exist. Also known as but for causation.

Indirect evidence: Also referred to as circumstantial evidence, indirect evidence helps to establish the main fact by inference.

Glossary terms adapted from Gutman et al. (2011); https://uslegal.com/, and merriamwebster.com/legal.

Cases Cited

Abnet v. UNIFAB Corporation (W.D. Mich. 2006).

Andujar v. General Nutrition Corporation (3rd Cir. 2019).

Babb v. Wilkie, 140 S. Ct. 1168 (2020).

Barber v. CSX Distribution Services, 68 F.3d 694 (1995).

Barnett v. PA Consulting Group, Inc., 715 F. 3d 354 (D.C. Cir. 2013).

Bennis v. Minnesota Hockey Ventures Group (D. Minn. 2013).

Benson et al. v. Tocco, Incorporated, 113 F. 3d 1203 (11th Cir. 1997).

Brown v. CSC Logic, Inc., 82 F. 3d 651 (5th Cir. 1996).

Buhrmaster v. Overnite Transportation Co., 61 F. 3d 461 (6th Cir. 1995).

Carras v. MGS, 782 Lex, Inc., 310 Fed. Appx. 421 (2d Cir.2008).

Connecticut v. Teal, 457 U.S. 440 (1982).

Coupe v. Federal Express, 121 F.3d 1022 (6th Cir. 1997).

Crawford v. Medina General Hospital, 96 F. 3d 830 (6th Cir. 1996).

Dediol v. Best Chevrolet, Incorporated, 655 F. 3d 435 (5th Cir. 2011)

Earl v. Nielsen Media Research, Inc., 658 F. 3d 1108 (9th Cir. 2011).

EEOC v. American Airlines, 48 F.3d 164 (5th Cir. 1995).

EEOC v. Borden's Inc., 724 F. 2d 1390 (9th Cir 1984).

EEOC. v. Exxon Mobil Corp., 560 F. App'x 282 (5th Cir. 2014).

EEOC v. McDonnell Douglas Corporation, 191 F. 3d 948 (8th Cir. 1999).

Fletcher v. Gulfside Casino, Incorporated (S.D. Miss, 2012).

France v. Johnson, 795 F. 3d 1170 (9th Cir. 2015).

Geller v. Markham, 635 F. 2d (2 Cir 1980).

Grosjean v. First Energy, 349 F.3d 332 (6th Cir. 2004).

Gross v. FBL Financial Services, 588 F.3d 614 (2009).

Hazen v. Biggens, 507 U.S. 604 (1993).

Healy v. New York Life Insurance Company, 860 F.2d 1209 (1988).

Hodgson v. Greyhound Lines, 499 F.2d 859 (7th Cir. 1974).

Houk v. Peoploungers, Inc., 214 F. App'x 379, 381 (5th Cir. 2007).

Karlo v. Pittsburgh Glass Works, LLC, 849 F. 3d 61 (3rd Cir. 2017).

Kentucky Retirement Systems v. EEOC, 128 S. Ct. 2361 (2008).

Kimel v. Florida Board of Regents, 528 U.S. 62 (2000).

Kleber v. Carefusion Incorporated, 914 F.3d 480, 485 (7th Cir. 2019).

Leftwich v. Harris-Stowe State College, 702 F.2d 686 (1983).

Lowe v. Commack Union Free School District, 886 F.2d 1364 (2nd Cir. 1989).

Madel v. FCI Marketing, Inc., 116 F.3d 1247 (1997).

McDaniel v. Progress Rail Locomotive Inc., 940 F.3d 360, 368 (7th Cir. 2019)

Meacham v. Knolls Atomic Power Laboratory, 461 F. 3d 134 (2nd Cir. 2006).

Meacham v. KAPL, 200 U.S. 321 (2008).

Meacham v. Knolls Atomic Power Laboratory, 627 F. Supp. 2d 72 (N.D. NY 2009)

Mereish v. Walker, 359 F.3d 330 (2004).

O'Connor v. Consolidated Coin Caterers Corporation, 517 U.S. 308 (1996).

Oubre v. Entergy Operations, 102 F.3d 551 (1998).

Proud v. Stone, 945 F. 2d 796 (4th Cir. 1991).

Rabin v. PriceWaterhouseCoopers LLP, 236 F. Supp. 3d 1126 (N.D. Cal. 2017).

Rand v. CF Industries, Inc., 42 F. 3d 1139 (7th Cir. 1994).

Reeves v. Sanderson Plumbing Products, Inc., 530 U.S. 133 (2000).

Smith v. City of Jackson, 544 U.S. 228 (2005).

Smith v. Tennessee Valley Authority, 948 F.2d 1290 (1991).

Snyder v. Pierre's French Ice Cream Co., 589 Fed. Appx. 767, 771 (6th Cir. 2014).

Tomassi v. Insignia Financial Group Inc., 478 F.3d 111, 115-16 (2d Cir. 2007).

Usery v. Tamiami Trail Tours Incorporated, 531 F.2d 224 (5th Cir. 1976).

Villarreal v. RJ Reynolds Tobacco Co., 839 F. 3d 958 (11th Cir. 2016).

Waldron v. SL Industries, Inc., 56 F. 3d 491(3d Cir. 1995).

Waters v. Logistics Management Institute, 716 F. App'x 194, 197 (4th Cir. 2018).

Western Airlines v. Criswell, 472 U.S. 400 (1985).

Wexler v. White's Fine Furniture, Inc., 317 F.3d 564 (2003).

Williams v. General Motors Corporation, 656 F.2d 120 (1981).

Williams v. Vitro Services Corp., 144 F. 3d 1438 (11th Cir. 1999).

Worden v. Interbake Foods LLC (D. SD 2012).

References

Beckles, T. M. (2008). Class of one: Are employment discrimination plaintiffs at an insurmountable disadvantage if they have no "similarly situated" comparators? *University of Pennsylvania Journal of Business and Employment Law, 10*, 459–482.

Dee, T. J. (1991). Plaintiffs cannot establish a prima facie case of age discrimination by showing disparate impact within the protected group. Lowe v. Commack Union Free School Dist., 886 F.2d 1364 (2d Cir. 1989). *Washington University Law Quarterly, 69*(1), 337–348.

Finkelstein, L. M., Burke, M. J., & Raju, N. S. (1995). Age discrimination in simulated employment contexts: An integrative analysis. *Journal of Applied Psychology, 80*, 652–663.

Finkelstein, L. M., Ryan, K. M., & King, E. B. (2013). What do the young (old) people think of me? Content and accuracy of age-based metastereotypes. *European Journal of Work and Organizational Psychology, 22*, 633–657.

Goldman, R. B. (2007). Putting pretext in context: Employment discrimination, the same-actor inference, and the proper roles of judges and juries. *Virginia Law Review, 93*, 1533–1571.

Gutman, A. (2005). Smith v. City of Jackson: Adverse impact in the ADEA—Well sort of. *The Industrial-Organizational Psychologist, 43*(1), 79–87.

Gutman, A., Koppes, L. L., & Vodanovich, S. J. (2011). *EEO law and personnel practices.* New York: Taylor and Francis.

Hartman, G. S., & Homer, G. W. (1990). *Personnel law handbook.* Winston-Salem, NC: University of Wake Forest Law School.

Harper, M. C. (2010). The causation standard in federal employment law: *Gross v. FBL Financial Services, Inc.,* and the unfilled promise of the Civil Rights Act of 1991. *Buffalo Law Review, 58*, 69–145.

Hunter, R. J. Jr., & Shannon, J. H. (2019). *Journal of Public Administration and Governance, 9*(1), 1–17.

Issacharoff, S., & Harris, E. W. (1997). Is age discrimination really age discrimination? The ADEA's unnatural solution. *New York University Law Review, 72*, 780–840.

Lidge, E. F. III (2002). Courts' misuse of the similarly situated concept in employment discrimination law. *Missouri Law Review, 67*, 831–882.

Mariani, R. C., & Robertson, K. E. (1997). Age discrimination litigation: Rifs, statistics and stray remarks. *Defense Counsel Journal, 64*(1), 88–98.

McAllister, M. C. (2019). Subgroup analysis in disparate impact age discrimination cases: Striking the appropriate balance through age cutoffs. *Alabama Law Review, 70*(4), 1073–1114.

Ng, T. W. H., & Feldman D. C. (2008). The relationship of age to ten dimensions of job performance. *Journal of Applied Psychology, 93*, 392–423.

Northup, J. S. (1998). The "same actor inference" in employment discrimination: Cheap justice? *Washington Law Review, 73*, 193–221.

Padilla, S. (2018). For clarity's sake: Redefining the knowing and voluntary standard in severance agreements. *Fordham Urban Law Journal, 45*, 839–874.

Perry, E. L., Kulik, C. T., & Bourhis, A. C. (1996). Moderating effects of personal and contextual factors in age discrimination. *Journal of Applied Psychology, 81*, 628–647.

Posthuma, R. A., Wagstaff, M. F., & Campion, M. A. (2012). Age stereotypes and workplace age discrimination. In J. W. Hedge & W. C. Borman (Eds.), *The Oxford handbook of work and aging* (pp. 298–312). New York: Oxford University Press.

Quintanilla, V. D., & Kaiser, C. R. (2016). The same-actor inference of nondiscrimination: Moral credentialing and the psychological and legal licensing of bias. *California Law Review, 104*(1), 1–74.

Rupp, D. E., Vodanovich, S. J., & Crede, M. (2006). Age bias in the workplace: The impact of ageism and causal attributions. *Journal of Applied Social Psychology, 36,* 1337–1364.

Van Ostrand, L. A. (2009). A close look at ADEA mixed-motives claims and *Gross v. FBL Financial Services, Inc. Fordham Law Review, 78,* 399–451.

Ventrell-Monsees, C. (2019). It's unlawful age discrimination: Not the natural order of the workplace. *Berkeley Journal of Employment and Labor Law, 40*(1), 91–134.

Vilella, S. (2018). ADEA disparate-impact claims: How the Third Circuit age-proofed comparators. *American University Business Law Review, 7*(1), 179–197.

Waldman, D. A., & Avolio, B. J. (1986). A meta-analysis of age differences in job performance. *Journal of Applied Psychology, 71,* 33–38.

Weber, Z. J. (2018). Disparate impact 2.0: *Karlo* provides a long-awaited update for ADEA subgroup plaintiffs. *University of Cincinnati Law Review, 86,* 1073–1097.

Wingate, P. H., Thornton, G. C. III, McIntyre, K. S., & Frame, J. H. (2003). Organizational downsizing and age discrimination litigation: The influence of personnel practices and statistical evidence on litigation outcomes. *Law and Human Behavior, 27,* 87–108.

8

Disability Discrimination

> Congress acknowledged that society's accumulated myths and fears about disability and disease are as handicapping as are the physical limitations that flow from actual impairment.
>
> **William J. Brenner, Jr., Former Supreme Court Justice's** statement in *School Board of Nassau City. v. Arline* (1987)

Overview of the Americans with Disabilities Act

The Americans with Disabilities Act of 1990 (ADA)[1] was signed into law by George W. Bush in an effort to reduce workplace discrimination on the basis

[1] https://www.ada.gov/archive/adastat91.htm

Table 8.1 Disability discrimination charges filed with the Equal Employment Opportunity Commission (EEOC) 2014–2020

Year	2014	2015	2016	2017	2018	2019	2020
Number of Charges	25,369	26,968	28,073	26,838	24,605	24,238	24,324

Retrieved from https://www.eeoc.gov/eeoc/statistics/enforcement/charges.cfm

of physical and mental disabilities. Despite the passage of the law, disability suits are some of the most frequent types filed with the Equal Employment Opportunities Commission (EEOC) (see Table 8.1 for the frequency of charges by year).

Besides the frequency of lawsuits, evidence exists that individuals with disabilities have a difficult time gaining employment. For instance, the Bureau of Labor Statistics (2020) concluded that the unemployment rate in 2019 for those with disabilities was 7.3% compared to an unemployment rate of 3.5% for individuals without disabilities. In addition, employees with disabilities are more likely to be employed on a part-time basis (32%) versus those without disabilities (17%).

The ADA is arguably one of the most complicated pieces of employment discrimination legislation that exists (e.g., Blanck, 2000). There are many definitional requirements that must be confronted (e.g., substantial limitation, essential job functions, reasonable accommodations), each of which involves various criteria. More recently, the Americans with Disabilities Act Amendments Act (ADAAA) was passed in 2008 to clarify several critical points within the ADA and to reflect Congress's original intention for passing the Act (see amended ADA with ADAAA language included).[2] One result of the ADAAA was the overturning of several controversial Supreme Court cases.

Rehabilitation Act of 1973

Coverage for individuals with disabilities began with the Rehabilitation Act of 1973 (RE-73, as amended)[3] although the term "handicapped" was

---

[2] https://www.ada.gov/pubs/adastatute08mark.htm
[3] https://www2.ed.gov/policy/speced/leg/rehab/rehabilitation-act-of-1973-amended-by-wioa.pdf

employed at the time. Some key parts of the Act include Sections 501, 504, and 508. Section 501 of RE-73[4] is limited to federal agencies and generally follows Title VII practices, including affirmative action and reasonable accommodation requirements. Federal entities and organizations receiving any federal funds are covered by Section 504 of RE-73.[5] This section bans discrimination against an "otherwise qualified individual with a disability." But Section 504 provides fewer safeguards as it is tied to Title VI of the Civil Rights Act, a comparatively weaker law than Title VII. Finally, Section 508 of RE-73[6] requires federal departments and agencies to provide individuals with disabilities access to electronic information.

Key Issues Involving the Americans with Disabilities (and Amendments) Act

As you may have noticed, the Rehabilitation Act focuses on federal agencies. Consequently, one purpose of the ADA was to fortify disability protections for applicants and employees of non-federal organizations. The goal of the ADA was to prevent discrimination against the estimated (at that time) 43 million individuals with disabilities. Specifically, the purpose of the ADA was, in part, "to provide a clear and comprehensive national mandate for the elimination of discrimination against individuals with disabilities" and "to provide clear, strong, consistent, enforceable standards addressing discrimination against individuals with disabilities."

Legal Definition of a Disability

To form a *prima facie* case under the ADA, plaintiffs must meet the legal definition of a disability by satisfying one or more of the following three prongs:

> *Prong 1*: They possess a physical or mental impairment that substantially limits one or more *major life activities.*

---

[4] https://www.eeoc.gov/laws/statutes/rehab.cfm
[5] https://www.dol.gov/agencies/oasam/centers-offices/civil-rights-center/statutes/section-504-rehabilitation-act-of-1973
[6] https://www.fcc.gov/general/section-508-rehabilitation-act

Table 8.2 Requirements for being considered disabled and qualified under the Americans with Disabilities Act (ADA)

Being considered as disabled	
Prong 1	Individuals must have a *current* physical or mental impairment that *substantially limits* a *major life activity.*
Prong 2	Individuals have a *record* of such an impairment (e.g., cancer survivor, past mental illness).
Prong 3	Individuals are *regarded as* having such an impairment.
Being considered as qualified	
Prerequisite 1	Individuals have the knowledge, skills, and ability to perform the *essential functions* of a job.
Prerequisite 2	Individual are able to perform the essential job functions with or without a *reasonable accommodation.*

Adapted from Gutman, Koppes, & Vodanovich (2011) (emphasis added).

> *Prong 2:* They have a record of such an impairment (e.g., cancer survivor, previous mental illness).
>
> *Prong 3:* They are regarded as having an impairment.

If plaintiffs meet one of these prongs, they must also demonstrate that they are *qualified* to perform the *essential functions of the job,* with or without a *reasonable accommodation.* Finally, plaintiffs must present evidence that an *adverse employment decision* was causally related to their disability. Table 8.2 outlines the disability definition and qualification components under the ADA.

Substantial Limitation and Major Life Activities

The majority of ADA suits are filed under the first prong (having a current disability). As the first prong conveys, for a disability to exist, an impairment must result in a substantial limitation of a major life activity. Two yardsticks have been used to assess whether individuals are substantially impaired. First, impairments must *not* be temporary in nature (this has been referred to as the *permanence standard*). Consequently, under the ADA, impairments with short durations will not count as disabilities. However, the Act provided no specific benchmarks for determining if impairments are substantially limiting or permanent. So, courts have used varying time frames to assess whether impairments qualified as being either permanent or not. Given the passage of the ADAAA, impairments with durations of six months or less are considered temporary and therefore they typically will not qualify as being a disability.[7]

However, in *Summers v. Altarium Institute Corp.* (2014),[8] the plaintiff (Carl Summers) received serious injuries to his legs while taking a train to work, which led to two separate operations. Summers's doctors instructed him to avoid putting weight on his left leg for about six weeks and that it would take approximately seven months before he could walk in a normal manner. Consequently, he requested accommodation from the organization (short-term disability, working remotely on a part-time or full-time basis). The organization failed to respond to his accommodation request and fired him less than two months later. As a result, Summers filed a disability lawsuit.

The District Court concluded that Summers's injuries were temporary and that working remotely was an unreasonable accommodation. The Court of Appeals for the 4th Circuit came to a different conclusion. The court stated that "A sufficiently severe temporary impairment may constitute a disability under the ADAAA." This position aligned with the EEOC's regulations after the ADAAA became law, which noted that the *duration* of an impairment is *one* of many factors used to determine the legal existence of a disability. The EEOC regulations also state that impairments of short durations can qualify as a disability if they are "sufficiently severe" in nature.

Notably, however, the court in *Summers* did not indicate *how* a "sufficiently severe" impairment ought to be determined or what *kind* of temporary impairments would be "sufficiently severe" to count under the Act. Also left unanswered was *how short* a temporary impairment can be to receive ADA protections (see Minter, 2014).

The other yardstick for assessing whether a disability exists is whether the restrictions emanating from impairments are severe enough compared to those experienced by the *average* person. This is referred to as the *average person standard*. Using this standard, courts have ruled that conditions such as fungus allergies, test anxiety, and moderate problems with walking, when judged against an average person, did not comprise substantial limitations. Therefore, they were not considered to be disabilities. As an example, in *Penny v. United Parcel Service Incorporated* (1997),[9] the plaintiff (James Penny) had moderate problems with walking due to a series of injuries. The

---

[7] The text from the ADAAA states that "A *transitory* impairment is an impairment with an actual or expected duration of 6 months or less." Interestingly, this text appears in the "regarded as" portion of the Act.

[8] https://scholar.google.com/scholar_case?case=7956725969330798863&hl=en&as_sdt=6&as_vis=1&oi=scholarr

[9] https://scholar.google.com/scholar_case?case=12512248574000330556&q=penny+v.+UPS&hl=en&as_sdt=40006

6th Circuit ruled against Penny stating that he "failed to create a triable issue of fact regarding whether he is substantially limited in the major life activity of walking." In coming to this conclusion, the court ruled that Penny did not produce evidence that "the nature and severity of his injury significantly restricted his ability to walk as compared with an average person in the general population." The average person standard was not addressed in the ADAAA. So the assumption is that this requirement is still in place.

Role of Mitigating (Correctable) Measures in Determining Disabilities

In 1999, several controversial decisions involving the ADA were announced by the Supreme Court (see *Albertsons Inc. v. Kirkingburg,* 1999[10,11]; *Murphy v. United Parcel Service, Inc.,* 1999[12,13]; *Sutton v. United Airlines, Inc.,* 1999[14,15]). In all three cases, the Court ruled that impairments need to be considered along with possible mitigating or correctable measures. That is, if individuals can successfully mitigate their impairments (e.g., by use of medication), their conditions would not qualify as being sufficiently severe or substantially limiting. Consequently, they would not be qualified disabilities under the ADA. Interestingly, the consideration of correctable measures was at odds with the guidance written by the EEOC after the ADA was passed.

In *Sutton v. United Airlines* (1999), the plaintiffs (twin sisters) were commuter plane pilots. They were both denied the opportunity to fly larger commercial jets because their vision was 20-200 in both eyes. When corrected, their eyesight was 20-20. United Airlines had a policy that required pilots to have a minimum of 20-100 uncorrected vision—a criteria that exceeded FAA regulations. The twins filed an ADA suit stating that they were substantially limited with respect to the major life activity of "working." As shown in the next section, working is considered to be a major life activity. However, to qualify as being disabled with respect to working, plaintiffs must pass the "broad-range test." That is, they must be significantly impaired across a wide range of jobs. The Sutton twins lost since they were qualified to perform other jobs besides being pilots, so they were *not* considered to be disabled with respect to working. Also, eyeglasses could readily correct their vision.

---

[10] https://www.law.cornell.edu/supct/html/98-591.ZO.html
[11] https://www.oyez.org/cases/1998/98-591
[12] https://www.law.cornell.edu/supct/html/97-1992.ZO.html
[13] https://www.oyez.org/cases/1998/97-1992
[14] https://www.law.cornell.edu/supct/html/97-1992.ZO.html
[15] https://www.oyez.org/cases/1998/97-1943

In the *Murphy* and *Kirkingburg* cases, both plaintiffs could effectively treat their conditions; the former by blood pressure medication, the latter by learning to adapt to "lazy eye" syndrome. Also, in *Murphy* and *Kirkingburg*, the plaintiffs erroneously believed their "diagnosis" alone was sufficient to be considered a legal disability under the ADA. In doing so, they failed to present evidence that their impairments substantially limited them on an *individual, case-by-case* basis, a requirement of the ADA. Therefore, under the ADA, it is possible for two employees to have the same diagnosis, such as diabetes or depression, and for one but not the other to be considered as having a disability (substantially limited). So plaintiffs must provide evidence that their impairment poses a significant limitation *for themselves* regarding a major life activity (e.g., seeing, hearing, speaking). A medical diagnosis, by itself, is insufficient. As such, the Courts ruled against the plaintiffs in both cases.

With the passage of the ADAAA, Congress clarified that impairments must be decided *without* consideration of available correctable measures such as medication, prosthetics, or other devices. For instance, individuals claiming to be disabled because of diabetes must be evaluated regarding how the disease affects them without the use of medication. However, under the ADAAA, it is legitimate to consider vision in its corrected state as long as this is accomplished with the use of regular eyeglasses or contact lenses.

Major Life Activities Listed in the ADAAA

As noted earlier, plaintiffs must prove they are significantly limited with respect to a *major life activity*. This begs the question: What are major life activities? The ADAAA provided an answer. The Act states that major life activities include the following:

- Caring for oneself, performing manual tasks, seeing, hearing, eating, sleeping, walking, standing, lifting, bending, speaking, breathing, learning, reading, concentrating, thinking, communicating, and working
- Functions of the immune system, normal cell growth, digestive, bowel, bladder, neurological, brain, respiratory, circulatory, endocrine, and reproductive functions

Essential Job Functions

Let's assume that plaintiffs prove that they have a disability under the ADA. That is, they successfully present evidence that they have an impairment that significantly limits their ability to perform a major life activity. In this instance, the plaintiffs still have another hurdle to overcome. They must prove that they are *qualified* to perform the work required by the job. Specifically, plaintiffs must demonstrate their ability to perform the *essential functions* of a job with or without a *reasonable accommodation*.

In *Toyota Motor Manufacturing, Ky., Inc. v. Williams* (2002),[16,17] Ella Williams was only able to perform two out of four essential job duties and claimed to be substantially limited in the performance of *manual tasks* due to carpal tunnel syndrome. Furthermore, she requested an accommodation for Toyota to limit her work to the two job functions she could successfully perform. Toyota refused her request. Following her doctor's orders to avoid performing her job duties, Williams was subsequently fired for missing work.

The Supreme Court agreed that manual tasks comprised a "major life activity" but stated that these tasks must be "central to daily life," like brushing one's teeth and caring for oneself. That is, the Court stated that to be substantially limited regarding performing manual tasks "an individual must have an impairment that prevents or severely restricts the individual from doing activities that are of central importance to most people's daily lives. The impairment's impact must also be permanent or long-term." Williams lost her case since she could successfully execute such daily tasks. In essence, the Court ruled that she did not possess a disability that qualifies under the ADA.

The text of the ADAAA separated manual tasks from caring for oneself, therefore reversing *Toyota v. Williams*. However, Williams likely still would have lost her case under the ADAAA because her inability to perform two out of four essential job functions would have rendered her unqualified for the position (Gutman, 2002). See Table 8.3 for a summary of the basic provisions under the ADAAA.

Since correctable measures cannot be considered in evaluating impairments, it is likely that plaintiffs will find it easier to meet the requirements for having a legal disability. Consequently, it is vital for organizations to determine and defend the essential functions of jobs. Although not required by law, conducting a systematic job analysis is invaluable in this regard (see Gutman & Dunleavy, 2012; Morgeson, Brannick, & Levine, 2019) since essential job functions must be supported by presenting factual evidence.

---

[16] https://www.law.cornell.edu/supct/html/00-1089.ZO.html
[17] https://www.oyez.org/cases/2001/00-1089

Table 8.3 Summary of requirements under the Americans with Disabilities Amendments Act (ADAAA)

Impairments that are episodic (or in remission) count as disabilities if they substantially limit a major life activity when active.

Disabilities must be considered in their *uncorrected* state, except the use of regular eyeglasses or contact lenses.

Working is supported as a major life activity.

Manual tasks and *caring for oneself* are considered separate major life activities.

An impairment must have a duration of 6 months or less to be considered *temporary*.

Recall that in *Summers v. Altarum* (2014) the court decided that temporary impairments (a duration of less than six months) can qualify as a disability if they are "sufficiently severe."

Reasonable Accommodation

Accommodations that impose an "undue hardship" on organizations are not considered "reasonable." The determination of hardship considers such criteria as the type and cost of accommodations, company resources, and the nature and structure of the organization. The ADAAA contains a list of eight types of accommodations required under the law:

1. Making facilities accessible
2. Restructuring jobs
3. Modifying work schedules (e.g., part -time work)
4. Reassignment to an open job
5. Modifying work equipment
6. Altering tests, training materials, and/or policies
7. Making readers or interpreters available
8. Other comparable accommodations

An example of an essential job function and reasonable accommodation is illustrated by a suit filed by professional golfer, Casey Martin (see *PGA Tour, Inc. v. Martin*, 2001).[18],[19] Martin suffered from a degenerative circulatory disorder (Klippel-Trenaunay-Weber syndrome), which caused swelling and pain in his right leg, making walking exceptionally difficult. He asked the Professional Golf Association (PGA) to accommodate his disability by allowing him to use a motorized golf cart during tournaments. His request was denied. The defense by the PGA was multifaceted. Two important

[18] https://www.law.cornell.edu/supct/pdf/00-24P.ZO
[19] https://www.oyez.org/cases/2000/00-24

defenses were that walking was an essential aspect of golf and that allowing the use of golf carts would result in a fundamental alteration of the game itself (e.g., unfair competition).

Casey Martin, like all professional golfers, was not an employee of the PGA but an independent contractor. The *PGA v. Martin* case was based on Title III of the ADA, which prohibits public facilities or venues (confusingly called "public accommodations" in the ADA) from discriminating against those with disabilities. As Title III states: "No individual shall be discriminated against on the basis of disability in the full and equal enjoyment of the goods, services, facilities, privileges, advantages, or accommodations of any place of public accommodation by any person who owns, leases (or leases to), or operates a place of public accommodation."

The Supreme Court ruled in favor of Martin by concluding that walking was *not* an essential aspect of golf and that the use of a golf cart by Martin was reasonable and would not fundamentally alter the nature of golf. As the Court noted, "we observe that the use of carts is not itself inconsistent with the fundamental character of the game of golf the essence of the game has been shotmaking." The Court further concluded that, "Under the ADA's basic requirement that the need of a disabled person be evaluated on an individual basis, we have no doubt that allowing Martin to use a golf cart would not fundamentally alter the nature of petitioner's tournaments." The Court's decision in the *Martin* case has been highly debated by legal scholars and within the sports industry (see Maitland, 1999; Resslar, 2002; Schauer, 2001; Spruill, 2001; Warden, 2002).

EEO in the Wild: Has the ADAAA Led to More Individuals Being Considered Disabled?

A major reason why the ADAAA was adopted was to expand the way courts were interpreting who qualified as having a disability and to be consistent with the intent of Congress in passing the ADA. As stated in the ADAAA, "While Congress expected that the definition of disability under the ADA would be interpreted consistently with how courts had applied the definition of a handicapped individual under the Rehabilitation Act of 1973, that expectation has not been fulfilled."

When the ADAAA was passed, most legal scholars believed that more people would count as having a disability and that the focus would be on whether individuals were qualified and/or if reasonable accommodations were available. This is partly because the ADAAA excluded correctable measures in defining disabilities, provided a comprehensive list of major life activities and accommodations, and stated that episodic illnesses should be considered as disabilities while in their non-active state (or in remission). This assumes the episodic impairment would substantially limit a major life activity when active. Some evidence exists that early court findings reflected the intent of the ADAAA but that such initial findings may have been short-lived.

For example, Porter (2014) studied all disability cases for five years after the ADAAA was enacted and concluded that the courts were adopting (as anticipated) the expanded view of the term "disability." After analyzing disability case law, the author concluded that "Despite my overall conclusion that courts seem to be following Congress' mandate for broad coverage under the ADAAA, there are a few cases that I believe were incorrectly decided by the courts." In this light, Porter summarizes cases where, in her view, the courts did not consider the more expansive conceptualization of disabilities contained in the ADAAA. Here, she cites cases where such conditions such as monocular vision, total hearing loss in one ear, and depression were not considered as disabilities—cases where Porter believed legal disabilities existed.

However, an investigation of disability cases over the next five years (2014–2018) yielded a different picture (Porter, 2019). Based on the facts involved, the author concluded that "mistakes" were made in defining disabilities in 210 out of 976 overall cases. Porter also notes that, in her view, "correct" decisions occurred in most cases and that this was a vast improvement from disability cases heard before the ADAAA, where 92% of cases were won by the defense (e.g., Colker, 2005). Still, the number of cases in which the author considered that errors were made (more than 200) was concerning.

One of the reasons for the errors identified by Porter (2019) was an apparent lack of knowledge of the ADAAA's passage. Here, the author identified 54 cases that did not cite any ADAAA cases several years after its passage. Another reason for "mistaken" decisions was deemed to be poor representation on the part of the plaintiff's lawyers. Some examples included (a) not indicating which major life activities (e.g., bodily functions) were affected, (b) failure to identify specific impairments possessed by plaintiffs, and (c) not demonstrating the manner in which impairments substantially limited a given major life activity.

The last rationale given for "incorrect" decisions identified by Porter includes courts using incorrect/outdated legal criteria in disability cases. For instance, some courts used a permanence standard of greater than six months as not being long enough to count as a disability. Other courts considered correctable (mitigating) measures in defining disabilities, while others failed to consider episodic illnesses as disabilities while they were inactive (in remission). Both are inconsistent with the provisions of the ADAAA. Porter concludes that another five-year analysis of disability cases would be beneficial to see if this trend continues.

It is important to note that organizations are only required to accommodate "*known*" disabilities, and they must "*flexibly interact*" with employees to arrive at accommodations that are both effective and reasonable (see Vodanovich & Piotrowski, 2008). Accommodation requests do not have to be made in writing—verbal requests that indicate a need for an accommodation are lawful. The need for an accommodation is usually generated by requests from individuals. But such requests are not needed if the impairment is obvious (e.g., presence of a prosthetic device). Also, a request for an accommodation may not be necessary if the company possesses enough information that someone has a disability and warrants an accommodation. This last point was addressed in *Kowitz v. Trinity Health* (2016).[20] Roberta Kowitz underwent a neck operation to correct spinal stenosis. At her request, she was given Family and Medical Leave Act (FMLA) leave, and her work hours were reduced after she returned. About a month after Kowitz returned to work the company stated that she had to obtain a basic life support (BLS) certification which required performing cardiopulmonary resuscitation (CPR) (BLS certification was deemed by the organization to be an essential job function). She informed the organization that her doctor stated that she needed physical therapy for a period of at least four months before doing CPR. Kowitz was subsequently fired. She filed an ADA claim stating that Trinity Health did not accommodate her disability. The 8th Circuit ruled that although Kowitz did *not* specifically ask for an accommodation, the organization had sufficient knowledge of her disability/work limitations and that she needed an accommodation. Consequently, they were required to participate in the interactive process of exploring potential reasonable accommodations.

The EEOC has issued interpretive guidance on how to engage in the interactive process.[21] The agency has listed the following four steps to assist in this endeavor:

1. Analyze the particular job involved and determine its purpose and essential functions;
2. Consult with the individual with a disability to ascertain the precise job-related limitations imposed by the individual's disability and how those limitations could be overcome with a reasonable accommodation;

---

[20] https://ecf.ca8.uscourts.gov/opndir/16/10/151584P.pdf
[21] https://www.law.cornell.edu/cfr/text/29/appendix-to_part_1630

3. In consultation with the individual to be accommodated, identify potential accommodations and assess the effectiveness each would have in enabling the individual to perform the essential functions of the position;

4. Consider the preference of the individual to be accommodated and select and implement the accommodation that is most appropriate for both the employee and the employer.

Finally, there are some activities *not* required of organizations. Organizations do not have to grant specific accommodations requested by individuals. The use of an alternate accommodation is fine as long as it is equally effective. Also, companies do not have to find alternative jobs for unqualified individuals, reduce quantity or quality standards, or eliminate essential job functions.

The need to reasonably accommodate applies to both applicants and employees. However, the type of accommodation needed for *applicants* during the selection process may be distinct from accommodations required for *employees* to perform their job. Therefore, organizations should *not* assume that an accommodation requested by an applicant would be also be required for carrying out the position if hired. After explaining what the hiring procedure entails (e.g., interview, performance test), it is legitimate to ask applicants if they need an accommodation to complete the selection requirements. The EEOC states that these accommodation requests should be handled separately from accommodation requests post-hire.

A question that is often asked is whether an organization can require someone to state whether they have a disability. The answer is "no." But it is allowable to inquire if they can perform essential job functions or perform critical job duties. Furthermore, given rules imposed by the Office of Federal Contract Compliance Programs (OFCCP), federal contractors are required to ask candidates and workers to voluntarily indicate the existence of disabilities. Indeed, it is appropriate for *any* organization (private or public) to ask applicants to *voluntarily* self-identify as having a disability. This is true as long as self-identification is for affirmative action purposes and that refusing to comply will not negatively affect applicants (to illustrate, see the OFCCP voluntary self-identification of disability form[22]).

---

[22] https://www.dol.gov/ofccp/regs/compliance/sec503/Self_ID_Forms/VoluntarySelf-ID_CC-305_ENG_JRF_QA_508c.pdf

Insights from Social Science: Discrimination Suits and Accommodations Based on Different Types of Disabilities

A study by Graham, McMahon, Kim, Simpson, and McMahon (2019) investigated the frequency of disability charges by impairment type (e.g., depression, orthopedic, vision, epilepsy) and the incidence of specific charges of discrimination using data provided by the EEOC across nearly 20 years (July 1992–December 2011). The authors collapsed specific disability types into four impairment categories: (1) physical (back injuries, cystic fibrosis), (2) behavioral (depression, anxiety), (3) neurological (epilepsy, learning disability), and (4) sensory (vision, hearing). The most common charges were those involving physical and behavioral impairments. Furthermore, the most prevalent forms of alleged disability discrimination for all impairment groups were involuntary discharge and lack of reasonable accommodation.

However, a slightly different picture emerged when the data were reported in terms of percentages rather than absolute number of charges. For instance, the percent of involuntary termination and harassment/intimidation was higher for individuals with behavioral impairments. The study also found that the percentage of specific allegations of discrimination were different for those with sensory impairments when compared to a combined group of people with non-sensory impairments (i.e., physical, behavioral, neurological). For example, individuals with sensory impairments were almost twice as likely (on a percentage basis) to allege discrimination regarding the lack of being hired, unlawful medical exams, denial of access to training programs, assignment to lower-level positions, and promotion opportunities. On the other hand, those with sensory impairments had the lowest percent of charges related to alleged illegal termination and transitory separations (e.g., temporary involuntary layoffs, failure to reinstate).

The authors conclude that disability-based termination decisions and requests for reasonable accommodations need to receive special attention. They also stated that individuals with certain types of impairments (e.g., sensory impairments) may be discriminated against in different ways. They argued that approaches to workplace disability issues need to focus on the nature of specific impairments to be most effective.

An investigation by Sundar (2017) reviewed nearly 50 studies to ascertain the types of accommodations employed by organizations. Overall, the results indicated that the most common accommodations used were assistive technology/equipment, altering job requirements, and modifying the work environment. However, types of accommodations were tied to the nature of disabilities. For instance, those with physical and sensory impairments were primarily accommodated by the use of technology/equipment while changing job requirements were more common for cognitive/psychiatric impairments.

Health and Safety Issues and the ADA

In determining whether individuals are qualified to carry out essential job functions, the ADA allows for the consideration of health and safety concerns. Essentially, individuals with disabilities may be deemed unqualified to perform a job due to their disability. In such a case, the organization would need to present evidence (e.g., medical data) that performing the job impaired by the disability would pose a "direct threat" to the health and safety of others and that the risks cannot be removed by the use of a reasonable accommodation.

A key pre-ADA case involving safety concerns is *School Board of Nassau County v. Arline* (1987),[23],[24] where an employee was fired without monetary relief for having recurring bouts of tuberculosis. Gene Arline alleged that the school board violated the Rehabilitation Act of 1973 in denying her financial relief because of her disability. The School Board admitted that Arline had a physical impairment but contended that Arline's impairment, per se, was not the reason for her termination. Rather, it was due to "the threat that her relapses of tuberculosis posed to the health of others." The School Board also consulted with a medical professional who recommended that Arline be fired due to the threat she posed to children, with whom she had regular contact.

The Supreme Court did not believe that the *effects* of a disease on an individual could be differentiated from the *contagious nature* of an impairment. As the Court stated, "Arline's contagiousness and her physical impairment each resulted from the same underlying condition, tuberculosis. It would be unfair to allow an employer to seize upon the distinction between the effects of a disease on others and the effects of a disease on a patient and use that distinction to justify discriminatory treatment." Not only did the Court rule that an individual with an infectious disease can be "handicapped" under the Rehabilitation Act, but the justices also issued guidance on how to assess if an individual is "otherwise qualified" under the Act—that is, whether someone with an infectious disease posed a direct threat to others. These criteria are:

1. Duration of the risk
2. Nature and severity of potential harm to others
3. Likelihood of potential harm
4. Probability of transmission—imminence of potential harm

---

[23] https://caselaw.findlaw.com/us-supreme-court/480/273.html
[24] https://www.oyez.org/cases/1986/85-1277?_

Another important early case involved a dentist, Randon Bragdon, who declined to fill a cavity of his patient (Sidney Abbot) after learning that she was HIV-positive (*Bragdon v. Abbott*, 1998).[25,26] Instead, Bragdon offered to treat Abbott in a hospital at no additional cost. The Supreme Court ruled that the ADA outlawed discrimination "on the basis of disability in the enjoyment of the services of any place of public accommodation by any person who operates [such] a place." Abbot was deemed to have a legitimate disability, as her HIV-positive status substantially limited her in the major life activity of reproduction. (See Mayer [1999–2000] for a review of the issues in *Bragdon v. Abbott*.) The Court further determined that Bragdon did not offer sufficient evidence that a significant risk existed by treating Abbott in his office. As the Court stated, "Petitioner failed to present any objective, medical evidence showing that treating respondent in a hospital would be safer or more efficient in preventing HIV transmission than treatment in a well-equipped dental office."

The Supreme Court sent the case back to the Court of Appeals for reevaluation of the medically based risk assessment evidence regarding HIV transmission (see *Abbott v. Bragdon*, 1998).[27] As before, the 1st Circuit ruled against Bragdon stating that, "Dr. Bragdon did not submit evidence demonstrating a genuine issue of material fact on the direct threat issue."

Direct threat cases have focused on the potential threat to *others*. An exception to this is *Chevron USA, Inc. v. Echazabal* (2002).[28,29] Mario Echazabal was not hired on two occasions after a physical exam conducted by the organization revealed liver damage that was later shown to be due to Hepatitis C. In the view of the company, exposing Echazbal to chemicals within the plant would exacerbate his condition and would entail a direct self-threat to Echazabal. Even though neither RE-73 or the ADA mention threats to one's *own* health (e.g., self-threats), the Supreme Court took an expansive view and asserted that self-threats are protected and ruled in favor of Chevron.

However, this was not a complete victory for Chevron. When the case was sent back to the Court of Appeals for the 9th Circuit, the decision focused on whether Chevron based its decision about Echazbal on sufficient, objective medical evidence. The 9th Circuit concluded that Chevron failed to do so. In the court's opinion, the company's individual assessment of the direct threat

---

[25] https://www.law.cornell.edu/supct/pdf/97-156P.ZO

[26] https://www.oyez.org/cases/1997/97-156

[27] https://scholar.google.com/scholar_case?case=1390916824061941863&q=Bragdon+v.+Abbott,+163+F.3d+87+&hl=en&as_sdt=40006

[28] https://www.law.cornell.edu/supremecourt/text/00-1406

[29] https://www.oyez.org/cases/2001/00-1406

to Echazbal's health was flawed. This was partly because the organization failed to fully consider three of the four factors for direct threat assessment specified in the *Arline* decision. The court also noted that Chevron did not adequately consider the opinions of Echazbal's medical experts, who concluded that working at the plant would not pose a substantial direct threat to his personal health (see *Echazabal v. Chevron USA, Inc.*, 2003).[30]

Medical Tests and the ADA

Under the ADA, organizations can legitimately require medical tests as long as they are given *after* a conditional job offer has been made (Feldblum, 1991). In this context, it is important to ensure that medical tests are part of a second, separate step in the decision-making process. Not doing so can lead to successful ADA challenges. For instance, in *Leonel v. American Airlines, Inc.* (2005),[31] after making conditional job offers, the company required medical tests, the completion of a medical history form, and background checks for the selection of flight attendants. Three applicants had their job offers rescinded after their blood tests indicated the presence of HIV, something they did not disclose previously. The medical tests and self-report medical data were collected at the same time as the background checks, not *after* (as a distinct phase), as required under the ADA. The 9th Circuit ruled against the airline since the collection of medical data was not an independent, post-offer assessment. As the Court stated, "The ADA requires that such examinations be conducted as a separate, second step of the selection process."

In *Karracker v. Rent-A-Center, Inc.* (1995),[32] the company administered a personality assessment (the Minnesota Multiphasic Personality Inventory [MMPI]) *before* making promotion decisions. The plaintiffs were three brothers (Steven, Michael, and Christopher Karracker) who were all denied promotions based on their MMPI scores. The plaintiffs filed an ADA suit claiming that the MMPI was a medical test (it can be used to diagnose certain personality disorders), a claim that was opposed by the defense. The court cited the EEOC's "ADA Enforcement Guidance: Preemployment Disability-Related Questions and Medical Examinations"[33] in its decision. The EEOC

---

[30] https://scholar.google.fr/scholar_case?case=1705753542995849145&hl=en&as_sdt=6&as_vis=1&oi=scholarr&sa=X&ved=0ahUKEwjBnKX6osvTAhVGz2MKHQ-YAt8QgAMIKSgBMAA

[31] https://scholar.google.com/scholar_case?case=12385648287772142702&q=Leonel+v.+American+Airlines+(2005),+&hl=en&as_sdt=40006

[32] https://caselaw.findlaw.com/us-7th-circuit/1486883.html

[33] https://www.eeoc.gov/policy/docs/guidance-inquiries.html

Guidance stipulates several criteria for determining if a test is considered as a medical exam.

The criteria are:

- whether the test is administered by a healthcare professional;
- whether the test is interpreted by a healthcare professional;
- whether the test is designed to reveal an impairment of physical or mental health;
- whether the test is invasive;
- whether the test measures an employee's performance of a task or measures his/her physiological responses to performing the task;
- whether the test normally is given in a medical setting; and
- whether medical equipment is used.

As the EEOC stated, "In many cases, a combination of factors will be relevant in determining whether a test or procedure is a medical examination. In other cases, one factor may be enough to determine that a test or procedure is medical."

The court determined that the MMPI was indeed a diagnostic tool and therefore a medical test. As the court concluded, "Because it is designed . . . to reveal mental illness . . . we think the MMPI is best categorized as a medical examination." Since the MMPI was considered to be a medical test, the company was found to have violated the ADA by administering it prior to making an employment decision.

Personality Tests and the ADA

A similar verdict would be expected for any assessment used in this way, and there currently exists debate over whether even more common employment-related personality assessments might also be considered in this light. This is because the so-called normal-level personality characteristics they assess tend to be correlated with scores on clinical assessments of personality disorders (Hopwood et al., 2018; Melson-Silimon, Harris, Shoenfelt, Miller, & Carter, 2019; Miller, Few, Lynam, & MacKillop, 2015; Trull & Widiger, 2013). Furthermore, some measures commonly used for personnel selection (e.g., the 16PF) can also be used to diagnose personality disorders (Gutman, 2015). In the *Karracker* decision, the court stated that "Psychological tests that are 'designed to identify a mental disorder or impairment' qualify as medical examinations, but psychological tests 'that measure personality traits such as honesty, preferences, and habits' do not." However, as stated by Melson-Silimon et al., "Ultimately, the horse is already out of the barn in terms of how personality data can be used to provide information on psychiatric disorders" (2019, p. 126). The authors state that the legality of measuring personality dimensions may be problematic (and could change), given the ADA's definition of a medical test.

On the other hand, researchers have argued that the intersection between normal personality traits and personality disorders alone is not congruent with the definition of a medical test as stated by the EEOC and case law (e.g., Saxena & Morris, 2019; Winterberg, Tapia, Nei, & Brummel, 2019). As Winterberg et al. (2019) noted, the intent and design of assessment devices are important considerations in categorizing measures as medical tests or personality measures. Furthermore, Saxon and Morris (2019) concluded that

> The mere existence of a characteristic on the same continuum as a disability does not imply that the test is being used for clinical diagnosis. There are many characteristics on which an extreme value could be considered a disability (as in the case of cognitive and physical abilities), and there is no indication in the EEOC guidelines or the case law that job-related tests of these characteristics would be considered a medical exam. (p. 138).

Alcoholism and Illegal Drug Use Under the ADA

Individuals who suffer from alcohol addiction are covered by the ADA, assuming they possess the ability to perform essential job functions. In this regard, organizations may need to accommodate those with alcoholism. With that being said, if the job performance of individuals with an alcohol abuse disorder is negatively affected, organizations can take action against them (e.g., termination, suspension).

Current users of illegal drugs are not protected by the ADA, but those who have been rehabilitated *are* covered. The determination of whether individuals are current users or have been rehabilitated is largely based on the passage of time (i.e., how long it had been since illegal drugs were used). However, the ADA is relatively vague on this point, indicating that a person is considered to be rehabilitated if they have refrained from using illegal drugs for a *considerable* amount of time. This has led courts to use varying time frames to determine rehabilitation status, from three weeks to several months of abstinence (see *Salley v. Circuit City Stores, Inc.*, 1997[34]; *McDaniel v. Mississippi Baptist Medical Center*, 1995[35]; *Collings v. Longview Fibre Company*, 1995[36]).

Physical Ability Tests Under the ADA

Tests that assess physical abilities using physiological measures (e.g., aerobic capacity, heart rate) are considered medical tests. Consequently, they must be administered after a conditional job offer is made. However, it is legitimate to ask job candidates, prior to a job offer, to demonstrate their ability perform physical activities that indicate such capabilities as muscular strength, endurance, and agility/coordination. This can be done by having applicants perform basic activities such as doing sit-ups, push-ups, running a mile, and placing round disks into holes quickly. Another common approach is to measure physical abilities by employing simulations of physical tasks required in jobs (e.g., carrying a fire hose, stair climbing, transporting goods using a dolly). When developed and used properly, these assessments can lead to fewer accidents, injuries, and greater productivity (e.g., Pate, Oria, & Pillsbury, 2010).[37] Positive benefits are more likely to occur if the physical ability tests are based on a job analysis and therefore representative of important job requirements. A job analysis can also help determine if reasonable accommodations are available to workers to assist with performing physical activities (e.g., lifting, standing, walking). Besides possibly increasing job performance, such an approach can help defend physical ability requirements against lawsuits (e.g., from those with physical impairments). For a detailed review of physical ability testing, see Murphy (2015).

Disability Claims and Arbitration

Some organizations have required employees to agree to resolve any complaints (such as alleged ADA violations) via *binding arbitration* (i.e., employees have been required to sign an agreement stating that they would

[34] https://scholar.google.fr/scholar_case?case=4778680570782884947&hl=en&as_sdt=6&as_vis=1&oi=scholarr&sa=X&ved=0ahUKEwjm86iTmcvTAhUQ12MKHZdBDIQQgAMIKCgAMAA

[35] https://scholar.google.fr/scholar_case?case=14907627147555768050&hl=en&as_sdt=6&as_vis=1&oi=scholarr&sa=X&ved=0ahUKEwjL5aGsmcvTAhVY-mMKHQRhAbkQgAMIKCgAMAA

[36] https://scholar.google.fr/scholar_case?case=15625217065002948568&hl=en&as_sdt=6&as_vis=1&oi=scholarr&sa=X&ved=0ahUKEwjkt6bQmcvTAhUVzmMKHVihCjgQgAMIJCgAMAA

[37] Physical ability tests are not without legal concerns. For instance, they can lead to adverse impact against certain groups, such as women (e.g., Courtright, McCormick, Postlethwaite, Reeves, & Mount, 2013).

not sue the organization for grievances but instead follow an arbitration process outside of the court system). This was the case in *EEOC v. Waffle House* (2002).[38,39] Eric Baker (like all applicants) was required to sign such an agreement as part of the application process. After being employed for just over two weeks, Baker had a seizure and was terminated. Consequently, he filed an ADA suit against Waffle House. The company contended that the plaintiff had waived his right to sue by signing the agreement. A key issue in this case was whether the existence of an arbitration agreement prevents the EEOC from pursuing victim-specific relief.

The Court decided that the EEOC can sue for damages even if an employee signed an agreement to only use arbitration to settle any future claims. One of the reasons for its ruling was the concern that giving more clout to arbitration agreements would weaken the EEOC's role in pursuing discrimination claims on behalf of individuals. As the Court stated, "To hold otherwise would undermine the detailed enforcement scheme created by Congress simply to give greater effect to an agreement between private parties that does not even contemplate the EEOC's statutory function." Regarding the *Waffle House* decision, Gutman (2002) concluded that it was a huge win for the EEOC. As Gutman wrote, "had the EEOC lost to Waffle House, the only mechanism for obtaining victim-specific relief would be through arbitration" and that "the EEOC is likely to use it to challenge future attempts by employers to force arbitration agreements as a condition of employment" (p. 64).

Supplemental Readings on the ADA/ADAAA

Beginner
Burgdorf, R. L. (July 24, 2015). Why I wrote the Americans with Disabilities Act. *Washington Post* article. https://www.washingtonpost.com/posteverything/wp/2015/07/24/why-the-americans-with-disabilities-act-mattered/

Americans with Disabilities Act. Department of Labor. https://www.dol.gov/general/topic/disability/ada

An overview of the Americans with Disabilities Act. https://adata.org/sites/adata.org/files/files/ADA_Overview_final2017.pdf

Intermediate
The ADA Amendments Act of 2008: FAQ, Department of Labor.https://www.dol.gov/ofccp/regs/compliance/faqs/ADAfaqs.htm

---

[38] https://www.law.cornell.edu/supct/pdf/99-1823P.ZO
[39] https://www.oyez.org/cases/2001/99-1823

Dunleavy, E., & Gutman, A. (2008). Understanding the ADA Amendments Act of 2008 (ADAAA): Back to the future? *The Industrial-Organizational Psychologist, 46*(3), 81–87. https://citeseerx.ist.psu.edu/viewdoc/download?doi=10.1.1.721.3100&rep=rep1&type=pdf

EEOC. Disability discrimination. https://www.eeoc.gov/laws/types/disability.cfm

EEOC. Enforcement guidance: Q&A: Disability-related inquiries and medical examinations of employees under the ADA. https://www.eeoc.gov/policy/docs/qanda-inquiries.html

EEOC. Enforcement guidance: Reasonable accommodation and undue hardship. https://www.eeoc.gov/policy/docs/accommodation.html

EEOC. The ADA: Your employment rights as an individual with a disability. https://www.eeoc.gov/facts/ada18.html

Advanced

Carlson, K. (2018). From storefront to dashboard: The use of the Americans with Disabilities Act to govern websites. *Catholic University Law Review, 67*(3), 521–547.

Papinchok, J. M. (2005). Title I of the Americans with Disabilities Act: The short but active history of the ADA enforcement and litigation. In F. J. Landy (Ed.), *Employment discrimination litigation: Behavioral, quantitative, and legal perspectives* (pp. 294–335). San Francisco, CA: Jossey Bass.

Proctor, P. (2003). Determining reasonable accommodation under the ADA: Understanding employer and employee rights and obligations during the interactive process. *Southwestern University Law Review, 33*(1), 51–74.

Zucker, D. K. (2003). The meaning of life: Defining "major life activities" under the Americans with Disabilities Act. *Marquette Law Review, 86*(5), 957–976.

Recommendations/Best Practices

- Avoid asking questions about the existence of disabilities (e.g., during job interviews).
- Identify essential job functions, preferably by conducting a systematic job analysis.
- Flexibly interact with applicants/employees regarding their requests for accommodations in a timely manner (e.g., communication about accommodation needs, consideration of preferred accommodations); begin the interactive process if a disability is clearly present.
- Involve external experts/organizations for how to best accommodate disabilities.
- Document all disability-relevant communication between appropriate parties.
- Record precise reasons why any accommodations were considered as unreasonable (e.g., an undue hardship) based on the type and

cost of requested accommodation, company financial data, and the accommodation's potential consequence(s) for the organization.

- Be specific when asking for documentation about the existence of a disability (e.g., clear, practical limitations of a disability; reason why an accommodation is needed); limit medical information to the disability itself.
- Use realistic job previews (RJPs) so applicants can assess whether they can perform the essential functions of jobs.

Summary and Take-Aways

Despite the fact that those with disabilities are protected by the ADA and the subsequent ADAAA, individuals with physical and mental disabilities still suffer from alleged discrimination. Indeed, disability claims were the second most common type of complaint to be filed with the EEOC in 2020. For five years prior to 2020, disability claims have consistently been among the top three or four most frequent types of EEOC discrimination charges (see also Table 8.4 for a list of settlement agreements).

As noted earlier, there is uncertainty regarding what criteria the courts will use to determine when/if temporary impairments are "sufficiently severe" to be considered a disability. Will certain types of disabilities be more likely to be deemed "sufficiently severe?" Also, will some durations be too short for sufficiently severe impairments to qualify as disabilities?

Another unsettled concern is the extent to which certain personality tests may be considered to be medical exams and therefore illegal if used before a conditional offer is extended. Although various measures of personality, such as those that assess "big five" personality traits, are used for non-diagnostic reasons, the data collected may be used to do so. In addition, some assessments of personality contain some possibly "intrusive" items (e.g., "I have frequent mood swings," "I get irritated easily").[40] Others argue that this concern is misplaced (see the 2019 issue, volume 12(2) of the *Industrial and Organizational Psychology: Perspectives on Science and Practice*, for a debate of this issue). Perhaps future court cases will clarify what is considered to be a medical test in light of these concerns.

---

[40] These sample items were obtained from a self-report inventory on the Open-Source Psychometrics Project website. As the site states, "the test uses the Big-Five Factor Markers from the International Personality Item Pool developed by Goldberg (1992)."

Table 8.4 Equal Employment Opportunity Commission disability discrimination settlements (listed in descending chronological order by year)

Organization (year of settlement)	Specific allegation(s)	Settlement and primary relief
KTF Enterprises, Inc. and Kirker Enterprises, Inc. (2020)[1]	Refused to approve of reasonable accommodations to three employees.	• Three-year content decree • $175,000 payment • ADA training for employees, management, and HR personnel
Prestige Care, Inc., Prestige Senior Living, LLC (2020)[2]	Company policy required employees to perform all job duties without accommodations or engaging in an interactive process; discharged disabled employees because of rigid leave policies.	• Five-year consent decree • $2 million payment • Revise ADA policies and procedures • ADA training; hire personnel to review accommodation and ADA complaints
Hawaii Medical Service Association (2020)[3]	Refused to allow intermittent leave for disabled employees; failed to engage in the interactive process.	• Three-year consent decree • $180,000 payment • Revise ADA policies and procedures
Big Lots Stores, Inc. (2019)[4]	Workplace harassment based on hearing and speech impairment disability (e.g., use of offensive terms, mocking speech); refusal to promote due to disability.	• $100,000 payment • Workplace ADA training • Send reports to EEOC regarding ADA harassment or discrimination charges
CROSSMARK, Inc. (2019)[5]	Refused to provide reasonable accommodations to employees (sit on a stool).	• Five-year consent decree • $2.65 million payment • Revise ADA policies/procedures • Workforce ADA training
G4S Secure Solutions (2018)[6]	Failure to offer a reasonable accommodation and termination of employee during medical leave.	• Two-year agreement • $90,000 payment • Hire an EEO constant to alter policies especially regarding need reasonable accommodations • Employee ADA training
M&R Consulting LLC (2018)[7]	Withdrew initial offer to hire applicant based on presence of perceived disability (tuberculosis).	• Two-year consent decree • $40,000 damage payment • Alter hiring process and post-offer assessment forms • ADA training for HR hiring personnel
Kessinger Hunter Management (2018)[8]	Denied 1-week extension of unpaid leave for employee after surgery. Employee fired for not returning.	• $50,000 damage award • Alter ADA policies • Employee training • EEOC compliance monitoring
Otto Candles (2018)[9]	Fired employee with ongoing pancreatitis though condition had no negative impact on job performance.	• Two-year consent decree • $165,000 damage payment • ADA training for employees

Table 8.4 Continued

Organization (year of settlement)	Specific allegation(s)	Settlement and primary relief
Home Depot (2018)[10]	Fired employee for alleged failure to provide company of her medical status after surgery (seen as subterfuge for disability discrimination by EEOC) and failure to provide reasonable accommodation.	• $100,000 damage payment • Anti-discrimination training • Requires company to not deny reasonable accommodations in future • Post notice of suit
Murphy Oil USA (2018)[11]	Forced long-term employee with back injury to perform certain work duties against advice of his doctor. Retaliation claim also filed after employee fired after complaining to management.	• Two-year consent decree • $100,000 damage award • Develop written ADA policy • ADA training • Post notice of settlement
Signature Industrial Services, LLC (2018)[12]	Firing three employees (brothers) with a genetic blood disorder (Hemophilia A) that had no effect on job performance.	• Two-year consent decree • Payment of $135,000
Zachry Industrial, Inc. (2018)[13]	Fired four workers based on medical history data without having an interactive discussion with them (e.g., determine ability to perform essential job functions).	• Three-year consent decree (2018) • Development of a anti disability discrimination policy • Yearly ADA training • Post a notice of the suit • Regular reporting to EEOC
Mueller Industries (2018)[14]	Fired employees with disabilities and/or failed to provide reasonable accommodations.	• $1 million payment (2018) • Reinstatement of disabled employees • ADA training; establish an ADA coordinator; revise complaint procedure policies • Send annual verification reports to the EEOC
Fresh Market (2018)[15]	Firing and/or disciplining employees with disabilities; failure to offer reasonable accommodations.	• $832,500 payment • Revision of ADA policies/procedures • Conduct ADA training
Jones Lang LaSalle Americas (2018)[16]	Refusal to hire applicant after being informed of her disability.	• $82,000 payment • Anti-discrimination training • Posting of anti-discrimination notices • Reporting/monitoring requirements to EEOC

(continued)

Table 8.4 Continued

Organization (year of settlement)	Specific allegation(s)	Settlement and primary relief
Lowe's (2016)[17]	Pattern and practice of terminating and refusing reasonable accommodations for those with disabilities.	• Four-year consent decree • $8.6 million payment • Amend company policies • ADA training • Centralized ADA accommodation request tracking system

[1] https://www.eeoc.gov/newsroom/ktf-enterprises-and-kirker-enterprises-settle-eeoc-disability-lawsuit-175000
[2] https://www.eeoc.gov/eeoc/newsroom/release/2-20-20a.cfm
[3] https://www.eeoc.gov/eeoc/newsroom/release/1-7-20b.cfm
[4] https://www.eeoc.gov/eeoc/newsroom/release/11-26-19a.cfm
[5] https://www.eeoc.gov/eeoc/newsroom/release/11-21-19a.cfm
[6] https://www.eeoc.gov/eeoc/newsroom/release/9-4-18.cfm
[7] https://www.eeoc.gov/eeoc/newsroom/release/9-4-18a.cfm
[8] https://www.eeoc.gov/eeoc/newsroom/release/8-31-18.cfm
[9] https://www.eeoc.gov/newsroom/otto-candies-pay-165000-resolve-eeoc-disability-discrimination-suit
[10] https://www.eeoc.gov/eeoc/newsroom/release/8-17-18.cfm
[11] https://www.eeoc.gov/eeoc/newsroom/release/8-13-18c.cfm
[12] https://www.eeoc.gov/eeoc/newsroom/release/8-13-18c.cfm
[13] https://www.eeoc.gov/eeoc/newsroom/release/8-13-18c.cfm
[14] https://www.eeoc.gov/eeoc/newsroom/release/7-17-18a.cfm
[15] https://www.eeoc.gov/eeoc/newsroom/release/7-2-18b.cfm
[16] https://www.eeoc.gov/eeoc/newsroom/release/7-3-18a.cfm
[17] https://www.eeoc.gov/eeoc/newsroom/release/5-13-16.cfm
Retrieved from EEOC Press Releases: https://www.eeoc.gov/newsroom/search

Glossary

Adverse employment practice: A disruptive and materially adverse change in working conditions that is more than an inconvenience or alteration of job responsibilities.

Average person standard: A yardstick for assessing if impairments count as a legal disability is that they must be greater than that experienced by the average person.

Binding arbitration: A process for resolving a dispute outside of the court system, in which the dispute is presented to a third party or panel that renders a decision that cannot be further challenged or brought to court in any way.

Essential job function: The primary duties that are fundamental to the job.

Interactive process: The steps taken when an employee and employer interactively determine a reasonable accommodation.

Major life activity: Functions central to life, such as caring for oneself, walking, seeing, breathing, learning, and working.

Medical test: A test administered and interpreted by a healthcare professional and designed to reveal physical or mental health impairments or measure task performance or a physiological response to performing the task.

Permanence standard: A way of assessing whether a person is substantially impaired; typically, impairments with a duration of more than six months are considered permanent.

Prima facie: Latin phrase for "at first glance." Consists of presenting evidence that is presumed to be true.

Reasonable accommodation: Adjusting or modifying a job application process or working conditions to enable a qualified person with a disability to be considered for the job.

Undue hardship: An accommodation that is overly demanding or costly for a given organization (i.e., creates a disproportionate or unreasonable burden or obstacle) when considering its resources, size, and nature of the business. Can partially or fully exempt an organization from providing the accommodation.

Glossary terms adapted from Gutman et al. (2011); https://uslegal.com/, and merriamwebster.com/legal.

Cases Cited

Abbott v. Bragdon, 163 F. 3d 87 (1st Cir. 1998).

Albertson's, Inc. v. Kirkingburg, 527 U.S. 555 (1999).

Bragdon v. Abbott, 524 U.S. 624 (1998).

Chevron USA Incorporated v. Echazabal, 536 U.S. 73 (2002).

Collings v. Longview Fibre Company, 63 F. 3d 828 (9th Cir. 1995).

Echazabal v. Chevron USA, Incorporated, 336 F. 3d 1023 (9th Cir. 2003).

EEOC v. Waffle House, Inc., 534 U.S. 279 (2002).

Karraker v. Rent-A-Center, Incorporated, 411 F. 3d 831 (7th Cir. 2005).

Kowitz v. Trinity Health, 839 F.3d 742, 33 A.D. Cases 1 (2016).

Leonel v. American Airlines, Incorporated, 400 F. 3d 702 (9th Cir. 2005).

McDaniel v. Mississippi Baptist Medical Center, 877 F. Supp. 321 (S.D.Miss. 1995).

Murphy v. United Parcel Service Incorporated, 527 U.S. 516 (1999).

Penny v. United Parcel Service Incorporated, 128 F. 3d 408(6th Cir. 1997).

PGA Tour, Incorporated v. Martin, 532 U.S. 661 (2001).

Salley v. Circuit City Stores, Inc., 160 F. 3d 977 (3rd Cir. 1998).

School Board of Nassau County v. Arline, 480 U.S. 273 (1987).

Summers v. Altarum Institute Corp. 740 F. 3d 325 (4th Cir. 2014).

Sutton v. United Air Lines, Incorporated, 527 U.S. 471 (1999).

Toyota Motor Manufacturing, Ky., Inc. v. Williams, 534 U.S. 184 (2002).

References

Blanck, P. D. (2000). Studying disability, employment policy, and ADA. In L. P. Francis & A. Silvers (Eds.), *Americans with disabilities: Exploring implications of the law for individuals and institutions* (pp. 209–220). New York: Routledge.

Bureau of Labor Statistics. (2020). *Persons with a disability: Labor force characteristics summary.* Retrieved on April 20, 2020, from https://www.bls.gov/news.release/disabl.nr0.htm

Colker, R. (2005). *The disability pendulum: The first decade of the Americans with Disabilities Act.* New York: New York University Press.

Courtright, S. H., McCormick, B. W., Postlethwaite, B. E., Reeves, C. J., & Mount, M. K. (2013). A meta-analysis of sex differences in physical ability: Revised estimates and strategies for reducing differences in selection contexts. *Journal of Applied Psychology, 98,* 623–641.

Feldblum, C. (1991). Medical examinations and inquiries under the Americans with Disabilities Act: A view from the inside. *Temple Law Review, 64,* 521–550.

Goldberg, L. R. (1992). The development of markers for the Big-Five factor structure. *Psychological Assessment, 4*(1), 26–42.

Graham, K. M., McMahon, B. T., Kim, J. H., Simpson, P., & McMahon, M. C. (2019). Patterns of workplace discrimination across broad categories of disability. *Rehabilitation Psychology, 64,* 194–202. http://dx.doi.org/10.1037/rep0000227

Gutman, A. (2002). Two January 2002 Supreme Court rulings: *Toyota v. Williams & EEOC v. Waffle House. The Industrial-Organizational Psychologist, 39,* 58–64.

Gutman, A. (2015). Disabilities: Best practices for vulnerabilities associated with the ADA. In C. Hanvey & K. Sady (Eds.), *Practitioner's guide to legal issues in organizations* (pp. 111–126). Cham, Switzerland: Springer International Publishing.

Gutman, A., & Dunleavy, E. (2012). Documenting job analysis projects: A review of strategy and legal defensibility for personnel selection. In M. Wilson, R. Harvey, G. Alliger, & W. Bennett (Eds.), *Handbook of work analysis* (pp. 139–168). New York: Routledge, Taylor & Francis Group.

Hopwood, C. J., Kotov, R., Krueger, R. F., Watson, D., Widiger, T. A., Althoff, R. R., . . . Bornovalova, M. A. (2018). The time has come for dimensional personality disorder diagnosis. *Personality and Mental Health, 12,* 82–86.

Maitland, P. (1999). Riding a cart of golf's "unfairways": *Martin v. PGA Tour. Golden Gate University Law Review, 29,* 627–681.

Mayer, C. (1999–2000). Is HIV a disability under the Americans with Disabilities Act: Unanswered questions after *Bragdon v. Abbott. Journal of Law and Health, 14,* 179–208.

Melson-Silimon, A., Harris, A. M., Shoenfelt, E., Miller, J. D., & Carter, N. T. (2019). Personality testing and the Americans with Disabilities Act: Cause for concern as normal and abnormal models are integrated. *Industrial and Organizational Psychology: Perspectives on Science and Practice, 12,* 119–132.

Miller, J. D., Few, L. R., Lynam, D. R., & MacKillop, J. (2015). Pathological personality traits can capture DSM-IV personality disorder types. *Personality Disorders Theory Research and Treatment 6,* 32–40.

Minter, S. (2014). *Summers v. Altarum:* Broadening the definition of disability under the ADA, and the impact of the new definition on employers. *North Carolina Central Law Review, 37,* 55–67.

Morgeson, F. P., Brannick, M. T., & Levine, E. L. (2019). *Job and work analysis: Methods, research, and applications for human resource management.* Thousand Oaks, CA: Sage Publications.

Murphy, K. R. (2015). Physical abilities. In C. Hanvey & K. Sady (Eds.), *Practitioner's guide to legal issues in organizations* (pp. 111–126). Cham, Switzerland: Springer International.

Pate, R., Oria, M., & Pillsbury, L. (2010). *Fitness measures and health outcomes in youth.* Washington DC: National Academy.

Porter, N. B. (2014). The new ADA backlash. *Tennessee Law Review, 82*(1), 1–82.

Porter, N. B. (2019). Explaining "not disabled" cases ten years after the ADAAA: A story of ignorance, incompetence, and possibly animus. *Georgetown Journal on Poverty Law and Policy, 26*(3), 384–414.

Resslar, M. A. (2002). *PGA Tour, Inc. v. Martin*: A hole in one for Casey Martin and the ADA. *Loyola University Law Review, 33*, 631–689.

Saxena, M., & Morris, S. B. (2019). Adverse impact as disability discrimination: Illustrating the perils through self-control at work. *Industrial and Organizational Psychology, 12*, 138–142.

Schauer, F. (2001). The dilemma of ignorance: *PGA Tour, Inc. v. Martin. The Supreme Court Review, 2001*, 267–297.

Spruill, W. E. (2001). Giving new meaning to handicap: The Americans with Disabilities Act and its uneasy relationship with professional sports in *PGA Tour, Inc. v. Martin. University of Richmond Law Review, 35*, 365–392.

Sundar, V. (2017). Operationalizing workplace accommodations for individuals with disabilities. *Work: Journal of Prevention, Assessment & Rehabilitation, 56*(1), 135–155. doi:10.3233/WOR-162472

Trull, T. J., & Widiger, T. A. (2013). Dimensional models of personality: The five-factor model and the DSM-5. *Dialogues in Clinical Neuroscience, 15*, 135–146.

Vodanovich, S. J., & Piotrowski, C. (2008). The interactive process requirement of the Americans With Disabilities Act: Implications for personnel managers. *Journal of Business Issues, 3*(1), 7–13.

Warden, A. I. (2002). Driving the green: The impact of *PGA Tour, Inc. v. Martin* on disabled athletes and the future of competitive sports. *North Carolina Law Review, 80*, 643–691.

Winterberg, C. A., Tapia, M. A., Nei, K. S., & Brummel, B. J. (2019). A clarification of ADA jurisprudence for personality-based selection. *Industrial and Organizational Psychology, 12*, 172–176.

9

Affirmative Action

The issue of affirmative action has sparked contention throughout history. Disagreements regarding its purpose and application stem from both a social and legal perspective (e.g., Crosby, Iyer, Clayton, & Downing, 2003; Wright & Garces, 2018). As Leiter and Leiter (2011) have contended, "Affirmative action is indisputably the flashpoint of America's civil rights movement" (p. 4). Judicial decisions have also been contentious. Disputes regarding affirmative action have spanned a wide spectrum of legal matters and have resulted in numerous close rulings by the Supreme Court (e.g., 5–4 votes). These cases are the focus of this chapter.

Employment Discrimination. Stephen J. Vodanovich and Deborah E. Rupp, Oxford University Press. © Oxford University Press 2022. DOI: 10.1093/oso/9780190085421.003.0010

Insights from Social Science: Support for Affirmative Action--A Question of Wording?

Many surveys have gauged support for affirmative action programs (AAPs) over the years. It appears that the wording of the questions and demographic characteristics of the samples may partly affect the findings. For instance, a Pew Research Center survey conducted in 2009[a] found that 31% of survey participants agreed with the statement, "we should make every effort to improve the position of blacks and minorities, even if it means giving them preferential treatment." When broken down by race, Hispanic (53%) and Black (58%) participants supported the use of preferential treatment as compared to 22% of White participants.

Another survey conducted in 2013 by the *Washington Post* and ABC News[b] asked the question, "Do you support or oppose allowing universities to consider applicants' race as a factor in deciding which students to admit?" The vast majority of respondents disagreed with this question (76%). In addition, approximately 80% of both White and Black respondents opposed using race in college admissions versus about 70% of Hispanic respondents.

A Post NBC News/*Wall Street Journal* poll conducted in 2013[c] concluded that 45% of participants thought that affirmative action programs are needed to thwart the effects of discrimination against underrepresented racial subgroups. In the same survey, 56% of White respondents were against affirmative action programs, while almost 70% of Hispanic and more than 80% of Black respondents supported such programs.

Greater support was found in a 2007 Pew Research survey,[d] where approximately 70% of respondents supported "affirmative action programs to help Blacks, women and other minorities get better jobs and education." In terms of demographics, support for this statement was 93% among Black respondents and 65% among White respondents. But only 34% of all respondents stated that they supported "preferential" treatment for "minorities."

Finally, a Pew Research Center survey in 2014[e] asked "In general, do you think affirmative action programs designed to increase the number of black and minority students on college campuses are a good thing or a bad thing?" Overall support for this statement was 63%. When broken down by race, this item was endorsed by 55% of White, 84% of Black, and 80% of Hispanic respondents.

A critical factor in surveys and ballot initiatives is the inclusion (or not) of the use of the words "preferential treatment." Nine states have banned the use of affirmative action in educational settings and public employment. All of these state bans on AAPs include the outlawing of "preferential treatment" based on various protected groups.

So, inserting the words "preferential treatment" in surveys (and ballot initiatives) regarding affirmative action reduces support for such programs.

a https://www.pewresearch.org/2009/06/02/public-backs-affirmative-action-but-not-minority-preferences/

b https://www.washingtonpost.com/politics/2013/06/11/4aee6cf8-d2b9-11e2-8cbe-1bcbee06f8f8_story.html

c https://www.nbcnews.com/news/world/nbc-news-wsj-poll-affirmative-action-support-historic-low-flna6C10272398

d https://www.pewresearch.org/fact-tank/2007/05/21/support-affirmative-action-programs/

e http://www.pewresearch.org/fact-tank/2014/04/22/public-strongly-backs-affirmative-action-programs-on-campus/

Office of Federal Contract Compliance Programs

The Office of Federal Contract Compliance Programs (OFCCP) is responsible for the administration of affirmative action via Executive Order 11246, as amended, which was issued in 1965.[1] The order pertains to federal agencies, contractors with government procurement contracts, and contractors with government construction contracts. Specifically, contractors who have federal contracts worth a minimum of $10,000, as well as federal entities, are required to (as stated in EO 11246) "take affirmative action to ensure that applicants are employed, and that employees are treated during employment, without regard to their race, color, religion, sex, sexual orientation, gender identity, or national origin."[2] Furthermore, contractors with 50 or more employees must submit an annual EEO-1 form, while those with contracts greater than $50,000 are required to develop affirmative action plans.

OFCCP Investigative Process

A primary goal of the OFCCP is to assess whether organizations affected by EO 11246 are compliant with affirmative action requirements and that underutilization of individuals from protected subgroups does not exist. This is accomplished through OFCCP compliance reviews. These are often carried out as "desk audits," which consist of examining information contained on

[1] https://www.dol.gov/agencies/ofccp/executive-order-11246/as-amended
[2] The initial version of EO 11246 did not cover women: they were included in EO 11375 issued in 1967.

Table 9.1 Organizational Requirements under Executive Order 11246

Company size/Contract amount	Requirement
Contractors with a minimum of $10,000 contracts	Must adhere to EO 11246 requirements
Contractors with 50 or more workers	EEO-1 form must be completed annually
Contractors with greater than $50,000 contracts	Affirmative action plans must be constructed to remedy underutilization
More than $1,000,000 contracts	Affirmative action plans must be approved before being implemented

Based on a 2019 decision by a district court judge in the District of Columbia in National Women's Law Center, et al., v. Office of Management and Budget, et al., Civil Action No. 17-cv-2458 (D.D.C.), employers and federal contractors with 100 or more employees must provide pay data on EEO-1 forms broken down by sex, race, and ethnicity. Pay data from 2017 and 2018 was due by September 30, 2019, but was moved to January 31, 2020. The EEOC has stated that it will not continue collecting pay data in the future due to cost concerns and the unproved utility of the information.

EEO-1 forms as well as an organization's affirmative action data. EEO-1 forms are required annually for private companies with 100 or more employees and federal contractors with 50 or more workers. A sample EEO-1 form is available from the Equal Employment Opportunity Commission (EEOC).[3] EEO-1 forms include questions about ethnicity, race, and sex representation across nine job categories. These categories include (1) managers and officials, (2) professionals, (3) technicians, (4) sales personnel, (5) administrative workers, (6) craft employees, (7) operatives, (8) laborers/helpers, and (9) service employees.

Specific obligations for organizations/contractors under EO 11246 are based on the number of employees and/or contract size in terms of dollar amount. The larger the company and/or contract, the more rigorous the requirements (see Table 9.1). The OFCCP estimates that federal contractors employ about 25% of the US workforce. On- and off-site reviews are also available to the OFCCP. If the OFCCP discovers noncompliance, it is obligated to attempt to achieve formal voluntary compliance by organizations. The OFCCP investigative process is quite different from that used by the EEOC in the enforcement of Title VII (see Table 9.2 for an overview of the OFCCP investigative process). For instance, one distinction is that the OFCCP can impose damages on organizations for noncompliance prior to going to court.

[3] https://www.eeoc.gov/sites/default/files/migrated_files/employers/eeo1survey/eeo1-2-2.pdf

Table 9.2 Overview of the Office of Contract Compliance Programs (OFCCP) investigative process

Step 1	OFFCP compliance review (e.g., desk audits using EEO-1 form, AAP data; onsite reviews)
Step 2	OFCCP tries to gain voluntary compliance if contractors are judged to be in violation
Step 3	If voluntary compliance is unsuccessful (e.g., no agreement), OFCCP can issue sanctions/fines
Step 4	Contractors may appeal OFCCP ruling; case goes to an Administrative Law Judge from the Department of Labor
Step 5	Contractors have to appeal to the Secretary of Labor (and lose) to have case forwarded to federal district court
Step 6	In federal district court, contractors must prove their innocence

Adapted from Dunleavy & Gutman (2010), https://www.siop.org/Portals/84/TIP/Archives/481.pdf?ver= 2019-08-20-115435-273

OFCCP Sanctions and Penalties

As indicated in Table 9.2, Step 3 of the OFCCP investigative process is enacted when voluntary compliance efforts fail. At that point, the OFCCP can levy sanctions and various remedies *before* a case goes to court. Table 9.3 contains a summary of the sanction/penalties available to the OFCCP. As shown, the OFCCP has successfully reached substantial financial settlements and compliance assistance with organizations. In 2019, monetary settlements reached by the OFCCP totaled more than $40 million—the most ever obtained by the agency.[4] Contributing to the

Table 9.3 Sanctions and penalties available to the Office of Contract Compliance Programs (OFCCP)

1	Publish the names of contractors or unions who have failed to comply
2	Recommend to the Department of Justice (DOJ) cases in which substantial violations exist (or the threat of such violations exist)
3	Recommend to the DOJ or Equal Employment Opportunity Commission (EEOC) that relevant proceedings be taken under Title VII
4	Recommend to the DOJ that criminal procedures be undertaken
5	Cancel, terminate, or suspend contracts
6	Eliminate the contractor from any future contracts with the government (e.g., debarment)

Information adapted from EO-11246 Subpart D - Sanctions and Penalties, Sec. 209, https://www.dol.gov/agencies/ofccp/executive-order-11246/as-amended

[4] https://www.dol.gov/newsroom/releases/ofccp/ofccp20191025

OFCCP's success in reaching these settlement agreements was the implementation the Early Resolution Procedures program, which allows some agreements to be reached early in the investigative process. For instance, in 2019, Bank of America, during a compliance review was alleged to have discriminated against female, Black, and Hispanic applicants in the hiring process. In an early conciliation agreement,[5] the bank agreed to pay $2 million in back pay and interest. An early resolution agreement was also reached with Dell Technologies for pay discrimination based on race and sex, which included a $7 million payout.[6] Similarly, an early conciliation resolution agreement was reached with Goldman Sachs to pay approximately 600 employees a total of $9,995,000 for race- and sex-based pay discrimination.[7] Additionally, the OFCCP answered a record number (greater than 4,500) of Help Desk questions during 2019. The Help Desk is an often-used vehicle to enhance compliance assistance.

Workforce and Availability Analyses

Several tools are critical to the implementation of successful affirmative action programs and the determination of underutilization. One such tool is *workforce analysis*. This analysis contains the number of individuals within protected demographic subgroups (e.g., race subgroups) within the organization (along with their associated pay rates), categorized by job titles or departments. Another tool is *availability analysis*. This incorporates information such as the percent of qualified women and underrepresented racial subgroups in the labor market and the percent of such individuals who can be trained, transferred, or promoted. Specific examples of affirmative action programs (e.g., forms, data collected) can be found at the OFCCP website.[8] Together, these analyses aid in judging how well organizations are reaching established goals and time tables for the employment of underrepresented demographic subgroups. The collection and analysis of these data can be quite time-consuming and complicated. As such, some organizations hire external firms that specialize in this type of work. Finally, the OFCCP's web site offers a variety of technical assistance (e.g., for small contractors, educational entities) and recordkeeping guides (e.g., applicant tracking) to assist organizations for compliance purposes.[9]

---

[5] https://www.dol.gov/newsroom/releases/ofccp/ofccp20190927
[6] https://www.dol.gov/newsroom/releases/ofccp/ofccp20190930-0
[7] https://www.dol.gov/newsroom/releases/ofccp/ofccp20190930
[8] https://www.dol.gov/sites/dolgov/files/ofccp/regs/compliance/AAPs/Sample_AAP_final_JRF_QA_508c.pdf
[9] https://www.dol.gov/agencies/ofccp/compliance-assistance

Strict Scrutiny

As mentioned earlier, *voluntary* affirmative action programs can face scrutiny for "reverse-discrimination," where individuals from a demographic subgroup that is in the numerical *majority* allege to be illegally disadvantaged by the program (e.g., White men). For an affirmative action plan to be legally defensible it must be able to stand up against two criteria that make up what is known as a *strict scrutiny* analysis.

1. Organizations must present evidence that a *compelling interest* was present (e.g., a critically important concern exists).
2. The means to attain diversity (e.g., specific procedures used) are *narrowly tailored* to accomplish the stated goal. For affirmative action, this includes evidence that the use of race is necessary and other less restrictive (e.g., race-neutral) alternatives are not workable.

Examples of a compelling interest include the goal of diversity in higher education; efforts to correct prior, intentional discrimination; and the existence of a glaring underrepresentation of protected group members in a given workforce. Criteria for determining narrow tailoring include the implementation of plans with definable end points (i.e., temporary plans), the use of protected group status as one of *several* factors in decision-making (e.g., as a "plus" factor), and the use of plans that do not *trammel* the interests of individuals in the opposing demographic group.

Voluntary Affirmative Action Programs

This chapter focuses on cases related to voluntary affirmative action programs (as opposed to those required as the result of a *consent decree* or *set-aside program*). Legal challenges to such programs are arguably more common and of greater relevance to most readers. For convenience, voluntary affirmative action cases are organized into the following sections: (1) educational settings, (2) private sector, and (3) noneducational government agencies (municipal, county, state, federal). Table 9.4 summarizes key affirmative action cases. Two other sections are also included. One pertains to affirmative action and consent decrees while the other relates to set-aside programs.

Table 9.4 Summary of key affirmative action cases (listed in chronological order)

Case	Major findings
California v. Bakke (1978)[1]	• A specific percent or number of openings based on race is illegal • Race is permissible as "plus" factor • Diversity can be a "compelling interest"
United Steelworkers v. Weber (1979)[2]	• Percent of Black skilled workers to around 39% • Plan was temporary and did not trammel the rights of the majority (white employees) • Goal was to eliminate *manifest racial imbalance*
Wygant v. Jackson Board of Education (1986)[3]	• Plan to keep percent of minority teachers (layoff senior nonminorities) not narrowly tailored • Role modeling is *not* a compelling state interest • Majority rights were trammeled upon (layoffs)
Johnson v. Transportation Agency (1987)[4]	• Plan was temporary and did not unnecessarily trample on the rights of the majority • Use of gender a "plus" factor to obtain minority representation (*manifest imbalance*)
United States v. Paradise (1987)[5]	• Strict promotional goals are legitimate to enhance representation of minorities in the police force (evidence of long-lasting race discrimination and plan had an end point)
City of Richmond v. Croson (1989)[6]	• City plan to allot a certain percentage of construction contracts to minority companies is illegal; no evidence of past discrimination and plan not narrowly tailored
Martin v. Wilkes (1989)[7]	• White firefighters could file a race discrimination suit after refusing to be a party in a consent decree. Decision overturned by the Civil Rights Act of 1991 (CRA-91)
Adarand Constructors, Inc. v. Pena (1995)[8]	• Federal government agencies must meet strict scrutiny when using race-based regulations to increase minority representation (construction contracts)
Gratz v. Bollinger (2003)[9]	• Giving 20 points for minority status to increase diversity not narrowly tailored; virtually guaranteed admission of minority applicants
Grutter v. Bollinger (2013)[10]	• Diversity is a compelling state interest • AAP was narrowly tailored (race only one factor) • AAP did not unduly harm nonminority applicants • Goal to terminate use of racial preferences as soon as practicable (achieving a "critical mass")
Petit v. City of Chicago (2003)[11]	• Legitimate to standardize test scores using race to increase diversity in the police force; a compelling interest was present and process was narrowly tailored (race used as a "plus" factor)

(continued)

Table 9.4 Continued

Case	Major findings
Parents v. Seattle School District (2007)[12]	• Use of race to balance racial composition of high schools is illegal (compelling interest not shown and not narrowly tailored)
Fisher v. University of Texas (2013)[13]	• Strict scrutiny *not* applied by lower courts
Schuette v. Coalition to Defend Affirmative Action (2014; a.k.a *Schuette v. BAMN*)[14]	• Voters in the States may choose to prohibit the consideration of racial preferences in state and local government agencies, and public education
Fisher v. University of Texas (2016)[15,16]	• The AAP was legitimate, it satisfied the requirements of strict scrutiny (e.g., compelling interest existed), race-neutral alternatives were ineffective, plan was narrowly tailored

[1] https://www.law.cornell.edu/supremecourt/text/438/265
[2] https://supreme.justia.com/cases/federal/us/443/193/
[3] https://supreme.justia.com/cases/federal/us/476/267/
[4] https://www.law.cornell.edu/supremecourt/text/480/616
[5] https://caselaw.findlaw.com/us-supreme-court/480/149.html
[6] https://caselaw.findlaw.com/us-supreme-court/488/469.html
[7] https://www.law.cornell.edu/supremecourt/text/490/755#writing-USSC_CR_0490_0755_ZO
[8] https://www.law.cornell.edu/supremecourt/text/515/200#writing-USSC_CR_0515_0200_ZO
[9] https://www.law.cornell.edu/supct/pdf/02-516P.ZO
[10] https://www.law.cornell.edu/supct/html/02-241.ZS.html
[11] https://caselaw.findlaw.com/us-7th-circuit/1061561.html
[12] https://www.law.cornell.edu/supct/pdf/05-908P.ZO
[13] https://www.law.cornell.edu/supct/pdf/11-345.pdf
[14] https://www.supremecourt.gov/opinions/13pdf/12-682_8759.pdf
[15] https://www.supremecourt.gov/opinions/15pdf/14-981_4g15.pdf
[16] https://www.oyez.org/cases/2015/14-981

Many affirmative action claims have alleged reverse discrimination, and cases in this area have generated their fair share of controversy. One source of tension is the perceived conflict between Title VII (nondiscrimination)/14th Amendment (equal protection) and the preferential treatment of protected, underrepresented subgroups (e.g., female, Black, or Latinx applicants) inherent to affirmative action programs. Affirmative action suits against governmental agencies can be filed using constitutional amendments (e.g., 5th, 14th) as well as Title VII (or Title VI[10] in some instances). Claims against private organizations are limited to Title VII challenges since the amendments only apply to governmental organizations.

[10] https://www.dol.gov/agencies/oasam/regulatory/statutes/title-vi-civil-rights-act-of-1964

Affirmative Action in Educational Settings

The use of specific numbers or percentages to ensure the representation of traditionally underrepresented subgroups (i.e., diversity) was found to be unlawful in the influential case of *Regents of University of California v. Bakke* (1978).[11,12] Allan Bakke (a White man) applied for admission to medical school at the University of California at Davis. At the time Bakke applied, the medical school used two committees to make admission decisions, referred to as *regular* and *special committees*. The special committee decided on the admissibility of economically and/or educationally disadvantaged individuals and "minority" applicants. Both committees employed numerous criteria in making their decisions (e.g., GPA, MCAT scores, recommendation letters). However, the minimum GPA requirement of 2.5 used by the regular committee was not employed by the special committee. Also, applicants considered by the special committee were only compared against each other—not versus those considered via the regular admissions process. Out of a total of 100 medical school slots, 16 were reserved for special committee applicants (those from underrepresented subgroups). Although many disadvantaged Whites applied through the special admissions process, only people of color were accepted.

Bakke was rejected by the regular admissions committee for two consecutive years, even though his scores were considerably higher than those admitted by the special admissions process. As a result, Bakke filed a race discrimination suit, contending that the procedure violated Title VI and the 14th Amendment's equal protection clause. In a 5–4 ruling, the Supreme Court in *Bakke* believed that the process of reserving 16 seats for minority admissions functioned as a quota. Consequently, it was judged to be illegal. It is notable that some justices on the Court in *Bakke* favored the use of race as a "plus" factor for minority status (e.g., allotting extra points) while also considering the goal of diversity to be a compelling government interest.

Justice Powell played a critical role in the *Bakke* decision, endorsing points from opposing sides in support of his vote. As Powell stated in the decision,

> While the goal of achieving a diverse student body is sufficiently compelling to justify consideration of race in admissions decisions under some circumstances,

[11] https://caselaw.findlaw.com/us-supreme-court/438/265.html
[12] https://www.oyez.org/cases/1979/76-811

petitioner's special admissions program, which forecloses consideration to persons like respondent, is unnecessary to the achievement of this compelling goal, and therefore invalid under the Equal Protection Clause. . . . [T]he purpose of overcoming substantial, chronic minority underrepresentation in the medical profession is sufficiently important to justify petitioner's remedial use of race.

(See the short video linked to the following footnote by Professor John Jeffries on the important influence of Justice Powell in *Bakke*.)[13]

Although the use of minority status as a "plus" factor is generally acceptable within affirmative action programs, its use does not guarantee legal compliance. Its legality depends on how the plus factor is used. For instance, the College of Literature, Science, and the Arts (LSA) at the University of Michigan used several factors when making undergraduate admission decisions. These included (among other criteria) high school GPA, standardized test scores, and rigor of high school curriculum, as well as minority status. The LSA awarded 20 points out of a required 100 within the admissions process for those belonging to "an underrepresented racial or ethnic minority group." Two White applicants who were denied admission to the College subsequently filed a race discrimination suit (*Gratz v. Bollinger*, 2003).[14,15] Although the College considered multiple factors in their decision-making approach, the Supreme Court determined by a 6–3 vote that giving 20 points toward the needed 100 effectively guaranteed that racial minority applicants would be accepted. As a result, the plan was not deemed to be narrowly tailored, a requirement under strict scrutiny, and the program was subsequently found to be illegal. As the Court concluded, "the LSA's automatic distribution of 20 points has the effect of making 'the factor of race . . . decisive' for virtually every minimally qualified underrepresented minority applicant." The Court further stated that,

We find that the University's policy, which automatically distributes 20 points, or one-fifth of the points needed to guarantee admission, to every single "underrepresented minority: applicant solely because of race, is not narrowly tailored to achieve the interest in educational diversity that respondents claim justifies their program.

[13] https://www.c-span.org/video/?c4459201/user-clip-justice-powell-bakke
[14] https://www.law.cornell.edu/supct/html/02-516.ZO.html
[15] https://www.oyez.org/cases/2002/02-516

A different scenario at the same university occurred in the case of *Grutter v. Bollinger* (2003).[16,17] To ensure diversity, the Law School at the University of Michigan used minority status as a factor in deciding whom to accept. As in *Gratz*, the Law School used numerous factors in addition to race in selecting applicants, such as LSAT scores, GPA, letters of recommendation, and quality of undergraduate institution. Barbara Grutter (a White applicant) was not admitted to law school and filed a 14th Amendment law suit alleging that race was a major factor in the school's admissions process, thus giving racial minorities a far better opportunity to be accepted. She further contended that the Law School did not have a "compelling interest" in using race in their selection process.

In contrast to the *Gratz* case, the Court sided with the university in a 5–4 decision (see Gutman, 2009; Heriot, 2004). Their ruling was based on several factors, which included the following:

- the use of race furthered a compelling interest (the attainment of diversity within law school classes),
- the plan was narrowly tailored in that it would end when a "critical mass" of individuals from underrepresented subgroups were admitted,
- race played a relatively minor role in admissions decisions,
- an individualistic assessment was made of each applicant that considered a wide range of applicant qualifications, and
- other subgroups (e.g., Whites) were not unduly harmed by the process.

Importantly, as the Court stated in *Grutter*, "Unlike the program at issue in Gratz v. Bollinger . . . the Law School awards no mechanical, predetermined diversity 'bonuses' based on race or ethnicity." It is noteworthy that Justice O'Connor believed that the need for affirmative action would not be permanent. To this point, she stated that the Supreme Court "expects that 25 years from now, the use of racial preferences will no longer be necessary to further the interest approved today."

As it turned out, the issue of achieving a "critical mass" would be addressed in future cases. In *Grutter*, university personnel and witnesses did not specifically state how a critical mass would be determined. One definition of "critical mass" in *Grutter* was "a number that encourages underrepresented minority students to participate in the classroom and not feel isolated" and that "there

---

[16] https://www.law.cornell.edu/supct/html/02-241.ZS.html
[17] https://www.oyez.org/cases/2002/02-241

is no number, percentage, or range of numbers or percentages that constitute critical mass." Another similar definition proposed that "critical mass means numbers such that underrepresented minority students do not feel isolated or like spokespersons for their race." Critical mass was also said to be attained when "racial stereotypes lose their force because nonminority students learn there is no 'minority viewpoint' but rather a variety of viewpoints among minority students." The concept of obtaining a critical mass would be a factor in another affirmative action case involving the University of Texas at Austin (UT Austin).

For several years, UT Austin employed a 10% rule to increase diversity at the undergraduate level. That is, all high school students who were in the top 10% of their high school graduating class in GPA scores were guaranteed admission to a Texas state university. This "race-neutral" approach improved underrepresentation. However, in lieu of the *Grutter* decision, the university decided to further examine whether a *critical mass* of traditionally underrepresented students existed in its undergraduate classes. An analysis of small, "participatory size" classes (5–24 students) indicated that various subgroups were enrolled at a low rate. For instance, 90% of students in these smaller classes contained only one or no Black students. When the smallest of these classes were excluded from analyses, 89% of classes still had one or no Black students enrolled. Other findings indicated that Hispanic and Asian American students were underenrolled in smaller classes, too, but not in as low numbers as Black students. Finally, a survey found that students comprising racial or ethnic minority groups reported feeling isolated and believed that such groups were not sufficiently represented at the university.

So, to achieve a critical mass of racial minorities at UT Austin, the school began to use race as one of many factors for students who were not admitted using the 10% rule (e.g., standardized tests scores, high school class rank, essays).[18] While employing this method, race was still used infrequently in admitting undergraduate students. Nonetheless, Abigail Fisher, a White student, was not admitted as an undergraduate student to UT Austin and sued the university. Her suit stated that the university did not specifically indicate how a critical mass would be determined, that the existing 10% rule had already achieved diversity so the use of race was unnecessary,

---

[18] For those not in the top 10%, UT Austin used standardized test scores and high school class rank to determine "academic achievement." Applicants could be admitted based on these criteria alone. Another factor was the "Personal Achievement Index" which consisted of two essays and an evaluation of an individual's complete file. Race was one part of the Achievement Index and was only used if "academic achievement" was high enough and essays were judged to be good.

and that the university had not adequately considered other race-neutral factors.

The case went to the Supreme Court twice, reaching an initial decision in 2013 and another in 2016. In *Fisher v. University of Texas* (2013),[19,20] the Supreme Court sent the case back to the lower courts by a margin of 7–1 (Justice Kagan recused herself). The justices concluded that a strict scrutiny analysis had not been properly applied and ruled that the lower courts had relied on the "good faith" of the school in considering race in admissions.

In *Fisher v. University of Texas* (2016),[21,22] the Court ruled in favor of the university (see *Washington Post* article that reviews the *Fisher* decision).[23] The vote was 4–3 due to Justice Kagan recusing herself as earlier and the death of Justice Antonin Scalia. Regarding the issue of determining a critical mass, the justices opined that it would be illegal for the University of Texas to use specific numbers or percentages of undergraduate racial minorities to indicate when a critical mass had been met. In lieu of this, the Court believed that the university had sufficiently presented clear, specific diversity-related goals. In addition, the Court decided that UT Austin proved it was necessary to use race as a factor in its admissions procedure. That is, the school performed two studies that indicated race-neutral practices were not successful in increasing diversity. Finally, the *Fisher* decision stated that the university adequately minimized the use of race in its admissions decisions and therefore the plan was narrowly tailored (see also Joshi, 2016).

Another important affirmative action case in the realm of academics is that of *Wygant v. Jackson Board of Education* (1986).[24,25] A collective bargaining agreement was established between the Board of Education and the teachers' union to protect employees with the most seniority in the event that layoff decisions needed to be made. Also, the agreement operated to keep intact the percent of racial minorities who were employed at the time of any layoffs. Given this later provision, when faced with layoffs, the school fired White teachers with more seniority while retaining those from underrepresented racial subgroups with less time on the job. Consequently, the discharged teachers filed suit asserting that the layoff procedure was an illegal violation of the 14th Amendment. The lower courts ruled for the

[19] https://www.law.cornell.edu/supremecourt/text/14-981
[20] https://www.oyez.org/cases/2012/11-345
[21] https://www.supremecourt.gov/opinions/15pdf/14-981_4g15.pdf
[22] https://www.oyez.org/cases/2015/14-981
[23] https://www.washingtonpost.com/politics/courts_law/supreme-court-upholds-university-of-texas-affirmative-action-admissions/2016/06/23/513bcc10-394d-11e6-8f7c-d4c723a2becb_story.html
[24] https://caselaw.findlaw.com/us-supreme-court/476/267.html
[25] https://www.oyez.org/cases/1985/84-1340

school board stating, in part, that the agreement was "an attempt to remedy societal discrimination by providing 'role models' for minority schoolchildren." The Supreme Court disagreed in a 5–4 decision. They ruled that if past discrimination on the part of the school board was *not* shown to exist, then the race-based layoff portion of the agreement was too broad (not narrowly tailored) and that other, less onerous options existed, such as the use of diversity-related hiring goals. The Court also found that the purpose of ensuring a fixed percent of Black teachers as role models for underrepresented students was not lawful.

The legality of racial balancing in high schools was addressed in *Parents Involved in Community Schools v. Seattle School District* (2007).[26,27] Seattle implemented a plan to prevent schools from being overly segregated by race (White vs. people of color) given racial imbalances that existed within geographically bound school districts. Students were given the opportunity to rank-order the high schools they wished to attend. However, if too many students picked a particular high school as their first choice, thus leading to a specific imbalance in the racial mix within the school, certain criteria ("tiebreakers") were employed to ensure racial diversity. The first was whether a sibling was also enrolled at the chosen school. The next factor consisted of the race of the student along with the racial composition of the school. A third factor was the proximity of the student's home to the selected school.

The parents of students who were denied admission to their chosen high school based on race filed a 14th Amendment suit. The Supreme Court decided (5–4) against the district's plan. The justices believed that the race-based approach to assigning students to schools did not pass strict scrutiny. The plan was not narrowly tailored and did not establish a compelling interest (see also Gutman & Dunleavy, 2007).[28] Indeed, the Court concluded that the primary goal of the plan was to have a sufficient racial makeup within schools rather than it being based on any definable educational benefits associated with a diverse student body. Quoting from the Court's decision,

The validity of our concern that racial balancing has no logical stopping point is demonstrated here by the degree to which the districts tie their racial guidelines

[26] https://www.law.cornell.edu/supct/pdf/05-908P.ZO
[27] https://www.oyez.org/cases/2006/05-908
[28] https://www.siop.org/Portals/84/TIP/Archives/452.pdf?ver=2019-08-20-115134-943

to their demographics. . . . Accepting racial balancing as a compelling state interest would justify the imposition of racial proportionality throughout American
society, contrary to . . . "the simple command that the Government must treat citizens as individuals, not as simply components of a racial, religious, sexual or national class.'"

Affirmative Action in the Private Sector

As mentioned earlier, suits alleging discrimination in the private sector are
filed under Title VII since constitutional amendment protections are limited
to government agencies. Also, in private organizations (vs. higher education),
it is unclear if the goal of diversity *alone* is sufficient to be considered as a compelling interest.

A key private sector case was *United Steelworkers v. Weber* (1979),[29,30]
where fewer than 2% of skilled positions within the organization located
in Gramercy, Louisiana were filled by Black employees. This was in comparison to the estimated 39% of skilled Black individuals in the relevant
labor market. A primary reason given for this underrepresentation was
that Black applicants lacked the prerequisite experience for skilled jobs.
This relative inexperience was due to the fact that the union (United
Steelworkers) had a long-standing history of denying Blacks access to essential training.

The United Steelworkers of America and the company (Kaiser Aluminum)
established a nationwide collective bargaining agreement to increase employment of persons of color. At the Gramercy plant, the agreement assured
that for every two openings in the training program, one White and one
Black individual would be selected. The plan would continue until Black
workers comprised roughly 39% of the skilled jobs in the organization (i.e.,
the estimated proportion of skilled Black workers in the relevant labor
market). This approach even applied to Blacks who had less seniority than
Whites.

Weber (a White employee), filed a Title VII class action suit alleging
that White employees with more seniority were denied admittance for
openings in the training program in favor of granting access to a certain
percent of Black employees. In the end, Weber lost in a 5–2 vote. The Court

[29] https://www.law.cornell.edu/supremecourt/text/443/193
[30] https://www.oyez.org/cases/1978/78-432

believed that the program was legitimate and did not violate Title VII. As the Court stated, "Title VII's prohibition . . . against racial discrimination does not condemn all private, voluntary, race-conscious affirmative action plans." Furthermore, the plan was viewed as a voluntary effort to offset long-standing racial discrimination in a manner that did not have an excessive negative effect on White employees (e.g., they did not lose their jobs). Furthermore, the plan was deemed to have a discernible end point (i.e., it was temporary).

Insights from Social Science: Can Recipients of Affirmative Action Programs Be Harmed by Its Implementation?

Many scholarly articles have addressed this question and the answer is largely "it depends." For instance, numerous studies by Heilman and her colleagues (among others) have shown that if the job qualifications of those who benefit from affirmative action are not made clear, then numerous undesirable effects may result. These effects, such as lower perceptions of self-competence, less job satisfaction, minimizing their own leadership abilities, and undervaluing performance on job tasks can occur among affirmative action recipients themselves.

Others can also hold a negative view of those selected via affirmative action, which generally results in lower ability assessments. Resentment by others for not being chosen over an affirmative action recipient can also occur. Therefore, one way to prevent these negative perceptions is to ensure that ability/merit is salient (or primary) in making affirmative action decisions. To quote from Heilman, Battle, Keller, and Lee (1998) in research on preferential selection based on sex, "By providing affirmation of competence to the beneficiaries themselves, it staved off negative self-evaluations and performance assessments. By directly negating the assumptions that allow for the beneficiary's qualifications to be discounted by onlookers, it precluded inferences of incompetence. And, by supplying information about the deservingness of the beneficiary, it precluded perceptions of inequitable outcomes on the part of those bypassed for the target position" (p. 203).

For more information, see also Heilman, Block, and Lucas (1992); Heilman, Block, and Stathatos (1997); Heilman, McCullough, and Gilbert (1996); Heilman, Rivero, and Brett (1991); and Heilman, Simon, and Repper (1987).

Affirmative Action in Noneducational Government Agencies

The use of a "plus" factor to achieve diversity was illustrated in *Johnson v. Transportation Agency of Santa Clara County* (1987).[31,32] The transportation company had a shortage of women in their workforce. Only 10% of those in technical jobs were women, and *no* women worked in skilled craft positions. Consistent with a recently developed plan to address the shortage of women, the agency promoted a female applicant (Dian Joyce) who received a marginally lower interview score compared to a White man (Paul Johnson). It is important to note that *both* candidates were considered to be qualified for the position.

Johnson filed a Title VII sex discrimination claim asserting that sex played a definitive role in his rejection for promotion and that the agency's affirmative action plan was not temporary as required. Johnson lost his suit. The Court decided (6–3) that a legitimate goal existed for the agency's affirmative action plan and the resulting promotion decision: to correct the relative scarcity of women who worked for the agency. Also, in the Court's view, sex was properly used as a "plus" factor in this context and did not overly harm those in the majority. From the Court's ruling,

> "substantial evidence shows that the Agency has sought to take a moderate, gradual approach to eliminating the imbalance in its work force, one which establishes realistic guidance for employment decisions, and which visits minimal intrusion on the legitimate expectations of other employees.

Another "plus factor" case that used diversity as a compelling interest is demonstrated by *Petit v. City of Chicago* (2003;[33] see also Gutman, 2004).[34] The city altered selection test scores based on race for promotion to police sergeant to increase racial and ethnic diversity as part of an affirmative action effort and also because the exam had not been validated. White candidates who were denied promotion by the standardization process alleged that their 14th Amendment rights were infringed upon. The 7th Circuit agreed with Chicago that the plan was constitutional to ensure a diverse police force. Referring to

---

[31] https://caselaw.findlaw.com/us-supreme-court/480/616.html
[32] https://www.oyez.org/cases/1986/85-1129
[33] https://caselaw.findlaw.com/us-7th-circuit/1061561.html
[34] https://www.siop.org/Portals/84/TIP/Archives/414.pdf?ver=2019-08-19-115654-973

the *Grutter* decision, the court reasoned that the goal of diversity in a police department qualified as a compelling interest. The court reasoned that,

> It seems to us that there is an even more compelling need for diversity in a large metropolitan police force charged with protecting a racially and ethnically divided major American city like Chicago. Under the *Grutter* standards, we hold, the City of Chicago has set out a compelling operational need for a diverse police department.

The court also believed that the promotional process was narrowly tailored. Some reasons for this conclusion were that the justices thought that race was not a decisive element in making promotion decisions. Rather, race was properly used as a "plus" factor since the score adjustments based on race were relatively minor. In addition, the alteration of test scores based on race stopped in 1991; it was not used in subsequent test administrations. Consequently, the plan was considered temporary in scope.

Employing a specific race-based solution was also supported in *United States v. Paradise* (1987).[35,36] The Alabama Department of Public Safety was found to have a clear pattern of race discrimination lasting about four decades regarding the job of state trooper. When several attempts to correct persistent race discrimination did not succeed, a district court issued an order mandating the use of rigorous hiring and promotional goals for increasing the number of qualified Black troopers hired, which operated as a quota. Specifically, the order stated "'for a period of time,' at least 50% of those promoted to corporal must be black, if qualified black candidates were available . . . and imposed a 50% promotional requirement in the other upper ranks, but only if there were qualified black candidates." The court's decision was contested by the Department of Justice, which alleged that the strict goals violated the 14th Amendment.

However, the Supreme Court ruled (5–4) in favor of the promotional goals. Their reasoning was that previous attempts did not eliminate race discrimination, so no viable alternatives remained. Also, the affirmative action plan was viewed by the Court as having an identifiable end point (i.e., it was temporary) and did not overly penalize the rights of other subgroups. As noted by the Court, "The one-for-one requirement did not impose an unacceptable burden on innocent third parties . . . the temporary and extremely limited nature of the requirement substantially limits any potential burden on white applicants for promotion." The majority of justices also stated that "The one-for-one

---

[35] https://caselaw.findlaw.com/us-supreme-court/480/149.html
[36] https://www.oyez.org/cases/1986/85-999

requirement does not require the layoff and discharge of white employees ... it only postpones the promotions of qualified whites." It is notable that the use of quotas to eradicate discrimination was controversial among the justices, with four members of the Court rejecting their use.

Finally, *Schuette v. Coalition to Defend Affirmative Action* (2014)[37,38] involved whether or not, at the state level, citizens can vote to eliminate affirmative action plans used by state and local government entities. Specifically, the Supreme Court ruled on the legality of Proposition 2 in the state of Michigan, which reads, in part, as follows:

Ban public institutions from using affirmative action programs that give *preferential treatment* to groups or individuals based on their race, gender, color, ethnicity or national origin for public employment, education, or contracting purposes. Public institutions affected by the proposal include state government, local governments, public colleges and universities, community colleges and school districts." (emphasis added)

The Court ruled (6–2; Justice Kagan did not participate in the ruling) in favor of the ban, stating that the 14th Amendment's equal protection clause was not violated by the proposition's passage. The majority of justices concluded that the law did not intend to discriminate and that it did not harm legally protected subgroups. It is essential to note that the Supreme Court did *not* decide on the legal merits of affirmative action programs in this case. Rather, *Schuette* was about "whether voters may determine whether a policy of race-based preferences should be continued. ... Michigan voters exercised their privilege to enact laws as a basic exercise of their democratic power, bypassing public officials they deemed not responsive to their concerns about a policy of granting race-based preferences" (see short video by ABC News on *Schuette* decision[39]).

To date, nine states have banned the use of affirmative action programs in public employment and education based on various factors (e.g., race, color, sex, national origin, ethnicity), with the majority (six) of these bans being approved by voters (see also Ledesma, 2019). Of the other three, two were passed by the legislature and another with an executive order signed by a governor (see Table 9.5).

---

[37] https://www.supremecourt.gov/opinions/13pdf/12-682_8759.pdf
[38] https://www.oyez.org/cases/2013/12-682
[39] https://abcnews.go.com/WNT/video/michigan-ban-college-affirmative-action-stands-23432058

Table 9.5 Affirmative action bans in the United States

Year	State	Method
2020	Idaho	Legislatively referred constitutional amendment
2012	Oklahoma	Legislatively referred constitutional amendment
2011	New Hampshire	Statute
2010	Arizona	Voter initiative: constitutional amendment
2008	Nebraska	Voter initiative: constitutional amendment
2006	Michigan	Voter initiative: constitutional amendment
1999	Florida	Executive order by governor
1998	Washington	Voter initiative: statute
1996	California	Voter initiative: constitutional amendment

Retrieved from the Pew Research Center, https://www.pewresearch.org/fact-tank/2014/04/22/supreme-court-says-states-can-ban-affirmative-action-8-already-have/.

Affirmative Action and Consent Decrees

The legitimacy of voluntary agreements between two parties (e.g., consent decrees) to address affirmative action has been disputed legally. For example, in *Firefighters v. Cleveland* (1986),[40,41] the Vanguards of Cleveland, a group of Black and Hispanic firefighters employed by the City of Cleveland, filed a Title VII class action suit alleging race discrimination. Subsequently, the city entered into settlement negotiations with the plaintiffs. During this time, the Firefighters Union (Local 93) inserted itself into the negotiations as a "party-plaintiff." The union opposed the implementation of potential affirmative action plans and therefore "overwhelmingly" rejected the negotiated consent decree. Despite this opposition, the Vanguards and the City sought court approval for a revised consent decree that included the negotiated affirmative action plan for promotional decisions but did not require the union's approval. This consent decree was approved by the district court and affirmed at appeal. The union then petitioned the Supreme Court for a *writ of certiorari* (a request for the Supreme Court to review the decisions of lower courts). Specifically, they requested that the Court consider their argument that the consent decree violated Section 706(g) of Title VII because the new proportional system did not benefit the actual victims of past race discrimination. Section 706(g) gave the courts the ability to make whole victims of past discrimination[42]—a

---

[40] https://caselaw.findlaw.com/us-supreme-court/478/501.html
[41] https://www.oyez.org/cases/1985/84-1999
[42] In this context, the phrase "make whole" refers to restoring victims to the position they were in prior to being discriminated against (e.g., by awarding sufficient damages).

section that some have interpreted as meaning that the courts are prohibited from ordering specific practices that benefit protected individuals who were not past victims. The union also argued that it was not a party to the agreement and, therefore, should not be held by its provisions.

In a 6–3 ruling, the Court concluded that although the union did not participate in the decree, the agreement did not mandate any requirements on its part. Also, the union could still pursue further legal action if it desired. Moreover, the Court stated that,

> The fact that the consent decree in this case was entered without petitioner's consent does not affect its validity. While an intervenor [*sic*] is entitled to present evidence and have its objections heard at the hearings on whether to approve a consent decree, it does not have power to block the decree merely by withholding its consent.

In addition, the Court ruled that Title VII does not prohibit parties from freely choosing to enter into agreements to remedy discrimination even though beneficiaries of the agreement were not affected by discrimination (i.e., actual victims). Quoting from the Court,

> Congress intended that voluntary compliance be the preferred means of achieving Title VII's objectives. Voluntary action available to employers and unions seeking to eradicate race discrimination may include reasonable race-conscious relief that benefits individuals who are not actual victims of that discrimination.

In *Martin v. Wilks* (1989),[43,44] the City of Birmingham's history of race discrimination in the hiring and promoting of firefighters eventually led to two consent decrees that stipulated hiring and promotion goals for firefighters of color. Several White firefighters refused to participate in the proceedings leading to the consent decrees. Years later, Robert Wilks, a White firefighter, filed a race discrimination suit alleging that the decree violated Title VII and the 14th Amendment in that lesser qualified Black firefighters were being favored over more qualified Whites. The Supreme Court took on the question of whether Wilks and other White firefighters had the right to challenge previously agreed-upon consent decrees.

The Court agreed with the White firefighters in a 5–4 decision. The Court stated, in part, that "a person cannot be deprived of his legal rights in a

[43] https://www.law.cornell.edu/supremecourt/text/490/755#writing-USSC_CR_0490_0755_ZO
[44] https://www.oyez.org/cases/1988/87-1614

proceeding to which he is *not* a party." However, the dissenting opinion argued that any party who had notice of pending litigation (e.g., a consent decree) and who had the chance to be involved should be held by its requirements. Otherwise, they believed that such "sideline sitters" could be rewarded after the fact by their inaction. Congress agreed with this dissenting opinion and overturned *Wilks* through the passage of the Civil Rights Act of 1991. Essentially, the Act stated that a party could *not* challenge a consent decree at a later date if they (1) were provided with sufficient notice of a proposed agreement and (2) had an opportunity to present their views (e.g., objections).

Affirmative Action and Set-Aside Programs

Set-asides are special programs aimed at increasing opportunities for small businesses and businesses owned by individuals from underrepresented groups to acquire government contracts. Typically, set-aside programs have very specific goals, whereby a certain number of opportunities are reserved for such businesses. In *City of Richmond v. Croson* (1989),[45,46] construction contracts in Richmond, Virginia, were virtually nonexistent for businesses run by Blacks. For instance, only 0.67% of contracts were given to contractors of color from March 1978 to March 1983.

To confront this issue, the city developed the Minority Business Utilization Plan. The plan mandated that principal contractors who received construction contracts with Richmond had to use subcontractor firms owned by persons of color for at least 30% of contract dollars. When attempts to hire subcontractors of color by J. A. Croson Company failed for a variety of reasons and the company ended up being the only bidder on an available contract, Croson requested a waiver of the 30% regulation. The city refused to waive the 30% rule and the company was denied the contract, leading Croson to sue under the 14th Amendment, arguing that the set-aside plan did not pass strict scrutiny.

The Supreme Court ruled that strict scrutiny requirements were *not* met by the city in issuing its 30% rule. The ruling stated that no evidence was presented of previous racial discrimination by the city in distributing construction contracts (lack of a compelling interest). In addition, the method to confront the lack of subcontractors of color was not narrowly tailored. Indeed,

---

[45] https://caselaw.findlaw.com/us-supreme-court/488/469.html
[46] https://www.oyez.org/cases/1988/87-998

the 30% figure was viewed as being applied indiscriminately. It was deemed to not be associated with any definable, applicable number, such as the availability of subcontractors of color in the city of Richmond.

In another case (*Adarand Constructors, Inc. v. Pena*, 1995),[47,48] the Department of Transportation (DOT) issued a directive that gave monetary rewards to general contractors who hired small businesses considered to be Disadvantaged Business Enterprises (DBE) for subcontracting work. Subcontractors who are owned by socially and economically disadvantaged individuals qualify for DBE status. The subcontracting clause under federal law states that contractors "shall *presume* that socially and economically disadvantaged individuals include Black Americans, Hispanic Americans, Native Americans, Asian Pacific Americans, and other minorities, or any other individual found to be disadvantaged by the [Small Business] Administration" (emphasis added).

The case involved a general contractor, Mountain Gravel and Construction Company, that selected a minority-owned subcontractor (Gonzales Construction Company) that was certified as a DBE. This decision was made despite the fact that another firm, Adarand Constructors, submitted a lower bid on the subcontract. Importantly, Adarand was not a DBE. Mountain Gravel stated that it hired Gonzalez Construction given the financial incentives involved in hiring them as a DBE.

After losing its bid, Adarand filed suit. A major point of contention by Adarand was that the government's practice of using ". . . race-based presumptions used in subcontractor compensation clauses was a violation of the equal protection component of the Fifth Amendment's Due Process Clause." At issue was which type of scrutiny should be used in evaluating the DOT's regulation. This issue was complicated since the 5th Amendment does not contain an "equal protection" clause. Rather, it guarantees "due process," a less obvious protection under the law.

The Supreme Court decided (6–3) that government directives using race-based approaches must be evaluated using a *strict scrutiny* approach. The case was consequently sent back to the lower courts for further review. In the end, the 10th Circuit concluded that a revised DBE program satisfied strict scrutiny. Thus, current case law suggests that race-based approaches at *all levels* of government (local, state, and federal) must be evaluated via strict scrutiny.

[47] https://www.law.cornell.edu/supremecourt/text/515/200#writing-USSC_CR_0515_0200_ZO
[48] https://www.oyez.org/cases/1994/93-1841

Insights from Social Science: Attracting Applicants of Color

Many organizations face challenges when it comes to recruiting diverse applicant pools. Consequently, one of the key aspects of affirmative action is the focus on recruitment. Several strategies have been advocated in this regard, such as including persons of color in job advertisements. This approach has received positive impressions from job seekers of color given that they are shown as being represented in organizations (e.g., Avery, Hernandez, & Hebl, 2004; Avery & McKay, 2006; Perkins, Thomas, & Taylor, 2000; Pietri, Johnson, & Ozgumus, 2018).

Another avenue is the use of recruiters of color. For instance, as Doverspike, Taylor, Shultz, and McKay (2000, p. 452) have stated, "organizations should deploy minorities as recruiters, particularly in settings where minorities are prevalent. . . . The presence of successful minority employees sends a signal to applicants that the organization is committed to diversifying its workforce, that potential role models exist, and that minorities have a strong likelihood of success" (see also, Avery, McKay, & Volpone, 2013).

However, recruiting for a more diverse workforce can lead to unintentional outcomes (e.g., greater turnover) if the climate of organizations fails to match the messages used to attract underrepresented applicants (McKay & Avery, 2005). Also, it has been suggested that an array of other factors can alter the effectiveness of recruiting a diverse workforce, such as the perceived reputation of organizations regarding diversity, how organizations are viewed as valuing diversity efforts, and the overall image of the organization (e.g., Avery & McKay, 2006). In contrast, some research has found that when a cooperative work environment exists, diversity climate is enhanced and can foster greater job performance, such as less turnover and better sales (e.g., McKay, Avery, Son, Rosado-Solomon, & Pustovit, 2017).

Other research has highlighted the importance of the specific wording of job qualifications in advertisements. For instance, some evidence exists that the wording of job ads can discourage individuals from underrepresented demographic groups from applying (e.g., Wille & Derous, 2018). Furthermore, the research of Purdie-Vaughns, Steele, Davies, Diltmann, and Crosby (2008) found that certain cues in recruiting materials, such as representation of persons of color (high or low) and diversity philosophy (a "color blind" vs. diversity emphasis) can affect, positively or negatively, the perceived levels of trust and comfort with management.

It has also been advocated that organizations should include their diversity policy in their job advertisements. This is opposed to having just a singular statement that a given organization is an equal opportunity employer and encouraging candidates from underrepresented demographic groups to apply (e.g., Williams & Bauer, 1994).

Finally, some researchers have contended that recruiting efforts solely aimed at increasing diversity in the applicant pool are often unsuccessful, especially if those attracted to apply are under qualified. One suggestion is to use targeted recruiting based on a combination of cognitive and personality factors, which can increase job performance and increase the number of individuals hired from underrepresented groups (e.g., Newman & Lyons, 2009;[a] Newman, Jones, Fraley, Lyon, & Mullaney, 2013).[b,c]

[a] https://psycnet.apa.org/doiLanding?doi=10.1037%2Fa0013472

[b] https://psycnet.apa.org/record/2013-34551-027

[c] https://www.oxfordhandbooks.com/view/10.1093/oxfordhb/9780199756094.001.0001/oxfordhb-9780199756094-e-022

Defining an "Applicant"

The definition of "applicant" can impact human resource practices (e.g., recruitment, selection) and legal issues (e.g., assessment of OFCCP compliance, disparate treatment, adverse impact). Given the increasing role the Internet plays in personnel practices (e.g., completing applications and other assessments online), both the EEOC and OFCCP developed different criteria for who qualifies as an applicant (see Reynolds, 2006). The primary distinction between the criteria is that the OFCCP requires individuals to be qualified for a given position (e.g., possess minimum qualification) to count as an applicant whereas the EEOC contains no such requirement (see Table 9.6).

Table 9.6 Distinction between Equal Employment Opportunity Commission (EEOC) and the Office of Contract Compliance Programs (OFCCP) definitions of an applicant

EEOC requirements

1	The organization has actively tried to fill a job (e.g., job posting, advertisement)
2	The job seeker has followed the organization's procedure for applying for jobs
3	The job seeker has expressed an interest in a *specific* job

OFCCP Requirements

1	The job seeker has expressed an interest in employment via the Internet or some related electronic process
2	The organization considers the job seeker for employment for a specific job
3	The job seeker's application indicates they have the basic qualifications for the job
4	Throughout the selection process, the job seeker does *not* (a) remove themselves from consideration or (b) indicate they are no longer interested in the job

Adapted from table 7.14 in Gutman, Koppes, & Vodanovich (2011).

The District Court decision in *Parker v. University of Pennsylvania* (2004)[49,50] illustrates the differences between the two sets of requirements. Gordon Parker sent in his resume (as requested) via the University of Pennsylvania's website expressing his interest in a range of positions, but he failed to express an interest in any *specific* job. Parker filed a disparate treatment suit after he was not contacted by the university for a follow-up interview for any of the jobs for which he applied. Although the judge ruled that Parker was successful in forming a *prima facie* case, she decided in favor of the university. That is, the school was found to have articulated a legal reason for the decision regarding Parker. As the judge concluded, the "defendant had met its burden of advancing a legitimate, non-retaliatory reason for not hiring plaintiff by offering proof that it did not consider plaintiff's application because plaintiff did not apply for specific positions."

Related to the discussion here is the fact that, under OFCCP criteria, the University of Pennsylvania would *not* have been required to articulate a legitimate business reason in defense of its actions. That is, Parker would have failed to establish a *prima facie* case: he would not meet the "qualification" component under OFCCP requirements since he failed to apply for a specific job.

Developing legally defensible affirmative action programs and adhering to the OFCCP's requirements can be a daunting task. Many steps are involved, which include (among others) recruitment efforts, accurate recordkeeping, and organizational-level actions. Therefore, the following recommendations are suggested to successfully implement affirmative action programs.

Recommendations/Best Practices

- Use recruitment methods that generate a large number of *qualified* applicants from underrepresented groups (e.g., women, persons of color) and that contain information that *accurately* illustrates a diverse workforce (e.g., pictures, videos, testimonials).
- Develop and communicate in sufficient detail how an affirmative action policy will affect job applicants and the decision-making process.

[49] https://scholar.google.com/scholar_case?case=12139050735079099615&q=Parker+v.+University+of+Pennsylvania+&hl=en&as_sdt=40006
[50] The Parker decision was rendered before the EEOC and OFCCP requirements were issued.

- Explain how *merit* was used in making decisions about individuals hired/ promoted via affirmative action programs.
- Use recruiters from underrepresented groups to enhance the appeal of organizations to such groups.
- Consider getting outside assistance with affirmative action requirements, such as workforce and availability analyses.
- Ensure that the affirmative action program meets the criteria for strict scrutiny (e.g., compelling interest, narrowly tailored).
- Use race and sex status as "plus" factors carefully (minor role) and in combination with additional job-related criteria.
- Do not use affirmative action plans that guarantee a fixed number (or percent) of women or persons of color in personnel decisions (e.g., hiring, promotion).
- Consider using targeted recruiting to enhance diversity (e.g., use both cognitive and personality factors).
- Create an organizational culture and climate that focuses on the value of a diverse workforce.

Summary and Take-Aways

Despite the social and legal challenges confronting affirmative action, the practice, when done properly (following the requirements of strict scrutiny), is still a viable mechanism to increase educational and workplace diversity. In this regard, the legality of race and/or sex as so-called "plus factors" is dependent on *how* it is used. Recall that race was used as such a factor in both *Gratz v. Bollinger* (2003) and *Grutter v. Bollinger* (2003). But the Court ruled against the affirmative action plan in *Gratz* while supporting the one used in *Grutter*.

As noted earlier, the OFCCP possesses ample power to investigate compliance with affirmative action requirements. To date, the agency has been successful in its enforcement role (e.g., via monetary conciliation agreements).

Court decisions pertaining to affirmative action (e.g., so-called "reverse discrimination" cases) have garnered their share of controversy. Despite this, affirmative action has survived legal analysis to date. How long this will last is an open question. For instance, in 2003, Justice O'Conner stated in the *Grutter* decision that "We expect that 25 years from now, the use of racial preferences will no longer be necessary to further the interest approved today." As we write this (Fall 2021), race-, sex-, and gender-based injustice seem both pervasive and apparent in all aspects of society. Thus, we unfortunately don't see this forecast coming to fruition in the immediate future, but do hope it becomes a reality at some point.

Also, the most recent case on affirmative action by the Supreme Court (*Fisher v. University of Texas at Austin,* 2016) ended with a 4–3 decision. The justice who wrote the opinion, Anthony Kennedy, is no longer on the Court. Nor is the late Justice Ginsburg, who voted in favor of UT Austin. Given the current composition of the Court, there is a chance that a majority of judges would have ruled differently in *Fisher* (with three having done so, i.e., Justices Alito, Roberts, and Thomas).

Finally, it will be interesting to see if the OFCCP and EEOC can agree on a definition of an applicant. The current differences can be confusing and lead to distinctions in who qualifies as an applicant, which can have implications for discrimination claims (e.g., adverse impact).

Supplemental Readings on Affirmative Action

Beginner
Affirmative Action History. https://web.uri.edu/affirmativeaction/affirmative-action-history/
American Association for Access, Equity, and Diversity (AAAED). https://www.aaaed.org/aaaed/default.asp
Hsu, H. (October, 2018). The rise and fall of affirmative action. *The New Yorker Magazine*. https://www.newyorker.com/magazine/2018/10/15/the-rise-and-fall-of-affirmative-action
National Public Radio. Debate: Does affirmative action on campus do more harm than good? Randall Kennedy and Theodore Shaw debaters. About 50-minute audio. https://www.npr.org/2014/03/26/293767851/debate-does-affirmative-action-on-campus-do-more-harm-than-good

Intermediate
Fullinwider, R. (2017) Affirmative action. In Edward N. Zalta (Ed.), *The Stanford encyclopedia of philosophy* (Summer 2017 Edition). https://plato.stanford.edu/archives/sum2017/entries/affirmative-action/
Plus, S. (1996). Ten myths about affirmative action. *Journal of Social Issues, 52*(4), 25–32.

Advanced
Barnes, C. B. (2016). Equal employment opportunity: *Strengthening oversight could improve federal contractor nondiscrimination compliance*. (GAO-16-750). Washington, DC: United States Government Accountability Office. https://www.gao.gov/assets/gao-16-750.pdf
Bridges, K. M. (2016). Class-based affirmative action or the lies we tell about the insignificance of race. *Boston University Law Review, 96*, 56–108. https://scholarship.law.bu.edu/cgi/viewcontent.cgi?article=1144&=&context=faculty_scholarship&=

&sei-redir=1&referer=https%253A%252F%252Fscholar.google.com%252Fscholar%25
3Fhl%253Den%2526as_sdt%253D0%25252C10%2526q%253DBridges%25252C%252
BK.%252BM.%252BClass-based%252Baffirmative%252Baction%2526btnG%253D#se
arch=%22Bridges%2C%20K.%20M.%20Class-based%20affirmative%20action%22
Zabel, J. (2019). Affirmative action, reaction, and inaction: Positive political theory analysis of affirmative action in higher education. *Connecticut Public Interest Law Journal,*
19(1), 221–243. https://cpilj.law.uconn.edu/wp-content/uploads/sites/2515/2020/
03/CPILJ-19.1-Affirmative-Action-Reaction-and-Inaction-A-Positive-Political-Theory-
Analysis-of-Affirmative-Action-in-Higher-Education-by-Joseph-Zabel.pdf

Glossary

Compelling interest: Necessary or essential, as opposed to being simply a discretion, preference, or choice (e.g., for affirmative action plans, the goal of achieving diversity in higher education).

Consent decree: Agreement or settlement between two parties that concludes a lawsuit instead of resolving the case through a hearing and/ or trial. Consent decrees and consent judgments are the same.

Make whole: Restoring victims to the position they were in prior to being discriminated against (e.g., by awarding sufficient damages).

Narrowly tailored: A practice or plan that attempts to achieve a compelling interest by employing the least restrictive means possible. For affirmative action programs, this includes evidence that plans are specific, temporary, and demonstrate that race-neutral alternatives are not workable.

Plaintiff: The party who initiates a lawsuit.

Prima facie: Latin phrase for "at first glance." Consists of presenting evidence that is presumed to be true.

Set-asides: Special programs aimed at increasing opportunities for small businesses and business owned by individuals from underrepresented groups to acquire government contracts.

Strict scrutiny: A legal standard applied when fundamental rights are in question. Under strict scrutiny, governmental or organizational practices or policies (e.g., affirmative action programs) are legally defensible only if they (1) advance a compelling interest (i.e., a crucially important concern) and (2) are narrowly tailored, using the least restrictive method to achieve the compelling interest.

Trammel: To unfairly impede, limit, or restrict.

Writ of certiorari: A request for the Supreme Court to review the decisions of lower courts.

Glossary terms adapted from Gutman et al. (2011); https://uslegal.com/, merriamwebster.com/legal; https://www.mtsu.edu/first-amendment/ encyclopedia.

Cases Cited

Adarand v. Pena, 151 U.S. 200 (1995).
City of Richmond v. Croson, 488 U.S. 469 (1989).
Firefighters v. Cleveland, 478 U.S. 501 (1986).
Fisher v. University of Texas at Austin, 133 S. Ct. 2411 (2013).
Fisher v. University of Texas at Austin, 136 S. Ct. 2198 (2016).
Gratz v. Bollinger, 539 U.S. 244 (2003).
Grutter v. Bollinger, 539 U.S. 306 (2003).
Johnson v. Transportation Agency of Santa Clara County, 480 U.S. 616 (1987).
Martin v. Wilks, 490 U.S. 755 (1989).
Parents Involved in Community Schools v. Seattle School District, 55 U.S. 701 (2007).
Petit v. City of Chicago, 352 F. 3d 1111 (7th Cir. 2003).
Regents of University of California v. Bakke, 438 U.S. 265 (1978).
Schuette v. Coalition to Defend Affirmative Action, 572 U.S. 291 (2013).
United States v. Paradise, 480 U.S. 149 (1987).
United Steelworkers. v. Weber, 443 U.S. 193 (1979).
Parker v. University of Pennsylvania (E.D. Penn. 2004).
Wygant v. Jackson Board of Education, 476 U.S. 267 (1986).

References

Avery, D. R., Hernandez, M., & Hebl, M. R. (2004). Who's watching the race? Racial salience in recruitment advertising. *Journal of Applied Social Psychology, 34,* 146–161.

Avery, D. R., & McKay, P. F. (2006). Target practice: An organizational impression management approach to attracting minority and female job applicants. *Personnel Psychology, 59,* 157–187.

Avery, D. R., & McKay, P. F., & Volpone, S. D. (2013). Diversity staffing: Inclusive personnel recruitment and selection practices. In Q. Roberson (Ed.), *The Oxford handbook of diversity and work* (pp. 282–299). New York: Oxford University Press.

Crosby, F. J., Iyer, A., Clayton, S., & Downing, R. A. (2003). Affirmative action: Psychological data and the policy debates. *American Psychologist, 58*(2), 93–115.

Doverspike, D., Taylor, M. A., Shultz, K. S., & McKay, P. F. (2000). Responding to the challenge of a changing workforce: Recruiting nontraditional demographic groups. *Public Personnel Management, 29,* 445–457.

Dunleavy & Gutman (2010). On the Legal Front: OFCCP settlement review: What was the burden on Bank of America? *The Industrial-Organizational Psychologist, 48*(1), 73–80.

Gutman, A. (2004). On the legal front: *Grutter* goes to work: The 7th Circuit Court's ruling in *Petit v. City of Chicago* (2003). *The Industrial-Organizational Psychologist, 41*(4), 71–77.

Gutman, A. (2009). Major EEO issues relating to personnel selection decisions. *Human Resource Management Review, 19,* 232–250.

Gutman, A., & Dunleavy, E. (2007). The Supreme Court ruling in *Parents v. Seattle School District*: Sending *Grutter* and *Gratz* back to school. *The Industrial-Organizational Psychologist, 45*, 41–48.

Gutman, A., Koppes, L. L., & Vodanovich, S. J. (2011). *EEO Law and personnel practices.* New York: Taylor and Francis.

Heilman, M. E., Battle, W. S., Keller, C. E., & Lee, R. A. (1998). Type of affirmative action policy: A determinant of reactions to sex-based preferential selection? *Journal of Applied Psychology, 83*, 190–205.

Heilman, M. E., Block, C. J., & Lucas, J. A. (1992). Presumed incompetent? Stigmatization and affirmative action efforts. *Journal of Applied Psychology, 77*, 536–544.

Heilman, M. E., Block, C. J., & Stathatos, P. (1997). The affirmative action stigma of incompetence: Effects of performance information ambiguity. *Academy of Management Journal, 40*(3), 603–625.

Heilman, M. E., McCullough, W. F., & Gilbert, D. (1996). The other side of affirmative action: Reactions of nonbeneficiaries to sex-based preferential selection. *Journal of Applied Psychology, 81*, 346–357.

Heilman, M. E., Rivero, J. C., & Brett, J. F. (1991). Skirting the competency issue: Effects of sex-based preferential selection on task choices of men and women. *Journal of Applied Psychology, 76*, 99–105.

Heilman, M. E., Simon, M. C., & Repper, D. P. (1987). Intentionally favored, unintentionally harmed? Impact of sex-based preferential selection on self-perceptions and self-evaluations. *Journal of Applied Psychology, 72*, 62–68.

Heriot, G. (2004). Thoughts on *Grutter v. Bollinger* and *Gratz v. Bollinger* as law and as practical politics. *Loyola University Chicago Law Review, 36*, 137–174.

Joshi, Y. (2016). Bakke to the future: Affirmative Action after *Fisher*. *Stanford Law Review, 69*, 17–27.

Ledesma, M. C. (2019). California sunset: O'Conner's post-affirmative action ideal comes of age in California. *The Review of Higher Education, 42*, 227–254.

Leiter, W. M., & Leiter, S. (2011). *Affirmative Action in Antidiscrimination Law and Policy: An Overview and Synthesis.* SUNY Press.

McKay P. F., & Avery D. R. (2005). Warning! Diversity recruitment could backfire. *Journal of Management Inquiry, 14*, 330–336.

McKay, P. F., Avery, D. R., Son, E., Rosado-Solomon, E., & Pustovit, S. (2017). Can cooperation help explain the demographic diversity–business performance relationship? *Academy of Management Proceedings, 2017*(1), 14775.

Newman, D. A., Jones, K. S., Fraley, R. C., Lyon, J. S., & Mullaney, K. M. (2014). Why minority recruiting doesn't often work, and what can be done about it: Applicant qualifications and the 4-group model of targeted recruiting. In K. Y. T. Yu & D. M. Cable (Eds.), *The Oxford handbook of recruitment* (pp. 492–556). New York: Oxford University Press.

Newman, D. A., & Lyon, J. S. (2009). Recruitment efforts to reduce adverse impact: Targeted recruiting for personality, cognitive ability, and diversity. *Journal of Applied Psychology, 94*(2), 298–317. https://doi.org/10.1037/a0013472

Perkins, L. A., Thomas, K. M., & Taylor, G. A. (2000). Advertising and recruitment: Marketing to minorities. *Psychology and Marketing, 17*, 235–255.

Pietri, E. S., Johnson, I. R., & Ozgumus, E. (2018). One size may not fit all: Exploring how the intersection of race and gender and stigma consciousness predict effective identity-safe cues for Black women. *Journal of Experimental Social Psychology, 74*, 291–306.

Purdie-Vaughns, V., Steele, C. M., Davies, P. G., Diltmann, R., & Crosby, J. R. (2008). Social identity contingencies: How diversity cues signal threat or safety for African Americans in mainstream institutions. *Journal of Personality and Social Psychology, 94*, 615–630.

Reynolds, D. (2006). OFCCP guidance on defining a job applicant in the Internet age: The final word? *The Industrial-Organizational Psychologist, 43*, 107–113.

Wille, L, & Derous, E. (2018). When job ads turn you down: How requirements in job ads may stop instead of attract highly qualified women. *Sex Roles, 79*, 464–475.

Williams, M. L., & Bauer, T. N. (1994). The effect of managing diversity policy on organizational attractiveness. *Group and Organization Management, 19*, 295–308.

Wright, D. K., & Garces, L. M. (2018). Understanding the controversy around race-based affirmative action in American higher education. In J. Blanchard (Ed.), *Controversies on campus: Debating the issues confronting American universities in the 21st Century* (pp. 8–17). Santa Barbara, CA: Praeger.

10

Retaliation

Forming a *Prima Facie* Case of Retaliation
Phase 1: Protected Activities
The Opposition Clause
- Hochstadt v. Worcester (1976)
- Rosser v. Laborers' International Union (1980)
- Crawford v. Metro. Government of Nashville (2009)
- Collazo v. Bristol-Myers Squibb Manufacturing Inc. (2010)
The Participation Clause
- Glover v. South Carolina Law Enforcement Division (1999)
- Risley v. Fordham University (2001)
Phase 2: Material Adverse Action
- Mattern v. Eastman Kodak (1997)
- Jensen v. Potter (2006)
- Washington v. Illinois Dept. of Revenue (2005)
- Burlington Northern Santa Fe Railway Company v. White (2006)
- Alvarez v. Royal Atlantic Developers, Inc. (2010)
- Roberts v. Roadway Express, Inc. (1998)
- Planadeball v. Wyndham Vacation Resorts, Inc. (2015)
- Millea v. Metro-North Railroad Co. (2011)
- Kessler v. Westchester City Department of Social Services (2006)
- Loya v. Sibelius (2012)
- O'Neal v. City of Chicago (2009)
- Walker v. Johnson (2015)
Phase 3: Establishing a Causal Connection
Time Elapsed
- Clark County School District v. Breeden (2001)
- Gorman-Bakos v. Cornell Coop of Schenectady County (2001)
- Oest v. Illinois Department of Corrections (2001)

- Evans v. City of Houston (2001)
- Cifra v. General Electric Co. (2001)
- Holava-Brown v. General Electric Co. (1999)
- Hudson v. Norris (2000)
Prior Knowledge
- Clark County School District v. Breeden (2001)
- Pomales v. Celulares Telefonico (2006)
- Robinson v. Jackson State University (2017)
Nassar and the Aftermath
- University of Texas Southwest Medical Center v. Nassar (2013)
- Woodson v. Scott Paper (1997)

Individuals Covered Under Retaliation
Former Employees
- Robinson v. Shell Oil (1997)
- Hillig v. Rumsfeld (2004)
- Third-Party Retaliation
- EEOC v. Bojangles Restaurant, Inc. (2003)
- Fogelman v. Mercy Hospital (2002)
- Holt v. JTM Industries (1996)
- Smith v. Riceland Foods, Inc. (1998)
- Singh v. Green Thumb Landscaping (2005)
- Thompson v. North American Stainless (2011)
- Antonelli v. Sapa Extrusions, Inc. (2015)
- Harrington v. Career Training Institute Orlando, Inc. (2011)
- Ali v. District of Columbia Government (2011)
- Sterner v. County of Banks (2014)

Filing a Complaint
- Kasten v. Saint-Gobain Performance Plastics (2011)
- Greathouse v. JHS Security Inc. (2015)

Recommendations/Best Practices

Summary and Take-Aways

Employment Discrimination. Stephen J. Vodanovich and Deborah E. Rupp, Oxford University Press. © Oxford University Press 2022. DOI: 10.1093/oso/9780190085421.003.0011

> Retaliation is related to nature and instinct, not to law.
> Law, by definition, cannot obey the same rules as nature.
>
> **Albert Camus**

Despite this sentiment by Camus, broad protections exist under the law against retaliation by organizations, most notably within Title VII. Section 704 A of Title VII provides legal protection against workplace retaliation by stating that it is unlawful for an employer to

> discriminate against any of his [*sic*] *employees* or *applicants* for employment . . . because he has *opposed* any practice made an unlawful employment practice by this subchapter . . ., or because he has made a charge, testified, assisted, or *participated* in any manner in an investigation, proceeding, or hearing.

Separate protections against retaliation exist within other laws such as the Age Discrimination in Employment Act (ADEA),[1] Americans with Disabilities Act (ADA),[2] Employment Retirement Income Security Act,[3] Fair Labor Standards Act,[4] National Labor Relations Act,[5] and Occupational Health and Safety Act,[6] which generally contain coverage consistent with Title VII (see Essary & Friedman, 1998).[7]

Forming a *Prima Facie* Case of Retaliation

Table 10.1 presents the phases required in establishing a *prima facie* case of retaliation. In the sections that follow, we cover each of these phases in depth along with their related concepts.

---

[1] https://www.eeoc.gov/statutes/age-discrimination-employment-act-1967
[2] https://www.eeoc.gov/statutes/titles-i-and-v-americans-disabilities-act-1990-ada
[3] https://www.dol.gov/general/topic/retirement/erisa
[4] https://www.dol.gov/agencies/whd/flsa#:~:text=The%20Fair%20Labor%20Standards%20Act%20(FLSA)%20establishes%20minimum%20wage%2C,%2C%20State%2C%20and%20local%20governme nts.&text=There%20is%20no%20limit%20on,may%20work%20in%20any%20workweek.
[5] https://www.nlrb.gov/guidance/key-reference-materials/national-labor-relations-act
[6] https://www.osha.gov/laws-regs
[7] https://scholarship.law.missouri.edu/cgi/viewcontent.cgi?article=3350&context=mlr

Table 10.1 Forming a prima facie case of retaliation

Phase 1	Plaintiff engages in protected activity by (1) complaining about an employer practice [*Opposition*] or (2) filing a formal claim of discrimination [*Participation*]. • Plaintiffs can be applicants, employees or former employees. • Participating in an investigation counts as "opposition." • Claims can be filed orally or in writing.
Phase 2	Plaintiff suffers a *materially adverse action* (one that deters a reasonable person from engaging in a protected activity).
Phase 3	Plaintiff demonstrates that *a causal connection* exists between engaging in a protected activity (phase 1) and the material adverse action (phase 2). To establish a causal connection, plaintiffs need to demonstrate: • a close temporal connection between engaging in a protected activity (Prong 1) and the alleged retaliation (Prong 2); • the company knew, or should have known, that an employee engaged in a protected activity; and • "*but for*" causation for the alleged retaliation.

Phase 1: Protected Activities

The preceding quote from Title VII highlights what have become known as the "opposition" and "participation" clauses, respectively. These concepts are critical to the first phase of establishing a *prima facie* case of discrimination.

The Opposition Clause

Not every organizational practice can be legitimately opposed. As interpreted by the Equal Employment Opportunity Commission (EEOC), opposition by a plaintiff must be based on an equal employment opportunity (EEO) practice *perceived* to be *illegal* (e.g., Title VII violation). There is no requirement that the opposed practice must be found to be unlawful in the end. Such a precondition would likely have the effect of thwarting employees in their efforts to oppose a questionable organizational practice. So, protected opposition must consist of a *good faith* belief by plaintiffs that an organization's actions were perceived to be illegal employment discrimination. As the EEOC has stated, "The manner of opposition must be reasonable, and the opposition must be based on a reasonable good faith belief that the conduct opposed is, or could become, unlawful."

Opposition by plaintiffs that consists of illegal or highly disruptive behaviors (e.g., hostile, antagonistic acts) may not be covered under Title VII. Such unreasonable opposition may provide organizations with a legitimate business reason for their actions. If so, the defense has an obligation to show that its decision was based on nondiscriminatory factors (see

Hochstadt v. Worcester Foundation for Experimental Biology, Inc., 1976[8]; *Rosser v. Laborers' International Union of North America*, 1980[9]).

Across the years, the Supreme Court has taken a rather firm stance against organizations with respect to workplace retaliation. Its decisions have indicated an intent to provide broad protections to those affected by retaliatory behavior (see Brake, 2014; Long, 2011). One example is the case of *Crawford v. Metro. Government of Nashville and Davidson County* (2009),[10,11] where the Supreme Court clarified what counts as opposition (see Kline, 2009; Nevin, 2010). As part of an investigation conducted by the human resources department, the plaintiff (Vicky Crawford) answered questions about sexual harassment and acknowledged incidents of such actions by a supervisor. She was fired soon after the investigation, and she filed a lawsuit alleging retaliation. The lower courts ruled in favor of the organization and concluded that Crawford had not opposed a practice but merely answered questions. However, the Supreme Court decided in favor of Crawford, stating that testimony from witnesses qualifies as opposition. As the Court noted,

> if an employee reporting discrimination in answer to an employer's questions could be penalized with no remedy, prudent employees would have a good reason to keep quiet about Title VII offenses.

Since the *Crawford* decision, other courts have supported the rather wide-ranging position on what constitutes opposition. For example, in *Collazo v. Bristol-Myers Squibb Manufacturing Inc.* (2010),[12] the court concluded that Luis Collazo opposed an employment practice when he helped one of his female subordinates file a sexual harassment complaint. As the court noted, the plaintiff's actions in helping the employee "purposefully communicated his opposition" to the sexual harassment complaint. Examples of opposition from the EEOC[13] include, but are not limited to

- complaining or threatening to complain about alleged discrimination against oneself or others,

---

[8] https://scholar.google.com/scholar_case?case=750170895929306990&q=Hochstadt+v.+Worcester,+1976&hl=en&as_sdt=40006&as_vis=1
[9] https://scholar.google.com/scholar_case?case=9304476411888538699&q=Rosser+v.+Laborers%27+International+Union,+1980&hl=en&as_sdt=40006&as_vis=1
[10] https://www.law.cornell.edu/supct/cert/06-1595
[11] https://www.oyez.org/cases/2008/06-1595
[12] https://caselaw.findlaw.com/us-1st-circuit/1533983.html
[13] https://www.eeoc.gov/laws/guidance/questions-and-answers-enforcement-guidance-retaliation-and-related-issues

- providing information in an employer's internal investigation of an EEO matter,
- advising an employer on EEO compliance,
- complaining to management about EEO-related compensation disparities, or
- talking to coworkers to gather information or evidence in support of a potential employment discrimination claim.

Insights from Social Science: The Impact of Workplace Retaliation

Research has indicated that experiencing mistreatment at work, including retaliation, can negatively affect the health and well-being of employees. A study by Cortina and Magley (2003) analyzed data from more than 1,100 employees. The authors classified workplace mistreatment as belonging to one of two categories: work retaliation victimization (WRV; e.g., "I was denied a promotion I deserved," "I was given less favorable job duties") and social retaliation victimization (SRV; e.g., "I was shunned or excluded by others at work," "I was gossiped about in an unkind way").

About 71% of the respondents indicated they had experienced interpersonal mistreatment across the past five years, with 27% of those having expressed "voice" about being mistreated. Three types of voice expression were considered (1) social support-seeking, (2) whistle-blowing, and (3) confrontation. Furthermore, 30% indicated they were victims of SRV alone, while 36% described being recipients of both SRV and WRV (WRV was never reported as occurring by itself).

The job status of both victims and so-called wrongdoers played an important role in the experience of retaliatory behavior. That is, employees in low-status positions received more SRVs and mistreatment, especially when such employees decided to confront their wrongdoers. The level of SRVs was also higher when victimized employees told others about their mistreatment by high-status/power wrongdoers if they confronted high-power offenders.

Victims who were the recipients of frequent SRVs and WRVs (and those experiencing only SRVs) reported low professional well-being (less job satisfaction, higher job stress, greater withdrawal behaviors). In addition, employees who received recurring mistreatment reported lower physical and psychological health, such as sadness, anxiety, and greater physical symptoms. A thought-provoking finding was that employees who remained silent about their mistreatment suffered the greatest physical and psychological problems. Ironically, employees who voice concerns, as well as those who remain silent, can both suffer mistreatment by others—quite a dilemma.

Given these findings, the authors suggest that greater attention needs to be given to organizational-level strategies to reduce workplace retaliation. Some possible interventions include the establishment (and modeling) of well-defined expectations for appropriate interpersonal behavior, as well as training regarding interpersonal skills. In addition, they note the importance of imposing penalties on retaliatory behavior. As the authors mention, "Rather than framing interpersonal mistreatment in organizations as a private problem for individuals to resolve, we should hold organizations responsible for managing misbehavior within."

The Participation Clause

As the EEOC has stated in its previously referenced guidelines (see note 13), "An employer must not retaliate against an individual for 'participating' in an EEO process. This means that an employer cannot punish an applicant or employee for filing an EEO complaint, serving as a witness, or participating in any other way in an EEO matter, even if the underlying discrimination allegation is unsuccessful or untimely." However, in contrast to opposition, the EEOC has noted that *participation* does *not* require a reasonable, good faith belief that an alleged claim is illegal. As Long (2011) stated, "Title VII's participation clause, unlike the opposition clause, does not impose any sort of good faith or reasonableness standard upon an employee seeking its protection. Thus, the protection afforded by the participation clause is virtually absolute" (p. 752). This position is consistent with several court decisions (e.g., *Glover v. South Carolina Law Enforcement Division*, 1999[14]; *Risley v. Fordham University*, 2001[15]). From the *Risley* case on the legal requirement for participation under Title VII,

Courts recognizing the difference between the opposition and participation clauses have consistently held that an employee who filed a charge or otherwise participated in

Title VII proceedings is protected from retaliation even if the charge was not meritorious or reasonable.

---

[14] https://caselaw.findlaw.com/us-4th-circuit/1441869.html
[15] https://casetext.com/case/risley-v-fordham-university

Phase 2: Material Adverse Action

Not every retaliatory behavior, if proven to have occurred, qualifies as illegal workplace retaliation. That is, alleged retaliatory actions must have a *material adverse impact* on individuals to be against the law. Trivial actions by companies would not meet this standard. Courts have disagreed on what standard should be used in determining a material adverse action. Some courts have required organizational actions to result in an ultimate, tangible *negative employment decision*, such as being terminated or demoted, to count as a material adverse action (e.g., *Mattern v. Eastman Kodak,* 1997).[16] This has been referred to as the *Ultimate Employment* standard. For instance, in *Mattern*, the plaintiff, Jean Mattern, lost because the alleged retaliatory behavior (being transferred to another team after complaining about sexual harassment by two senior coworkers) was not considered to be serious enough in that it did not result in an "ultimate employment decision."

Other courts determined that the action must *interfere* with terms/conditions/privileges of employment, but not result in a specific adverse employment action to qualify as a material adverse action. This so-called *Adverse Employment* standard was illustrated in *Jensen v. Potter* (2006),[17] where the plaintiff was harassed by coworkers for almost two years. The Court of Appeals for the 3rd Circuit believed that the harassment against Anna Jensen rose to the level of having a negative effect on the terms and conditions of her employment, so Jensen won.

Finally, some courts have opined that a material adverse impact only needs to *deter* someone from performing a protected activity—a relatively easier standard for plaintiffs to meet. This point was exemplified in *Washington v. Illinois Dept. of Revenue* (2005).[18] Chrissie Washington had been given a flextime schedule to care for her special-needs child. After filing a race discrimination suit, she was removed from flextime and placed on a regular shift, which she refused to work. Afterward, her position was eliminated, and Washington was transferred to work with a new boss on a 9–5 schedule. To take care of her child, Washington had to use her vacation and sick leave. She filed a retaliation suit and won. From the Court's ruling:

---

[16] https://scholar.google.com/scholar_case?case=17436726420327842333&q=Mattern+v.+Eastman+Kodak,+1997&hl=en&as_sdt=40006&as_vis=1
[17] https://scholar.google.com/scholar_case?case=9534460769915884300&hl=en&as_sdt=6&as_vis=1&oi=scholarr
[18] https://scholar.google.fr/scholar_case?case=15005791135078037904&hl=en&as_sdt=6&as_vis=1&oi=scholarr&sa=X&ved=0ahUKEwi45Lf0scvTAhVHNiYKHb44Aj4QgAMIJygAMAA

By and large a reassignment that does not affect pay or promotion opportuni-ties... is not actionable. But "by and large" differs from "never." . . . "Context matters. . . . A schedule change in an employee's work schedule may make little difference to many workers, but may matter enormously to a young mother with school-age children.

These conflicts regarding the proper criteria for a material adverse action were resolved by the Supreme Court in *Burlington Northern Santa Fe Railway Company v. White* (2006).[19],[20] Sheila White was given the job of forklift op-erator at BNSF by Marvin Brown. Some of her coworkers did not approve of this decision. They were upset that White (a woman) was hired instead of a man with greater seniority. Later, White alleged that she experienced sexual harassment by her immediate supervisor (Bill Joiner). After an investiga-tion, BNSF suspended Joiner and mandated that he attend sexual harassment training. However, Brown removed White from the forklift job, and she was demoted to her previous laborer position. After her demotion, White filed a retaliation suit. Later that year, after a disagreement with her immediate su-pervisor, Brown suspended White for more than a month without pay for al-leged insubordination.[21] Consequently, White filed a retaliation suit based on her suspension.

The lower courts did *not* believe that White suffered a material adverse action. They concluded that there was no interference with the terms and conditions of her employment. However, the Supreme Court concluded that a material adverse action exists if the retaliatory behavior has the effect of *preventing* or *deterring* a reasonable person from *engaging* in a protected activity (see Dunleavy, 2007; Savage, 2004;[22] Valenti & Burke, 2010). This criterion has been referred to as the *EEOC Deterrence Standard*. As stated by the EEOC in its enforcement guidelines (see note 13): "Retaliation ex-pansively reaches any action that is 'materially adverse,' meaning any ac-tion that might well deter a reasonable person from engaging in protected activity". Not surprisingly, retaliation claims increased after the *BNSF v. White* decision, and this trend has generally continued over recent years (see Tables 10.2 and 10.3).

Examples of material adverse actions include, but are not limited to, the refusal to promote or hire, loss of job benefits, demotion, suspension, and

---

[19] https://www.law.cornell.edu/supct/html/05-259.ZO.html
[20] https://www.oyez.org/cases/2005/05-259
[21] An internal investigation by BNSF concluded that White was not guilty of insubordination.
[22] https://lawdigitalcommons.bc.edu/bclr/vol46/iss1/5/

Table 10.2 Equal Employment Opportunity Commission (EEOC) retaliation claims after *BNSF v. White* 2006–2010 (all statues)

Year	2006	2007	2008	2009	2010
Number of Charges	22,555	26,663	32,690	33,613	36,258

Retrieved from https://www.eeoc.gov/eeoc/statistics/enforcement/charges.cfm.

termination (e.g., *Alvarez v. Royal Atlantic Developers, Inc.*, 2010[23]; *Roberts v. Roadway Express, Inc.*, 1998[24]). Other adverse actions include work-related threats (*Planadeball v. Wyndham Vacation Resorts, Inc.*, 2015[25]), warnings, reprimands (*Millea v. Metro-North Railroad Co.*, 2011[26]), undesirable transfers (*Kessler v. Westchester City Department of Social Services*, 2006[27]; *Loya v. Sibelius*, 2012[28]; *O'Neal v. City of Chicago*, 2009[29]), and negative/reduced performance evaluations (*Walker v. Johnson*, 2015[30]).

Phase 3: Establishing a Causal Connection

After a material adverse action has been established, plaintiffs face another hurdle to form a *prima facie* case. That is, plaintiffs must prove a

Table 10.3 Retaliation charges filed with the Equal Employment Opportunity Commission (EEOC) 2015–2020 (all statues)

Year	2015	2016	2017	2018	2019	2020
Number of Charges	39,757	42,018	41,097	39,469	39,110	37,632

Retrieved from https://www.eeoc.gov/eeoc/statistics/enforcement/charges.cfm.

[23] https://scholar.google.com/scholar_case?case=18068689615178326552&q=Alvarez+v.+Royal+Atlantic+Developers,+Inc.,&hl=en&as_sdt=40006
[24] https://scholar.google.com/scholar_case?case=11960307772189036158&q=Roberts+v.+Roadway+Express,+Inc.,+1998&hl=en&as_sdt=40006&as_vis=1
[25] https://scholar.google.com/scholar_case?case=10315003351709533260&q=Planadeball+v.+Wyndham+Vacation+Resorts,+Inc.,+2015&hl=en&as_sdt=40006&as_vis=1
[26] https://scholar.google.com/scholar_case?case=9769752998359921823&q=Millea+v.+Metro-North+Railroad+Co.,+2011&hl=en&as_sdt=40006&as_vis=1
[27] https://scholar.google.com/scholar_case?case=17451376192210962879&q=Kessler+v.+Westchester+City+Department+of+Social+Services,+2006&hl=en&as_sdt=40006&as_vis=1
[28] https://scholar.google.com/scholar_case?case=15114898234322248235&q=Loya+v.+Sebelius,+2012&hl=en&as_sdt=40006&as_vis=1
[29] https://scholar.google.com/scholar_case?case=10482454420963111944&q=O%27Neal+v.+City+of+Chicago,+2009&hl=en&as_sdt=40006&as_vis=1
[30] https://scholar.google.com/scholar_case?case=13412285100804404444&q=Walker+v.+Johnson,+2015&hl=en&as_sdt=40006&as_vis=1

causal connection exists between engaging in a protected activity and the organization's retaliatory behavior.

Time Elapsed

One important factor influencing the assessment of a causal link is the time that has elapsed between performing a protected activity and the alleged retaliatory behavior. In general, the closer in time the two events have occurred, the easier it is for plaintiffs to meet their burden. However, there is no established amount of time that proves a causal link. The Supreme Court stated that the covered behavior must occur "very close" in time to the claimed retaliatory behavior (*Clark County School District v. Breeden*, 2001).[31] Consistent with the Court's decision in Breeden, the 2nd Circuit noted that they have *not* used "a bright line to define the outer limits beyond which a temporal relationship is too attenuated to establish a causal relationship between the exercise of a federal constitutional right and an allegedly retaliatory action" (*Gorman-Bakos v. Cornell Coop of Schenectady County*, 2001).[32] Similar logic was employed in *Oest v. Illinois Department of Corrections* (2001),[33] where the court stated that, "A mechanistically applied time frame would ill serve our obligation to be faithful to the legislative purpose of Title VII."

However, given this ambiguity, courts have differed about how *close* in time the protected activity and retaliatory behavior must be to establish a causal connection (see O'Brien, 2002).[34] For instance, in *Richmond v. Oneok* (1997) the 10th Circuit ruled that the passage of two months was too long.[35] Earlier, the 7th Circuit concluded that a timeframe of four months was too long to establish a connection between engaging in a protected behavior and the alleged retaliatory action by the company (*Hughes v. Derwinski*, 1992).[36] On the other hand, in *Evans v. City of Houston* (2001),[37] the passage of five days between engaging in a protected activity (being part of a coworker's grievance proceeding) and an adverse employment action (being recommended for a demotion) was judged to be close enough to form a retaliation claim.

[31] https://scholar.google.com/scholar_case?case=6107069847960066476&q=Clark+County+School+District+v.+Breeden+(2001)&hl=en&as_sdt=40006&as_vis=1

[32] https://caselaw.findlaw.com/us-2nd-circuit/1306593.html

[33] https://scholar.google.com/scholar_case?case=17913246114243755095&hl=en&as_sdt=6&as_vis=1&oi=scholarr

[34] https://core.ac.uk/download/pdf/71454814.pdf

[35] https://scholar.google.com/scholar_case?case=15837751263585243125&q=Richmond+v.+Oneok+1997&hl=en&as_sdt=40006

[36] https://scholar.google.com/scholar_case?case=6588586558836854937&q=hughes+v.+derwinski+1992&hl=en&as_sdt=40006

[37] https://caselaw.findlaw.com/us-5th-circuit/1146988.html

In *Cifra v. General Electric Co.* (2001),[38] the court stated that Kathleen Cifra, who was fired 20 days after complaining about sexual harassment by her supervisor, had adequately established causation.

It is important to note that *prima facie* efforts can still be successful when the temporal proximity is longer, especially if other factors exist to indicate retaliation on the part of organizations. As an example, in *Hudson v. Norris* (2000),[39] the 8th Circuit concluded that several adverse actions taken by the company against Paul Hudson (e.g., refusal to promote, two internal investigations, denial of vacation) that occurred four months after the plaintiff offered evidence in a suit filed by a coworker adequately established a causal link. As the court stated,

> While we agree that the mere coincidence of close timing is generally not enough to create an inference of causation, there is more than a simple concurrence of two events here: The large number of adverse actions that occurred hard on the heels of the protected activity in this case, particularly when juxtaposed with Mr. Hudson's previously strong employment record, is significant evidence that what happened here was more than just coincidence.

In addition, Hudson presented evidence that the reasons provided by the company for their actions against him were baseless.

Prior Knowledge

Finally, for a plaintiff's claim to succeed, organizations must have *prior knowledge* that an employee opposed or engaged in a protected behavior. In other words, organizations must have known or should have known that a protected activity occurred (e.g., plaintiff filing a lawsuit) for retaliation to materialize. This lack of prior knowledge was an issue in *Clark County School District v. Breeden* (2001).[40] Shirley Breeden was reassigned to a different school with less supervisory responsibility (an alleged retaliatory behavior) after filing a sexual harassment complaint with the EEOC. But the evidence indicated that the school district did not learn of Breeden's complaint until a day *after* they made their reassignment decision. So, a causal connection could not be established in this case and Breeden lost.

---

[38] https://caselaw.findlaw.com/us-2nd-circuit/1306543.html
[39] https://caselaw.findlaw.com/us-8th-circuit/1401435.html
[40] https://scholar.google.com/scholar_case?case=6107069847960066476&q=Clark+County+School+District+v.+Breeden+(2001)&hl=en&as_sdt=40006&as_vis=1

The lack of knowledge defense was also supported in *Pomales v. Celulares Telefonico* (2006).[41] Here, the plaintiff (Magdalena Pomales) was fired after complaining to management about the sexually oriented behavior of her supervisor. The court concluded that the individual who made the termination decision had no knowledge of the complaint made by the plaintiff, so the suit was unsuccessful.

A different scenario played out in *Robinson v. Jackson State University* (2017).[42] In an interview with the EEOC, Frederick Robinson provided corroborating information of sexual harassment by athletic director, Vivian Fuller. Robinson was fired without any explanation approximately one month after his EEOC interview and subsequently filed a retaliation suit against the university and Dr. Fuller. Dr. Fuller denied any knowledge of Robinson's unfavorable EEOC interview. In addition, nonretaliatory reasons were given for Robinson's firing—a reorganization effort of the athletic department and Robinson's lack of availability while at work. So, two main issues were involved here: prior knowledge of the decision-maker and whether the reasons given for Robinson's firing were legitimate or a pretext for retaliation.

In the end, the 5th Circuit ruled in favor of the Robinson. Regarding the prior knowledge requirement, the court relied on (1) the first-hand knowledge of Robinson's interview by Fuller's attorneys (whom she met with regularly), (2) threats made by the president of the university that she would terminate anyone who testified against Dr. Fuller, and (3) the fact that Dr. Fuller avoided contact with Robinson after his interview.

Additional evidence was presented that cast doubt on the reasons given for Robinson's firing. These included the short time frame between Robinson's interview and his firing, inconsistent reasons given for his termination, the failure to follow university procedures for making termination decisions, and the fact that the reorganization plan (signed by Fuller) recorded Robinson as Director of Sports Medicine.

Nassar and the Aftermath

The process for establishing a causal connection in retaliation cases was altered in the case of *University of Texas Southwest Medical Center v. Nassar* (2013).[43,44] Giving the possible implications of this decision, it will be

---

[41] https://scholar.google.com/scholar_case?case=16177378394777538353&hl=en&as_sdt=6&as_vis=1&oi=scholarr
[42] https://caselaw.findlaw.com/us-5th-circuit/1881840.html
[43] https://www.law.cornell.edu/supct/pdf/12-484.pdf
[44] https://www.oyez.org/cases/2012/12-484

described in some detail (for legal reviews of *Nassar*, see Grossman & Brake, 2013; Krimski, 2014; Zimmer, 2014).

Nassar, a physician, was employed as a faculty member at a university medical center and physician at Parkland Memorial Hospital. The university and the hospital had an agreement to give faculty preference for open positions at the hospital. Nassar, who was Egyptian-born and Muslim, asserted that one of his supervisors at the university harassed him because of his race and religious beliefs. Given this, Nassar decided to quit his faculty position. He received a verbal agreement that he could remain at the hospital despite not being employed by the university. However, after he sent a letter to his supervisor's boss (and others) about the alleged harassment at the university, Nassar's job at the hospital was cancelled. He filed a *constructive discharge*[45] and retaliation suit.

The Supreme Court's decision centered around charges of retaliation by the medical center. In a divided decision (5–4) the Supreme Court concluded that to prove a causal connection, plaintiffs must demonstrate that the alleged retaliatory behavior by an organization was the *but for* reason for its employment decision. In other words, proof is needed that the adverse action would not have occurred "but for" retaliation, which is a high bar for plaintiffs to reach.

One reason for the Court's ruling is that retaliation is *not* contained in the portion of the Civil Rights Act of 1991 (CRA-91) regarding mixed-motive cases,[46] which stipulates that it is illegal if race, color, religion, sex, or national origin was a *motivating factor* for any employment practice. In addition, the majority of justices noted that the anti-retaliation language is included within a different section of Title VII (Section 704) rather than Section 703, which covers race, color, religion, sex, or national origin—referred to as "status group" protections. From Section 704(a) of the Civil Rights Act:

> It shall be an unlawful employment practice for an employer to discriminate against any of his [*sic*] employees or applicants for employment, for an employment agency to discriminate against any individual, or for a labor organization to discriminate against any member thereof or applicant for membership, because he has opposed any practice made an unlawful employment practice by this title,

---

[45] Constructive discharge occurs when a situation is so bad that a reasonable individual is compelled to quit.

[46] Mixed-motive scenarios are discussed in more detail in Chapter 2, "Basic Discrimination Scenarios," Chapter 5 on sex discrimination, and Chapter 7 on age discrimination.

or because he has made a charge, testified, assisted, or participated in any manner in an investigation, proceeding, or hearing under this title.

The Court concluded that since the retaliation provision was located in a separate section of the CRA, individuals alleging retaliation were not meant to receive the same treatment as the original five protected groups. Consequently, retaliation claims currently need to show "but for" causation.

The Supreme Court's decision was not a complete surprise. Several previous lower court decisions reflected the logic of the majority in *Nassar* (e.g., *Woodson v. Scott Paper Co.*, 1997). For instance, these decisions declared that the mixed-motive section of CRA-91 (e.g., demonstrating that an illegal factor motivated an employment decision) was *not* applicable to retaliation claims. Lower courts also found that the placement of the retaliation provision within a *different* section of Title VII was intentional; thus, retaliation was meant to receive different protection than race, color, religion, sex, or national origin.

At the time of the *Nassar* decision, the EEOC had adopted a contrary view which stated that retaliation claims ought to be treated the same as "status" factors (e.g., race, sex). Also, the dissent in *Nassar* countered that the goal of the CRA-91 was to broaden or strengthen (not reduce) protections for workplace discrimination. Furthermore, in her dissent, Justice Ginsburg noted that the Court artificially separated retaliation from status-based allegations. In her view, the two were fundamentally connected. Ginsberg also mentioned that the Court appeared motivated to reduce the ever-growing number of retaliation claims. She ended with a call for Congress to amend the Civil Rights Act. Time will tell if Congress adopts her position.

As a result of the *Nassar* case, the EEOC's guidance states that "For retaliation claims against private sector employers and state or local government employers, the Supreme Court has ruled that the causation standard requires that 'but for' a retaliatory motive, the employer would not have taken the adverse action." It is important to note that a different standard exists for showing a causal connection in retaliation cases filed against *federal* employers. Here, plaintiffs only need to demonstrate that the alleged retaliatory behavior was a motivating factor—"but for" causation is not required. The agency's rationale is that for federal sector retaliation suits under Title VII (and the ADA) "due to different statutory wording, . . . the 'motivating factor' causation standard applies. The 'motivating factor' standard can be met even if the employer would have taken the same action absent a retaliatory motive."

Individuals Covered Under Retaliation

Former Employees

Overall, court decisions have taken an expansive view regarding *who* is covered by Title VII's retaliation provisions. A key example of this is *Robinson v. Shell Oil* (1997).[47,48] Charles Robinson was terminated by Shell Oil, and he subsequently filed a race discrimination charge against the organization. While his discrimination charge was ongoing, Robinson applied for another job. The company to which he applied asked for a letter of recommendation from Shell Oil. After learning that the letter was negative, Robinson sued for retaliation. The defense by the company argued that retaliation does not apply to *former* employees, only to applicants and employees. Strictly speaking, the retaliation section within Title VII only mentions applicants and employees, not former workers. Consequently, lower court rulings determined that former employees were *not* covered by Title VII's retaliation provisions. But the Supreme Court reversed the decision and concluded that former employees are protected in addition to current workers and applicants.

In *Hillig v. Rumsfeld* (2004),[49] Terrie Hillig filed two race discrimination suits during a five-year timeframe. As a result, a settlement was reached that involved raising Hillig's performance appraisals and removing deleterious content from her personnel file. The plaintiff eventually applied for a new job and was informed by her interviewer that she would be "a perfect fit." However, after she was not offered the position, Hillig learned that a supervisor had indicated to the prospective employer (Department of Justice) the she was a very poor worker. A retaliation suit was filed, and the court ruled in favor of Hillig even though she did not have proof that she would have been hired without the negative reference (see also Baker, 2005).[50] The following statement by the EEOC captures the essence of *who* is covered in retaliation cases:

> Anti-retaliation protections extend to many individuals, including those who make formal or informal allegations of EEO violations (whether or not successful), those who serve as witnesses or participate in investigations, those who exercise rights such as requesting religious or disability accommodation, and even those who are retaliated against after their employment relationship ends.

[47] https://www.law.cornell.edu/supct/html/95-1376.ZO.html
[48] https://www.oyez.org/cases/1996/95-1376
[49] https://scholar.google.com/scholar_case?case=746751790223357652&q=Hillig+v.+Rumsfeld+(2004),+&hl=en&as_sdt=40006&as_vis=1
[50] https://core.ac.uk/download/pdf/62548648.pdf

Finally, individuals are protected from retaliation if their employer *believes* they have been involved in a protected activity even if they have not done so.

Third-Party Retaliation

Let's say that a husband and wife both work for the same organization. The wife files a discrimination charge against the company, and her husband is fired soon after the suit was initiated. In this situation, can the husband sue for retaliation? Recall that retaliation provisions protect individuals who have opposed or participated in a protected activity themselves. In this scenario, the husband did not participate in a protected activity—his wife did. Such claims are referred to as *third-party retaliation* cases.

Traditionally, the courts did not allow third-party retaliation claims (e.g., *EEOC v. Bojangles Restaurant, Inc.*, 2003[51]; *Fogelman v. Mercy Hospital, Inc.*, 2002[52]; *Holt v. JTM Industries*, 1996[53]; *Smith v. Riceland Foods, Inc.*, 1998[54]). Generally, the courts concluded that an individual who files a retaliation claim must be the *same* person who engaged in a protected activity. Third parties were viewed as not being protected under Title VII (also see Hegerich, 2010; Sharone, 2010). As an example, in *Holt v. JTM Industries* (1996),[55] after a wife filed an ADEA suit, her husband (employed by the same company) was put on leave and then transferred to another location. He sued for retaliation and lost on the basis of not having engaged in the protected activity. That being said, some lower courts (e.g., *Singh v. Green Thumb Landscaping, Inc.*, 2005)[56], as well as the EEOC, have accepted the viability of third-party retaliation claims.

The Supreme Court's unanimous decision (8–0) in *Thompson v. North American Stainless* (2011)[57,58] formalized the legality of third-party retaliation suits. Here, Eric Thompson and his fiancée (then wife) Miriam Regalado worked for the same organization. Regalado filed a sex discrimination suit against the organization. Not long after she filed the suit, Thompson was fired, and then he sued for retaliation. Lower courts in this case decided that

[51] https://law.justia.com/cases/federal/district-courts/FSupp2/284/320/2562029/
[52] https://caselaw.findlaw.com/us-3rd-circuit/1441672.html
[53] https://scholar.google.com/scholar_case?case=5846710717716286410&q=Holt+v.+JTM+Industries&hl=en&as_sdt=40006&as_vis=1
[54] https://caselaw.findlaw.com/us-8th-circuit/1397072.html
[55] https://scholar.google.com/scholar_case?case=5846710717716286410&hl=en&as_sdt=6&as_vis=1&oi=scholarr
[56] https://scholar.google.com/scholar_case?case=2732311136966853193&q=Singh+v.+Green+Thumb+Landscaping,+2005&hl=en&as_sdt=40006&as_vis=1
[57] https://www.law.cornell.edu/supct/pdf/09-291P.ZO
[58] https://www.oyez.org/cases/2010/09-291

third-party claims were not protected. But the Supreme Court supported the retaliation claim by Thompson. In doing so, they supported a rather expansive view of retaliation claims under Title VII and concluded that any action by an organization that may reasonably deter an employee from performing a protected activity (such as firing someone's fiancé/spouse) is actionable under Title VII's retaliation section. As the Court stated: "We think it obvious that a reasonable worker might be dissuaded from engaging in protected activity if she knew that her fiancé would be fired." The Court further commented that "we conclude that Thompson falls within the zone of interests protected by Title VII. Thompson was an employee of NAS, and the purpose of Title VII is to protect employees from their employers' unlawful actions. Moreover, accepting the facts as alleged, Thompson is not an accidental victim of the retaliation—collateral damage, so to speak, of the employer's unlawful act."

It is important to note that the Supreme Court in *Thompson* declined to specify how close the relationships must be to be covered (e.g., Cavico & Mujaba, 2011; Lucas, 2016). As the Court noted in *Thompson*,

> We must also decline to identify a fixed class of relationships for which third-party reprisals are unlawful. . . . Given the broad statutory text and the variety of workplace contexts in which retaliation may occur, Title VII's anti-retaliation provision is simply not reducible to a comprehensive set of clear rules.

The Court in *Thompson* noted that terminating a close family member will likely always count as retaliation while a lesser adverse action against a friend or colleague would not. However, in the EEOC's Questions and Answers: Enforcement Guidance on Retaliation and Related Issues,[59] the agency states, "If an employer takes an action against someone else, such as a family member or close friend, in order to retaliate against an employee, both individuals would have a legal claim against the employer." Also, some courts have allowed third-party claims of retaliation for coworkers who were dating (*Antonelli v. Sapa Extrusions, Inc.,* 2015[60]; *Harrington v. Career Training Institute Orlando, Inc.,* 2011). For instance, in *Harrington* the court reasoned that "The present case can be distinguished because the complaint alleges that the Plaintiffs are dating and in *Thompson*, the employees were engaged to be married. However, it should be noted that the Court's ruling in *Thompson* does not exclude third party reprisal claims for individuals who are merely dating."

---

[59] https://www.eeoc.gov/laws/guidance/questions-and-answers-enforcement-guidance-retaliation-and-related-issues

[60] https://scholar.google.com/scholar_case?case=11685133767420607834&q=Antonelli+v.+Sapa+Extrusions,+Inc.,+2015&hl=en&as_sdt=40006

In addition, courts have allowed third-party claims when coworkers professed to be friends (*Ali v. District of Columbia Government*, 2011; *Sterner v. County of Banks*, 2014).[61] For readers interested in detailed legal reviews of third-party retaliation claims, see Long (2007), Lucas (2016), McCambridge (2013), Naquin (2013), Plain (2011), Strawbridge (2012), and Underwood (2013).

Filing a Complaint

Another case, *Kasten v. Saint-Gobain Performance Plastics, Corp.* (2011),[62,63] concerned what standard should be used for "filing" a complaint. After being fired, Kevin Kasten sued for retaliation under the Fair Labor Standards Act (FLSA),[64] alleging that his termination occurred after he *orally* complained about an organizational practice (location of time clocks). He complained that the placement of the clocks cost employees money by not allowing them to get paid for the time they spent changing into and removing required protective clothing. As before, the lower courts ruled for the organization, stating that oral complaints are *not* covered under the FLSA, which makes it illegal for employers "to discharge . . . any employee because such employee has filed any complaint." Once again, the Supreme Court overturned the lower courts and stated that oral complaints are protected under the law (also see *Greathouse v. JHS Security Inc.*, 2015).[65]

In making its decision, the majority of the Court stressed that oral arguments were not uncommon when the FLSA was passed in 1938. Also, the Court's decision aligned with the position of other agencies (EEOC, Department of Labor) that have recognized oral complaints as legitimate. Finally, the justices reasoned that requiring individuals to file a claim in writing could disadvantage certain groups, such as those who were illiterate or had less education. See Table 10.4 for a summary of the key retaliation cases just discussed.

The burden shifting process of a retaliation case is consistent with that used within disparate treatment cases (i.e., the McDonnell-Douglas framework). For instance, plaintiffs must establish a *prima facie* case, the defense must then articulate a legitimate (nondiscriminatory) reason for its actions, and, if the defense is successful, plaintiffs must prove that the reason(s) articulated by the organization was a pretext for retaliation. See the "EEO in the Wild" box

[61] https://casetext.com/case/sterner-v-cnty-of-berks
[62] https://www.supremecourt.gov/opinions/10pdf/09-834.pdf
[63] https://www.oyez.org/cases/2010/09-834
[64] https://www.dol.gov/whd/regs/statutes/FairLaborStandAct.pdf
[65] https://caselaw.findlaw.com/us-2nd-circuit/1697996.html

Table 10.4 Summary of important retaliation cases (listed in chronological order)

Court case	Central legal issue
Robinson v. Shell Oil (1997)[1]	Retaliation claims are *not* limited to applicants and current employees; former employees are also protected
BNSF v. White (2006)[2]	Actions by organizations that would deter a reasonable person from engaging in protected activities establishes a "material adverse action." Court supported the so-called Equal Employment Opportunity Commission (EEOC) Deterrence standard
Crawford v. Metro Gov't of Nashville (2009)[3]	Participating in an investigation (e.g., as a witness) counts as "opposition."
Thompson v. North American Stainless (2011)[4]	Retaliation protections extend to actions against closely-related third parties (e.g., fiancés).
Kasten v. Saint-Gobain Performance Plastics (2011)[5]	Oral complaints are covered in retaliation cases, not just written, formal complaints.
University of Texas Southwestern Medical Center v. Nassar (2013)[6]	Plaintiffs must show that an organization's retaliation was the "but for" reason for its adverse employment action.

[1] https://www.law.cornell.edu/supct/html/95-1376.ZO.html
[2] https://www.law.cornell.edu/supct/html/05-259.ZO.html
[3] https://www.law.cornell.edu/supct/pdf/06-1595P.ZO
[4] https://www.law.cornell.edu/supct/pdf/09-291P.ZO
[5] https://www.law.cornell.edu/supct/pdf/09-834P.ZO
[6] https://www.law.cornell.edu/supct/pdf/12-484.pdf
Adapted from Vodanovich & Piotrowski (2014).

for a discussion of the relevancy of the disparate treatment scenario given the Court's decision in *Nassar*.

EEO in the Wild: Is the McDonnell-Douglas Disparate Treatment Framework Appropriate for Retaliation Cases?

Some legal scholars have argued that the McDonnell-Douglas disparate treatment scenario does not fit comfortably with Title VII retaliation cases given the decision in *Nassar* (e.g., Rosenthal, 2016; Teal, 2018). As noted by Kremer (2017), the need to show "but for" causation to establish a prima facie case is not explicitly part of the McDonnell-Douglas burden shifting framework. Basically, a *prima facie* case in disparate treatment cases requires evidence that plaintiffs belong to a protected class, they are qualified for the position in question, are recipients of a negative employment decision despite being qualified, and others not in the protected group were treated more favorably (e.g., hired, not terminated, received requested accommodation) or that the search process continued for similarly qualified individuals. The burden for plaintiffs under the disparate treatment scenario is to present evidence that is presumed to be true—a relatively light requirement. The need for "but for" causation is not inherent to the process. In this regard, the framework has been reconfigured (and inconsistently so) for use in retaliation claims.

For instance, the *Nassar* decision (which required "but for" causation) did not include any reference to the McDonnell-Douglas framework, let alone how it should be used in Title VII retaliation cases. As noted by Rosenthal (2016), this has led to a split among the courts, with some deciding that Nassar raised the burden on plaintiffs for establishing a *prima facie* case and others holding that Nassar did not affect the standard process.

Kremer (2017) provided examples of courts that believed that "but for" causation must be met in the *prima facie* phase in retaliation cases (e.g., *Wheat v. Florida Parish Juvenile Justice Commission*, 2016; *Walker v. Mod-U-Kraf Homes*, 2014), as well as those that have not set such a standard (e.g., *Foster v. University of Maryland-Eastern Shore*, 2015), and also emphasized that if "but for" causation is required to establish a *prima facie* case of retaliation, then the next two steps of the McDonnell-Douglas framework are artificially applied. As noted earlier in the text, the second step of the framework requires the defense to articulate (produce) a legitimate reason for its actions. If this succeeds, plaintiffs must prove that the reason given by the defense is a pretext for discrimination. So, if "but for" causation is required in the *prima facie* phase, Kremer contended that the case is functionally decided (for either side) in phase 1. As Kremer stated,

> If the plaintiff is able to demonstrate a but for causal link between the protected conduct and the adverse employment action, he [sic] has apparently proven his claim, establishing a non-rebuttable presumption of discriminatory retaliation.... Conversely, where the plaintiff could not establish but for causation in his prima facie case, a court would necessarily be required to find in favor of the defendant employer. If the evaluation ends after the prima facie case, whether satisfied or not, there is no need for the McDonnell Douglas burden-shifting framework in Title VII retaliation claims.

Teal (2018) similarly argued that "applying the ultimate causation standard, but for, at the prima facie stage would be tantamount to eliminating the McDonnell Douglas framework in retaliation cases altogether. It would force plaintiffs to prove their ultimate case before they even get their cases off the ground." In any event, the applicability for retaliation claims under the burden shifting framework of McDonnell-Douglas is intriguing and worth further commentary and analysis.

Consistent with other types of discrimination, many retaliation claims are settled between the EEOC and various organizations. A representative list of such settlements is presented in Table 10.5. As you can see, these settlements can be costly to companies, and they typically require alterations to the way human resource functions are performed.

Table 10.5 Representative Equal Employment Opportunity Commission (EEOC) retaliation settlements (listed in descending chronological order by year)

Organization (year of settlement)	Specific allegation(s)	Settlement and primary relief
Whataburger Restaurants, LLC (2020)[1]	Plaintiff complained after being told by her general manager (on several occasions) to only hire White applicants. Plaintiff then received verbal and physical abuse, threats, change in schedule, and more work duties. Plaintiff claimed she was compelled to quit.	• $180,000 damage award • Three-year consent decree • Develop new HR policies, perform employee training, establish an anonymous complaint hotline, and post notices in the workplace about the suit
Erikson Living Management, LLC (2020)[2]	Director complained to HR about perceived poor treatment of one of her subordinate employees due to their disability and questioned the performance assessment process, which she believed was discriminatory. Both the director and her subordinate were fired.	• $150,000 damage award • Two-year consent decree • ADA training; post anti-discrimination notice in the workplace
Global Ministries, Inc. (2020)[3]	Employee complained on numerous occasions about alleged instances of race discrimination and retaliation against individuals who complained. She was subsequently fired.	• $50,000 damage award • Anti-discrimination training for employees • Post anti-retaliation policy; post anti-discrimination notice
Herbruck Poultry Ranch, Inc. (2019)[4]	Constructive discharge after employee was subjected to hostile work environment based on her disability.	• $93,000 settlement • Update company harassment and retaliation policies
Louisiana Credit Union (2018)[5]	Plaintiff fired after opposing an alleged racist video for training.	• $110,000 settlement • Retaliation training
Jewish Board of Family and Children's Services (2018)[6]	Plaintiff asked company to remove her disability information from a log to which other employees had access. Company refused, she filed an ADA suit and was fired.	• $60,000 settlement • Mandatory management and HR training

(continued)

Table 10.5 Continued

Organization (year of settlement)	Specific allegation(s)	Settlement and primary relief
Aloha Auto Group, Ltd. (2018)[7]	Fired worker for encouraging a group of employees to complain about a racially discriminatory statement.	• $30,000 settlement • Choose individual to function as an equal employment opportunity (EEO) monitor • Develop a complaint process • Managerial training
Plastipak Packaging, Inc. (2018)[8]	Female employee fired after complaining of sexual harassment.	• $90,000 settlement • Develop comprehensive policy regarding sexual harassment and retaliation • Training for all personnel
Rite Way Service, Inc. (2017)[9]	Terminated employee for participating in an internal sexual harassment investigation.	• $70,000 settlement • Develop anti-discrimination policies and implement policies • Train managers and supervisors regarding workplace discrimination,
Bass Pro Outdoor World, LLC (2017)[10]	Pattern and practice discrimination regarding hiring of African Americans and Hispanics; retaliation for opposing company practices.	• $10.5 million settlement • Update EEO policies and hiring procedures • Yearly management training
ABL Management, Inc. (2017)[11]	Employee fired for complaining about sexual harassment.	• $35,000 settlement • Develop policies and procedures to stop sex discrimination and retaliation • Anti-discrimination training

Note: Retaliation suits and settlements are often combined with other claims of discrimination (e.g., sexual harassment, disability discrimination, race discrimination).

[1] https://www.eeoc.gov/newsroom/whataburger-pay-180000-settle-eeoc-retaliation-suit
[2] https://www.eeoc.gov/newsroom/erickson-living-management-will-pay-151000-settle-eeoc-retaliation-lawsuit
[3] https://www.eeoc.gov/newsroom/global-ministries-pay-50000-settle-eeoc-retaliation-discrimination-suit
[4] https://www.eeoc.gov/newsroom/herbruck-poultry-ranch-inc-pays-93000-settle-eeoc-harassment-and-retaliation-suit
[5] https://www.eeoc.gov/eeoc/newsroom/release/12-19-18b.cfm
[6] https://www.eeoc.gov/eeoc/newsroom/release/9-17-18b.cfm
[7] https://www.eeoc.gov/eeoc/newsroom/release/1-10-18.cfm
[8] https://www.eeoc.gov/newsroom/plastipak-packaging-will-pay-90000-settle-eeoc-retaliation-suit
[9] https://www.eeoc.gov/eeoc/newsroom/release/3-23-17.cfm
[10] https://www.eeoc.gov/eeoc/newsroom/release/7-25-17b.cfm
[11] https://www.eeoc.gov/eeoc/newsroom/release/4-10-17a.cfm

Retrieved from EEOC Press Releases: https://www.eeoc.gov/newsroom/search.

Recommendations/Best Practices

- Develop a policy to ban workplace retaliation that includes components such as specific complaint procedures and training for investigating employee opposition/grievances.
- Train supervisors to use organizational justice principles (e.g., procedural, interactional) in making personnel decisions and managing opposition and participation activities.
- Keep records of all communication between parties and organizational responses to protected activities.
- Cooperate with the EEOC on retaliation investigations; give investigators timely and truthful information.
- To the extent possible by law, keep employee complaints about alleged retaliation confidential.
- Process claims of retaliation as soon as possible.
- Train all personnel on what constitutes retaliation and the effects this behavior can have on employees and organizations.
- Educate employees of their rights under the law regarding Title VII retaliation claims.
- Develop an organizational culture that values a diverse and inclusive workforce.
- Reward behaviors that foster workplace civility and respect for diverse views.
- Develop clearly delineated expectations for proper interpersonal behavior; consider workforce training on interpersonal skills.

Summary and Take-Aways

Retaliation claims continue to be the most common suits filed with the EEOC (see Tables 10.2 and 10.3). This does not mean that they are easy to win. The "but for" causation requirement stipulated in *Nassar* is a difficult burden for plaintiffs. However, even prior to the Nassar case, retaliation cases often failed to meet the causal connection criteria (e.g., Gutman, 2007).

Although third-party retaliation is a viable claim, it is unclear how *close* the relationship must be to be challenged legally. As stated by Strawbridge, "While the *Thompson* opinion's language provides some guidance, it stops predictably short of articulating any fixed point of reference for practitioners and courts to evaluate third-party retaliation, thus requiring further litigation to flesh out the skeleton of third-party retaliation claims under Title VII."

The lack of clarity for evaluating the required closeness of third-party relationships has led to mixed court decisions and varying reactions among legal scholars (e.g., Long, 2007), and some scholars have stressed the need for a clear standard regarding who qualifies for third-party claims (e.g., Plain, 2011). Some have noted that such clarification could be done by Congress (e.g., Long, 2011) and the EEOC (e.g., McCambridge, 2013; Underwood, 2013). As McCambridge has indicated, "The EEOC is perfectly positioned to help employers who need user-friendly, easy-to-follow instructions for determining who qualifies as a third-party with standing to sue for retaliation." Without greater specificity on who qualifies as a legally covered third party, researchers have predicted an increase in the number of retaliation suits[66] (e.g., Fink, 2012; Naquin, 2013). However, Lucas (2016) has articulated that the decision in *Thompson* aligns with the overall purpose of Title VII, which avoids fixed rules in lieu of providing general standards, thus allowing courts to judge the merit of cases on the facts within individual claims. At this point, it is unknown whether Congress and/or the EEOC (and perhaps the Supreme Court) will interject more specific criteria for assessing third-party retaliation claims. So, the guidance set forth in *Thompson* is controlling.

Finally, it will also be interesting to see if Congress will address the "but for" causation standard stipulated by the Court's decision in *Nassar*. As noted earlier, this standard is harsher for plaintiffs than that required for discrimination based on race, color, religion, sex, and national origin.

Supplemental Readings on Workplace Retaliation

Beginner

McElgunn, T. (November, 12, 2018). EEOC sees retaliation claims rise: How to stay off its radar. HR Morning.com. http://www.hrmorning.com/eeoc-sees-retaliation-workload-rise-how-to-stay-off-its-radar/

Nagele-Piazza, L. (March 26, 2018). How to prevent workplace retaliation claims. Society for Human Resource Management (SHRM). https://www.shrm.org/resourcesandtools/legal-and-compliance/employment-law/pages/how-to-prevent-a-workplace-retaliation-claim.aspx

Shappel, C. (February 17, 2016). EEOC's new retaliation guidance should concern you— and here's why. HRMorning,com. https://www.hrmorning.com/articles/eeoc-retaliation-guidance-should-concern-you/

---

[66] The EEOC does not separate third-party retaliation claims from overall retaliation suits.

Veirs, K. (2017, Spring). Avoiding workplace retaliation: Guidance for employers. Employee Relations Today, 57–63. https://www.bassberry.com/wp-content/uploads/Employment-Relations-Today-Spring-2017.pdf

Intermediate
EEOC. Guidance on retaliation and related issues.https://www.eeoc.gov/laws/guidance/enforcement-guidance-retaliation-and-related-issues

EEOC. Questions and answers: Enforcement guidance on retaliation and related issues. https://www.eeoc.gov/laws/guidance/questions-and-answers-enforcement-guidance-retaliation-and-related-issues

Sammons, D. E. (2011). Retaliation. In M. A. Paludi, E. R. DeSouza, & C. A. Paludi (Eds.), *Praeger handbook on understanding and preventing workplace discrimination* (pp. 183–194). Santa Barbara: CA., Praeger Publishers.

Smith, A. (January 27, 2016). EEOC cracks down on retaliation. Society for Human Resource Management (SHRM). https://www.shrm.org/resourcesandtools/legal-and-compliance/employment-law/pages/retaliation-proposed-guidance.aspx

Advanced
Cooney, J. (2003). Understanding and preventing workplace retaliation. *Massachusetts Law Review, 88*(1), 3–23.

Long, A. B. (2018). Retaliation backlash. *Washington Law Review, 93*, 715–766.

Taylor, H. (2019). The other 20 cents isn't worth it: The inadequacy of Title VII's anti-retaliation framework. *Duke Journal of Gender Law & Policy, 26*, 65–83. https://scholarship.law.duke.edu/djglp/vol26/iss2/1/

Twomey, D. P. (2011). Employee retaliation under the Supreme Court's Burlington, Crawford, and Thompson decisions: Important implications for employers. *Labor Law Journal, 62*, 57–66.

Glossary

Adverse employment standard: To qualify as a material adverse action, the behavior by the organization must interfere with the terms/conditions/privileges of employment but not have to result in a specific adverse employment action.

But for analysis: Frequently used to assess causation. It is often referred to as the actual or factual cause. For instance, "but for" a retaliatory motive, the employer would not have taken the adverse action. Also known as but for causation.

Constructive discharge: Discrimination or harassment so egregious that would compel a reasonable person in the same position to resign.

EEOC Deterrence Standard: Retaliatory behavior that has the effect of preventing or deterring a reasonable person from engaging in a protected activity.

Good faith: Using honesty, due diligence, and best efforts in dealing with others.

Motivating factor: One of the reasons, but may not be the only reason, for an adverse employment practice.

Opposition clause: Appears in Section 704 A of Title VII and provides legal protection against workplace retaliation by stating that it is unlawful for employers to discriminate against employees or applicants for opposing unlawful employment practices.

Participation clause: Appears in Section 704 A of Title VII and provides legal protection against workplace retaliation by stating it is unlawful for employers to discriminate against employees or applicants who participate in an investigation, proceeding, or hearing.

Prima facie: Latin phrase for "at first glance." Consists of presenting evidence that is presumed to be true.

Third-party retaliation: The act of seeking revenge against an employee indirectly through adverse actions against a third party who is connected to the individual, typically a friend or relative working within the same organization.

Ultimate employment standard: To qualify as materially adverse, the organization's action must result in an ultimate, tangible negative employment decision (e.g., being terminated or demoted).

Glossary terms adapted from Gutman et al. (2011)/ https://uslegal.com/.

Cases Cited

Ali v. District of Columbia Government, 810 F. Supp. 2d 78 (D.C. Cir. 2011).
Alvarez v. Royal Atlantic Developers, Inc., 610 F. 3d 1253 (11th Cir., 2010).
Antonelli v. Sapa Extrusions, Inc. (MD Pa, 2015).
Burlington Northern Santa Fe Railway Company v. White, 548 U.S. 53 (2006).
Cifra v. General Electric Co., 252 F.3d 205 (2nd Cir 2001).
Clark County School District v. Breeden, 532 U.S. 268 (2001).
Collazo v. Bristol-Myers Squibb Manufacturing Inc., 617 F.3d 39, 49 (1st Cir. 2010).
Crawford v. Metropolitan Government of Nashville and Davidson County, 555 U.S. 271 (2009).
EEOC v. Bojangles Restaurants, Inc., 284 F. Supp. 2d 320 (M.D.N.C. 2003).
Evans v. City of Houston, 246 F. 3d 344 (5th Cir. 2001).
Fogelman v. Mercy Hospital., Inc., 283 F. 3d 561 (3d Cir. 2002).
Glover v. South Carolina Law Enforcement Division, 170 F.3d 411 (4th Cir. 1999).
Gorman-Bakos v. Cornell Coop of Schenectady County, 252 F.3d 545 (2d Cir. 2001).
Greathouse v. JHS Security Inc., 784 F. 3d 105 (2d Cir. 2015).
Harrington v. Career Training Institute Orlando, Inc. (M.D. Fla., 2011).
Hillig v. Rumsfeld, 381 F.3d 1028 (10th Cir. 2004).
Hochstadt v. Worcester Foundation for Experimental Biology, Inc., 545 F.2d 222 (1st Cir. 1976).
Holava-Brown v. General Electric Company, 189 F.3d 461 (2nd Cir. 1999).

Holt v. JTM Industries Inc., 89 F.3d 1224 (5th Cir. 1996).

Hudson v. Norris, 227 F. 3d 1047 (8th Cir. 2000).

Hughes v. Derwinski, 967 F. 2d 1168 (7th Cir. 1992).

Jensen v. Potter, 435 F. 3d 444 (3rd Cir. 2006).

Kasten v. Saint-Gobain Performance Plastics Corp., 563 U.S. 1 (2011).

Kessler v. Westchester City Department of Social Services, 461 F.3d 199 (2 Cir. 2006).

Loya v. Sebelius, 840 F. Supp. 2d 245 (D.D.C. 2012).

Mattern v. Eastman Kodak Co., 104 F. 3d 702 (5th Cir. 1997).

Millea v. Metro-North Railroad Co., 658 F.3d 154 (2nd Cir. 2011).

Oest v. Illinois Department of Corrections, 240 F.3d 605 (7th Cir. 2001).

O'Neal v. City of Chicago, 588 F.3d 406 (7th Cir. 2009).

Planadeball v. Wyndham Vacation Resorts, Inc., 793 F.3d 169 (1st Cir. 2015).

Pomales v. Celulares Telefonico Inc., 447 F. 3d 79 (1st Cir. 2006).

Richmond v. Oneok Inc. 120 F. 3rd 205 (10th Cir. 1997).

Risley v. Fordham University, 99 CIV. 9304 (DLC) (S.D.N.Y. Feb. 13, 2001).

Roberts v. Roadway Express, Inc., 149 F.3d 1098 (10th Cir. 1998).

Robinson v. Jackson State University, 714 Fed.App'x, 354 (5th Cir. 2017).

Robinson v. Shell Oil, 519 U.S. 337 (1997).

Rosser v. Laborers' International Union of North America, 616 F. 2d 221 (5th Cir. 1980).

Singh v. Green Thumb Landscaping, Inc., 390 F. Supp. 2d 1129 (M.D. Fla. 2005).

Smith v. Riceland Foods, Inc., 151 F. 3d 813 (8th Cir. 1998).

Sterner v. County of Banks, Civil Action No. 13-1568 (E.D. Pa. Mar. 28, 2014).

Thompson v. North American Stainless, LP 562 U.S. 170 (2011).

University of Texas Southwestern Medical Center v. Nassar, 570 U.S. 338 (2013).

Walker v. Johnson, 798 F.3d 1085 (D.C. Cir. 2015).

Washington v. Illinois Dept. of Revenue, 420 F. 3d 658 (7th Cir. 2005).

Woodson v. Scott Paper, Co., 109 F.3d 913 (3rd Cir. 1997).

References

Baker, S. C. W. (2005). A choice of rules in Title VII retaliation claims for negative employer references. *Duke Law Review*, *55*, 153–178.

Brake, D. L. (2014). Retaliation in the EEO office. *Tulsa Law Review*, *50*(1), 1–42.

Cavico, F. J., & Mujaba, B. G. (2011). Managers be warned: Third-party retaliation lawsuits and the United States Supreme Court. *Contemporary Issues in Business and Economics*, *2*, 8–17.

Cortina, L. M., & Magley, V. J. (2003). Raising voice, risking retaliation: Events following interpersonal mistreatment in the workplace. *Journal of Occupational Health Psychology*, *8*(4), 247–265.

Dunleavy, E. M. (2007). What is all the fuss about: The implications of the EEOC Deterrence Standard after *BNSF v. White*. *The Industrial-Organizational Psychologist*, *44*, 31–39.

Essary, M. A., & Friedman, T. D. (1998). Retaliation claims under Title VII, the ADEA, and the ADA: Untouchable employees, uncertain employers, unresolved courts. *Missouri Law Review*, *63*, 115–153.

Fink, J. K. (2012). Protected by association? The Supreme Court's incomplete approach to defining the scope of the third-party retaliation doctrine. *Hastings Law Journal*, *63*, 521–566.

Grossman, J. L., & Brake, D. L. (2013). Revenge: The Supreme Court narrows protection against workplace retaliation in *University of Texas Southwestern Medical Center v. Nassar* verdict. Retrieved November 27, 2019, from https://scholarlycommons.law.hofstra.edu/faculty_scholarship/977/

Gutman, A. (2007). *BNSF v. White*: Early returns. *The Industrial-Organizational Psychologist*, *44*, 97–110.

Hegerich, R. M. (2010). Employment law: Title VII does not extend to third-party retaliation claim by fiancée of discrimination claimant. *Suffolk University Law Review*, *43*, 1059–1069.

Kline, B. (2009). Oppose by any other name: The Title VII opposition clause and *Crawford v. Metropolitan Government of Nashville and Davidson County, Tennessee*. *Oklahoma City University Law Review*, *34*(3), 591–608.

Kremer, C. (2017). McDonnell-Douglas burden shifting and judicial economy in Title VII retaliation claims: In pursuit of expediency, resulting in inefficiency. *University of Cincinnati Law Review*, *85*, 857–876.

Krimski, M. A. (2014). *University of Texas Southwestern Medical Center v. Nassar*: Undermining the national policy against discrimination. *Maryland law Review Endnotes*, *73*, 132–160.

Long, A. B. (2007). The troublemaker's friend: Retaliation against third parties and the right of association in the workplace. *Florida Law Review*, *59*(5), 931–990.

Long, A. B. (2011). Employment retaliation and the accident of text. *Oregon Law Review*, *90*(2), 525–582.

Lucas, K. E. (2016). How close is close enough? Examining the relationships in Title VII third party retaliation claims. *Labor Law Journal*, *67*(3), 445–458.

McCambridge, S. (2013). Third-party retaliation: The shoes of an employer. *John Marshall Law Journal*, *7*(1), 41–88.

Naquin, L. (2013). Closing the floodgates: Defining class of third-party plaintiffs for Title VII retaliation claims. *Louisiana Law Review*, *73*(2), 669–702.

Nevin, R. (2010). Title vii antiretaliation: The United States Supreme Court's decision in Crawford v. Metropolitan Government of Nashville & Davidson County, Tennessee on the scope of the opposition clause. *Richmond Journal of Law and Public Interest*, *13*(2), 291–314.

O'Brien, J. P. (2002). Weighing temporal proximity in Title VII retaliation claims. *Boston College Law Review*, *43*, 741–781. Retrieved November 27, 2019, from https://lawdigitalcommons.bc.edu/cgi/viewcontent.cgi?article=2207&context=bclr

Plain, G. L. (2011). I'll get you my pretty and your little associate too: The expansion of employee protection in Title VII retaliation claims. *Cumberland Law Review*, *42*(3), 549–584.

Rosenthal, L. D. (2016). Timing isn't everything: Establishing Title VII retaliation prima facie case after *University of Texas Southwestern Medical Center v. Nassar*. *SMU Law Review*, *69*(1), 143–186.

Savage, J. M. (2004). Adopting the EEOC deterrence approach to the adverse employment action prong in a prima facie case for Title VII retaliation. *Boston College Law Review*, *46*, 215–250.

Sharone, J. B. (2010). For better or worse: Spouses left unprotected by the anti-retaliation provision of Title VII. *Suffolk Journal of Trial and Appellate Advocacy*, *15*, 289–307.

Strawbridge, D. D. (2012). Thy fiancé doth protest too much: Third-party retaliation under Title VII after *Thompson v. North American Stainless, LP*. *Mercer Law Review*, *63*(2), 767–790.

Teal, J. (2018). A survivor's tale: McDonnell Douglas in a post-Nassar world. *San Diego Law Review*, *55*(4), 937–968.

Underwood, B. (2013). Tread lightly: Third-party retaliation claims after *Thompson v. North American Stainless*. *Journal of Corporation Law*, *38*(2), 463–486.

Valenti, A., & Burke, L. A. (2010). Post-*Burlington*: What employers and employees should know about retaliation. *Employee Responsibilities and Rights Journal*, *22*, 235–251. doi:10.1007/s10672-009-9137-z

Vodanovich, S. J., & Piotrowski, C. (2014). Workplace retaliation: A review of emerging case law. *The Psychologist-Manager Journal*, *17*(2), 71–78.

Zimmer, M. J. (2014). Hiding the statute in plain view: *University of Texas Southwestern Medical Center v. Nassar*. *Nevada Law Journal*, *14*(3), 705–722.

Glossary

Adverse employment practice A disruptive and materially adverse change in working conditions that is more than an inconvenience or alteration of job responsibilities.

Adverse employment standard To qualify as a material adverse action, the behavior by the organization must *interfere* with terms/conditions/privileges of employment but does *not* have to result in a specific adverse employment action.

Adverse impact When facially neutral selection criteria disproportionately exclude a higher percentage of one group relative to another. These differences are often assessed by using the four-fifths rule or statistical significance tests.

Affirmative defense A defense raised that contains facts contrary to those stated by the plaintiff and which justifies the challenged actions.

Applicant flow data The number of people who apply to positions and are accepted from each demographic group.

Applicant flow statistics Calculating and comparing the total number of applicants to the number of applicants selected/hired in each demographic group.

Applicant stock statistics Statistics that compare organizational data (e.g., number of hires by demographic groups) with the number of qualified individuals in the relevant labor market.

Average person standard A yardstick for assessing if impairments count as a legal disability is that they must be greater than that experienced by the *average* person.

Ban the box proposals Laws that prohibit the use of criminal background data prior to making an initial job offer.

Bennett Amendment An amendment inserted into Title VII to ensure that violations of the Equal Pay Act would also violate Title VII.

Beyond a reasonable doubt The strictest standard of proof that can be met. This standard is required to convict a criminal defendant of a crime.

Binding arbitration A process for resolving a dispute outside of the court system where the dispute is presented to a third party or panel that renders a decision that cannot be further challenged or brought to court in any way.

Bona fide occupational qualification Defense that applies to facial discrimination (i.e., "need not apply" rules) based on sex, national origin, religion, and age but only if the defendant can prove it is reasonably necessary for the essence of the business to exclude all or most members of these protected classes.

Bona fide seniority systems An established system in companies giving individuals with more years of tenure preference for a promotion and/or terminating these individuals last when layoffs are implemented.

But for analysis Frequently used to assess causation. It is often referred to as the *actual* or *factual cause*. For instance, "but for" a retaliatory motive, the employer would not have taken the adverse action. Also known as *but for causation*.

But for causation See *But for analysis*

Class action One or more plaintiffs who represent a group of plaintiffs similarly affected by the defendant's actions, along with their counsel, bring a lawsuit against one or more defendants.

Class protection The plaintiff(s) will sufficiently protect the interests of the class.

Cognizable A viable claim or a claim that is capable of being judicially heard and determined.

Collective bargaining agreement A contract or agreement between an employer and one or more unions that creates the terms of employment for the employees who belong to that labor union. The contract may include provisions regarding wages, paid time off, working hours and conditions, health insurance, and other benefits.

Commonality requirement The requirement, applied in class action certification, that questions of law or fact are common to the entire class.

Comparable worth The concept that women and men should receive equal pay for jobs requiring comparable (not equal) work.

Compelling interest Necessary or essential, as opposed to being simply a discretion, preference, or choice (e.g., achieving diversity in higher education).

Compensatory damages Awarding of payments for costs incurred (e.g., lost wages, bonuses, pain and suffering).

Consent decree Agreement or settlement between two parties that concludes a lawsuit instead of resolving the case through a hearing and/or trial. Consent decrees and consent judgments are the same.

Constructive discharge Discrimination or harassment so egregious that would compel a reasonable person in the same position to resign.

Daubert motion A motion to exclude the presentation of unqualified evidence by questioning the expertise or methodology of an expert witness.

Daubert standard Rule of evidence used as a standard in determining the admissibility of expert witness testimony. The factors include if the technique or theory can be or has been tested, whether it has been subject to peer review and publication, the known or potential rate of error of the technique or theory, the existence and maintenance of standards and controls, and whether the technique or theory has been generally accepted within the scientific community.

De minimis Something so small or trivial that it is not considered by the law; this is often used to describe exemptions to legal rules and regulations.

Declarative relief A decision of the rights of those involved in a suit under a given law. No monetary awards are involved.

Defense The arguments and evidence presented by the defendant in opposition to the allegations or charges brought against them by the plaintiff(s). Term is also used to refer to the party sued by a plaintiff.

Deposition The written testimony of a sworn witness presented during discovery before the trial.

Direct evidence Evidence which proves the existence of an alleged fact without needing inference or presumption. Direct evidence cannot only suggest discrimination (or retaliation) or be subject to more than one interpretation.

Discovery The fact-finding process that allows parties to prepare for settlement or trial that occurs after a lawsuit has been filed and before the trial takes place. During this period, evidence is obtained through formal requests between plaintiff(s) and the defense or through subpoenas.

Disparate treatment Intentionally treating an individual or group less favorably than another due to protected group status (e.g., race, religion, national origin, sex, disability).

Dissent A disagreement or difference of opinion with the majority opinion among judges.

Ecological validity Research conducted in a naturalistic setting and involving materials and activities from everyday life.

EEOC Deterrence Standard Retaliatory behavior that has the effect of preventing or deterring a reasonable person from engaging in a protected activity.

Equal work Under the Equal Pay Act, this is defined as jobs that are substantially equal with respect to effort, skill, responsibility, and work conditions.

Essential job function The primary duties that are fundamental to the job.

Establishment Often, but not limited to, a physical location. According to the Equal Pay Act, a place where central decisions are made.

Factor other than sex (FOS) A defense available to organizations that their decision(s) were based on any factor other than sex in Equal Pay Act cases.

Good faith Using honesty, due diligence, and best efforts in dealing with others.

Hostile work environment An environment that is intimidating, offensive, or unreasonably interferes with an employee's work performance.

Indirect evidence Also referred to as *circumstantial evidence*, indirect evidence helps to establish the main fact by inference.

Injunction A court order that prevents or commands an action from the defense. To receive an injunction, the plaintiff must show that monetary damages will not suffice and that an irreparable injury will result unless the injunction is issued.

Injunctive relief A court-ordered remedy that requires a given party to do, or not do, a given activity.

Liquidated damages Typically included within contracts and specifies a given monetary award if contracts are broken. Often used when actual damages are difficult to determine.

Major life activity Functions central to life, such as caring for oneself, walking, seeing, breathing, learning, and working.

Make whole Restoring victims to the position they were in prior to being discriminated against (e.g., by awarding sufficient damages).

McDonnell-Douglas framework A three-step burden shifting process used for cases of intentional discrimination.

Medical test A test administered and interpreted by a healthcare professional designed to reveal physical or mental health impairments or measure task performance or a physiological response to performing the task.

Mixed-motive cases Cases where illegal and legal factors motivate an employment decision.

Monetary damages/relief Compensation given to an injured party by a liable party (e.g., back pay, lost salary, fringe benefits, bonuses, pain and suffering).

Motivating factor One of the reasons, but may not be the only reason, for an adverse employment practice.

Narrowly tailored A practice or plan that attempts to achieve a compelling interest by employing the least restrictive means possible (e.g., specific plans that are temporary; race-neutral alternative not available).

Natural experiments Research that examines outcomes from observations of treatment and control groups that are not randomly assigned.

Numerosity clause The class is so numerous that claims by individuals are unrealistic.

Opposition clause Appears in Section 704 A of Title VII and provides legal protection against workplace retaliation by stating that it is unlawful for employers to discriminate against employees or applicants for opposing unlawful employment practices.

Participation clause Appears in Section 704 A of Title VII and provides legal protection against workplace retaliation by stating that it is unlawful for employers to discriminate against employees or applicants who participate in an investigation, proceeding, or hearing.

Permanence standard A way of assessing whether a person is substantially impaired; typically, impairments with a duration of more than six months are considered permanent.

Plaintiff The party who initiates a lawsuit.

Plurality Receiving the greatest number, but not a majority, of votes.

Practical significance Concerns whether a disparity is of a magnitude that is meaningful.

Precedent Deference to a prior reported opinion (often of an appeals court) to form the basis of a legal argument in a subsequent case; the principle announced by a higher court that should be followed in later cases.

Preponderance of evidence Evidence that indicates that a violation of law (e.g., discrimination) was more likely than not to be true. This is the type of evidence commonly used in civil trials and is the least strict standard of evidence, as compared to beyond a reasonable doubt and clear and convincing evidence.

Presumptive evidence Evidence that the alleged discrimination was "more likely than not" to have transpired.

Prima facie Latin phrase for "at first glance." Consists of presenting evidence that is presumed to be true.

Privileged Information that is not legally discoverable by the opposing party and is covered by statutory or common law protections.

Protected class Groups protected by anti-discrimination laws, including race, color, national origin, religion, sex (or gender), age (older than 40), and disability.

Punitive damages Used to punish employers for discriminatory acts committed with malice or reckless indifference and to prevent the reoccurrence of comparable discriminatory behavior.

Quid pro quo Latin phrase literally meaning "something for something." Getting something of value in exchange for giving something of value. Often seen in sexual harassment cases.

Reasonable accommodation Adjusting or modifying a job application process or working conditions to enable a qualified person with a disability to be considered for the job.

Reasonable person standard Standard often used to determine whether a hostile work environment exists in sexual harassment cases. Consists of assessing whether behavior would be considered as hostile from the perspective of a reasonable person (or a reasonable person from the point of view of the victim).

Set-asides Special programs aimed at increasing opportunities for small businesses and business owned by individuals from underrepresented groups to acquire government contracts.

Statistical significance Evaluates the probability that group differences are due to chance, often using null hypothesis significance testing.

Strict liability Cases where *no* affirmative defense is available to organizations to limit or negate liability, as is the case with *quid pro quo* cases.

Strict scrutiny A legal standard applied when fundamental rights are in question. Under strict scrutiny, governmental or organizational practices or policies (e.g., affirmative action programs) are legally defensible only if they (1) advance a compelling interest (i.e., a crucially important concern) and (2) are narrowly tailored, using the least restrictive method to achieve the compelling interest.

Summary judgments Decisions by a judge that resolve lawsuits in favor of a given party.

Third-party retaliation The act of seeking revenge against an employee indirectly through adverse actions against a third party who is connected to the individual; typically, a friend or relative working within the same organization.

Trammel To unfairly impede, limit, or restrict.

Typicality Claims of the plaintiff(s) are representative of those of the class parties.

Ultimate employment standard To qualify as materially adverse, the organization's action must result in an ultimate, tangible *negative employment decision* (e.g., being terminated or demoted).

Undue hardship An accommodation that is overly demanding or costly for a given organization (i.e., creates a disproportionate or unreasonable burden or obstacle) when considering its resources, size, and nature of the business. Can partially or fully exempt an organization from providing the accommodation.

Vicarious liability Cases where organizations are responsible for the behavior of their supervisors or "agents" of the company.

Writ of certiorari A request for the Supreme Court to review the decisions of lower courts.

Glossary terms adapted from Bronfenbrenner (1977), Cohen & Aamodt (2010), Gutman et al. (2011), https://uslegal.com/; https://www.mtsu.edu/first-amendment/encyclope dia; merriamwebster.com/legal; and Mueller, Dunleavy, & Buonasera (2008).

Cases Cited

Abbott v. Bragdon, 163 F. 3d 87 (1st Cir. 1998).

Abnet v. UNIFAB Corporation (W.D. Mich. 2006).

Adarand v. Pena, 151 U.S. 200 (1995).

Albermarle Paper Company. v. Moody, 422 U.S. 405 (1975).

Albertson's, Inc. v. Kirkingburg, 527 U.S. 555 (1999).

Alexander v. Chattahoochee Valley Community College, 345 F. Supp. 2d 1306 (M.D. Ala. 2004).

Ali v. District of Columbia Government, 810 F. Supp. 2d 78 (D.C.Cir. 2011).

Alicea-Hernandez v. Catholic Bishop of Chicago, 320 F. 3d 698 (7th Cir. 2003).

Alvarez v. Royal Atlantic Developers, Inc., 610 F. 3d 1253 (11th Cir., 2010).

American Federation etc. (AFSCME) v. State of Washington, 770 F.2d 1401 (9th Cir. 1985).

Andujar v. General Nutrition Corporation (3rd Cir. 2019).

Ansonia Board of Education v. Philbrook, U.S. 41 EPD q 36,565 (1986).

Antonelli v. Sapa Extrusions, Inc. (MD Pa, 2015).

Apsley v. Boeing, 691 F.3d 1184 (10th Cir. 2012).

Automobile Workers v. Johnson Controls, Inc., 499 U.S. 187 (1991).

Babb v. Wilkie, 140 S. Ct. 1168 (2020).

Barber v. CSX Distribution Services, 68 F.3d 694 (1995).

Barker v. Taft Broadcasting Co., 549 F.2d 400 (6th Cir. 1977).

Barnett v. PA Consulting Group, Inc., 715 F. 3d 354 (D.C. Cir. 2013).

Bennis v. Minnesota Hockey Group (D. Minn. 2013).

Benson v. Tocco, Incorporated, 113 F. 3d 1203 (11th Cir. 1997).

Bew v. City of Chicago, 252 F.3d 891 (7th Cir. 2001).

Bibby v. Philadelphia Coca-Cola Bottling Co., 260 F.3d 257, 260-61 (3rd Cir. 2001).

Bostock v. Clayton County Board of Commissioners, 894 F.3d 1335 (11th Cir. 2018).

Bostock v. Clayton County, Georgia, 140 S. Ct. 1731, 1739 (2020).

Bragdon v. Abbott, 524 U.S. 624 (1998).

Brennan v. City Stores, Inc., 479 F.2d 235 (5th Cir. 1973).

Brennan v. Goose Creek Consolidated Independent School District, 519 F.2d 53 (5th Cir. 1975).

Bridgeport Guardians, Inc. v. City of Bridgeport, 933 F.2d 1140, 1149 (2nd Cir. 1991).

Brown v. CSC Logic, Inc., 82 F. 3d 651 (5th Cir. 1996).

Buhrmaster v. Overnite Transportation Co., 61 F. 3d 461 (6th Cir. 1995).

Burlington Industries v. Ellerth, 524 U.S. 742 (1998).

Burlington Northern Santa Fe Railway Company v. White, 548 U.S. 53 (2006).

Burwell v. Hobby Lobby Stores, Inc., 134 S. Ct. 2751 (2014).

California Federal Savings and Loan Association v. Guerra, 479 U.S. 272 (1987).

Carras v. MGS, 782 Lex, Inc., 310 Fed. Appx. 421 (2d Cir. 2008).

Carroll v. Talman Federal Savings & Loan Association of Chicago, 604 F. 2d 1028 (7th Cir. 1979).

Carter v. Gallagher, 452 F. 2d 315 (8th Cir. 1971).

Castello v. Donahue, EEOC DOC 0520110649, 2011 WL 6960810 (2011).

Chevron USA Incorporated v. Echazabal, 536 U.S. 73 (2002).

Cifra v. Gen. Electric Co., 252 F.3d 205 (2nd Cir 2001).

City of Boerne v. Flores, 521 U.S. 507 (1997).

City of Richmond v. Croson, 488 U.S. 469 (1989).

Clark County School Dist. V. Breeden, 532 U.S. 268 (2001).

Glover v. South Carolina Law Enforcement Division, 170 F.3d 411 (4th Cir. 1999).

Gorman-Bakos v. Cornell Coop of Schenectady County, 252 F.3d 545 (2d Cir. 2001).

Gratz v. Bollinger, 539 U.S. 244 (2003).

Greathouse v. JHS Security Inc., 784 F. 3d 105 (2d Cir. 2015).

Green v. Missouri Pacific Railroad Company, 523 F.2nd 1290 (8th Cir. 1975).

Griggs v. Duke Power Co., 401 U.S. 424 (1971).

Grosjean v. First Energy, 349 F.3d 332 (6th Cir. 2004).

Gross v. FBL Financial Services, 588 F.3d 614 (2009).

Grutter v. Bollinger, 539 U.S. 306 (2003).

Guzman v. Brown County, 884 F.3d 633, 641 (7th Cir. 2018).

Harper v. Blockbuster Entertainment Corporation, 139 F.3d 1385 (11th Cir. 1998).

Harrington v. Career Training Institute Orlando, Inc. (M.D. Fla., 2011).

Harris v. Forklift Sys. Inc., 510 U.S. 17 (1993).

Hayden v. Nassau County, 180 F.3d 42 (2nd Cir. 1999).

Hazelwood School District v. United States, 433 U.S. 299 (1977).

Hazen v. Biggens, 507 U.S. 604 (1993).

Healy v. New York Life Insurance Company, 860 F.2d 1209 (1988).

Hillig v. Rumsfeld, 381 F.3d 1028 (10th Cir. 2004).

Hively v. Ivy Tech Community College, South Bend, 830 F.3d 698 (7th Cir. 2016).

Hochstadt v. Worcester Foundation for Experimental Biology, Inc., 545 F.2d 222 (1st Cir. 1976).

Hodgson v. Brookhaven General Hospital, 423 F.2d 719; 470 F.2d 729 (5th Cir. 1970).

Hodgson v. Greyhound Lines, 499 F.2d 859 (7th Cir. 1974).

Hogancamp v. County of Volusia, 316 F. Supp. 3d 1354 (M. D. Fla. 2018).

Holava-Brown v. General Electric Company, 189 F.3d 461 (2nd Cir. 1999).

Holman v. Indiana, 211 F.3d 399 (7th Cir. 2000).

Holt v. JTM Industries Inc., 89 F.3d 1224 (5th Cir. 1996).

Hosanna-Tabor Evangelical v. EEOC, 565 U.S. 171 (2012).

Houk v. Peoploungers, Inc., 214 F. App'x 379, 381 (5th Cir. 2007).

Hudson v. Norris, 227 F. 3d 1047 (8th Cir. 2000).

Hughes v. Derwinski, 967 F. 2d 1168 (7th Cir. 1992).

International Brotherhood of Teamsters v. United States, 431 U.S. 324 (1977).

Isabel v. City of Memphis, 404 F. 3d 404 (6th Cir. 2005).

Jensen v. Potter, 435 F. 3d 444 (3rd Cir. 2006).

Jespersen v. Harrah's Operating Co., 280 F. Supp. 2d 1189 (D. Nev. 2002).

Johnson v. Transportation Agency, 480 U.S. 616 (1987).

Jones v. City of Boston, 752 F.3d 38, 60 (1st Cir. 2014).

Karlo v. Pittsburgh Glass Works, LLC, 849 F. 3d 61 (3rd Cir. 2017).

Karraker v. Rent-A-Center, Incorporated, 411 F. 3d 831 (7th Cir. 2005).

Kasten v. Saint-Gobain Performance Plastics Corp., 563 U.S. 1 (2011).

Kentucky Retirement Systems v. EEOC, 128 S. Ct. 2361 (2008).

Kessler v. Westchester City Department of Social Services, 461 F.3d 199 (2nd Cir. 2006).

Kimel v. Florida Board of Regents, 528 U.S. 62 (2000).

Kirkland v. New York St. Dept. of Correctional Services, 374 F.Supp. 1361 (S.D.N.Y. 1974).

Kouba v. Allstate, 691 F.2d 873 (9th Cir. 1982).

Kowitz v. Trinity Health, 839 F.3d 742, 33 A.D. Cases 1 (2016).

Laffey v. Northwest Airlines, Inc., 740 F.2d 1071 (D.C. Cir. 1984).

Laffey v. Northwest Airlines, Inc., 366 F. Supp. 763 (D.D.C. 1973).

Laffey v. Northwest Airlines, Inc., 567 F.2d 429 (D.C. Cir. 1976).

Lanigan v. Bartlett and Company Grain, 466 F. Supp. 1388 (W.D. Mo. 1979).

LeBoon v. Lancaster Jewish Community Center Association, 503 F. 3d 217 (3d Cir. 2007).

Ledbetter v. Goodyear Tire & Rubber Co., Inc., 550 U.S. 618 (2007).

Rafael Ortiz v. DMD Florida Restaurant Group, Southern District of Florida, Case number 0:16-cv-61375. (2016).

Rand v. CF Industries, Inc., 42 F. 3d 1139 (7th Cir. 1994).

Reeves v. Sanderson Plumbing Products, Inc., 530 U.S. 133 (2000).

Regents of University of California v. Bakke, 438 U.S. 265 (1978).

Ricci v. DeStefano, 129 S. Ct. 2658 (2009).

Richmond v. Oneok Inc. 120 F. 3rd 205 (10th Cir. 1997).

Risley v. Fordham University, 99 CIV. 9304 (DLC) (S.D.N.Y. Feb. 13, 2001).

Rizo v. Yovino, 887 F.3d 453 (9th Cir. 2018).

Roberts v. Roadway Express, Inc., 149 F.3d 1098 (10th Cir. 1998).

Robinson v. Jackson State University, 714 Fed.App'x, 354 (5th Cir. 2017).

Robinson v. Shell Oil, 519 U.S. 337 (1997).

Rosser v. Laborers' International Union of North America, 616 F. 2d 221 (5th Cir. 1980).

Salley v. Circuit City Stores, Inc., 160 F. 3d 977 (3rd Cir. 1998).

School Board of Nassau County v. Arline, 480 U.S. 273 (1987).

Schuette v. Coalition to Defend Affirmative Action, 572 U.S. 291 (2013).

Schultz v. American Can Co., 424 F.2d 356 (8th Cir. 1970).

Shepherd v. Slater Steels Corporation, 168 F.3d 998, (7th Cir. 1999).

Sherbert v. Verner, 374 U.S. 398 (1963).

Singh v. Green Thumb Landscaping, Inc., 390 F. Supp. 2d 1129 (M.D. Fla. 2005).

Smith v. City of Jackson, 544 U.S. 228 (2005).

Smith v. City of Salem, Ohio, 378 F.3d 566 (6th Cir. 2004).

Smith v. Riceland Foods, Inc., 151 F. 3d 813 (8th Cir. 1998).

Smith v. Tennessee Valley Authority, 948 F.2d 1290 (1991).

Snyder v. Pierre's French Ice Cream Co., 589 Fed. Appx. 767, 771 (6th Cir. 2014).

Spaulding v. University of Washington, 740 F.2d 686, 692 (9th Cir. 1984).

Spearman v. Ford Motor Company, 231 F.3d 1080, (7th Cir. 2000).

Steiner v. Showboat Operating Co., 25 F.3d 1459, 1463 (9th Cir. 1994).

Sterner v. County of Banks, Civil Action No. 13-1568 (E.D. Pa. Mar. 28, 2014).

St. Mary's Honor Center v. Hicks, 509 U.S. 502 (1993).

Starkman v. Evans, 198 F. 3d 173 (5th Cir. 1999).

State of Washington v. Arlene's Flowers, Inc., 389 P. 3d 543 (Wash: Supreme Court 2017).

State v. Arlene's Flowers, Inc., 441 P. 3d 1203 (Wash: Supreme Court 2019).

Strickland v. Water Works and Sewer Board of the City of Birmingham, 239 F.3d 1199 (11th Cir. 2001).

Summers v. Altarum Institute, Corporation, 740 F. 3d 325 (4th Cir. 2014).

Sutton v. United Air Lines, Incorporated, 527 U.S. 471 (1999).

Tavora v. New York Mercantile Exchange, 101 F.3rd 907 (2nd Cir. 1996).

International Brotherhood of Teamsters vs. United States, 431 U.S. 324 (1977).

Teamsters Local Union No. 117 v. Washington Department of Corrections, 789, F.3rd, 979 (9th Cir., 2015).

Texas Dept. of Community Affairs v. Burdine, 450 U.S. 248 (1981).

Thompson v. North American Stainless, LP 562 U.S. 170 (2011).

Thompson v. Sawyer, 678 F.2d 257, 264 (D.C. Cir. 1982).

Tomassi v. Insignia Financial Group Inc., 478 F.3d 111, 115-16 (2d Cir. 2007).

Toyota Motor Manufacturing, Ky., Inc. v. Williams, 534 U.S. 184 (2002).

Trans World Airlines, Inc. v. Hardison, 432 U.S. 63 (1977).

Trans World Airlines, Incorporated v. Hardison, 432 U.S. 63 (1977).

United States v. Paradise, 480 U.S. 149 (1987).

United Steelworkers. v. Weber, 443 U.S. 193 (1979).

University of Texas Southwestern Medical Center v. Nassar, 570 U.S. 338 (2013).

US Airways, Inc. v. Barnett, 535 U.S. 391 (2002).
Usery v. Tamiami Trail Tours Incorporated, 531 F.2d 224 (5th Cir. 1976).
Vance v. Ball State University, 570 U.S. 421 (2013).
Villarreal v. RJ Reynolds Tobacco Co., 839 F. 3d 958 (11th Cir. 2016).
Waldron v. SL Industries, Inc., 56 F. 3d 491(3d Cir. 1995).
Walker v. Johnson, 798 F.3d 1085 (D.C. Cir. 2015).
Wal-Mart v. Dukes, 564 U.S. 338, 350 (2011).
Wards Cove Packing Co. v. Atonio, 490 U.S. 642 (1989).
Washington v. Illinois Dept. of Revenue, 420 F. 3d 658 (7th Cir. 2005).
Waters v. Logistics Management Institute, 716 F. App'x 194, 197 (4th Cir. 2018).
Western Airlines v. Criswell, 472 U.S. 400 (1985).
Wexler v. White's Fine Furniture, Inc., 317 F.3d 564 (2003).
Williams v. General Motors Corporation, 656 F.2d 120 (1981).
Williams v. Vitro Services Corp., 144 F. 3d 1438 (11th Cir. 1999).
Wilson v. Chertoff, 699 F.Supp.2d 364 (D. Mass. 2010).
Wisconsin v. Yoder, 406 U.S. 205 (1972).
Woodson v. Scott Paper, Co., 109 F.3d 913 (3rd Cir. 1997).
Worden v. Interbake Foods LLC (D. SD 2012).
Wygant v. Jackson Board of Education, 476 US 267 (1986).
Wysong v. Dow Chemical Company, 503 F. 3d 441 (6th Cir. 2007).
Yates v. Avco Corporation, 819 F. 2d 630 (6th Cir. 1987).
Young v. United Parcel Service, 135 U.S. 338 (2015).
Zarda v. Altitude Express, Inc., 883 F. 3d 100 (2nd Cir. 2018).

References

Aamodt, M. (2017). Really, I come here for the food: Sex as a BFOQ for restaurant servers. *The Industrial-Organizational Psychologist*, *54*(3). https://www.siop.org/Research-Publications/TIP/TIP-Back-Issues/2017/January/ArtMID/20301/ArticleID/1624/Really-I-Come-Here-for-The-Food-Sex-as-a-BFOQ-for-Restaurant-Servers

Agan, A., & Starr, S. (2018). Ban the box, criminal records, and racial discrimination: A field experiment. *The Quarterly Journal of Economics*, *133*(1), 191–235.

Alliger (Eds.), Handbook of work analysis *Methods, systems, applications and science of work measurement in organizations* (pp. 139–168). New York: Routledge, Taylor & Francis Group.

Anderson, C. L. (2002). Neutral employer policies and the ADA: The implications of *US Airways, Inc. v. Barnett* beyond seniority systems. *Drake Law Review*, *51*, 1–43.

Antecol, H., & Cobb-Clark, D. (2003). Does sexual harassment training change attitudes? A view from the federal level. *Social Science Quarterly*, *84*, 826–842.

Avery, D. R., & McKay, P. F. (2006). Target practice: An organizational impression management approach to attracting minority and female job applicants. *Personnel Psychology*, *59*, 157–187.

Avery, D. R., & McKay, P. F., & Volpone, S. D. (2013). Diversity staffing: Inclusive personnel recruitment and selection practices. In Q. Roberson (Ed.), *The Oxford handbook of diversity and work* (pp. 282–299). New York: Oxford University Press.

Avery, D. R., Hernandez, M., & Hebl, M. R. (2004). Who's watching the race? Racial salience in recruitment advertising. *Journal of Applied Social Psychology*, *34*, 146–161.

Baker, S. C. W. (2005). A choice of rules in Title VII retaliation claims for negative employer references. *Duke Law Review*, *55*, 153–178.

Barkacs, L. L., & Barkacs, C. B. (2009). The time is right—or is it? The Supreme Court speaks in *Ledbetter v. Goodyear Tire & Rubber Co. Journal of Legal, Ethical and Regulatory Issues*, *12*, 1–7.

Bartlett, K. T. (1994). Only girls wear barrettes: Dress and appearance standards, community norms, and workplace equality. *Michigan Law Review*, *92*, 2541–2582.

Beckles, T. M. (2008). Class of one: Are employment discrimination plaintiffs at an insurmountable disadvantage if they have no "similarly situated" comparators? *University of Pennsylvania Journal of Business and Employment Law*, *10*, 459–82.

Becton, J. B., Gilstrap, J. B., & Forsyth, M. (2017). Preventing and correcting workplace harassment: Guidelines for employers. *Business Horizons*, *60*, 101–111.

Bernerth, J. B. (2012). Demographic variables and credit scores: An empirical study of a controversial selection tool. *International Journal of Selection and Assessment*, *20*, 242–246.

Bernerth, J. B., Taylor, S. G., Walker, H. J., & Whitman, D. S. (2012). An empirical investigation of dispositional antecedents and performance-related outcomes of credit scores. *Journal of Applied Psychology*, *97*, 469–478.

Berry, L. M. (2003). *Employee selection*. Belmont, CA: Wadsworth.

Bertrand, M., & Mullainathan, S. (2004). Are Emily and Greg more employable than Lakisha and Jamal? A field experiment on labor market discrimination. *American Economic Review*, *94*, 991–1013.

Beschle, D. L. (2018). Are two clauses really better than one: Rethinking the religion clause(s). *University of Pittsburgh Law Review*, *80*(1), 1–32.

Bezrukova, K., Jehn, K. A., & Spell, C. S. (2012). Reviewing diversity training: Where we have been and where we should go. *Academy of Management Learning & Education, 11*, 207–227.

Bible, J. (2007). *Ledbetter v. Goodyear Tire & Rubber Co.*: Supreme Court places roadblock in front of title VII pay discrimination plaintiffs. *Labor Law Journal, 58*, 170–182.

Blackhurst, E., Congemi, P., Meyer, J., & Sachau, D. (2011). Should You Hire BlazinWeedClown@ Mail. Com?. *TIP: The Industrial-Organizational Psychologist, 49*(2), 27–37. https://cornerstone.lib.mnsu.edu/cgi/viewcontent.cgi?article=1185&context=psyc_fac_pubs

Blanck, P. D. (2000). Studying disability, employment policy, and ADA. In L. P. Francis & A. Silvers (Eds.), *Americans with disabilities: Exploring implications of the law for individuals and institutions* (pp. 209–220). New York: Routledge.

Blumenthal, J. A. (1998). The reasonable woman standard: A meta-analytic review of gender differences in perceptions of sexual harassment. *Law and Human Behavior, 22*, 33–57.

Board of Governors of the Federal Reserve System. (2007). *Report to the Congress on credit scoring and its effects on the availability and affordability of credit*. Washington, DC: US Federal Reserve. Retrieved from: https://www.federalreserve.gov/boarddocs/rptcongress/creditscore/creditscore.pdf

Bobko, P., Roth, P. L., & Potosky, D. (1999). Derivation and implications of a meta-analytic matrix incorporating cognitive ability, alternative predictors, and job performance. *Personnel Psychology, 52*, 561–589.

Brake, D. L. (2014). Retaliation in the EEO office. *Tulsa Law Review, 50*(1), 1–42.

Bronfenbrenner, U. (1977). Toward an experimental ecology of human development. *American Psychologist, 32*, 513–531.

Bryan, L. K., & Palmer, J. K. (2012). Do job applicant credit histories predict performance appraisal ratings or termination decisions? *The Psychologist-Manager Journal, 15*, 106–127.

Bureau of Labor Statistics. Persons with a disability: Labor force characteristics summary. Retrieved on April 20, 2020, from https://www.bls.gov/news.release/disabl.nr0.htm

Burgess, D., & Borgida, E. (1997). Sexual harassment: An experimental test of sex-role spillover theory. *Personality and Social Psychology Bulletin 23*, 63–75.

Campbell, D. T., & Stanley, J. C. (1966). *Experimental and quasi-experimental designs for research*. Chicago: Rand McNally.

Campion, M. A., Outtz, J. L., Zedeck, S., Schmidt, F. L., Kehoe, J. F., Murphy, K. R., & Guion, R. M. (2001). The controversy over score banding in personnel selection: Answers to 10 key questions. *Personnel Psychology, 54*, 149–185.

Cascio, W. F., Outtz, J., Zedeck, S., & Goldstein, I. L. (1991). Statistical implications of six methods of test score use in personnel selection. *Human Performance, 4*, 233–264.

Cascio, W. F., Outtz, J., Zedeck, S., & Goldstein, I. L. (1995). Selected science or selective interpretation? *American Psychologist, 50*, 881–882.

Cavico, F. J., & Mujaba, B. G. (2011). Managers be warned: Third-party retaliation lawsuits and the United States Supreme Court. *Contemporary Issues in Business and Economics, 2*, 8–17.

Cimpl-Wiemer, A. (2008). *Ledbetter v. Goodyear*: Letting the air out of the continuing violations doctrine? *Marquette Law Review, 92*(2), 355–382.

Claussen, C. L. (1996). Gendered merit: Women and the merit concept in federal employment, 1864–1944. *The American Journal of Legal History, 40*, 229–252.

Coady, R. P. (1986). An analysis of state library job application forms for compliance with EEOC Guidelines. *Journal of Library Administration, 7*(1), 49–55.

Cohen, D. B., & Aamodt, M. G. (2010). *Technical advisory committee report on best practices in adverse impact analyses*. Washington, DC: Center for Corporate Equality.

Colker, R. (2005). *The disability pendulum: The first decade of the Americans with Disabilities Act*. New York: New York University Press.

Cook, T. D., & Campbell, D. T. (1979). *Quasi-experimentation: Design & analysis for field studies*. Boston: Houghton Mifflin.

Coon, L. L. (2001). Employment discrimination by religious institutions: Limiting the sanctuary of the constitutional ministerial exception to religion-based employment decisions. *Vanderbilt Law Review, 54*, 481–546.

Cooper, E. A., & Barrett, G. A. (1984). Equal pay and gender: Implications of court cases for personnel practices. *Academy of Management Journal, 9*, 84–94.

Copeland, R. W., & Schmake, M. (2016). Protected classes, credit histories and criminal background checks: A new twist to old-fashioned disparate impact cases? *Journal of Business and Behavioral Sciences, 28*, 129–144.

Copus, D., Ugelow, R. S., & Sohn, J. (2005). A lawyer's view. In F. J. Landy (Ed.), *Employment discrimination litigation: Behavioral, quantitative, and legal perspectives.* (pp. 450–502). San Francisco: Jossey-Bass.

Cortina, L. M., & Magley, V. J. (2003). Raising voice, risking retaliation: Events following interpersonal mistreatment in the workplace. *Journal of Occupational Health Psychology, 8*, 247–255.

Courtright, S. H., McCormick, B. W., Postlethwaite, B. E., Reeves, C. J., & Mount, M. K. (2013). A meta-analysis of sex differences in physical ability: Revised estimates and strategies for reducing differences in selection contexts. *Journal of Applied Psychology, 98*, 623–641.

Crampton, S. M., Hodge, J. W., & Mishra, J. M. (1997). The Equal Pay Act: The first 30 years. *Public Personnel Management, 26*, 335–344.

Creswell, J. W., & Creswell, J. D. (2018). *Research design: Qualitative, quantitative, and mixed methods approaches.* Thousand Oaks, CA: Sage Publications.

Crosby, F. J., Iyer, A., Clayton, S., & Downing, R. A. (2003). Affirmative action: Psychological data and the policy debates. *American Psychologist, 58*(2), 93–115.

De Corte, W., Lievens, F., & Sackett, P. R. (2007). Combining predictors to achieve optimal trade-offs between selection quality and adverse impact. *Journal of Applied Psychology, 92*, 1380–1393.

De Corte, W., Lievens, F., & Sackett, P. R. (2008). Validity and adverse impact potential of predictor composite formation. *International Journal of Selection and Assessment, 16*, 183–194.

Dee, T. J. (1991). Plaintiffs cannot establish a prima facie case of age discrimination by showing disparate impact within the protected group. Lowe v. Commack Union Free School Dist., 886 F.2d 1364 (2d Cir. 1989). *Washington University Law Quarterly, 69*(1), 337–348.

Dofner, E. K. (2016). The Supreme Court acknowledges Title VII's relaxed standard in favor of plaintiffs: *Equal Employment Opportunity Commission (EEOC) v. Abercrombie & Fitch Stores, Inc. Duquesne Business Law Journal, 18*, 81–102.

Doleac, J. L., & Hansen, B. (2016). Does "ban the box" help or hurt low-skilled workers? Statistical discrimination and employment outcomes when criminal histories are hidden. (NBER Working Paper No. 22469). Cambridge, MA: National Bureau of Economic Research.

Doverspike, D., Taylor, M. A., Shultz, K. S., & McKay, P. F. (2000). Responding to the challenge of a changing workforce: Recruiting nontraditional demographic groups. *Public Personnel Management, 29*, 445–457.

Drogan, O., & Yancey, G. B. (2011). Financial utility of best employee selection practices at organizational level of performance. *The Psychologist-Manager Journal, 14*(1), 52–69.

Dunleavy, E. M. (2007). What is all the fuss about: The implications of the EEOC Deterrence Standard after *BNSF v. White. The Industrial-Organizational Psychologist, 44*, 31–39.

Dunleavy, E. M. (2010). A consideration of practical significance in adverse impact analysis. *Washington, DC: DCI Consulting Group, July.*

Dunleavy, E. M., & Gutman, A. (2008). *Ledbetter v. Goodyear Tire Co.:* A divided Supreme Court causes quite a stir. *The Industrial-Organizational Psychologist, 45*, 55–63.

Dunleavy, E. M., & Gutman, A. (2009). What's new in compensation discrimination enforcement: A review of the Ledbetter Fair Pay Act and Paycheck Fairness Act. *The Industrial-Organizational Psychologist, 47*, 49–57.

Dunleavy, E. M., & Gutman, A. (2010). On the Legal Front: OFCCP settlement review: What was the burden on Bank of America? *The Industrial-Organizational Psychologist,48*(1), 73–80.

Dunleavy, E. M., & Gutman, A. (2010). OFCCP settlement review: What was the burden on Bank of America? *The Industrial-Organizational Psychologist, 48*, 73–80.

Dunleavy, E. M., & Gutman, A. (2011). An update on the statistical versus practical significance debate: A review of *Stagi v. Amtrak* (2010). *The Industrial-Organizational Psychologist, 48*, 121–130.

Dyer, R. W. (2011). Qualifying for the Title VII religious organization exemption: Federal circuits split over proper test. *Missouri Law Review, 76*. 545–573.

Employment Law—Title VII—EEOC Affirms Protections for Transgender Employees—Macy v. Holder. (2013). *Harvard Law Review, 126*, 1731–1738.

Equal Employment Opportunity Commission. (2017). *Policy guidance documents related to sexual harassment*. Retrieved from https://www.eeoc.gov/laws/types/sexual_harassment_guidance.cfm

Essary, M. A., & Friedman, T. D. (1998). Retaliation claims under Title VII, the ADEA, and the ADA: Untouchable employees, uncertain employers, unresolved courts. *Missouri Law Review, 63*, 115–153.

Fallon, R. (2017). Tiers for the establishment clause. *University of Pennsylvania Law Review, 166*(1), 59–128.

Feldblum, C. (1991). Medical examinations and inquiries under the Americans with Disabilities Act: A view from the inside. *Temple Law Review, 64*, 521–550.

Fibbi, R., Lerch, M., & Wanner, P. (2006). Unemployment and discrimination against youth of immigrant origin in Switzerland: When the name makes the difference. *Journal of International Migration and Integration, 7*, 351–366.

Finch, D. M., Edwards, B. D., & Wallace, J. C. (2009). Multistage selection strategies: Simulating the effects on adverse impact and expected performance for various predictor combinations. *Journal of Applied Psychology, 94*, 318–340.

Findley, H., Fretwell, C., Wheatley, R., & Ingram, E. (2006). Dress and grooming standards: How legal are they? *Journal of Individual Employment Rights, 12*, 165–182.

Fink, J. K. (2012). Protected by association? The Supreme Court's incomplete approach to defining the scope of the third-party retaliation doctrine. *Hastings Law Journal, 63*, 521–566.

Finkelstein, L. M., Burke, M. J., & Raju, N. S. (1995). Age discrimination in simulated employment contexts: An integrative analysis. *Journal of Applied Psychology, 80*, 652–663.

Finkelstein, L. M., Ryan, K. M., & King, E. B. (2013). What do the young (old) people think of me? Content and accuracy of age-based metastereotypes. *European Journal of Work and Organizational Psychology, 22*, 633–657.

Fitzgerald, L. F., Swan, S. C., & Fischer, K. (1995). Why didn't she just report him? The psychological and legal implications of women's responses to sexual harassment. *Journal of Social Issues, 51*, 117–138.

Flake, D. F. (2019). Interactive religious accommodations. *Alabama Law Review, 71*(1), 67–114.

Freeman, J. (1991). How sex got into Title VII: Persistent opportunism as a maker of public policy. *Law & Inequality: A Journal of Theory and Practice, 9*, 163–184.

Garrow, D. J. (2014). Toward a definitive history of *Griggs v. Duke Power Co. Vanderbilt University Law Review, 67*(1), 197–237.

Gasperson, S. M., Bowler, M. C., Wuensch, K. L., & Bowler, J. L. (2013). A statistical correction to 20 years of banding. *International Journal of Selection and Assessment, 21*(1), 46–56.

Gevertz, D. E., & Dowell, A. C. (2014 March). Are English-only policies in the workplace discriminatory of national origin? American Bar Association. https://www.americanbar.org/groups/litigation/committees/civil-rights/articles/2014/are-english-only-policies-in-the-workplace-discriminatory-of-national-origin/

Ghumman, S., Ryan, A. M., Barclay, L. A., & Markel, K. S. (2013). Religious discrimination in the workplace: A review and examination of current and future trends. *Journal of Business and Psychology*, *28*(4), 439–454.

Gold, M. E. (1980). A tale of two amendments: The reasons congress added sex to Title VII and their implication for the issue of comparable worth. *Duquesne Law Review*, *19*, 453–477.

Goldberg, L. R. (1992). The development of markers for the Big-Five factor structure. *Psychological Assessment*, *4*(1), 26–42.

Goldman, R. B. (2007). Putting pretext in context: Employment discrimination, the same-actor inference, and the proper roles of judges and juries. *Virginia Law Review*, *93*, 1533–1571.

Graham, K. M., McMahon, B. T., Kim, J. H., Simpson, P., & McMahon, M. C. (2019). Patterns of workplace discrimination across broad categories of disability. *Rehabilitation Psychology*, *64*, 194–202. http://dx.doi.org/10.1037/rep0000227

Greenawalt, K. (1995). Quo Vadis: The status and prospects of tests under the Religion Clauses. *Supreme Court Review*, *8*, 323–392.

Grossman, J. L. (2009). Pregnancy, work, and the promise of equal citizenship. *Georgetown Law Journal*, *98*, 567–628.

Grossman, J. L. (2016). Expanding the core: Pregnancy discrimination law as it approaches full term. *Idaho Law Review*, *52*, 825–866.

Grossman, J. L., & Brake, D. L. (2013). Revenge: The Supreme Court narrows protection against workplace retaliation in *University of Texas Southwestern Medical Center v. Nassar* verdict. Retrieved November 27, 2019, from https://scholarlycommons.law.hofstra.edu/faculty_scholarship/977/

Guerin, L., & England, D. D. (2018). *The essential guide to family & medical leave.* Berkeley, CA: Nolo.

Guion, R. M. (1998). *Assessment, measurement, and prediction for personnel decisions.* Mahwah: NJ: Erlbaum.

Gutek, B. A. (1995). How subjective is sexual harassment? An examination of rater effects. *Basic and Applied Social Psychology*, *17*(4), 447–467.

Gutek, B. A., & O'Connor, M. (1995). The empirical basis for the reasonable woman standard. *Journal of Social Issues*, *51*(1), 151–166.

Gutek, B. A., & Stockdale, M. S. (2005). In F. Landy (Ed.), *Employment discrimination litigation: Behavioral, quantitative, and legal perspectives.* (pp. 229–254). San Francisco: Jossey-Bass.

Gutman, A. (2002). Two January 2002 Supreme Court Rulings: *Toyota v. Williams & EEOC v. Waffle House. The Industrial-Organizational Psychologist*, *39*, 58–64.

Gutman, A. (2003). Adverse impact: Why is it so difficult to understand? *The Industrial-Organizational Psychologist*, *40*, 42–50.

Gutman, A. (2004). Ground rules for adverse impact. *The Industrial-Organizational Psychologist*, *41*, 109–119.

Gutman, A. (2004). On the legal front: *Grutter* goes to work: The 7th Circuit Court's ruling in *Petit v. City of Chicago* (2003). *The Industrial-Organizational Psychologist*, *41*(4), 71–77.

Gutman, A. (2005). Smith v. City of Jackson: Adverse impact in the ADEA—Well sort of. *The Industrial-Organizational Psychologist*, *43*(1), 79–87.

Gutman, A. (2005). Unresolved issues in same-sex harassment. *The Industrial-Organizational Psychologist*, *42*, 67–75.

Gutman, A. (2007). *BNSF v. White*: Early returns. *The Industrial-Organizational Psychologist*, *44*, 97–110.

Gutman, A. (2009). Major EEO issues relating to personnel selection decisions. *Human Resource Management Review*, *19*, 232–250.

Gutman, A. (2015). Disabilities: Best practices for vulnerabilities associated with the ADA. In C. Hanvey & K. Sady (Eds.), *Practitioner's guide to legal issues in organizations* (pp. 111–126). Cham: Springer International Publishing.

Gutman, A., & Dunleavy, E. (2007). The Supreme Court ruling in *Parents v. Seattle School District*: Sending *Grutter* and *Gratz* back to school. *The Industrial-Organizational Psychologist, 45*, 41–48.

Gutman, A., & Dunleavy, E. (2009). The Supreme Court Ruling in *Ricci v. DeStefano. The Industrial-Organizational Psychologist, 47*, 57–71.

Gutman, A., & Dunleavy, E. (2011). A review of the Supreme Court ruling *Wal-Mart v. Dukes*: Too big to succeed? *The Industrial-Organizational Psychologist, 49*(2), 75–80.

Gutman, A., & Dunleavy, E. (2012). Documenting work analysis projects: A review of strategy and legal defensibility for personnel selection. In M. A. Wilson, W. Bennett Jr., S. G. Gibson, & G. M. Alliger (Eds.), *The handbook of work analysis: Methods, systems, applications and science of work measurement in organizations* (pp. 139–168). New York: Routledge/Taylor and Francis.

Gutman, A., Koppes, L. L., & Vodanovich, S. J. (2011). *EEO law and personnel practices* (3rd ed.). New York: Psychology Press/Routledge/Taylor & Francis Group.

Gutman, A., Outtz, J. L., & Dunleavy, E. (2017). An updated sampler of legal principles in employment selection. In J. L. Farr & N. T. Tippins (Eds.), *Handbook of employee selection* (pp. 631–658). New York: Routledge, Taylor & Francis Group.

Hamburg, J. (1989). When prior pay isn't equal pay: A proposed standard for the identification of "factors other than sex" under the Equal Pay Act. *Columbia Law Review, 89*, 1085–1110.

Harper, M. C. (2010). The causation standard in federal employment law: *Gross v. FBL Financial Services, Inc.*, and the unfilled promise of the Civil Rights Act of 1991. *Buffalo Law Review, 58*, 69–145.

Hart, M. (2004). Will employment discrimination class actions survive? *Akron Law Review, 37*, 813–846.

Hartman, G. S., & Homer, G. W. (1990). *Personnel law handbook*. Winston-Salem, NC: University of Wake Forest Law School.

Hattrup, K., Rock, J., & Scalia, C. (1997). The effects of varying conceptualizations of job performance on adverse impact, minority hiring, and predicted performance. *Journal of Applied Psychology, 82*, 656–664.

Hegerich, R. M. (2010). Employment law: Title VII does not extend to third-party retaliation claim by fiancée of discrimination claimant. *Suffolk University Law Review, 43*, 1059–1069.

Heilman, M. E., Battle, W. S., Keller, C. E., & Lee, R. A. (1998). Type of affirmative action policy: A determinant of reactions to sex-based preferential selection? *Journal of Applied Psychology, 83*, 190–205.

Heilman, M. E., Block, C. J., & Lucas, J. A. (1992). Presumed incompetent? Stigmatization and affirmative action efforts. *Journal of Applied Psychology, 77*, 536–544.

Heilman, M. E., Block, C. J., & Stathatos, P. (1997). The affirmative action stigma of incompetence: Effects of performance information ambiguity. *Academy of Management Journal, 40*(3), 603–625.

Heilman, M. E., McCullough, W. F., & Gilbert, D. (1996). The other side of affirmative action: Reactions of nonbeneficiaries to sex-based preferential selection. *Journal of Applied Psychology, 81*, 346–357.

Heilman, M. E., Rivero, J. C., & Brett, J. F. (1991). Skirting the competency issue: Effects of sex-based preferential selection on task choices of men and women. *Journal of Applied Psychology, 76*, 99–105.

Heilman, M. E., Simon, M. C., & Repper, D. P. (1987). Intentionally favored, unintentionally harmed? Impact of sex-based preferential selection on self-perceptions and self-evaluations. *Journal of Applied Psychology, 72*, 62–68.

Heller, L. (2007). Modifying the ministerial exception: Providing ministers with a remedy for employment discrimination under Title VII while maintaining First Amendment protections of religious freedom. *St. John's Law Review, 81*, 663–699.

Henle, C. A. (2004). Case review of the legal status of banding. *Human Performance, 17*, 415–432.

Heriot, G. (2004). Thoughts on *Grutter v. Bollinger* and *Gratz v. Bollinger* as law and aspractical politics. *Loyola University Chicago Law Review, 36*, 137–174.

Highhouse, S., & Gutman, A. (2011). Was the addition of sex to Title VII a joke? Two viewpoints. *The Industrial-Organizational Psychologist, 48*, 102–107.

Holloway, H. (2019 September). Robot hires human being in world first as AI conducts job interview. Daily Star. https://www.dailystar.co.uk/news/world-news/robot-hires-human-being-world-19572551

Hopwood, C. J., Kotov, R., Krueger, R. F., Watson, D., Widiger, T. A., Althoff, R. R., . . . Bornovalova, M. A. (2018). The time has come for dimensional personality disorder diagnosis. *Personality and Mental Health, 12*, 82–86.

Hulin, C. L., Fitzgerald, L. F., & Drasgow, F. (1996). Organizational influences on sexual harassment. In M. S. Stockdale & M. S. Stockdale (Eds.), *Sexual harassment in the workplace: Perspectives, frontiers, and response strategies* (pp. 127–150). Thousand Oaks, CA: Sage Publications.

Hunter, R. J. Jr., Shannon, J. H., & Amoroso, H. J. (2019). Employment discrimination based on age: part II: applying the ADEA in employment scenarios: discrimination, idle chatter, or something else? *Journal of Public Administration and Governance, 9*(1), 1–17.

Hyman, J. (2019). A pox on the box. Retrieved form Workforce.com at: https://workforce.com/news/a-pox-on-ban-the-box

Issacharoff, S., & Harris, E. W. (1997). Is age discrimination really age discrimination? The ADEA's unnatural solution. *New York University Law Review, 72*, 780–840.

Jackson, D. J. R., Lance, C. E., & Hoffman, B. J. (2012). *The psychology of assessment centers*. New York: Routledge.

Jackson, J. R. (2011, September 12). *Class actions and the implications of Rule 23*. SCOTUSBLOG. https://www.scotusblog.com/2011/09/class-actions-and-the-implications-of-rule-23/

Jacobs, R., Murphy, J., & Siva, J. (2012). Unintended consequences of EEO enforcement policies: Being big is worse than being bad. *Journal of Business and Psychology, 28*, 467–471. doi:10.1007/s10869-012-9268-3

Jolly, J. P., & Frierson, J. G. (1989). Playing it safe. *Personnel Administrator, 34*, 44–50.

Joshi, Y. (2016). Bakke to the future: Affirmative Action after *Fisher*. *Stanford Law Review, 69*, 17–27.

Kanda, K. S. (2002). Validity and application of the Religious Freedom Restoration Act in the Tenth Circuit after *City of Boerne v. Flores*. *Denver University Law Review, 79*(3), 295–330.

Katz, R. C., Hannon, R., & Whitten, L. (1996). Effects of gender and situation on the perception of sexual harassment. *Sex Roles, 34*(1-2), 35–42.

Kelly, E. (2008). Accommodating religious expression in the workplace. *Employee Responsibilities and Rights Journal, 20*, 45–56.

Kline, B. (2009). Oppose by any other name: The Title VII opposition clause and *Crawford v. Metropolitan Government of Nashville and Davidson County, Tennessee*. *Oklahoma City University Law Review, 34*(3), 591–608.

Kravitz, D. A. (2008). The diversity-validity dilemma: Beyond selection—the role of affirmative action. *Personnel Psychology, 61*, 173–193.

Kremer, C. (2017). McDonnell-Douglas burden shifting and judicial economy in Title VII retaliation claims: In pursuit of expediency, resulting in inefficiency. *University of Cincinnati Law Review, 85*, 857–876.

Krimski, M. A. (2014). *University of Texas Southwestern Medical Center v. Nassar*: Undermining the national policy against discrimination. *Maryland Law Review Endnotes, 73*, 132–160.

Landy, F. J. (2005). Phases of employment litigation. In F. J. Landy (Ed.), *Employment discrimination litigation: Behavioral, quantitative, and legal perspectives*. San Francisco, CA: John Wiley & Sons.

Lax, J. (2007). Do employer requests for salary history discriminate against women? *Labor Law Journal, 58,* 47–52.

Ledbetter, L., & Isom, L. S. (2012). *Grace and grit: My fight for equal pay and fairness at Goodyear and beyond.* New York: Three Rivers Press.

Ledesma, M. C. (2019). California sunset: O'Conner's post-affirmative action ideal comes of age in California. *The Review of Higher Education, 42,* 227–254.

Leiter, W. M., & Leiter, S. (2011). *Affirmative Action in Antidiscrimination Law and Policy: An Overview and Synthesis.* SUNY Press.

Lesley, C. M. (2019). Making Rule 23 ideal: Using a multifactor test to evaluate the admissibility of evidence at class certification. *Michigan Law Review, 118,* 149–171.

Levi, J. L. (2007). Some modest proposals for challenging established dress code jurisprudence. *Duke Journal of Gender Law and Policy, 14,* 243–255.

Levine, E. L., Ash, R. A., Hall, H., & Sistrunk, F. (1983). Evaluation of job analysis methods by experienced job analysts. *Academy of Management Journal, 26,* 339–348.

Liao, H., & Rupp, D. E. (2005). The impact of justice climate and justice orientation on work outcomes: Across-level multifoci framework. *Journal of Applied Psychology, 90,* 242–256.

Lidge, E. F. III. (2002). Courts' misuse of the similarly situated concept in employment discrimination law. *Missouri Law Review, 67,* 831–882.

Linsted, J. L. (2006). The Seventh Circuit's erosion of the Equal Pay Act. *Seventh Circuit Review, 1,* 129–151.

Little, L., Hinojosa, A., & Lynch, J. (2017). Make them feel: How the disclosure of pregnancy to a supervisor leads to changes in perceived supervisor support. *Organization Science, 28,* 618–635.

Long, A. B. (2007). The troublemaker's friend: Retaliation against third parties and the right of association in the workplace. *Florida Law Review, 59*(5), 931–990.

Long, A. B. (2011). Employment retaliation and the accident of text. *Oregon Law Review, 90*(2), 525–582.

Lucas, K. E. (2016). How close is close enough? Examining the relationships in Title VII third party retaliation claims. *Labor Law Journal, 67*(3), 445–458.

Lund, C. C. (2011). In defense of the ministerial exception. *North Carolina Law Review, 90*(1), 1–72.

Maitland, P. (1999). Riding a cart of golf's "unfairways": *Martin v. PGA Tour. Golden Gate University Law Review, 29,* 627–681.

Malos, S. (2010). Post-9/11 backlash in the workplace: Employer liability for discrimination against Arab- and Muslim-Americans based on religion or national origin. *Employee Responsibilities and Rights Journal, 22,* 297–310.

Mariani, R. C.; Robertson, K. E. (1997). Age discrimination litigation: Rifs, statistics and stray remarks. *Defense Counsel Journal, 64*(1), 88–98.

Mayer, C. (1999–2000). Is HIV a disability under the Americans with Disabilities Act: Unanswered questions after *Bragdon v. Abbott, Journal of Law and Health, 14,* 179–208.

McAllister, M. C. (2019). Subgroup analysis in disparate impact age discrimination cases: Striking the appropriate balance through age cutoffs. *Alabama Law Review, 70*(4), 1073–1114.

McCambridge, S. (2013). Third-party retaliation: The shoes of an employer. *John Marshall Law Journal, 7*(1), 41–88.

McDonald, P. (2012). Workplace sexual harassment 30 years on: A review of the literature. *International Journal of Management Reviews, 14*(1), 1–17.

McKay, P. F., & Avery, D. R. (2005). Warning! Diversity recruitment could backfire. *Journal of Management Inquiry, 14,* 330–336.

McKay, P. F., Avery, D. R., Son, E., Rosado-Solomon, E., & Pustovit, S. (2017). Can cooperation help explain the demographic diversity–business performance relationship? *Academy of Management Proceedings, 2017*(1), 14775.

Melson-Silimon, A., Harris, A. M., Shoenfelt, E., Miller, J. D., & Carter, N. T. (2019). Personality testing and the Americans with Disabilities Act: Cause for concern as normal and abnormal models are integrated. *Industrial and Organizational Psychology: Perspectives on Science and Practice, 12,* 119–132.

Meyer, A. (1992). Getting to the heart of sexual harassment. *HR Magazine, 37*(7), 82–84.

Meyer, B. D. (1995). Natural and quasi-experiments in economics. *Journal of Business & Economic Statistics, 13*(2), 151–161.

Miller, J. D., Few, L. R., Lynam, D. R., & MacKillop, J. (2015). Pathological personality traits can capture DSM-IV personality disorder types. *Personality Disorders Theory Research and Treatment 6,* 32–40.

Miller, E. (1980). An EEO examination of employment applications. *Personnel Administrator, 25,* 63–81.

Miller, K. R. (2016). The Ninth Circuit's decision in *Escriba v. Foster Poultry Farms, Inc.* may limit the use of involuntary leave and why that is okay. *University of Cincinnati Law Review, 84,* 307–326.

Miller, M. (2006). Lost in the balance: A critique of the Ninth Circuit's unequal burdens approach to evaluating sex-differential grooming standards under Title VII. *North Carolina Law Review, 84,* 1357–1372.

Minter, S. (2014). *Summers v. Altarum*: Broadening the definition of disability under the ADA, and the impact of the new definition on employers. *North Carolina Central Law Review, 37,* 55–67.

Morgeson, F. P., Brannick, M. T., & Levine, E. L. (2019). *Job and work analysis: Methods, research, and applications for human resource management.* Thousand Oaks, CA: Sage Publications.

Morris, S. B. (2015). Statistical inference testing in adverse impact cases. In C. Hanvey & K. Sady (Eds.), *Practitioner's guide to legal issues in organizations* (pp. 71–91). New York: Springer.

Morris, S. B. (2017). Statistical significance testing in adverse impact analysis. In S. B. Morris and E. M. Dunleavy (Eds.), *Adverse impact analysis: Understanding data, statistics, and risk* (pp. 113–125). New York: Routledge. doi.org/10.4324/9781315301433

Morris, S., Dunleavy, E. M., & Howard, E. (2015). Measuring adverse impact in employee selection decisions. In C. Hanvey & K. Sady (Eds.), *Practitioner's guide to legal issues in organizations* (pp. 1–27). New York: Springer.

Mueller, L. M., Dunleavy, E. M., & Buonasera, A. K. (2008). Analyzing personnel selection decisions in employment discrimination litigation settings. *New Directions for Institutional Research, 138,* 67–83.

Murphy, K. R., & Jacobs, R. R. (2012). Using effect size measures to reform the determination of adverse impact in equal employment litigation. *Psychology, Public Policy, & Law, 18,* 477–499.

Murphy, K. R., & Jacobs, R. R. (2017). When and why do different indices lead to different conclusions about adverse impact. In S. B. Morris and E. M. Dunleavy (Eds.), *Adverse impact analysis: Understanding data, statistics, and risk* (pp. 113–125). New York: Routledge. doi.org/10.4324/9781315301433

Murphy, K. R. (2015). Physical abilities. In C. Hanvey & K. Sady (Eds.), *Practitioner's guide to legal issues in organizations* (pp. 111–126). Cham: Springer International.

Murphy, K. R., Osten, K., & Myors, B. (1995). Modeling the effects of banding in personnel selection. *Personnel Psychology, 48,* 61–84.

Musa, A. (2016). "A motivating factor": The impact of *EEOC v. Abercrombie & Fitch Stores, Inc.* on Title VII religious discrimination claims. *Saint Louis University Law Journal, 61,* 143–164.

Naquin, L. (2013). Closing the floodgates: Defining class of third-party plaintiffs for Title VII retaliation claims. *Louisiana Law Review, 73*(2), 669–702.

Nasuti, J. (2017). *E.E.O.C. v. Abercrombie & Fitch Stores, Inc.*: Reexamining the notice requirement in religious accommodation cases. *North East Journal of Legal Studies, 36,* 102–130.

Nevin, R. (2010). Title VII antiretaliation: The United States Supreme Court's decision in Crawford v. Metropolitan Government of Nashville & Davidson County, Tennessee on the scope of the opposition clause. *Richmond Journal of Law and Public Interest, 13*(2), 291–314.

Newman, D. A., & Lyon, J. S. (2009). Recruitment efforts to reduce adverse impact: Targeted recruiting for personality, cognitive ability, and diversity. *Journal of Applied Psychology, 94*(2), 298–317. https://doi.org/10.1037/a0013472

Newman, D. A., Jones, K. S., Fraley, R. C., Lyon, J. S., & Mullaney, K. M. (2014). Why minority recruiting doesn't often work, and what can be done about it: Applicant qualifications and the 4-group model of targeted recruiting. In K. Y. T. Yu & D. M. Cable (Eds.), *The Oxford handbook of recruitment* (pp. 492–526). New York: Oxford University Press.

Ng, T. W. H., & Feldman D. C. (2008). The relationship of age to ten dimensions of job performance. *Journal of Applied Psychology, 93*, 392–423.

Northup, J. S. (1998). The "same actor inference" in employment discrimination: Cheap justice? *Washington Law Review, 73*, 193–221.

O'Brien, J. P. (2002). Weighing temporal proximity in Title VII retaliation claims. *Boston College Law Review, 43*, 741–781. Retrieved November 27, 2019, from https://lawdigitalcommons.bc.edu/cgi/viewcontent.cgi?article=2207&context=bclr

O'Leary-Kelly, A., Bowes-Sperry, L., Bates, C., & Lean, E. (2009). Sexual harassment at work: A decade (plus) of progress. *Journal of Management, 35*, 503–536.

Oswald, F. L., Dunleavy, E. M., & Shaw, A. (2017). Measuring practical significance in adverse impact analysis. In S. B. Morris & E. M. Dunleavy (Eds.), *Adverse impact analysis: Understanding data, statistics, and risk* (pp. 92–112). New York: Routledge. doi.org/10.4324/9781315301433

Outtz, J. L. (Ed.). (2010). *Adverse impact: Implications for organizational staffing and high-stakes selection.* New York: Routledge.

Outtz, J. L., & Newman, D. A. (2010). A theory of adverse impact. In J. L. Outtz (ed.), *Adverse impact: Implications for organizational staffing and high stakes selection* (pp. 80–121). New York: Routledge.

Padilla, S. (2018). For clarity's sake: Redefining the knowing and voluntary standard in severance agreements. *Fordham Urban Law Journal, 45*, 839–874.

Paludi, M. A., Ellens, J. H., & Paludi, C. A. (2011). Religious discrimination. In M. A. Paludi, C. A. Pauldi & E. R. DeSouza (Eds.), *Praeger handbook on understanding and preventing workplace discrimination* (vol. 1, pp. 157–182). Santa Barbara, CA: Praeger.

Park, J., Malachi, E., Sternin, O., & Tevet, R. (2009). Subtle bias against Muslim job applicants in personnel decisions. *Journal of Applied Social Psychology, 39*, 2174–2190.

Pate, R., Oria, M., & Pillsbury, L. (2010). *Fitness measures and health outcomes in youth.* Washington DC: National Academy.

Perkins, L. A., Thomas, K. M., & Taylor, G. A. (2000). Advertising and recruitment: Marketing to minorities. *Psychology and Marketing, 17*, 235–255.

Perry, E. L., Kulik, C. T., & Bourhis, A. C. (1996). Moderating effects of personal and contextual factors in age discrimination. *Journal of Applied Psychology, 81*, 628–647.

Pietri, E. S., Johnson, I. R., & Ozgumus, E. (2018). One size may not fit all: Exploring how the intersection of race and gender and stigma consciousness predict effective identity-safe cues for Black women. *Journal of Experimental Social Psychology, 74*, 291–306.

Plain, G. L. (2011). I'll get you my pretty and your little associate too: The expansion of employee protection in Title VII retaliation claims. *Cumberland Law Review, 42*(3), 549–584.

Ployhart, R. E., & Holtz, B. C. (2008). The diversity-validity dilemma: Strategies for reducing racioethnic and sex subgroup differences and adverse impact in selection. *Personnel Psychology, 61*, 153–172.

Popovich, P. M., Gehlauf, D. N., Jolton, J. A., & Somers, J. M. (1992). Perceptions of sexual harassment as a function of sex of rater and incident form and consequence. *Sex Roles, 27*, 609–625.

Porter, N. B. (2014). The new ADA backlash. *Tennessee Law Review, 82*(1), 1–82.

Porter, N. B. (2019). Explaining "not disabled" cases ten years after the ADAAA: A story of ignorance, incompetence, and possibly animus. *Georgetown Journal on Poverty Law and Policy, 26*(3), 384–414.

Posthuma, R. A., Wagstaff, M. F., & Campion, M. A. (2012). Age stereotypes and workplace age discrimination. In J. W. Hedge & W. C. Borman (Eds.), *The Oxford handbook of work and aging* (pp. 298–312). New York: Oxford University Press.

Potter, E. E. (1989). Employer's burden of proof may be reduced in testing cases. *The Industrial-Organizational Psychologist, 26*, 43–47.

Potter, E. E. (1999). Supreme Court's Wards Cove Packing decision redefines the adverse impact theory under Title VII. *The Industrial-Organizational Psychologist, 27*, 25–31.

Purdie-Vaughns, V., Steele, C. M., Davies, P. G., Diltmann, R., & Crosby, J. R. (2008). Social identity contingencies: How diversity cues signal threat or safety for African Americans in mainstream institutions. *Journal of Personality and Social Psychology, 94*, 615–630.

Pyburn, K. M., Ployhart, R. E., & Kravitz, D. A. (2008). The diversity-validity dilemma: Overview and legal content. *Personnel Psychology, 61*, 143–151.

Quintanilla, V. D., & Kaiser, C. R. (2016). The same-actor inference of nondiscrimination: Moral credentialing and the psychological and legal licensing of bias. *California Law Review, 104*(1), 1–74.

Ravishankar, K. (2016). The establishment clause's hydra: The Lemon Test in the circuit courts. *University of Dayton Law Review, 41*(2), 261–302.

Report of the Scientific Affairs Committee. (1994, July). An evaluation of banding methods in personnel selection. *The Industrial-Organizational Psychologist, 32*, 80–86.

Resslar, M. A. (2002). *PGA Tour, Inc. v. Martin*: A hole in one for Casey Martin and the ADA. *Loyola University Law Review, 33*, 631–689.

Reynolds, D. (2006). OFCCP guidance on defining a job applicant in the Internet age: The final word? *The Industrial-Organizational Psychologist, 43*, 107–113.

Riccucci, N. M., & Riccardelli, M. (2015). The use of written exams in police and fire departments: Implications for social diversity. *Review of Public Personnel Administration, 35*(4), 352–366. doi:10.1177/0734371X14540689

Riger, S. (1991). Gender dilemmas in sexual harassment policies and procedures. *American Psychologist, 46*, 497–505.

Rosenthal, L. D. (2016). Timing isn't everything: Establishing Title VII retaliation prima facie case after *University of Texas Southwestern Medical Center v. Nassar*. *SMU Law Review, 69*(1), 143–186.

Roth, P. L., BeVier, C. A., Bobko, P., Switzer III, F. S., & Tyler, P. (2001). Ethnic group differences in cognitive ability in employment and educational settings: A meta-analysis. *Personnel Psychology, 54*, 297–330.

Roth, P. L., Bobko, P., & Switzer, F. S. III. (2006). Modeling the behavior of the 4/5 rule for determining adverse impact: Reasons for caution. *Journal of Applied Psychology, 91*(3), 507–522.

Rotundo, M., Nguyen, D.-H., & Sackett, P. R. (2001). A meta-analytic review of gender differences in perceptions of sexual harassment. *Journal of Applied Psychology, 86*, 914–922.

Rubino, C., Avery, D. R., McKay, P. F., Moore, B. L., Wilson, D. C., Van Driel, M. S., . . . McDonald, D. P. (2018). And justice for all: How organizational justice climate deters sexual harassment. *Personnel Psychology, 71*, 519–544.

Rupp, D. E., Song, Q. C., & Strah, N. (2020). Addressing the co-called validity-diversity trade-off: Exploring the practicalities and legal defensibility of pareto-optimization for reducing adverse impact within personnel selection. *Industrial and Organizational Psychology: Perspectives on Science and Practice, 13*, 246–271.

Rupp, D. E., Vodanovich, S. J., & Crede, M. (2006). Age bias in the workplace: The impact of ageism and causal attributions. *Journal of Applied Social Psychology, 36*, 1337–1364.

Sackett, P. R., & Ellingson, J. E. (1997). The effects of forming multi-predictor composites on group differences and adverse impact. *Personnel Psychology, 50*, 707–721.

Sanchez, J. I., & Levine, E. L. (1989). Determining important tasks within jobs: A policy-capturing approach. *Journal of Applied Psychology, 74*, 336–342.

Savage, J. M. (2004). Adopting the EEOC deterrence approach to the adverse employment action prong in a prima facie case for Title VII retaliation. *Boston College Law Review, 46*, 215–250.

Savage, M. (2019 March). Meet Tengai, the job interview robot who won't judge you. BBC News.https://www.bbc.com/news/amp/business-47442953

Saxena, M., & Morris, S. B. (2019). Adverse impact as disability discrimination: Illustrating the perils through self-control at work. *Industrial and Organizational Psychology, 12*, 138–142.

Schauer, F. (2001). The dilemma of ignorance: *PGA Tour, Inc. v. Martin. The Supreme Court Review, 2001*, 267–297.

Schlanger, M., & Kim, P. (2014). The Equal Employment Opportunity Commission and structural reform of the American workplace. *Washington University Law Review, 91*, 1519–1590.

Schmidt, F. L. (1991). Why all banding procedures are logically flawed. *Human Performance, 4*, 265–278.

Semuels, A. (2016, August 4). When banning one kind of discrimination results in another. *The Atlantic*. https://www.theatlantic.com/business/archive/2016/08/consequences-of-ban-the-box/494435/

Shadish, W. R., Cook, T. D., & Campbell, D. T. (2002). *Experimental and quasi-experimental designs for generalized causal inference.* New York: Houghton Mifflin.

Shaman, J. M. (2012). Rules of general applicability. *First Amendment Law Review, 10*, 419–464.

Sharone, J. B. (2010). For better or worse: Spouses left unprotected by the anti-retaliation provision of Title VII. *Suffolk Journal of Trial and Appellate Advocacy, 15*, 289–307.

Shoenfelt, E. L., Maue, A. E., & Nelson, J. (2002). Reasonable person versus reasonable woman: Does it matter? *Journal of Gender, Social Policy and Law, 10*, 633–672.

SHRM. (2012a July). Background checking—The use of criminal background checks in hiring decisions. *Society for Human Resource Management.* https://www.shrm.org/hr-today/trends-and-forecasting/research-and-surveys/Pages/criminalbackgroundcheck.aspx

SHRM. (2012b July). Background checking: The use of credit background checks in hiring decisions. *Society for Human Resource Management.* https://www.shrm.org/hr-today/trends-and-forecasting/research-and-surveys/pages/creditbackgroundchecks.aspx

Simson, G. J. (2018). Permissible accommodation or impermissible endorsement? A proposed approach to religious exemptions and the establishment clause. *Kentucky Law Journal, 106*(4), 535–601.

Siskin, B. R., & Trippi, J. (2005). Statistical issues in litigation. In F. J. Landy (Ed.), *Employment discrimination litigation: Behavioral, quantitative, and legal perspectives* (pp. 132–166). San Francisco: Jossey-Bass.

Smith, G., & Duda, S. (2010 September). Bridging the gap: Credit scores and economic opportunity in Illinois communities of color. *Woodstock Institute.* 1–25. https://woodstockinst.org/wp-content/uploads/2013/05/bridgingthegapcreditscores_sept2010_smithduda.pdf

Song, Q., Wee, S., & Newman, D. A. (2017). Diversity shrinkage: Cross-validating pareto-optimal weights to enhance diversity via hiring practices. *Journal of Applied Psychology, 102*, 1636–1657.

Spruill, W. E. (2001). Giving new meaning to handicap: The Americans with Disabilities Act and its uneasy relationship with professional sports in *PGA Tour, Inc. v. Martin. University of Richmond Law Review, 35*, 365–392.

Strah, N., & Rupp, D. E. (in press). Are there cracks in our foundation? An integrative review of diversity issues in job analysis. *Journal of Applied Psychology.*

Strawbridge, D. D. (2012). Thy fiancé doth protest too much: Third-party retaliation under title VII after *Thompson v. North American Stainless, LP. Mercer Law Review, 63*(2), 767–790.

Suddath, C. (2016). Why can't we stop sexual harassment at work? *Bloomberg Business Week*. Retrieved from https://www.bloomberg.com/features/2016-sexual-harassment-policy/#/

Sundar, V. (2017). Operationalizing workplace accommodations for individuals with disabilities. *Work: Journal of Prevention, Assessment & Rehabilitation, 56*(1), 135–155. doi:10.3233/WOR-162472

Tam, A. P., Murphy, K. R., & Lyall, J. T. (2004). Can changes in differential dropout rates reduce adverse impact? A computer simulation study of a multi-wave selection system. *Personnel Psychology, 57*, 905–934.

Teal, J. (2018). A survivor's tale: McDonnell Douglas in a post-Nassar world. *San Diego Law Review, 55*(4), 937–968.

Thompson, D. E., & Thompson, T. A. (1982). Court standards for job analysis in test validation. *Personnel Psychology, 35*, 865–874.

Thornton, G. C., III, & Rupp, D. E. (2006). *Assessment centers in human resource management: Strategies for prediction, diagnosis, and development*. Mahwah, NJ: Lawrence Erlbaum.

Thornton, G. C., III, Mueller-Hanson, R. A., & Rupp, D. E. (2017). *Developing organizational simulations*. New York: Routledge.

Thornton, G. C., III, Rupp, D. E., & Hoffman, B. (2015). *Assessment center perspectives for talent management strategies*. New York: Routledge.

Thornton, G., III, & Potemra, M. (2010). Utility of assessment center for promotion of police sergeants. *Public Personnel Management, 39*, 59–69.

Tonowski, R. (2014). On the legal front. *The Industrial-Organizational Psychologist, 52*, 21–26.

Trull, T. J., & Widiger, T. A. (2013). Dimensional models of personality: The five-factor model and the DSM-5. *Dialogues in Clinical Neuroscience, 15*, 135–146.

Underwood, B. (2013). Tread lightly: Third-party retaliation claims after *Thompson v. North American Stainless*. *Journal of Corporation Law, 38*(2), 463–486.

Uniform guidelines on employee selection procedures. *Federal Register, 43*(38), 290–238, 315 (1978).

Vaas, F. J. (1966). Title VII: Legislative history. *Boston College Law Review, 7*, 431–458.

Valenti, A., & Burke, L. A. (2010). Post-*Burlington*: What employers and employees should know about retaliation. *Employee Responsibilities and Rights Journal, 22*, 235–251. doi:10.1007/s10672–009-9137-z

Van Ostrand, L. A. (2009). A close look at ADEA mixed-motives claims and *Gross v. FBL Financial Services, Inc*. *Fordham Law Review, 78*, 399–451.

Ventrell-Monsees, C. (2019). It's unlawful age discrimination—not the natural order of the workplace. *Berkeley Journal of Employment and Labor Law, 40*(1), 91–134.

Vilella, S. (2018). ADEA disparate-impact claims: How the Third Circuit age-proofed comparators. American *University Business Law Review, 7*(1), 179–197.

Vodanovich, S. J., & Lowe, R. H. (1992). They ought to know better: The incidence and correlates of inappropriate application blank inquiries. *Public Personnel Management, 21*, 363–370.

Vodanovich, S. J., & Piotrowski, C. (2008). The interactive process requirement of the Americans with Disabilities Act: Implications for personnel managers. *Journal of Business Issues, 3*(1), 7–13.

Vodanovich, S. J., & Piotrowski, C. (2014). What constitutes the definition of supervisor in workplace harassment cases? *Journal of Instructional Psychology, 41*, 97–99.

Vodanovich, S. J., & Piotrowski, C. (2014). Workplace retaliation: A review of emerging case law. *The Psychologist-Manager Journal, 17*(2), 71–78.

Waldman, D. A., & Avolio, B. J. (1986). A meta-analysis of age differences in job performance. *Journal of Applied Psychology, 71*, 33–38.

Wallace, J. C., Tye, M., & Vodanovich, S. J. (2000). Applying for jobs online: Examining the legality of Internet-based application forms. *Public Personnel Management, 29*, 497–504.

Wallace, J. C., & Vodanovich, S. J. (2004). Appropriateness of personnel application blanks: Persistence and knowledge of application blank items. *Public Personnel Management, 33*, 331–345.

Wallace, J. C., Tye, M. G., & Vodanovich, S. J. (2000). Applying for jobs online: Examining the legality of Internet-based application forms. *Public Personnel Management, 29*, 497–504.

Wang, X., & Yancey, G. G. (2012). The benefit of a degree in I-O psychology or human resources. *The Industrial-Organizational Psychologist, 50*, 45–50.

Warden, A. I. (2002). Driving the green: The impact of *PGA Tour, Inc. v. Martin* on disabled athletes and the future of competitive sports. *North Carolina Law Review, 80*, 643–691.

Weber, Z. J. (2018). Disparate impact 2.0: *Karlo* provides a long-awaited update for ADEA subgroup plaintiffs, *University of Cincinnati Law Review, 86*, 1073–1097.

Wee, S., Newman, D. A., & Joseph, D. L. (2014). More than g: Selection quality and adverse impact implications of considering second-stratum cognitive abilities. *Journal of Applied Psychology, 99*, 547–563.

Widner, D., & Chicoine, S. (2011). It's all in the name: Employment discrimination against Arab Americans. *Sociological Forum, 26*, 806–823.

Wiener, R. L., Watts, B. A., Goldkamp, K. H., & Gaspar, C. (1995). Social analytic investigation of hostile work environments: A test of the reasonable woman standard. *Law and Human Behavior, 19*, 263–281.

Wille, L., & Derous, E. (2018). When job ads turn you down: How requirements in job ads may stop instead of attract highly qualified women. *Sex Roles, 79*, 464–475.

Williams, M. L., & Bauer, T. N. (1994). The effect of managing diversity policy on organizational attractiveness. *Group and Organization Management, 19*, 295–308.

Wingate, P. H., Thornton, G. C. III, McIntyre, K. S., & Frame, J. H. (2003). Organizational downsizing and age discrimination litigation: The influence of personnel practices and statistical evidence on litigation outcomes. *Law and Human Behavior, 27*, 87–108.

Winterberg, C. A., Tapia, M. A., Nei, K. S., & Brummel, B. J. (2019). A clarification of ADA jurisprudence for personality-based selection. *Industrial and Organizational Psychology, 12*, 172–176.

Wright, D. K., & Garces, L. M. (2018). Understanding the controversy around race-based affirmative action in American higher education. In J. Blanchard (Ed.), *Controversies on campus: Debating the issues confronting American universities in the 21st Century* (pp. 8–17). Santa Barbara, CA: Praeger.

Zalesne, D. (2007). Lessons from equal opportunity harasser doctrine: Challenging sex-specific appearance and dress codes. *Duke Journal of Gender Law and Policy, 14*, 535–560.

Zedeck, S. (2009). Adverse impact: History and evolution. In J. L. Outtz (Ed.), *Adverse impact: Implications for organizational staffing and high stakes selection*. New York: Taylor & Francis.

Zimmer, M. J. (1980). Title VII: Treatment of seniority systems. *Marquette Law Review, 64*, 79–102.

Zimmer, M. J. (2014). Hiding the statute in plain view: *University of Texas Southwestern Medical Center v. Nassar. Nevada Law Journal, 14*(3), 705–722.

Index

Tables and figures are indicated by *t* and *f* following the page number.